Stefansson's "The Friendly...

PRINCIPLES OF EDUCATION

PRINCIPLES OF EDUCATION

*

JAMES L. MURSELL, Ph.D.

Professor of Education
Lawrence College

W · W · NORTON & COMPANY, INC ·
NEW YORK

Copyright, 1934, by
W · W · NORTON & COMPANY, INC.
70 Fifth Avenue, New York

PRINTED IN THE UNITED STATES OF AMERICA
BY THE VAIL-BALLOU PRESS, INC., BINGHAMTON, N. Y.

I DEDICATE THIS BOOK TO
PROFESSOR WILLIAM H. KILPATRICK

Table of Contents

Part One
FOUNDATIONS

1. WHAT IS EDUCATION? — 3
2. HOW IS EDUCATION RELATED TO SOCIETY? — 23
3. WHAT IS THE RELATION OF EDUCATION TO MENTAL GROWTH? — 46
4. WHAT IS THE SIGNIFICANCE OF FORMAL DISCIPLINE? — 74
5. WHAT IS THE PLACE OF THE SCHOOL IN EDUCATION? — 94

Part Two
OUTCOMES

6. HOW MAY EDUCATION ADJUST MAN TO HIS CIVIC INSTITUTIONS? — 121
7. HOW MAY EDUCATION ADJUST MAN TO HIS ECONOMIC INSTITUTIONS? — 141
8. HOW MAY EDUCATION ADJUST MAN TO FAMILY LIFE? — 166
9. HOW MAY EDUCATION PROMOTE RECREATION? — 185
10. HOW MAY EDUCATION PROMOTE HEALTH? — 204

Part Three
PROBLEMS

11. HOW MAY WE DEAL WITH THE PROBLEM OF EDUCATIONAL OPPORTUNITY? — 231

12.	HOW MAY WE DEAL WITH THE PROBLEM OF THE INDIVIDUAL?	256
13.	HOW MAY WE DEAL WITH THE PROBLEM OF INTEREST?	280
14.	HOW MAY EDUCATION SERVE THE ENDS OF CULTURE AND VOCATION?	301
15.	HOW MAY EDUCATION STIMULATE THINKING?	326
16.	HOW MAY EDUCATION DEAL WITH THE PROBLEM OF MORALITY?	350

Part Four

Instrumentalities

17.	HOW SHALL WE PLAN THE CURRICULUM?	375
18.	WHAT ARE THE IMPLICATIONS OF THE EDUCATIONAL LADDER?	403
19.	WHAT USE SHOULD BE MADE OF MEASUREMENT IN EDUCATION?	427
20.	WHAT IS THE SIGNIFICANCE OF METHOD?	450
21.	HOW SHALL WE INTERPRET THE WORK OF THE TEACHER?	471

Preface

I OFFER this book to the public with a deep sense of insufficiency, both in it, and in myself. To present what is here attempted—a comprehensive account of the process of education—is surely no mean task. What is involved is nothing less than a philosophy of human life and its values. To face such a task without self-questioning seems hardly possible. And as one seeks to carry it out, one becomes increasingly aware of the limitations of one's own knowledge and insight, and the necessarily tentative nature of many of one's views.

Yet I am convinced that one of the greatest needs of our educational life today is a more wide-spread canvassing of fundamental issues. In the multiplicity of special studies which are appearing, essential though they be, we too easily neglect those broad integrating principles on which the effectiveness of our whole enterprise depends. Insight into such principles is needed far beyond the professional training of the teacher, though it is, perhaps, the most important single item in his equipment. There is an urgent necessity that the public which must support our schools shall be brought to some intelligent appreciation of the immense significance of this great social and cultural phenomenon, and some understanding of its present defects, and of the directions in which progress must be sought. And I believe that multitudes who enter our institutions of higher learning may benefit greatly from some instructed consideration of such matters. If anyone who reads these pages, whether or no his life work is to be that of a teacher, is brought to a clearer comprehension of what education means, and a better recognition of how it may be made more vital, even though he come there by the road of disagreement with what I have to say, I shall be well content.

In preparing this book, I have made an effort to avoid the technical terminology of education, which, in spite of its real values, often seems to interpose a barrier between the student's mind and the realities which are being discussed. I have sought to use illustrative material which might bring home to the reader the actual human problems under consideration. And I have not hesitated to use the first personal singular. The aim has been to avoid remoteness of treatment, and to leave no doubt as to what is meant when a principle is discussed and applied. It is a familiar dictum that education in general should come to grips with current and even contentious issues. This surely applies to the presentation of the theory of education. That theory touches current practice at all points, and is best comprehended in terms of such contacts. This involves what may seem to some a dangerous directness, and full agreement is not likely to be had. But at least it brings before the student the current and compelling problems which must be met if we are to find a better way of education.

In determining what topics should be treated, I sent out a questionnaire to 210 teachers of courses in Principles of Education. This questionnaire was made up of 118 topics taken from textbooks in the field. The respondents were asked to indicate by checks (a) which topics they treated *in extenso* in their courses (b) which topics they treated incidentally and briefly (c) which topics they did not treat at all, but still regarded as appropriate for such courses. Ninety-three replies were received, and of these 64 proved of immediate value. The procedure, naturally, was rough; but it gave at least some indication of what was being done.

I list below the topics treated by 30 or more teachers, both *in extenso* and incidentally. The numbers in parentheses indicate the frequency of each item, checked under (a) and (b) combined.

Definitions of education (53): education and democracy (51): education and society (50): education and nationalism (50): education and the family (48): education and the economic system (48): education and health (47): education and recreation (47): liberal education (46): Dewey (44): elementary school (44): junior high school (44): education and the state (44): education and culture (44): education and the home (43): education and morality (43): teacher ideals (43): education and the church (42): vocational education (42): individual differences (42): teacher training (42): senior high school (41): education and the community (41): education and religion (41): education and personality (41): curricular aims (40): motivation (40): task of teacher (40): kindergarten (39): mental growth (39): thinking (39): provision for individual differences (39): junior college (38): teacher status (38): Froebel (37): Winnetka (37): aim of education (37): laws of learning (37): play (37): Pestalozzi (36): Dalton Plan (36): infancy (36): interest (36): senior college (35): curricular evolution (35): physical basis of learning (35): complete act of thought (35): intelligence tests (35): guidance (35): Rousseau (34): education and class distinction (34): education and industry (34): curriculum organization (34): curriculum construction (33): thought and language (33): athletics (33): heredity (32): intelligence as hereditary (32): nature of intelligence (32): general nature of method (32): Batavia (31): Gestalt (31): associationism (31): project method (31): private school (30): progressive school (30): social science (30): natural science (30): fine arts (30): drill (30): ideas and concepts (30): socialized recitation (30): testing (30).

It is clear that there is substantial agreement between this ranking of topics, and the contents of this book. There are of course omissions and variations, but not of an extreme kind. Replies to certain general questions clearly indicate that the course in Principles of Education is usually set up as an elementary study of educational philosophy, and that general and educational psychology are usually prerequisites.

A word should be said concerning the workbook which has been prepared to accompany this text. Study aids at the ends of chapters have the dual disadvantage of breaking up the continuity of an extensive exposition, and of presenting mechanical difficulties to effective use. Experience would indicate that many teaching problems may be solved by the use of an independent workbook.

In conclusion I wish to acknowledge with gratitude the assistance of those who have made contributions to the enterprise of preparing this book. I thank those who so kindly gave their time to filling in the questionnaires which were sent out. In particular I wish to acknowledge the stimulation I have received from the work of Professor Ross Finney, whose vigorous book, *A Sociological Philosophy of Education,* I found most valuable, and whose dictum that the aims of education are the institutions of society I have adopted and sought to apply. The influence of Dewey and Kilpatrick, amongst many others, is manifest throughout. And I am indebted to many friends and associates of the staff of Lawrence College for numerous discussions concerning matters here treated, from which I have learned much.

JAMES L. MURSELL

Part One

FOUNDATIONS

*

Chapter 1

WHAT IS EDUCATION?

1. How should we think of education?

When one puts the question: What is education? most people's minds are apt to fill with a host of vague memories of the mill through which they passed when they were young. Thoughts crowd upon them of starting off from home in the morning with books and lunches, of lines forming and ringing bells, of classrooms, teachers, and subjects, of recitations, homework and examinations, and of the amiable glories of commencements. In a word, people are apt to think of education as *schooling*.

Now as long as our minds continue at this level, we shall reach no very deep understanding, nor achieve any very helpful and illuminating insight. For all such things are the outward forms rather than the inner essence of the affair. And it is the inner essence which we seek. In setting out upon a study of the principles of education, which is obviously an investigation of its central meaning, the very first demand upon us is to break up this conventional pattern of ideas. We must at the very outset make the effort necessary to think of it all in a far larger and deeper way. We must stand farther back from the detail, so as to secure a better perspective, and a broader, more inclusive sweep of view. If one wishes really to know a tract of country, one must not only explore it bit by bit; one must also seek a vantage point from which it can be surveyed as a whole, and where the relationship of all its parts to one another can be seen. At first one will feel a certain strangeness. Familiar objects take on an unexpected look, and do not lie just where one thought they did. Such is quite likely to be your experience, more particularly as you study the opening chapters of the book. You may perhaps sometimes have the feeling that what is said here has little relation to education as you yourself have known it. So much, however, is necessary and even desirable. Anyone who has looked over a landscape from a mountain top knows very well that an inclusive view gained for the first time always works somewhat of a revolution. And you may be assured that nothing is more worth while, nothing indeed is more essential, for any kind of practical intelligent appreciation, than to make the effort to see education steadily and to see it whole.

What then is the best vantage ground from which to survey this field? We find it in the summary statement that a person's education consists of the total of those formative influences which determine how he shall live. Education is the shaping of life. This, of course, is no new thought. You may even find it commonplace. Yet it is infinitely fruitful. And furthermore, like so many valuable commonplaces, people constantly repeat it in words, and forget it in action. And it is, without question, the best, the most central, the most strategic of all points of view.

The thought that the whole meaning of education is the shaping of life has inspired teachers of every age. From classical antiquity there comes the word: *Non scholæ sed vitæ*. In the first prospectus of what is now one of America's most famous private schools, the central purpose is set forth as the preparation of pupils for "the great business of living." And we constantly hear it said that the task of all teachers and all schools is not to cram subject matter into unwilling minds, but to make men and women.

But within recent years, this ancient, fructifying idea has been endowed with new vividness and new wealth of meaning. This has come about through the rise of the biological sciences. These are the sciences which deal specifically with life and its conditions. The point of contact is obvious. Our fuller understanding of the economy of life leads directly to a better understanding of the nature and task of education. If science can tell us what the conditions of life are, and how it rises to new and higher levels, we can see, far better than was possible in earlier times, how education may take hold upon it. So it is that our conception, which, notice again, has been held by many of the greatest teachers and thinkers of all ages, has come now to be known as the "biological approach" to education. The complete, rich, diversified meaning of this approach we shall try to explain in the following pages. But always you should remember that it stands for the central, the essentially simple claim that we think of education best as that process by which the business of living is determined.

2. *What is the essential nature of the life process?*

The statement that it is the task of education to determine how we shall live, may seem to you very indefinite and general. In this you are perfectly right. "Life," after all, is a very vague term, and includes any and every kind of activity. And a process which determines the way we live, may be almost any kind of a process. Perhaps this is the chief reason why so many teachers have assented to our claim in words, while ignoring it in action. It has not seemed to lead to any concrete proposals about the management of schools, or to any clear cut program of teaching, which one could distinguish with certainty and authority from any other program. This is just where the modern biologist becomes helpful. For he brings to us an authentic account of the nature of life, which shows us what is really involved in any attempt to mould and determine it. For biological science, the essential characteristic of the life process is summed up in the word *adjustment*. A living being is distinguished from a dead thing by its capacity for adjusting itself to its environment. Let us try, by means of a few concrete illustrations, to explain this idea.

Suppose we begin with the tiny unicellular, aquatic animal, the *paramecium*. If we introduce a drop of dilute acid into the water where a number of these creatures are living, we find that, as they approach the outer edge of the drop, they pause, and begin to change the direction of their movement. This happens again and again, in a sequence of trials, until at last they are able to find the way to swim around and beyond the drop. Contrast this with what happens if we pour some acid onto a marble slab. It would seem ridiculous to say that the marble "adjusts itself" to the acid, or in any way "finds out how to deal with it." All that takes place is a chemical reaction, a change. Or again, to descend considerably from even this low point in the scale, contrast the effect light has upon a tree with that which it has upon a photographic plate. If the tree stands in thick woods, so that most of its light comes from above, this profoundly affects the way it grows. It becomes tall, and has little spread and few low branches. Its whole appearance is different from what it would have been if it had grown in the open, illuminated freely from all sides. If one has no objection to picturesque language, one might say that it adapted its inner purpose, the purpose to grow, to its surroundings. With the photographic plate, however, nothing of the sort happens. The plate automatically, passively, and fatally receives the imprint produced by the light falling upon it. In one case we have adjustment, and in the other not. So instances could be multiplied. At one time in geological history, certain species of mammals grew to enormous size; but the rocks did not! There was a point in the growth of the animals, because it enabled them to survive. An inner purpose was fulfilled. A problem was met, and for the time being, solved. But there was no point in the growth of the rocks, because they had no inner tendency or purpose to realize. When a water hole in central Africa dries up, the mud becomes hard. In its own right as mud, it is just as well one way as the other, hard and dry, or soft and moist. But the animals migrate. They do not merely succumb to altered conditions. They find another way of living. If I stick a pin into a cushion, it is just a physical event, and nothing further happens. But if I stick it into my arm, I jump, make a remark, hastily pull it out, and look for a bandage. With me, there is an accommodation of inner tendency to outer circumstance. With the cushion, there is not. Again we have the contrast between adjustment and its absence; between a living being, and a dead thing.

For the biologist then—the scientist whose special field is the study of the phenomena of life—the essential business of living is

WHAT IS EDUCATION? 7

the (accommodation of inner tendency to outer circumstance.) And this he calls adjustment. Notice how much more definite this already makes our conception of education. The word life has in a considerable measure ceased to be vague, and has gained a clear cut meaning. We regard it as the accommodation of inner and outer. Where there is no inner tendency there is no life. Whenever inner tendency fails to adjust itself to outer circumstance, life is threatened, and may cease. And the aim of education now appears as the moulding, the determining of this adjustment between the living being with its wants and purposes, and the world round about it. Putting the matter in slightly different words, *the aim of education, as a process of readjustment, is to produce fitness for the problems of life.* What the great reptiles did by developing enormous body size and prodigious armament; what the mammoth achieved by his hairy coat, and tusks, and trunk; what the sabre tooth tiger won by his formidable fangs; what every species of plant and animal has brought about by some means or other; that very thing man has done, and done far better than they, by means of education. By it he has met the challenge which the environment presents to his wants and purposes, and has achieved a measure of victory greater than that of any other creature. He has won for himself a way of living at once the fullest and the most secure that has ever appeared upon the earth.

3. *What are some implications of our conception of education?*

Of course the purpose of this entire book is to bring out the wide and striking implications of this biological conception of education. But for the sake of making the idea more meaningful, we may find it worth while to pause for a moment here at the outset, to see how broad, significant, and impressive our central doctrine is.

A. In the first place, it is clear that the more limited, the more static any creature's adjustment, the more precarious will be its life. In spite of their tremendous strength and fearful weapons, the great reptiles and mammals of other epochs have vanished from the scene. They had developed into specialists, so to speak. And when the particular conditions with which their powers enabled them to cope passed away, they were unable to solve the problems of a new situation, and so were doomed. This consideration applies precisely to human affairs, both for the individual and the group. It would be quite possible to take a child, and educate him intensively for one specialized vocation, and one only. We could find out exactly what skills and abilities he would need, and see to it that he had them. And we would probably produce a first rate expert. But to do this would be monstrously unwise. For by the time the child was grown up, the vocation for which he was trained might no longer exist. His powers of adjustment would be gravely limited. And he might have the alternative of starvation or charity. In the same way, a whole society can destroy itself by persisting in certain modes of action and feeling which are no longer appropriate to the conditions of its existence. The obvious instance is that of chauvinistic patriotism, and the obsessions of militarism, in an industrial civilization. And so when the schools of some countries concentrate, as in fact they do, on producing a jingo patriotism, they are working towards a limited, rigid adjustment, which makes it harder and harder to accommodate to actuality, and which may be the ruin of us all. Thus one great and immediate conclusion, which we shall develop more fully as we proceed, is that the best adjustment is that which is most free and most flexible.

B. The next implication of our point of view is that education must, in its very nature, begin always with the purpose of the person who is being educated. Remember that the very difference between a living creature and a non-living object, lies in the presence or absence of an inner trend or tendency. Adjustment is precisely the accommodation of the inner to the outer. And where we have no inner trend, no purpose, no activity self-initiated, there can be no adjustment, no life, no education. Education starts when one wants something, and runs into difficulties in getting it.

This idea is very widely recognized in our schools of today. It is part of the creed of the "progressive schools," which are becoming so numerous both here and abroad. It is an essential element in the kindergarten idea. And it is behind certain reorganizations of college and university teaching. We may say that the best teachers everywhere believe in it, and seek to put it into operation, and that every year it is becoming more influential. But it is still far more widely ignored than practiced. A vast number of teachers still sit in darkness, and believe—or act as if they believed—that education is a matter of task setting, lesson hearing, and forced memorizing, in which the active purpose of the pupil counts for nothing. A child who begins to learn through activity and purpose in the kindergarten, is often treated like a chicken to be stuffed, as soon as he enters the first grade. A pupil whose mental growth has been stimulated by a well considered sequence of vital projects in a junior high school, goes backward through fifty years of educational evolution between the ninth grade and the tenth, and in senior high school finds himself subjected to the "good old rule, the simple plan" of imposed textbook recitation learning. One of the fundamental ideas we derive from the biological conception of education is, that in teaching, our task is not to stuff things into people's heads, but to build adjustment on the only possible foundation—inner purpose.

C. But we have only told half the story when we say that adjustment necessarily involves inner purpose. Let us take a concrete case. A girl in the tenement district of a great city was brought up under very unfavorable home conditions. Her parents cared little for her, and exercised no supervision. About all she got from them was her food, and an occasional beating when they happened to be irritated. She played truant as much as she could from the none too excellent neighborhood school. She was thrown in with highly undesirable acquaintances. Before she was ten she was initiated into the technique of shop-lifting. She became a sexual delinquent at the age of twelve. At sixteen she was committed to a reformatory, and was headed, probably with little chance of salvation, towards some sort of criminal career. What was the matter? Her "inner purposes" as in infant were just as good as anyone's. She had no inherited pathological taint. Her tendencies were everybody's tendencies. But her environment was such that she could achieve only the most disastrous, and ultimately, of course, destructive adjustment. She was like some poor plant, twisted, warped, blanched by insufficient light and hostile soil. As a bundle of human potentialities, she was just as good as you and I. But the problems the world presented to her were such, that their obvious solution was by becoming a thief and a prostitute. This was the best adjustment she could make.

So we see that while education begins in part with the inner impulse of the person to be educated, it also has another point of origin—the creation and maintenance of a proper environment. This is where the school comes in. And our biological conception shows us just how we ought to think about its work and place. The school has the same relationship to the child that the hot-house in a cold climate has to a rose-plant. It furnishes an environment where the proper adjustment is possible. It brings inner impulse, inner purpose, into contact with the right sort of challenge and opportunity.

D. In the fourth place, our conception of education as a process for securing a favorable adjustment of inner to outer, furnishes us with a touchstone for deciding what school studies, and what out-of-school experiences are valuable. Only those studies and those experiences which contribute to the strengthening and widening of life are worth while. Herbert Spencer long ago put the matter with a force and clarity on which we cannot improve.

"How to live?—that is the essential question for us. Not how to live in the mere material sense only, but in the widest sense. The general problem which comprehends every special problem is—the right ruling of conduct in all directions under all circumstances. In what way to treat the body; in what way to treat the mind; in what way to manage our affairs; in what way to bring up a family; in what way to behave as citizens; in what way to utilize all those sources of happiness which nature supplies—how to use all our faculties to the greatest advantage of ourselves and others—how to live completely? And this, being the great thing needful for us to learn, is, by consequence the great thing which education has to teach. To prepare us for complete living is the function which education has to discharge; and the only rational mode of judging any educational course, is to judge in what degree it discharges this function."

E. Lastly, our central conception implies a certain ideal of the educated man. Very often this ideal consists of a list of items of knowledge and types of accomplishment conventionally thought desirable. One hears it said—or finds it implied—that the educated man ought to be able to speak good English, that he ought to appreciate good music and art, that he ought to know something of science and history, that he ought to be able to read, and perhaps write and speak, one or more foreign languages, that he ought to be a good conversationalist. And so on. Now all this may easily be a symptom of a completely wrong line of thought. Education is no more a decorative luxury than is the long neck of the giraffe, or the illuminating device of a deep-sea fish. Like these things, it is an affair of adjustment to the demands of the environment, which is the essence of living, as well in its most literal sense of sheer ability to survive, as in its wider sense of breadth of interest, and flexibility of mental grasp. To make our own ideal of the educated man concrete by an example, we would insist that no person can be considered as having an adequate adjustment, who is a vocational incompetent, or who lacks the knowledge and skill needed to look after his health. Vocational competence, and good health practices, therefore, are essential items in the picture of the well educated man—far more essential than a great deal ordinarily included. An educated human being does not have for his essential distinguishing mark a preoccupation with "the finer things of life," in the narrow, snobbish sense. In essence he is biologically competent, fitted to survive and grow, possessed of a firm grip upon life.

Let me close this section with the hope that even such a brief and preliminary survey will make you see how rich with practical meaning is our biological conception, which treats education as a process of adjustment between inner purpose and outer need, or as the promotion of a better way of life.

4. *What are the other agencies of adjustment besides education?*

Education is only one of the agencies by which a living creature adjusts himself to the demands of his environment. It is the agency most typical of human beings. But the others are important too.

And it is valuable in many ways for us to understand their place in the economy of life. Besides education, the other agencies of adjustment are inherited structure, reflexes, and instincts.

A. What is the part played by inherited structure in securing adjustment? We have already mentioned some of the most obvious, dramatic instances. Great size, a thick skin, a ponderous skeleton, formidable teeth, powerful wings—the value of these possessions in coping with the world hardly needs elaboration. Such physical structures are the tools and weapons, by which the creature subdues nature to his purposes. Now, while man is not very strong, and is by inheritance quite lightly armed, he possesses two of the most marvelous bodily structures which have ever appeared in the whole course of evolution—his hand, and his vocal organs. Only the highest apes possess a hand with an opposed thumb; and without such a hand, most of the manipulations by which we control our machines and tools, would be vastly more difficult, if not completely impossible. Moreover, the best ape-hand is so much cruder than the human hand, that it could hardly be disciplined to the adjusting of delicate precision instruments, or complicated mechanisms. As for the vocal organs, it has been said that man alone, of all living beings, possesses a sound-producing equipment refined enough to make possible any highly developed language. So, quite without reference to any higher mental powers, we may well believe that without the structures of the human body, the most triumphant of all types of adjustment, which we call civilization, could hardly have been attained.

B. What is the part played by reflexes in securing adjustment? A reflex is usually defined as an inherited mode of response, characterized by simplicity, definiteness, and inevitability. That is to say, it is very clear cut and easy to recognize. When the proper stimulus is given, the reaction almost certainly occurs. A good instance is the "knee jerk," the automatic kick produced by tapping the tendon below the knee cap. Most of the reflexes must be accounted indispensable agencies for adjustment. When we eat, a whole chain of automatic responses is set in motion. Saliva and gastric juices flow; the muscular lining of the stomach and intestines becomes active; and without this balanced sequence, digestion could not take place. Food being eaten constitutes, as it were, the challenge given, or the problem set, by the environment. And the body proceeds to meet the situation by reflex response. But it would not be quite true to say that all reflexes are aids to adjustment. For instance, a new born baby will grasp tightly any stick-like object—a finger for instance—which touches its hand. And this reflex vanishes about the one hundred and fiftieth day of life. Such a performance might be useful to a creature destined to be carried through the tree tops by its mother; but hardly to a human baby. Indeed, if it did not die out, many of our manipulative skills would be quite impossible because of this fatal convulsive grasping. Nor does the knee jerk seem to serve any very obvious purpose. Still, in the main, the reflexes are necessary agencies in the economy of human life.

C. What part is played by instinct in securing adjustment? Here we come upon a very different matter. And our answer is: With human beings, very little, perhaps none.

Like a reflex, an instinct is an inherited mode of response. In some cases an animal may need a little practice to bring an instinct to full efficiency; but essentially it remains an unlearned response. An instinct differs from a reflex by being vastly more complex, and far less certain. Compare the migration of birds with the knee jerk, and the differences between instinct and reflex are obvious at once.

Now it is likely that with the lower animals, instinct does play a great part in bringing about adjustment. I say that it is likely, because, as we shall see in a moment, even this is not quite certain. The insect world is particularly rich in marvelous instances of what seems like instinctive behavior. Ants are able to carry on a most intricate community life, taking care of military defence, providing far in advance for food supplies, seeing to architectural and engineering needs, and maintaining arrangements for the care of the young—all, so far as we know, without any learning whatsoever. The migratory impulse of birds, the gregarious tendencies of certain animals, the constructional activities of beavers, are a few examples from higher levels of life. It certainly seems as though everywhere we were in the presence of life adjustments brought about through the agency of instinct. And yet the evidence is not conclusive. We know nothing—less than nothing—about what takes place in the animal's mind when it goes through a performance which we call instinctive. All we can do is to watch its overt behavior, and draw conclusions, necessarily limited, necessarily conjectural. And even at that, our opportunities are very narrow, because it is rarely possible to observe the creature when at home in his natural habitat. Our actual, certain knowledge of the psychology of animals is really very small. What controls the behavior of the migrating bird, or how the beaver feels when he selects trees for his dam, we simply do not know. Even with animals, the term "instinctive" as applied to some instance of behavior, is pretty much a label for our ignorance. So, plausible though the concept be, the part of wisdom remains hesitation.

When we come to human beings, the case is much clearer. Many important authorities now believe that human beings have virtually no true instincts. I shall not discuss this at length, because it is a topic which belongs to systematic psychology. But I shall maintain that very, very few human actions are determined by instinct—indeed, probably none. Perhaps the best way to make clear the reasons for this position, will be to take two much talked-of instincts, and analyze their influence in the economy of human life.

Have human beings a sex instinct? Most people would instantly say, yes. There is, of course, no doubt that we are endowed with a sequence of reflexes connected with sexual behavior, just as we have a sequence of reflexes connected with digestive behavior. But there is all the doubt in the world as to whether we have a sex *instinct* at all comparable, let us say to the migratory tendency of a bird, or the dam building tendency of a beaver. We might imagine each new generation of birds feeling a strong traditional urge to get together and fly south in the fall, or each new generation of beavers feeling a strong traditional urge to work together on a dam. And we believe that such animal traditions are innate rather than acquired. But are our traditions about marriage and mating instinctive? No one who has read such a book as Westermarck's *History of Human Marriage,* can easily believe it, simply because

WHAT IS EDUCATION?

other races have traditions differing from our own all the way to extreme opposition. Are our traditional sex taboos instinctive? Certainly not. The normal sex life of an educated Athenian of the age of Pericles would seem shocking even in this sophisticated age; but it shocked nobody then. What therefore can we conclude? Surely that whether or no a sex instinct really exists, its manifestations, which vary with tradition, with race, with education, with social expectation, are infinitely more important than the instinct itself. Notice that this makes the whole project of sex education more hopeful. If we were in the presence of a definite and powerful instinct, there would be little we could do. Nature would have to be given its course, even though individuals, and social systems, were wrecked thereby. But sex behavior certainly can, and certainly should, be moulded by education. Our adjustment here is not by instinct, but by learning. About all we have in the way of native endowment is the mere reflex mechanism of the sex process. The part played by sex in our lives is determined by the uses and the social setting of the process, and this depends on education.

Have human beings a maternal instinct? The sentimentalist cries, yes. The psychologist is not so sure. We must always bear in mind that every woman with a baby is under enormous social pressure to behave like a "natural mother"—which of course means, like a conventional one. Any refusing to do so, meets with violent disapprobation, and is even made highly inconvenient in many ways. A cynical observer has remarked that if one wishes to lose one's belief in the maternal instinct, one should work for a while in the free ward of a maternity hospital. And it is perfectly true that we find great variations in maternal behavior among different classes and different races. Once again, as with sex, what we seem to have as a gift of nature, is only the reflex mechanism of motherhood—that is, the sequence of reflexes which constitute nursing. The rest we learn. Notice again the hopefulness of this view. If a woman's adjustment to the great environmental problem of a young infant were brought about by some inevitable instinct, which "taught" her what to do and what not to do, then how would progress be possible? Would not motherhood mean exactly the same thing today as it did in the stone age? And would not this be disastrous? If, on the other hand, maternal behavior is mostly learned, then we can hold wise motherhood to be one of the greatest and most desirable of educational outcomes. Surely the creed that education is the shaping of life should include also a belief in its applicability to this most significant of all life's problems.

Of course I have not here presented any complete or adequate criticism of what is known as the "instinct theory." To obtain this, you must turn to modern treatises on systematic psychology. All I have done is to indicate the grounds on which we must question the doctrine of instinct, and which lead us to regard those long lists of instincts which used to adorn the pages of old fashioned texts in psychology, as simply so much mythology. And of course our rejection of the notion that human beings have a great many instincts, has a most important educational bearing. It forbids us to believe that the art of teaching consists largely of connecting up something to be learned with the child's instincts. This was a piece of advice often given to teachers in the past. But it falls to the ground if we deny the presence of specific instincts. As we shall see later, we must work along very different lines when we seek to improve and render more vital the teaching process.

So to sum up, inherited structure necessarily plays a great part in man's adjustment to life: reflex a considerable one: instinct a very slight and doubtful one. Our major resource in dealing with the problems which the world presents, is learning. In this, man probably differs very much from the lower creatures. And here we come upon our next principal question.

5. *What are the unique characteristics of human adjustment?*

Through long ages of conflict, humanity has emerged as the supreme animal type. Our ancestors of the stone age barely competed for the right to live with the formidable creatures which shared their habitat. The American Indian had no overwhelming advantage over the bison and the bear. The Hindu villager still fears the tiger as a foe to be met on not unequal terms. But civilized man has established an absolute dominance. If the most powerful and intelligent of the lower creatures are not wholly cer-

WHAT IS EDUCATION?

tain victims of the express rifle in the hands of the expert hunter, yet the general advance of civilization spells their sure doom. Only the insect, with its vast fecundity and insidious attack, in any way threatens man's complete command of the resources of the earth, and the means of livelihood. Why is this? The question is one of the most momentous we can ask. The conditions which, working over tens of thousands of years, have brought mankind to its present mastery of life, are exactly those to which we must continue to look for further progress. If we wish our race to continue in the ascending pathway trodden for so long, we must know what it is that has given humanity this commanding advantage, and then we must set to work to accelerate and intensify its operation, and to guard it from perversion.

What then are the unique characteristics of human adjustment? What unique power for dealing with environmental problems is possessed by man? What is the secret of his biological supremacy? Certainly not superiority in size, or strength, or swiftness. Certainly not a more efficient repertoire of instincts. The answer is that man, far more than any other living creature, is able to *acquire,* or *learn* his adjustment, instead of inheriting it. And an acquired adjustment has certain great advantages, which I am about to point out. You should observe that in doing this, I am really stating the conditions of an educational program. If education is to do what it should in the way of moulding and improving life, it must concentrate on those advantages in adjusting and living, which have given man his supremacy, and which, if rightly used, can increase it.

A. In the first place, an acquired adjustment may be *flexible,* while an inherited adjustment is fixed or rigid. When the migratory season comes, the birds travel over the same old route, in spite of manifold new dangers from gun and decoy. But when the patrol reports icebergs in the North Atlantic, the liners steer on a different course. When, in the last geological epoch, the climate of northern Europe changed, many of the lower animal types were exterminated. But mankind developed a new way of living. This flexibility, this power to alter radically a manner of action in the face of a new environmental challenge, is the most precious human capacity. And a wisely conceived scheme of education will cherish it above everything.

In all our racial history there has never been a time when the lure of specialization was so great. It is one of the great perils of education today. There is a widely held notion that schools should devote most of their effort to training young people for specific jobs, and that anything else is in the way of ornament, frill, or luxury. This is entirely contrary to a biological conception of the essential task of education. What we urgently need is a greater amount, not of specialized but of general training—training, that is, which seeks to equip the individual to meet new problems, and face demands which cannot be foreseen, rather than to make him efficient in a limited routine. Taking it on the lowest level of selfish practicality, a general education offers the best chance of a personal success, simply because failure in one line may be recouped by success in another, if we are flexible enough. And the perpetuation of our civilization, and the improvement of its institutions, patently demands a generation able to deal broadly with circumstance, and to cope flexibly with the problems of life. Let us not forget that the dinosaur and the mammoth were two of nature's masterpieces of specialization, and that the outcome is written in the record of the rocks.

B. In the second place, an acquired adjustment may take place at any time in an individual's life history, while an inherited adjustment is over once for all when a certain period closes. So human adjustment may continue as long as a person lives. It has the characteristic of being *progressive*.

We know that not all instincts make their appearance at birth. But when once an animal's complete repertoire of instinctive responses has fully emerged, it is just about as efficient as it ever will be. This, of course, is not absolutely true, because all the higher mammals are capable of some learning, so that a wolf of seven years may be a wiser hunter than he was at three; and so on. But the amount of improvement that can take place after the inherited adjustment has established itself, is not very great.

With man, the case is utterly different. It used to be thought that human beings learned best when they were young, and that after they reached early maturity, their capacity for radical improvement was at an end. We now know this to be entirely false. One can learn better at twenty-five than one could at fifteen; and one can continue to learn, almost as well as ever, at least to the age of fifty, and probably far beyond it. Recently a distinguished and successful author has publicly stated that he began his career as a writer after he was forty. A popular magazine, a short time ago, printed the story of a business man, ruined at sixty, who built up a striking success in an entirely new line of activity. And the great sociologist, William Graham Sumner, is a notable example of a man who reorganized his whole mental life after the age of forty, learning many new languages, acquiring a mastery of higher mathematics, and developing a body of theory which deeply influences contemporary thought.

There cannot be a doubt that the power of continuing to learn has been an enormous advantage to the human race, partly because its elders have been able to accumulate a wisdom and an insight which was a precious asset. An old dog may not be able to learn new tricks, but an elderly man can. And this is one reason why he is a superior creature. Now the schools can hinder or help this projection of adjustment late into life. If we take the short view, if we think that the only "practical" kind of education is one that prepares us for a job immediately after graduation, then we are going contrary to one of the major influences upon which human progress must depend. Again, such an attitude is stupid, even on the grounds of a purely selfish interest. Our best guarantee of success and happiness in life, is to have, during youth, the kind of experience and education which will enable one to make continuous readjustments, even into old age. Education best serves the individual and the race, by seeking to preserve flexibility later and later into life; by creating in the individual the power and will *to go on learning*.

C. In the third place, human adjustment is *creative* rather than passive. Man solves the problems of existence, not only by changing himself, but also by changing the environment. The human being has been defined as the tool using animal, or the fire using animal; and there is a basic truth in this, though inadequately stated. We have, perhaps, in this chapter, seemed to think of adjustment too exclusively as *finding* a way, whereas, with human beings at least, it should rather mean *creating* a way. Man, in adjusting himself to the universe, makes tools, and weapons, and buildings, and social institutions. He takes the stuff of nature, and moulds it to his need. And this is yet another secret of his supremacy.

This idea is so important, and will influence so much of our thinking about educational problems, that I will try to put it in another way. It may help us more vividly to understand what is meant by creative adjustment, if we say that man often deals with life's problems, not by submission, nor by compromise, but by invention. "The head of a big industrial plant which has joint committees of management and workmen said to me, 'I find that we come to agreement . . . not by reconciling our ideas but by finding the new idea which is always something different from the addition of the previous ideas.'"[1] When a social case worker has to deal with an individual whose life relationships are profoundly unsatisfactory, she does not just advise him to put up with things as they are, to make the best of a bad job, just to fit in with iron circumstances; rather she should seek for him some new constructive interests and ways of living. The Reconstruction Finance Corporation is an invention for dealing with the problems of a business depression; and it is a very different affair from simply sitting down and waiting for the clouds to roll by. If you will think of your own way of meeting difficulties, you will find that your most satisfying successes have come, not from putting up with adverse conditions, but from discovering ways of changing the conditions, from inventing some new course of action, from altering not only yourself, but also your environment. It is just because man is able to do this sort of thing, that he has established himself as a master of life.

Once again, education may help or hinder. If we treat the person to be educated as a passive recipient into whom knowledge must be poured, or on whom habits must be impressed, our ideas and practices run counter to the distinctive character of human adjustment. Education that is true to its genius and function, must

[1] M. P. Follett: *Creative Experience:* Longmans, Green and Co. 1924.

clearly stimulate the experimental attitude, the creative approach. It is the creative man, rather than the conforming one, who is best and most triumphantly adjusted to the universe in which we live, and who most strongly carries, from the dim past towards the unknown future, the torch of human progress.

D. In the fourth place, acquired adjustment tends to exalt the individual, while inherited adjustment tends to exalt the species. We often hear inherited adjustment called "racial." And so it is. Certain lower forms of life, more particularly insects, and fish, provide for the continuity of the stock by producing monstrous hordes of young. Multitudes are slain by enemies and accidents. But it does not matter, because the racial adjustment is, on the average, and for the majority, effective. So also with animal instinct at higher levels, which may ruthlessly sacrifice the individual for the species. In all such cases, we behold nature "red in tooth and claw," careless of the single life, careful only of the race.

But as soon as we have an acquired type of adjustment, the picture changes. The individual, and his acquisitions of experience and wisdom, becomes the agent of racial progress and perpetuation. When a herd of musk oxen abandon a defeated leader to certain death, they gain an actual advantage. But when a man of ripe powers, wide knowledge, and deep insight, dies or is submerged, there is a racial loss with no offsetting gain.

This is the reason why education is bound to respect individuality, if it is true to itself. And it also shows how individuality should be sanely respected, a point of great importance, for here is a matter on which many enthusiasts run amuck. A human being, merely as so many pounds of protoplasm, has no particular value. But as a person who can be led to acquire a flexible, creative, ever-continuing adjustment, he has a unique and absolute worth. So the individual child in the school should be respected, not for what he is, but for what he may become. One of the errors that we find in the present day "progressive school" movement, is the tendency to suppose that every whim of every child is sacred, merely because he has it. For this there is no rational defence. It is individualism run to seed. Each person is of value, either for what he now possesses in the way of mental and moral quality and insight, or for what he may come to possess. And the child inevitably has little, though he may come to have much. What is wholly true, however, is that through the very nature of human adjustment, the individual acquires an absolute worth as the only hope of progress. Whenever we subordinate him to propaganda, to class interest, to any form of exploitation, or above all to treatment as a mere unit in a mass, we sink towards the sub-human level.

Chapter 2

HOW IS EDUCATION RELATED TO SOCIETY?

1. What is the importance of society in human life?

Everyone takes it as a truism that society is enormously important for the individual. But it needs some reflection to see how profoundly, how completely, our social experiences and opportunities mould and make us.

Every human being becomes the kind of person he is through the influence of his social environment. Primitive man lives in a small and narrow group. He is dominated and shaped by tribal custom. His life is an affair of compulsion and taboo. He feels that certain ways of conduct are perfectly right and "natural," which we would regard as wrong and horrible; for instance, he is likely to be hostile and treacherous to all strangers, or willing to kill off the old and helpless. His ideas about the nature of the world in which he lives hardly deserve to be called ideas at all; they are crude, animistic myths and superstitions, which provide a sort of rationalized support for the tribal way of life. When this being, so closely kin to us in his biological inheritance but the product of a social environment thus limited, comes into contact with our modern civilization, we perceive with a shock the gulf that divides him from us, and gain some intimation of the extent to which society schools us into the persons that we are. On a less dramatic scale, the same thing happens all around us. The social environment of the peasant produces the peasant type. English upper class life has given the world generations of men, indelibly and unmistakably marked in character and outlook. Every occupational group, in so far as it moves in a social world distinctively its own, develops its distinguishing personal characteristics. If it were possible to pick out a Solomon Islander, an English aristocrat, a New York stock broker, an Arab tribesman, and a southern Negro field laborer—all of precisely the same native ability, all exactly equal in direct biological inheritance—we would find ourselves dealing with human beings so enormously different that it would be almost hopeless for them to understand one another, or to enter into any genuine communion. And these vast differences would come from social background and experience.

We may go even further than this. For without society, human personality itself would be impossible. There is no such thing as a person apart from society. If a man were set down in the wilderness, with absolutely no social aids and facilities, he would swiftly and miserably perish. Not only would he be naked, foodless, weaponless, and without tools or shelter; he would also be destitute of all mental equipment, all knowledge, all skill; for these also he gains from society. Or if a human being could be brought up with just the bare minimum of help from others needed to keep him alive, he would, at the age of twenty, be human only in bodily shape. He would be unable to talk; he would have none of the concepts which organize and implement our mental life; he would not possess the skill to use the simplest, commonest, most necessary articles; he would have none of the habits on which our social decencies depend. Could we deprive anyone of every last thing he owes to society, there would be nothing left but so many pounds of helpless protoplasm, which could not even put food into its mouth, and whose highest achievement would be the chain reflexes of swallowing, digestion, and elimination.

Let us state the case somewhat differently. Human adjustment is made to the social environment, to social demand, to social expectation. This is so, even when we seem to be responding to physical objects. When I sit down on a chair, I am not just responding to a physical thing which in and of itself suggests sitting. I am accommodating myself to a social regime which, among other matters, expects people to sit on chairs. If a person has grown up in a chairless society, he will merely gaze at the strange object in bewilderment. Or if his tribal mythology has taught him that only devils sit on chairs, he will scare his host by shrinking away in horror, or by smashing the infamous thing. His adjustment is always not to the physical object itself, but to the physical object as part of a social setting. In the same way, a farmer in the harvest field, or the miner at the coal face, are not simply reacting to immediate physical reality. Their behavior is an adjustment to a complex whole of social and economic pressures, demands, and considerations.

So we move forward a step beyond the idea of our first chapter. Not only is education a process of adjustment. It is a process of social adjustment. Not only is education the shaping of life. It is the shaping of a life lived in society, sustained and determined by society. Society makes demands. Education fits the individual to meet them, and in so doing, makes him what he is.

2. How does society set the goals of education? *By its institutions*

The institutions of society are the goals of education. If at first this statement may seem unusual and dubious, it is because we understand the term "institution" too narrowly. This word is apt to call up in our minds visions of bricks and mortar and concrete, and of persons in uniform. We think of a prison as one kind of a building, a school as another, a home for crippled children as another, and a hospital as still another. But a little reflection shows us that all this is very superficial. A prison, in essence, is not made of stone walls, but is a way of living and acting. A school is not a specimen of architecture, but a group of learners and teachers coming together and working for a common purpose in a particular manner. And we may have a superb hospital which does not look like a hospital at all; or conversely, one that looks very fine, and is very poor. So understood, an institution seems to be nothing more than a very widely recognized, well established, and permanent mode or habit of acting and living together. Indeed, sociologists point out that the difference between an institution and a custom is only one of degree. It is a custom to return a social call, or to wear certain clothes at certain gatherings, or to send out wedding invitations in form. The behavior of pupils and teachers in school, and all that goes with it; the organized life of an office or a factory; or the great mass of human activity which, taken together, constitutes what we call a democratic state, are customs, but on a vastly grander, more complicated, and more established scale. Human beings have to learn to adjust themselves to custom at both levels; but in the first instance, about all they need is a book on etiquette and a little coaching, while in the second, only a lengthy and most carefully considered process of education will suffice. Social institutions, regarded as established, customary ways of acting, constitute the demand which our human environment makes upon the individual. And in this sense, they are the goals of all education.

This idea is so very significant, and will be the foundation of so much of our thinking, that I am anxious to explain it as clearly and cogently as possible. Suppose an immigrant from some backward country comes to the United States; we feel it very important that he shall become "Americanized." This means that he must become adjusted to the social institutions of America. When first he lands from Ellis Island, he is like some crude and awkward being in a laboratory full of delicate and powerful machinery. Unless he is helped and guided, he will either stand still in bewildered fear, or else hurt himself and damage the equipment. Little by little he comes to find his way about in the intricate social tangle. And with good fortune, he becomes at last adapted to our ways of social living, and feels a spiritual kinship with his new fatherland. In many respects, the little child is in a similar case. Australia has a saying that the baby is the best immigrant, because the native born child has a better chance of complete adjustment than any grown person coming in from a differet social order. In any case, the great task, the great challenge, which society puts before its new recruit, is that of adjustment to its institutions.

But does not this mean that education has almost numberless goals? It does. And if we tried to make a complete list of all the institutions of society, we should never finish. Yet if a person has a radically faulty adjustment to any one of them, his education is a failure to that degree; and the importance of the failure is directly proportional to the importance of the institution concerned. One of the greatest teachers of social ethics has told of a student whose work in his courses was of the highest excellence, but who later became a vicious grafter in a political gang. This was a tragic educational failure, a failure to adjust to what is, in one sense, the most important single institution in the modern social order, the political state. Now certainly many of us never become grafters or gangsters, and would not, even if we had the opportunity. But there is not one of us who is not imperfectly adjusted to some of the major, and a whole host of the minor, social institutions. And to that extent we are educational failures, no matter what kind of academic honors our sheepskins may attest.

In suggesting that some institutions are more important than others, we have a clue which must be used in the practical working out of our further discussions. To attempt to discuss fully the ideal adjustment of a human being to all social institutions would mean writing a book as large as the *Encyclopaedia Britannica;* and it would call for a knowledge compared to which my own is an extremely small drop in a very large bucket. What I can hope to do, however, is to pick out the most salient institutions, and show how education, as a process of adjustment, is related to them. In this way, perhaps, you may be helped to understand the method which sound, fundamental educational analysis and thinking must always follow. The institutions which I shall pick out for particular study are these: The state; the family; the economic system; the recreational institutions; the institutions which exist to preserve and promote health. My argument will be that the well educated man is one who is adjusted adequately to all of these. They are, in fact, the educational goals which we are to discuss.

There is a great advantage in thinking of the goals of education in institutional terms, and also a certain danger. The advantage consists in making our discussions very realistic. To talk in general terms about social adjustment may be all very well. Much that we say may be true enough. But we can hardly hope to envisage an educational program until we specify exactly what kind of social adjustment we have in mind. And when we deal with the state, the family, the economic system, the recreational institutions, and the health preserving institutions, we eliminate much vagueness. But also a certain danger of error is involved. For no man adjusts himself separately to each separate institution. A man whose recreational interests are defective cannot be a first rate member of a family. A person who cannot take care of his health is not likely to be a completely effective citizen of the economic republic. And a man who is content with a very tedious and confining job, or a job which is inimical to physical well being, cannot be well adjusted in matters of health or recreation or political interest. We must remember that life is not divided into different water-tight compartments, but that it is an integrated whole. And we must not think that our institutional view implies a curriculum which gives now a little bit of home training, now a little bit of civic training, now a little bit of health education, and so on. Rather we must have a general, integrated curriculum which still makes definite contacts with, and has definite outlets upon, specific institutions and their problems.

But you may interpose an objection to this entire point of view. You may say that this notion of the goals of education as the institutions of society seems to leave wholly out of account the individual private life of the human being. Can any scheme of education be at all adequate, you may ask, which simply ignores personal, private experience, enrichment, and development? This indeed is a most weighty and far reaching question. Moreover, it is a question which I cannot, at this stage, answer fully or very convincingly. Still, when we pointed out the importance of society for the individual, we gained at least the glimmering of an adequate reply. We saw that all those things which make a human being truly human, were wholly impossible without society. And now we push this thought one step farther. There is no individual experience, there is no private personal culture, apart from society. You, and I, and all of us, do not live lives which are partly social and partly individual. There is no bulkhead between the social and the individual portions of our experience. That experience is wholly social—and at the same time wholly individual. And as our discussions advance, it will become more and more clear that the enrichment, the uniqueness, and the creative freedom of the individual is best served by an education which brings home to him the significance of his social relationships, and leads him to feel deeply his kinship with his fellows.

Conceptions of education which begin by dividing human life into separate individual and social aspects, are always defective. So are conceptions of education which work in terms of the individual considered as something in himself, apart from society. The aims of education have often been so conceived. And this leads us to our next question, which will, perhaps, throw fuller light upon this problem of the individual and social aspects of life and education.

3. *In what other ways have the aims of education been stated?*

All writers on the fundamentals of education are likely to deal, more or less explicitly, with educational aims. So we have, in the literature, a great many statements on the matter, which are often quite conflicting. It is important for us to know some of these, because, in comparing them with our own position, we come to understand it better.

A. Of all statements of educational aims, that which has probably influenced most deeply the thought and practice of school people within recent years, is the one known as "The Seven Cardinal Principles of Secondary Education," though it applies very well to elementary and higher education also.[1] It was drawn up by an official group, the Commission on the Reorganization of Secondary Education. In the opinion of this committee, the secondary school should bring about the following seven results:

i. It should safeguard and promote the pupil's physical health.
ii. It should perfect his command of the fundamental processes; that is, reading, writing, arithmetical computation, and oral and written expression.
iii. It should train for worthy home membership.
iv. It should equip him vocationally, so that he may be able to earn a living.

[1] United States Department of the Interior; Bureau of Education; *Bulletin,* 1918, no. 35.

v. It should develop in him desirable civic qualities.
vi. It should equip him for the worthy use of leisure time.
vii. It should definitely promote ethical character.

We need to understand that this sevenfold statement did not originate with the commission. It is, indeed, a reworking of a much earlier formulation of aims, put forward by the philosopher, Herbert Spencer.[2] This, as a matter of fact, makes it all the more valuable and authoritative. For it represents the consensus of much of the best thinking over a period of years, rather than a sort of special revelation which burst upon the world in 1918. School people have everywhere recognized its excellence. It gives a splendid picture of what a really educated man should be. And it tells the schools what they should try to do. In the main, one cannot but agree with it. Yet we are unable to find it wholly acceptable.

By far the most important objection to it is that the statement seems largely individualistic. It appears to divide human life into private functions, and social functions, though this may not have been the actual intent of the commission. Health, for instance, is treated as though it were an individual problem; whereas as a matter of fact, one's physical and mental well being depend on properly using the institutional conveniences and modes of action provided by society for their promotion and establishment. Vocational fitness, again, calls for something not only more than, but different from, the equipment of the individual with certain skills and insights; rather it demands a broad, competent adjustment to economic institutions. The worthy use of leisure time, too, seems desirable enough, but it is rather intangible. "Leisure time," of course, means time when one is not occupied in earning a living. But its "worthy use" does not mean doing purely private things. It means satisfactory, active adjustment to civic, domestic, and recreational institutions, and must be so handled educationally. Ethical character, once more, is certainly of essential importance. No educational scheme which fails to produce it, can be considered good. But it is by no means a separate part of life. Nor is it an individual matter. It is the total outcome of a favorable adjustment to all social institutions.

[2] *Education;* 1900.

When we consider worthy home membership and good civic qualities, we certainly seem to be dealing with social ideals. But the commission did not formulate them in social terms, as adjustments to specific institutions. To sum up our whole point, the Seven Cardinal Principles of Secondary Education furnish us with a splendid outline of a valid educational ideal. But it is not so realistic, nor so concrete, and therefore not so useful, as a statement of educational aims in terms of institutional adjustment.

B. Let us now consider a statement of aims which is interesting and significant, but not so important or so excellent as the foregoing. This is the one advanced by Alexander Inglis.[3] According to him, education ought to equip one for "social-civic" activities, for "economic-vocational" activities, and for "cultural-avocational" activities. Many serious objections can be urged against this. In the first place, it seems as if only civic activities are supposed to be social. Culture and vocation appear to be individual matters, and on a different footing. And this is a profound defect. In the second place, there is a very strong objection to thinking of culture as having to do essentially with avocations or hobbies. This tends to treat it as an individual possession, a private adornment. Such a belief is the tap root of one of the most vicious educational developments of modern times, the treatment of culture in terms of elegance rather than of life. In the third place, it is absurd to divide human life into vocation, avocation, and citizenship, which is just what Inglis proposes. One might almost as well divide it into sleeping and waking, and say that education exists to prepare us for them. The claim would be true, but ridiculous and irrelevant. It ignores a whole host of vital matters. What about one's relationship to one's family, to the state, to the economic system, to the public press, to the institutions which exist to provide recreation? Has education nothing to do with these? Need it not take them into consideration? The reply is obvious. Once more, the really significant subdivisions of human life are those in terms of institutional adjustments and relationships.

C. Let us now consider some of the older, classic statements of educational aim. They are far simpler, far more in the nature of blanket formulas, than those which we have been discussing. But

[3] *Principles of Secondary Education:* Houghton Mifflin Company, 1916.

it will not be a waste of time to review one or two of them, because we still hear them repeated, and they influence educational thought and practice.

First take the famous dictum that education should seek a harmonious development of all the powers and faculties of the individual. This conception does not lack a certain nobility; and it has inspired some of the most devoted and enthusiastic teaching the world has ever seen. But for us it remains woefully inadequate. So long as we think merely in terms of the individual, which it invites us to do, we can have no concrete idea of what "harmonious" development is, or how it differs from one that is not "harmonious." One supposes it to mean that a person ought not to have a one-sided development, or excessive and exaggerated interests in science, or in literature, or in art, or in vocational matters, and so on. But how much interest along any line is just enough? And what shall determine when someone has too much? We cannot say. A personality which might be "harmonious" both inwardly and outwardly in ancient Athens, would probably be out of tune with life, and inwardly conflicting, if transferred to the modern world. A "harmoniously developed" and balanced Bulgarian peasant is apt to become a jangle of misery and dissonance on the lower East Side of New York. The only feasible interpretation would be to say that a "well rounded personality" is one adequately adjusted to a wide range of social situations, demands, and institutions. And this brings us back once more to our own position, that the goals of education are the institutions of society.

Again, it has been said that education means the universal distribution of extant knowledge. But what about skills? What about appreciations? What about a recognition of civic duties? Moreover one would think that education has something to do with the person who knows, as well as with the knowledge. Also we must insist, and insist most strongly, that all knowledge does not have equal worth; so that the choice of what is best to know becomes a most essential educational responsibility. And our last, and most fundamental criticism is that knowledge for its own sake has no value. Knowledge must be transmuted into power, or it is not worth having or worth distributing. So we must disagree with this statement of the "knowledge aim" of education as exceedingly misleading.

Then there are various statements often lumped together as formulations of the "bread and butter aim" of education. Their common idea is that the chief business of education is to enable a person to earn a living. This, of course, gives us an easy target. Earning a living is certainly part of life, but hardly the whole of it. No one could be considered biologically or socially very well adjusted, who starved to death because he could not procure food, clothes, and shelter. But neither would anyone who could do nothing but earn, and who was hopelessly inept in all other life relationships.

Lastly, there are various statements of the aim of education which we classify as disciplinary. Their common thought is that education exists to train the mind, to develop power in general, or to strengthen the faculties. Behind these views there is a theory so broad and elaborate, that we shall postpone their fuller discussion for a separate chapter. All that I will now say is that they present, although imperfectly, a great truth, which much contemporary discussion fails to recognize. The truth is that the well disciplined, well developed mind really depends upon, and even means the same thing as, adequate social adjustment. To be sure, the disciplinary aims do not, in their original form, seem to involve this idea at all. But later on I shall try to show that in this lies all the force, all the truth which they possess.

4. *What type of institutional adjustment is desirable?*

When we say that the goal of education is to adjust the individual to the institutions of society, there is a danger that our principle will be quite wrongly understood. As a matter of educational history, it has in fact been thus wrongly understood, and perversely and destructively applied, many and many a time. Often all that the guides and rulers of mankind have seen in the school, is a powerful engine for producing conformity and docility, ideals perfectly expressed in the rote prayer of the English peasant child:

"God bless the squire and his relations,
And keep us in our proper stations."

Translated into terms of educational policy, this meant a stingy rationing to the lower classes of just enough education to be suitable to their humble position, without giving them any dangerous thoughts, or culpable longings for some fuller way of life. Moreover the doctrine of institutional adjustment as conformity has jumped the Atlantic, and infected a good deal of our educational thought and practice. A priceless instance was furnished by a certain educational authority, who rebuked the head of a vocational school for introducing such subjects as English and history, which he regarded as considerably worse than useless, and who insisted that the job of the school was to train boys to stand nine hours a day at a lathe for a dollar and a half and like it. Moreover there are fashionable schools and colleges in this country which influence their students strongly, whether deliberately or not, in the direction of a social outlook which is a sort of stall-fed, complacent, rigid conservatism.

If you will recall our analysis of the special and distinctive characteristics of human adjustment, you will readily see what line our criticism must take. Institutional adjustment as conformity, is rigid adjustment. But human adjustment—by which our race has made all its progress so far, and come to a dominant position in the world—is precisely *not* rigid. It has the qualities of flexibility, creativeness, and progressiveness. This is the type of adjustment to social institutions which we ought to seek.

Concretely, what does this mean? We can perhaps answer the question best by taking a few specific cases.

Let us begin with our educational authority's boy at the lathe. If he is simply trained to operate the lathe, and no more, his whole adjustment to the shop as an institution is highly limited and rigid, however efficient it may be within its boundaries. He can do his one routine chore, and nothing else. But suppose he has behind him the right kind of study of general science. His aroused curiosity and critical tendencies may lead him to see better ways of doing his job. Such cases have often enough occurred. And if he has a really living, functioning background of social science, which means an actual insight into the operations, mechanisms, and values of group life, he may well become a helpful factor in improving the whole organization. Here we have flexibility and inventiveness, rather than rigidity and blind conformity. The boy is not a worse workman because he is more than a mere conformist. Indeed he is a far more valuable one.

Or again, take the teaching profession. Early in the nineteenth century, a scheme of school organization arose, which was known as the Monitorial Plan. It was a system by which a single teacher could handle a very large number of pupils—even many hundreds—with a corresponding reduction in school costs. The teacher taught a standardized lesson to a group of older pupils, the monitors. They, in turn, were supposed to teach it, exactly as it was given to them, each to his own group of younger pupils. The mob of learners was handled by a sort of semi-military squad drill. Everything was most orderly and convenient. Now the adjustment of the monitors to their pupil groups, and to the school as a whole, was as rigid as it could be. On this depended the efficiency of the institution, which was the efficiency of a Ford assembly line. The monitors were emphatically not encouraged to ask fundamental questions, to try experiments, or to suggest improvements. We still have some hang-overs of this philosophy in present day education, whenever teachers are taught or required to use an invariant method without question.

"Theirs not to reason why
Theirs but to do, and—"

Contrast this with the adjustment expected of teachers in a first rate modern school. A background knowledge of education and psychology, and a real mastery of the subject they are teaching, makes it possible for them to find better methods, and to fit procedures to individual needs. An insight into educational principles and the fundamentals of school organization enables them to offer valuable suggestions as to the general management of the institution, and to coöperate intelligently with administrative plans, rather than blindly conforming. Moreover, such teachers are expected to grow, and to keep on growing, in skill, insight, and power. Our whole conception of the sort of person a teacher ought to be involves the idea of an adjustment which is flexible, inventive, and progressive rather than rigid and limited.

Instances might be multiplied at length, but there is no need. You can think of them for yourself. The good citizen is not a person who passively obeys the laws; he is one who enters into civic life—local, state, and national—offering suggestions, concurring, differing, choosing. The good mother is one who discovers and understands the needs of her children, and finds ways to meet them, rather than doing all things by rote and tradition.

The value of education lies precisely in producing individuals who deal with social institutions in terms of initiative, intelligence, and a willingness to go on learning. These are the virtues which the school must seek to engender. It must plan all its work, organize all its contacts, with these ends in view. Education must supply the individual not with a groove, but an orientation.

5. *Why is flexible, creative, progressive social adjustment needed?*

You have probably tended to agree with the claim that a flexible, creative, progressive adjustment of the individual to society is in fact more desirable than one which is rigid and invariant. But suppose you were challenged by an intelligent Hindu, who held the contrary opinion, and who argued that human welfare is best served by an ironclad caste system, in which every person moves in a fixed orbit, and has his course in life determined absolutely from birth onwards. Or suppose that you have to deal with some of our American believers in a caste system, who insist that a great many people ought to be educated as passive followers, and only a few as creative leaders. How would you defend your position? In replying to such people, there are two strong points which can be made.

A. A flexible, creative, progressive adjustment is better than one which is rigid, because it enables the group to fulfill far better its essential purpose, which obviously is to serve and strengthen its members. A wolf pack is able collectively to defy the larger carnivorous animals, which could easily overcome the individual wolves.

And human society is the great agency by which a creature, individually feeble and defenceless, has made himself the dominant species. As it has become organized into larger and larger units, the biological advantage it offers becomes greater and greater. This securing for the individual of a more established way of life, is the essential function both of society as a whole, and of its constituent groups.

Now suppose we consider the group of people who operate a factory, all the way from the unskilled laborer to the chief executive. If each person is allowed only to perform his allotted task, and never thinks of anything else in connection with his work, we may have efficiency of a sort. But suppose each employe is encouraged to think and to criticize, to invent and to grow, then surely there is a great potential advantage. The task of management may become much harder; but its results may also be much greater. For now the undertaking as a whole has a chance of deriving benefit from the full contribution of each person in it. The individual ceases to be a mere "hand," and becomes a complete person, and thus a potential source of improved group efficiency.

This is one great argument for flexible, creative, and progressive adjustment. It enables the entire group to take the fullest advantage of the powers of its members. A rigid caste system, a scheme of things where each person has his definite status from which he can never depart, is much simpler to manage and easier to live in. This is exactly the reason why some people prefer it. But it has vastly lower potentialities as a society, than one where each individual is encouraged to make his maximum contribution to the common good. Imagine, if you can, a football team each one of whose members knew absolutely nothing about the game except how to play one position. It would not be a very promising group mechanism. Perhaps the most nearly perfect example which our imperfect world has yet known of a society, which, as a whole, benefits by the contribution of each individual, is a working group of scientists. Each man works freely and creatively with regard to the past and present achievements of the group, and his new results are made promptly and fully available to his fellow investigators.

B. The second point which can be made against the argument

for social rigidity, is that the individual has the best chance for a satisfying and full existence in a society where he has the fullest freedom to discover new ways of living, and acting, and thinking, and feeling, and is expected to work for alterations and improvements in existing institutions. Social rigidity means individual limitation. When we say that a small farmer, or an artisan only "needs" a rudimentary education, and that for him, any wide culture would be out of place, we assume that he is fatally and utterly fixed in his groove as farmer or artisan. His caste label becomes more important than his humanity. But if we think that, outside his day's work, he should sustain interests in family life, in recreational and health matters, in religious and civic concerns, which cannot but bring him into all sorts of relationships with human affairs—and if we are even rash enough to imagine that intelligence and insight should have some conceivable bearing on his job, so that even this should not be a mere matter of routine—then, indeed, it would appear that his mental horizons can hardly be too wide. This is precisely the faith which inspires one of the most notable educational movements in the world, namely the rural Folk High School system of Denmark, which undertakes to give the farming population a very wide cultural education, something which seems the height of perverse foolishness to the caste-minded person. Both Danish and foreign observers, however, agree that in these schools and in the education they provide, lies much of the true secret of the notable agricultural prosperity of that none too favored land. And as one old peasant remarked: "The Folk High School helps the farmer to be a human being."

The essence of these two points is that we believe a society most effective where there is the fullest reciprocity between the individual and the group, where each person makes his maximum contribution to the common good, which in turn is his own chief support and source of strength. Notice too, that this conception of the free, creative interrelationship of the individual with the social group, is exactly what we mean by the democratic idea. More than two thousand years ago that idea was expressed with a masterly simplicity by the great Athenian leader, Pericles: ". . . we Athenians are able to judge at all events, if we cannot originate; and instead of looking on discussion as a stumbling-block in the way of action, we think it an indispensable preliminary to any wise action at all. . . . In short, I say that as a city we are the school of Hellas; while I doubt if the world can produce a man, who, where he has only himself to depend on, is equal to so many emergencies, and graced by so happy a versatility as the Athenian."

6. *How does society furnish the means of institutional adjustment?*

It is, of course, hopeless to try to bring about a favorable institutional adjustment by saying that it should exist. The undeveloped human being cannot sustain a free, creative group relationship. He must be educated. He must have at his command certain mental tools. And society provides the tools whereby the individual may adjust himself effectively to its institutions. It has done so by accumulating a body of intellectual resources, which it is the peculiar task of education to transmit and render available. Ross Finney [4] presents a useful list of these resources and describes them as follows:

i. The means of communication. These include "facial expression, gesture, language, the arts of writing and printing, the fine arts considered as means of expressing feeling, and all the mechanical devices and social arrangements for communicating at a distance, besides those repositories by which we leave records for subsequent generations.

ii. The techniques of industry. By these he means ". . . the knowledge of how to perform the processes of all branches of economic production. And that includes not only the manual and mental skills, but the applications of the arts and sciences, as well as the industrial organizations of various sorts"—in a word, technology in its widest sense.

iii. The techniques of amusement. "The great athletic sports . . . the field sports . . . indoor amusements . . . assembly hall entertainments . . . sociable gatherings . . . besides many other recreations that will occur to the reader."

iv. The sciences.

v. The fine arts.

vi. The body of current beliefs, which are zealously maintained and dutifully transmitted and accepted. Though often with-

---

[4] *A Sociological Philosophy of Education,* The Macmillan Company, 1928.

out any sufficient basis of evidence, they produce very profound effects upon human welfare. Thus the belief that the earth was the center of the universe permeated mediaeval life and institutions like an invisible but potent vapor; and resistance to Copernicus and Gallileo came from a dim perception of how the new astronomy threatened the entire structure of society.

vii. Prevailing wants and ideals. Part of the mind set of modern America, which helps to make our social picture very different from that of Europe, is the general desire, transmitted to our rising generation, to own an automobile. Here we see an intellectual factor, a wish or idea, deeply affecting the pattern of social life.

viii. A vast, vague, ill defined body of conventions, made up of the "folkways" or traditional modes of acting, which include such matters as "ringing the door bell or knocking before entering, tipping the porter of a sleeping car . . ." and so on; and the "mores" or conventions regarding what is right and wrong, as for instance, our notions of decency and indecency in dress.

These are the agencies, Finney tells us, by which we operate the institutions of society. They are the means, rather than the ends of education. Where such resources are abundantly available, institutional life is copious and satisfying, and individual adjustment to society is effective and creative. Where they are meager, the whole social level falls. Consider those dark centuries after the collapse of the Western Empire, when Gregory of Tours lamented in ungrammatical Latin the decline of learning. All the resources of communication were depleted; the techniques of industry and recreation were at the lowest ebb; the fine arts and the sciences hardly existed; prevailing beliefs were crude and superstitious; prevailing wants were of the humblest; and life was governed by a body of convention and tradition which seemed like a return to primitive ways. What was the result? In a word, pernicious social anaemia. The family was housed, if not with contentment, at least with resignation, in a wattle and daub hut which but typified its institutional condition. The state was an ineffective hodge-podge of do-nothing royal puppets and conspiring grand viziers. The offices of the Faith were discharged in crude structures, unserved by the enriching and humanizing arts. The industrial mechanism, founded upon an inefficient agriculture, faltered, and seemed about to fall to bits. The paucity of intellectual capital had as its inevitable counterpart an unexampled social and cultural depression.

Moreover, the contrary relationship also holds. Bagley has cogently argued, in his *Determinism in Education,* that whenever intellectual resources are copiously available at a high level, there institutional life is abundant and effective, and individual life full and rich. Here we come upon the vital, the central point of connection between education and social welfare. For the educational institutions have as their special purpose the accumulation and distribution of this intellectual capital. They are the banking houses of the social order. And just as banks are not stores of bullion, but mechanisms for the support of industrial life through credit, so the schools perform a far greater and different function from the mere storing of knowledge and preservation of learning. Their personnel adds to our intellectual resources through research, and makes these resources available through re-synthesis, re-interpretation, popularization, and teaching.

Perhaps the significance of the intellectual accumulations of a society can be made more impressively clear if we take two striking modern instances. A few years ago there burst upon post-war Paris an apparition in the form of a Senegalese prize fighter known as "Battling Siki." After a whirlwind career of almost incredible whoopee and violence, during which he defeated the French heavyweight champion, and, of course, gained quite enough money to set himself up for life—but which he incontinently squandered—he miserably collapsed. Newspaper comment referred to him as a pathetic figure despite his prowess—a barbarian disgracefully exploited by a world he could not understand. Here we have a first rate example of a person projected into a sophisticated society, who was utterly lacking in the background of intellectual resources necessary for successful adjustment to its complex institutions. What happens is a brief, deafening episode, and then extinction. The man is torn to bits by a mechanism which he utterly fails to comprehend. His failure lies in this; he is confronted with complex institutional problems without the intellectual wherewithal to cope with them. Society sets him a task of adjustment, but does not provide him with those resources which alone make success possible.

For a contrary case consider the famous explorer Steffansson. Here is a man who learned to cope with the forbidding Arctic environment actually better than the natives. What they unanimously thought impossible, he achieved. He made his way for great distances over the frozen ocean, carrying no food supplies, and living entirely "off the country." Here we see the essential advantage of the civilized man. Society had endowed Steffansson with its richest intellectual resources. His capital, in this respect, was far greater than that of any native of the Arctic. And it made possible for him a supremely flexible, creative, progressive adjustment. In a most fascinating narrative he has told us how he solved the problems of securing food and fresh water many miles from land; of building snow houses, a thing which no white man was thought able to do; of finding his way in blizzards, and so on. All that he writes on such matters in his *The Friendly Arctic* is testimony to the unexampled value of the intellectual capital of civilization. Steffansson in the Arctic is a splendid type case of the conception presented in these pages of the educated man.

7. *What specific and urgent educational problem is here raised?*

This catalog of the intellectual resources of civilization exhibits what we might call the mental core of social living. The more fully anyone inherits these resources, the more completely will he be able to share in the enterprises of social life, and the better will he be able to adjust himself to social institutions. And conversely, there is no better and surer way of keeping a man down, and tying him to a limited and rigid adjustment, than to deprive him of his full share of these intellectual goods.

So much should be clear from what we have already said. But here emerges what is certainly the most central problem of practical education. *We must find ways of conveying these intellectual possessions to the individual, not as things valuable in and of themselves, but in such a manner that they will, in fact, facilitate his social adjustment, which, after all, is the only reason for their existence and transmission.* These things are means, not ends, and must be treated as such. Here we have a most crucial point. For always school people tend towards the primrose path of conveying the intellectual tools of civilization, simply and merely as ends in themselves, rather than as social utilities. When this happens, education becomes sterile.

Whenever there is a proposal to establish schools in other lands, and for other races, we are likely to have a dramatic case of transmitting intellectual resources as ends in themselves, deprived of immediate social reference. Many years ago, English liberal politicians were instrumental in setting up schools, more or less of the English type, in British India. The purpose was noble and altruistic. But the execution was seriously at fault. It was assumed that the same subjects of study which were the stock-in-trade of English education, would be appropriate for India. What could being educated mean, if not the study of these subjects? Such was the simple question implicitly involved. So Hindu youths were subjected to the English curriculum, modified and tempered, to be sure, but as little as might be. There can be no doubt that these schools, begun with such excellent intentions, have been one great cause of the present day unrest in India. They turned legions of young men out with a certain contempt for their own people and its ancient ways; spoiled for old modes of life, and hoping for some sort of clerkship or other white collar job. And when the demand for these positions began greatly to exceed the supply, education became a trouble breeder. Does this mean that England was unwise in establishing schools of any kind in her Indian domain? Far from it; for only so could she hope to discharge her great governmental responsibility of raising the social level of the population. But every effort should have been made to develop schools which would connect directly with and grow out of local conditions and the indigenous culture; and which would work directly for the reconstruction of Indian social life by teaching a curriculum calculated to fit young men for better adjustment in their own environment, rather than to alienate them from it. The worship of subject matter for its own sake, the belief that education consists in knowing certain things, rather than in possessing certain social aptitudes, perverted the schools.

This is exactly the mistake which the most intelligent educators in the British possessions in Africa are doing their best to avoid. The policy of conveying intellectual content to the youngsters of an African tribe, just as if they were rather duller counterparts of English schoolboys, is seen to be futile and dangerous. Its result is an unhappy being who is neither fish, flesh, nor good red herring —who is adjusted to no social order at all. What the best of the African schools try to do is not to shatter, but to improve the pattern of native life. The effort is to assist the native to a better and more scientifically controlled agriculture, a more sanitary and effective home life, a wider range of recreation, a more enlightened ethic. The only possible agency for doing this is an intellectual capital more copious than he possesses. But this intellectual capital must be conveyed to him in the closest connection with his own needs and situation.

The problem which we see dramatized in the schools of British India and Africa is just as cogent in those of America. But our perception of it is blunted by custom. A quotation here may serve to bring home the point, of which every teacher should be acutely conscious.

> "If one will ask himself in just what way the history he has studied or the history he is teaching, is affecting, or could be expected to affect one's civic reactions, he will find himself able to locate very few actual contributions. What did he learn about Lincoln or Washington or Jackson that could induce him to go to the polls when otherwise he would have stayed at home? What political event or economic principle was so discussed in his school history as to change his vote from a particular Republican to a particular Democratic congressman? The claim of contribution to citizenship seems very plausible until one presses for details; then it vanishes into thin air. Similarly, it has never been shown that a study of Latin necessarily contributes toward the improvement of English style. Such scientific studies as have been made are very far from confirming this claim, and some of them point in exactly the opposite direction. When one stops to think, one recognizes that the way in which circles are studied in geometry could not con-

tribute to the development of aesthetic appreciation of circles as used in buildings or linoleum designs. And so with numberless other claims." [5]

Here we have one of the great, crucial outcomes of our discussion of educational principles, so far. Just as soon as we admit that the intellectual resources of civilization are the agencies through which alone human beings may achieve a flexible, creative, progressive social adjustment to institutions, we confront the great problem of conveying them to the individual in such a way that they may really apply or, to use the stock term, "function." The body of intellectual capital amassed by the race is precisely the same in Equatoria, in the Madras Presidency, in Thibet, in the English country-side, or the Iowa prairie, in the Arctic wilderness, or on the icy shores of the Bay of Whales. But its application to the problems of human living differs in each case, because the problems are different. As something which exists for its own sake, it is suitable only for a glass case in a museum. Properly understood and used, it is the grand tool of social living.

[5] C. C. Peters: *Foundations of Educational Sociology:* The Macmillan Company, 1924, p. 77.

※

Chapter 3

WHAT IS THE RELATION OF EDUCATION TO MENTAL GROWTH?

1. *What is the nature of mental growth?*

A man's education is the course of his mental growth. As you think over your life, you can pick out certain experiences which, somehow, have educated you. Some of these may have come to you in the processes of your schooling—taking a course of study, making contact with a teacher, reading a book, preparing a thesis, and so on. But many of them may have had nothing to do with school work at all—meeting and knowing some person, organizing some piece of work, hearing some musical composition, seeing some picture, taking some journey. However such an experience came to you, it was educative for just this reason: It contributed to your mental growth. And very often what we do, or have done to us, in school has no permanent educative effect at all. We merely go through certain motions, obey certain orders, conform to certain requirements. We do not grow. And this means that we are not really becoming educated.

So it is of the highest importance to understand the nature and conditions of mental growth. A school, or a teacher, or a textbook, or a method of instruction, or a course of study, or a curriculum, or a system of marking—all these are good or bad, succeed or fail, simply in so far as they satisfy the conditions of mental growth, and so bring it about. Thus, we should be anxious to know its essence, and also how to avoid the numerous wrong ideas about it which beset our thought and spoil our educational practice.

It may seem to you that when, after discussing education as social adjustment, I now speak of it as mental growth, I am being inconsistent. But this is not so. In fact such a belief is the very first of those besetting wrong ideas of which we must energetically rid our thinking. What I have to say in this chapter is not inconsistent with, but a logical continuation of, the discussions of the last. Or rather, it is an attempt to look at and explain the very same things from a somewhat different point of view, and with an altered emphasis which will help us to a further comprehension of their rich significance. *For mental growth, properly understood, means precisely growth in social insight and outlook, and in power to deal flexibly and creatively with life's problems.* It is, so to speak, the inner aspect of social adjustment.

Such a statement, of course, looks very strange. It is foreign to our ordinary ideas. Very likely when you think about mental growth, it seems to mean something which has no relationship at all to social attitudes. Indeed, it often appears to mean the very opposite. The typical "intellectual" person, who may be supposed to have achieved effective mental growth, often seems anti-social rather than social. The "good student," beloved of teachers, is apt not to be a shining figure in the general life of the school. As he develops, he often becomes more and more a recluse, even an oddity. With the strengthening of his intellectual interests, his concern with the ordinary doings of mankind becomes less and less. And the popular picture of the man whose mental development has reached its zenith, is the absent-minded professor, who lives wholly in his study or his laboratory, who deals only with recondite matters, who is wrapped up in a sort of intellectual game, and whose social ineptitude is a standing joke. Very readily do we think of mental power merely as the possession of various techniques, such as those of mathematics, and of various kinds of knowledge; and of mental growth as something which goes on wholly inside the mind, so to speak.

Now when the schools hold up such an ideal, and further, when they actually organize their work to achieve it, they falsify the first condition of their own success. I am sure that one reason why all of us have gained far less real education than we have a right to expect from much of our school experience, is that teachers have gone to work to produce in us mental growth by giving us knowledge and technique, rather than significant and ever broadening social insight and outlook. For here we have false doctrine, leading straight to destructive practice. So let me try to explain why I believe that mental growth must be understood as growth towards flexible, creative social adjustment, and then point out some of the consequences of this view for education.

Ask yourself this question: Why would we all agree (as I think we would), that a great mathematical physicist like Einstein is far more of a figure in the human drama than a great chess player like Capablanca? So far as intellectual technique is concerned, there may not be much difference. To look thirty moves ahead in a game of chess may take quite as much sheer skill of mind as to work out the theory of physical relativity. But we hardly consider the work of Capablanca particularly significant, whereas the work of Einstein may and will have enormously important human and social consequences, which as yet we only dimly see. So with all the great minds of history. They are not great simply because they are clever, but because they deal with significant material. There may have been many routine mathematicians just as smart as Newton at solving problems. But that is not the right place to look for Newton's kingly supremacy. It lies in the content, the meaningfulness, of what he did, not in its manipulative skill; in his establishment of the foundations on which the entire intellectual structure of three hundred years was to be erected. There may have been formal teachers of counterpoint who were as skilled as Bach; there surely have been many who were as skilled as Schubert. But Bach and Schubert are greater minds and greater men than the cleverest mere contrapuntist who ever lived, simply because they have a message to proclaim through music, which has charmed and moved mankind ever since it was uttered. The quiet monk Mendel towers above a whole host of well equipped biologists who may have been his superiors in knowledge and technique, because he was dealing with matters so essential, and formulating doctrines so basic to the whole business of human life. Some dramatists have excelled Shakespeare in range of vocabulary, and others in facility with blank verse. But this does not save them from partial oblivion, or place them on an equal pedestal. Shakespeare's greatness lies in the human universality of his message to the world. Intellectual greatness does not consist of cleverness, but in dealing clearly and strongly with the issues of human life. And the mind grows towards greatness not by accumulating knowledge or perfecting technique, but by perceiving ever more clearly and comprehensively where those issues lie, and what they mean.

But here you may perceive a seeming difficulty. "Are not many of these great men really very unsocial beings?" You may ask. "Are they not often very hard to get on with, very difficult, very odd? And are they not, for instance, often very disappointing teachers?" Let us bring the question to a concrete point. You may have had a course with some man who was world renowned as a creative scholar and thinker, and found that in the classroom he was a grievous bore. Every great university has on its faculty such men; men who are eminent in research, but poor as teachers. What about this? Does it not show that intellectual supremacy may go hand in hand with social incompetence? Does it not destroy our argument that mental growth means growth in social outlook and insight? No, it means no such thing. Are these men really poor teachers? I answer: They are not. They may not teach a class very well, and to that extent there is a weakness in them. But the glory of their greatness far outshines it. For they teach, not a small group of students, but a whole generation of their fellows, and in supreme cases, many generations. Newton, Darwin, Shakespeare, Beethoven, Michael Angelo—these are numbered among the great teachers of the human race, and must be so accounted, be they never so wretched as classroom hands, and never so odd and difficult as personalities. Of course there is research and research. Some men are mere pedants, and make their pedantry an excuse for shoddy instruction and lazy teaching. But the truly great mind is a phenomenon of the utmost social significance. He is the guide who blazes the trail, the creator of new ways of thought and life and feeling. His adjustment to society is really on the highest constructive human level. It is the very stuff of his intellectual greatness. And compared with it, his small defects are no more than spots upon the sun.

Now all this may seem remote. It seems a far cry from the supreme champions of the human mind to teaching arithmetic, and history, and science to children, or even to the kind of work your college requires of you as an undergraduate student. Of course the distance is enormous; but so is the distance between a wanderer in the woods and the Pole Star. What he needs, and what we need, is *direction*. So here is the practical outcome. If teachers and schools are really to educate in all they do, they must chart a course by the great luminaries of the intellectual firmament. They must perceive that those very conditions of mental growth which show forth so wonderfully in the Newtons, the Darwins, the Einsteins, the Beethovens, and the Shakespeares, have application also to the youngest child and the dullest child. The lesson to be learned is this. Mental growth depends upon dealing with significant matters, and not upon an inner accumulation of knowledge and technique.

How can the study of arithmetic educate a child? How can it be a factor in his mental growth? Not by teaching it to him with the chief emphasis upon technique and mental manipulations. The reason why so much arithmetic is not educative at all, is that it is so often presented in just this way. Rather we must teach arithmetic so that the child gains an increasing sense of competency in using it in the actual concerns and problems of living. He gains a true feeling for mathematics—and such a feeling may be acquired very early—by recogizing in it an intellectual tool for mastering the intricacies of environmental problems, by seeing it as a means rather than an end. How can learning history be educative? If it is chiefly a matter of facts and dates, memorized for examination, it will not be educative at all. The reason why many students come to hate history, that most human and fascinating of all subjects, is that their teachers have completely falsified the most essential condition of mental growth. They have taught the subject as though its chief mission were the storing of the mind, rather than the achievement of new outlooks and insights. How can science be educative? Certainly not by being made an affair of formal laboratory techniques, and the learning of textbook material for recitation. Science is an agent for mental growth when, and only when, its vast significance as an interpretation of the world in which we live and of the social mechanisms which support us, comes to be appreciated.

So I could go on with all the subjects of the curriculum, and indeed with every detail and device of education. If you look back over your own education, and notice the dead and the living spots in it, and want to know why some are dead and some are living, here is the reason. A bit of learning is educationally dead if it is no more than the mastery of technique or the acquisition of knowledge, without any sense of its human significance. A bit of learning is educationally living if and as the learner appreciates the importance, the worth whileness of the thing learned. And I say this with all emphasis: *Our great endeavor should be to have all school learning come to life*. We do this by recognizing the nature and fulfilling the conditions of mental growth.

Such being the nature of the process of mental growth, we must now go on to ask how it begins, by what means it continues, and where it ends, and then deal with a certain incorrect theory regarding it.

2. *How does mental growth begin?*

Mental growth can begin in only one way—in a state of things where we want to accomplish something; where we are, so to speak, challenged by the environment. In other words, it must always start with a sense of imperfect adjustment to the world about us. A child of a year, toddling about his home, is continually drawn onward by a need for better and clearer ways of communicating; and he learns to talk with wonderful speed and thoroughness. A girl of eight hears one of her friends play the piano at a junior recital; and at once she is all eagerness for music lessons, and throws herself into work on the instrument with an enthusiasm and effect which the most tactful parental nagging could never produce. A boy of fourteen owns a light Remington rifle. He notices certain statements in the company's advertising which for some reason he doubts. To check up on them requires considerable mathematics; but he goes ahead and succeeds in mastering it on his own initiative. A student in a great European university spends his summer vacations in the Near East, disguised as an Arab. Through his perfect mastery of the languages, he is able to visit every one of the military ruins left by the Crusaders, in spite of the Turkish ban on investigators. He writes a thesis on the subject; and his university, recognizing the validity of his intellectual achievement, waives all other requirements, and grants him his degree. An astronomer notices a deviation in the orbit of the planet Uranus. The environment has issued its challenge; he has no adequate response. For months he pursues intricate calculations. Then he instructs the observatories to turn their telescopes to a certain spot in the heavens at a certain instant; and for the first time human eyes catch the far off gleam of Neptune.

Every one of these instances is an actual case of mental growth, an incident which has taken place. And they reveal its essence. It is a conquest of the environment, a raising of human adjustment to a new level of power and fullness. And always the point of origin is the same—the sense of a real, compelling problem. No person directly intervenes to set a task, or to find out whether it has been done. The environment challenges. The individual responds. A life problem is presented; and mental growth is the way of solving it.

The best and most thoughtful teachers have long acknowledged the truth of these ideas, and many are the experiments which have been made in applying them to the work of the school. I suppose the most striking, and for our immediate purpose the most instructive, though not necessarily the soundest of these, is what is known as the project method. Its use in an experimental rural school has been described by Ellsworth Collings in his book *An Experiment with a Project Curriculum*.[1] In this school, the children were not taught organized subjects at all. Their whole work consisted in carrying out a large number of projects of various kinds. They undertook to discover the causes of typhoid fever in a local farm home where the disease was recurrent. They studied in detail

[1] The Macmillan Company, 1923.

the course of a local criminal trial, and the subsequent life of the prisoner in the penitentiary. They investigated the issues of a political campaign, making an excursion to hear the candidate for the presidency. They set out to prepare cocoa for the school lunch, to dramatize the story of the first Thanksgiving, to beautify the school grounds, to manage the school garden, and so on. The question of the full educational value, and proper purpose and possibilities of the project method will occupy us in our later discussions. And we shall find something to criticize as well as much to commend. But for the moment, I use this merely to illustrate the way in which educative processes are started off. Contrast these procedures with the ordinary formal teaching of the elementary school, where subjects are set up as if they ought to be learned purely for their own sake, and where the applications of what is learned to actual life situations are treated quite incidentally, or not at all. What the staff of the experimental school did was to select environmental problems or challenges which might be expected to have meaning and appeal for a child. They brought these into the lives of the pupils. And mental growth was organized about them.

It would, of course, be a capital mistake to think that in order to stimulate and initiate a truly educational course of mental growth, we must always have projects of the type used by Collings, or that we must always deal with the current and the immediate. Here, as invariably, the letter kills, and it is the spirit which brings life. What we must have is a stimulation, a challenge, the undefinable but unmistakable sense of something real, something worth thinking about. One attempt to achieve this is the so-called "situation organization" of subject matter, which is now being used in many high schools and colleges. Courses are blocked out which do not attempt to follow the logic of some special subject, or indeed even to stay within its bounds. Instead they select a series of massive problems, perhaps from the immediate environment, perhaps from the remote past. One such course presents as its sequence, the civilization of Greece, the civilization of Rome, and the civilization of the Middle Ages. Another presents the water supply, the forests, dietetics, and so forth. To what extent they succeed, and what dangers beset them, is not now the question before us. The point is that they try to subject the pupil's mind to a series of impacts, to produce the inward exclamation: "Here is something I would like to know and master!" And whether they succeed or not, their obvious endeavor is to put into practice our principle that mental growth always begins with the sense of a genuine and appealing problem. The case method of teaching law, where legal principles are developed, not in a systematic manner, but through the kind of concrete problems which might face a practicing lawyer, is in certain ways another instance of the same attempt. So is the use of clinical experience in the training of physicians. And the thing can be done without any ostentation, or elaborate parade of brand new procedures. Perhaps it is then done best of all. May not the reading of a brilliantly and humanely written book provide just the vital spark of which I have been speaking? Read such a book as *New Russia's Primer,* and ask yourself whether it may not well initiate a life long course of mental growth, whatever may be your opinion of the probable direction of that growth. May not the inspiration of a teacher, even working under adverse and routine conditions, vivify a pupil's mind perhaps as well as some pretentious project?

The thing we really want is not something far fetched, or elaborate, or esoteric. Its very simplicity often baffles us. It is like a grain of mustard seed that falls inconspicuous into the ground. It is like that still, small voice which may often be heard when all the noise and fire and whirlwind of educational reorganization has passed by. What we must contrive to do, in order to inaugurate mental growth, is to tempt the mind to exploration and adventure among genuine and compelling issues. We must make learning seem worth while.

3. *How does mental growth continue?*

Two men see an apple fall to the ground. One of them vaguely wonders about it for a moment, and then dismisses it from his mind. The other ponders and toils and learns, and after years of labor, gives to the world an account, embracing and profound, of the whole physical universe. Two college students prepare themes on the preservation of learning in the monasteries of the Middle Ages. One writes his paper, hands it in, and turns to other things with a sigh of relief. The other is haunted by the half hidden, half revealed intimations he has found in his reading. And in his early maturity he writes a book which is a prophetic interpretation of mediaeval life. Two teachers work in a rural school. Both feel from time to time the insistent, mysterious challenge of the child mind. One jogs along in the regular routine, not ill satisfied with herself, nor, indeed, unsatisfactory to the community she serves. The other cannot leave the problem alone. She experiments, and reads, and ponders, and seeks new light on every hand. And at last she attains a creative vision of a new way of education; and all the world, and generations of children, are in her debt.

In each of these contrasts we have the beginning, the possibility, of a sequence of mental growth. In each we have the impact of a genuine, intriguing problem. But in one case, the sleeper is restless for but a moment, while in the other he awakens to new worlds. The priest and the Levite pass by, with only an uneasy glance. The Samaritan stops, and his whole life is changed. Mental growth starts always with a challenge which one feels as real, which somehow actually matters. Without this, it will never occur at all. But so far we have only a beginning. The seed must be planted, or the ground will remain barren. But long and careful culture is required before we have flower or fruit. In education we must do all in our power to provide for the initiation of mental growth. But we must not stop with this. Also we must provide for its continuation. How then does mental growth continue?

If the sense of a challenging problem is actually to lead to a course of mental growth, there is one imperative condition which must be fulfilled. *It must lead to an acquisition by the individual of a fuller measure of the intellectual resources of civilization.* These are the means, and indeed the only possible means, by which the raw, crude human creature becomes transformed into the civilized man. By calling them in, the felt maladjustment which we have spoken of as the challenge, or the problem, is cured, and adjustment becomes increasingly flexible and creative. Here we see the entire picture of mental growth, the essence of the educative process.

Consider the transformation which takes place in the little child during the first three or four years of his life. Anyone who has watched it knows how wonderful and complete it is. What is its essential character? Of course the child grows physically; but this is not all. He grows mentally. He learns. What does he learn? One of his most important acquisitions is his mother tongue. He comes to be able to express himself to others in it, and also to use it as an instrument for thinking. And it makes his whole adjustment to his home utterly different, and far more coöperative and effective, than it could possibly be otherwise. He begins to inherit a great racial possession, which transforms, and renders far more effective his whole adaptation to his social surroundings. He begins to grow up towards the full stature of civilized humanity. And of course, there are many other items of the social heredity which he begins to possess. He learns a great many conventional ways of doing things, such as how to behave at table, how to ask "nicely" for what he wants, and so forth. These folkways are not "mere" conventions. They are part of the heritage of civilization, whose possession is necessary if he is to become a civilized person. Again, he begins to discover that there is such a thing as music, such a thing as art, and such a thing as literature. He acquires a few of the more elementary techniques of amusement, and thereby begins to be independently able to enjoy himself, without needing his parents constantly. Such are the inner causes of his mental growth, which is at the same time a social growth. Few errors can be greater than to think of the little child as merely learning routine habits. On the contrary, his mind becomes enlightened by an increasing possession of the intellectual resources of civilization. This is the reason why his conduct becomes more and more typically human. A home is an educational success just in the measure to which it stimulates the child to seek new and ever better adjustments, and at the same time mediates to him the means of all human adjustment, which are always intellectual means. Here we have a prototype of the entire course of education.

The student who begins a thesis on the preservation of learning, and mounts onward till he becomes a distinguished mediævalist, does so because he ties in to his problem an ever wider range of historical knowledge and technique. The young man who enters his father's business, progresses towards the status of a "big, broad gauge merchant" (to quote the letters of Mr. Lorimer's self made merchant to his son), by mastering the techniques of industry, as well as a whole range of conventions and insights essentially involved in the management of men and the direction of affairs. It is precisely this connection between the sense of a problem, the feeling of an inadequate adjustment, and the solving of it by a mastery of intellectual resources, that determines whether or no any given problem, any given challenge, is to have an educative issue. The most attractive project, the most interestingly written chapter, the most inspiring and potentially suggestive lesson—these things in themselves are nothing but starting points, necessary indeed, but not sufficient to insure mental growth. Their value in education depends entirely on that to which they lead. Is their outcome a progressive and increasing mastery of some part of the intellectual resources of civilization? If so, they stand justified. But not otherwise.

This account of the nature of mental growth enables us to understand and guard against two prevalent errors in educational thought and practice. On the one hand, some "progressive" schools are open to criticism because they provide for the beginning of mental growth, but not for its continuation. You may often hear it said about such a school that the children are simply allowed to run wild, and to do anything they like. Oftentimes these complaints are no more than the peevishness of people who dislike any new way, and suspect liberty. But they involve a momentous issue. A school may botch the job of education just as badly by failing to build any continuous, orderly, significant intellectual grasp, as by trying to force subject matter upon pupils who feel not the slightest inner necessity for it. There is no inherent virtue in working in the school garden, or visiting the fire department, or disassembling an automobile engine, or attending a political rally. All such things are opportunities, valuable only in so far as we take advantage of them. A certain very worthy gentleman wanted to convey a moral lesson to a group of boys, and to do it impressively. So he artfully began by showing them a camera he had with him, and telling them a few things about it. Having caught their interest, and gained a promising momentum, he turned to the edifying part of his discourse. But one little fellow put up his hand and piped out: "Please mister, leave off that, and tell us more about your camera!" This illustration strikes to the root of one kind of educational error, the error committed by some, but by no means all, progressive schools.

The opposite error is to treat subject matter as an end in itself, without relating it to those very life situations which it was developed to interpret and meet. Language, literature, art, mathematics, science, history, all are treated simply as so much content to be memorized, instead of as intellectual tools invented for the purpose of improving human adjustment. It is as if we should try to teach a tiny child to talk, to behave at table, to play with his toys, and to dress himself, in a series of formal lessons with tests at the end of each one, rather than in a social situation which actually demands the acquisition of these techniques, tendencies, insights, and abilities. The error, again, is to treat mental growth as growth in mere cleverness or knowledge or technique, rather than in significant insight.

Life problems without intellectual content are not educative. Nor is intellectual content educative when divorced from life problems. Human adjustment to the demands of living is an intellectual process. It is the process of mental growth, the educative process itself.

4. *When does mental growth end?*

Is there any time in one's life when mental growth, like bodily growth, comes to an end? Can we tell when this time comes? Is it the same for all? Such questions are obviously important for many educational purposes and plans.

One answer commonly given is to say that mental growth comes to an end about the age of sixteen. This idea is so very well known that you are apt to come upon it, stated as an accepted fact, in quite popular literature. But it is very misleading indeed, and unless we qualify and explain it with great care, entirely false. It really comes from the work which has been done on the measurement of intelligence. Experts in this field have discovered that when a person has gone beyond a certain age, his ability to do more and more difficult mental tests ceases. He reaches an upper limit, above which he cannot go. Imagine a series of problems, all of the same type, but steadily increasing in difficulty —say, for instance, a series of completion items (paragraphs with various words omitted), which is a common and very excellent form of mental test material, beginning with very easy specimens and ending with very hard ones. Now as a child grew older, he would be able to go higher and higher on such a scale, just as his height measured by pencil marks on a door frame steadily increases year by year. But neither growth in height, nor in ability to solve problems, would increase forever. A time would come when there would be no more advance. This is what is called the *age of arrest of intelligence*. Different investigators have located it at different ages, varying all the way from thirteen to nineteen or more; but the most familiar claim, though perhaps not the best founded, is for sixteen.

Another piece of work along similar lines is that reported by Thorndike in his book, *Adult Learning*. He raised the question as to when the capacity to learn, apart from all special training, reaches a maximum. And his decision was for an upper limit somewhere between the ages of twenty-two and twenty-three.

But can we really say that these "ages of arrest" are points in one's life history when one's mind ceases to grow? After all, we still have all our intelligence left with us after the age of sixteen, even though we may not, in some special sense, go on gaining more and more of it. And intelligence, surely, is the power to deal adequately with new situations and difficulties. In the same way, we do not lose our power to learn the day after it reaches its maximum. On the contrary, it declines very gradually indeed. And the power to learn is the power to grow mentally. What these various statements about the age of arrest actually mean is simply that whatever year is chosen is the time when we achieve *our maximum power of mental growth*. Growth of intelligence, or of power to learn, is really growth of the power to grow. Whether or no we use that power, and actually continue to grow, is another question.

This point about the true meaning of statements concerning the age of arrest has not often been made as clear as it ought to be. And as a result, people have taken such statements to imply all sorts of things which they really do not. They have a definite meaning, usually, in connection with a given set of mental tests. They simply tell us that, on investigation, it appears that children above a certain age do not continue to improve in their ability to meet the test requirements. But we certainly must not understand them as general, sweeping assertions of the impossibility of mental growth beyond certain age levels.

All this preliminary discussion was needed to clear the way for a definite reply to the question which stands at the head of this section. When does mental growth end? Our specific answer is that it need never end. Of course each particular sequence of mental development comes to an end. The little girl works at her music lessons for a while, and then is able to play at a children's concert. The class locates the causes of typhoid fever, and the project terminates. But the point is that each new achievement, in fact, opens up a new vista. As soon as a person becomes able to do any particular thing, he thereby becomes able to see new things to be done. The little girl becomes aware of new and more exacting pieces, and of more demanding and repaying situations. The class becomes conscious in a new way, of the social and communal problems of hygiene, and of the endless possibilities of improvement through applied science. Kilpatrick has brilliantly illustrated the point by showing the change brought about in a little child by his acquiring the simple skill of dressing himself. His whole attitude towards time is thrown into a creative flux, because he must now plan to rise early enough to dress himself, instead of leaving all this planning to his mother. His social attitudes undergo a subtle, far reaching change, for he becomes more of a coöperative person, less of a passive baby. Every new power we achieve, every success we gain, every sequence of mental growth brought to finality, opens up new possibilities, and renders us sensitive to new challenges. Mental development is like climbing a range of mountains. We see ahead of us a ridge, which looks like the top. We climb it, only to find another slope ahead, which before we could not see. The only difference is that one ultimately reaches the summit of a mountain, but one never exhausts the possibilities of mental advance.

As a matter of fact, however, a great many people do cease to grow mentally. They land a job in a store, or a shop, or an office, and become either content with or resigned to a vocational routine, doing pretty much the same thing from one year's end to another. Their point of view is aptly expressed by the term used for such jobs in England, where they are called "berths" which seems to indicate slumber. Their amusements show little variation or advance. Their civic horizons do not expand. Their home life jogs along without experimentation or radical change. Their calibre at sixty is not notably greater than it was at twenty-five. The world is full of such oysters, outwardly resembling human beings. Why do they stop growing? Not because they must. Not because of the coming of some day of doom, or "age of arrest." The reason is that their minds lose touch with the vast and inexhaustible treasury of human intellectual goods. And that means stopping readjustment in terms of insight. They become beings of a fixed routine, rather than inheritors of intellectual enlightenment.

Now such people are educational failures, which is the proper classification for everyone whose education stops as soon as he leaves school, or indeed, while he is alive. It is the very nature of human mental growth to continue without limit. Or, putting it in the way we have done before, adequate human adjustment to the environment is progressive, rather than static and limited. When the school just fits a person into a niche, and boasts about it— when it deliberately produces a type of being who will stand nine hours a day at a lathe without another thought or aspiration—it has simply ceased to be an adequate educational institution, and becomes a menace rather than an aid to human life.

So, if our schools are to be guided and inspired by a living faith that all genuine education is mental growth, and that their great business is to produce it and to fulfill its conditions, they must educate for continuing growth. What does this mean as a practical proposition? It means chiefly that we should avoid narrowness. When we concentrate on teaching a child just those things which he needs to become a plumber, or a machinist, or even a lawyer or a physician, we limit him. He may never become any of these things. And even if he does, there will be plenty of problems he will have to meet outside his vocational capacity. And his vocational adjustment itself is most effective when it is no mere matter of routine. He is likely to be a better, a more progressive, a more successful plumber, or machinist, or lawyer, or physician, if he is aware of horizons broader than those of the vocational techniques of those jobs. Our best chance of helping a child to continue his mental growth throughout life is to give him a general education, which means precisely bringing him as widely as possible into touch with human intellectual resources, always taught in terms of social meanings.

5. *What is the place of background in mental life?*

The whole account of the nature and conditions of mental life which I have been trying to convey is in essence a restatement of the classic doctrine of apperception. Inasmuch as we are dealing with an issue of momentous and far-reaching importance, it will repay us to look at the matter in the new perspective of that doctrine. To do so will help us to a more fruitful and adequate insight.

The doctrine of apperception is the doctrine of mental background. Its central insistence is that we never merely *perceive* anything. Always we *apperceive* it. What is before our minds is not just the mere, bare impression which an object makes upon our senses. It is always the sensory impression interpreted according to a background of experience. And on the interpretation we give to any object before us, will depend our course of action regarding it.

When a primitive savage sees his first aeroplane, he flees in terror. He interprets the swooping apparition, with its roaring voice, as an appalling monster. His whole background makes this necessary and dictates his adjustment. If we lived in a chairless civilization, the first chair we saw would not be an object upon which to sit. It would be a puzzling conglomeration of lines, and masses, and colors; and we would probably stand and gape. When the British troops in the World War underwent their first gas attack, they failed entirely to grasp the meaning of the strange dark cloud sweeping down upon them. It was not a set of routine habits they lacked, but a mental background adequate to interpret the omen. Their response was too late, too stupid. And the penalty was death.

The whole of our power to deal with the challenges of life flexibly and inventively, depends upon mental background, upon apperception. The great soldier can invent expedients and strategies at once new and sound, because of his mastery of military techniques. The trained engineer can deal with unprecedented problems, which would certainly defeat the layman, just because of his mathematical, scientific, and technological backgrounds which enable him to understand and interpret a situation. A man without business and financial experience is not a safe person at the head of a bank. His lack of knowledge is a practical defect, which will lay him open to making wrong and ruinous decisions. A peasant who comes to the United States from some venal and tyrannous autocracy is at a loss when he must deal with an honest and considerate government official. He is unable to understand, to interpret. And all the things he does—his fear, his efforts to placate by backsheesh, his very manners and bearing—betray and express his intellectual inadequacy.

So the great problem of civilizing and humanizing men, of helping them towards an effective adjustment to the institutions of society, which of course is the educational problem itself, can be thought of as the development of mental background. This is the only true and effective control of action. We must build up adequate apperceptions. We must deepen, widen, and render more precise, our perception of the meanings of experience. We must foster the growth of mind.

So much is abundantly and evidently true. But now we come upon a question which brings us to a parting of the ways. How is mental background to be developed? A high school freshman cannot possibly deal with the problems of a business depression, not merely because he is young, but chiefly because he is insufficiently educated. He lacks the necessary coördinated intellectual grasp and insight to understand what his eyes see and his ears hear, and to reach the proper decisions. So much we admit. But what ought we to try to do about it? How shall we seek to develop his mentality? How shall we transform crudity into strong finesse, superficiality into deep insight, weakness into power? Once more, how shall we go about building up in him a more and more adequate mental background?

One clear answer which has been made, an answer which expresses itself both in theory and practice, is that we should begin by trying to give him a knowledge of the fundamental and the general, so that later on he may be able to deal with the particular and the concrete. Such was unquestionably the thought behind the recommendations made years ago by the American Historical Association, that high school pupils should start with ancient history in their freshman year, and lead up through the history of the intervening ages to a study of American developments when they became seniors. In the field of science our principle would mean beginning with pure sciences as the proper preparation for applications. In geometry, it would mean beginning with the axioms and postulates which are supposed to be the intellectual foundations of the subject, and passing on to the deductive development of a sequence of theorems. In language work, it would mean beginning with an intensive study of grammar before one tried to read, or speak, or write. In English literature, it might well mean beginning with a general survey course before taking up any particular author or movement. This is the doctrine of building always on a complete and adequate logical foundation. It is the exact opposite of beginning with projects, or concrete and fragmentary experiences of any kind.

Now bluntly, is this doctrine true? Certainly there are a number of very cogent considerations which make us doubt it.

A. First of all, it is manifest that some of the most effective learning we ever do seems to require no careful organization of background. When we began to learn to speak English, we were aware only of a need for communication; and we plunged right in and learned whatever we had to learn to meet that need. Quite a good deal of the growing which our minds do out of school seems rather evidently to be of this type. It is very certain that the development of more adequate and intelligent adjustment does not *always* depend upon the prior elaboration of mental background.

B. Second, experimental teaching has abundantly proved that one need not concern oneself a great deal with the organized elaboration of mental background in order to achieve a working mastery. This is the case even with so logically organized a subject as mathematics. Modern schools often begin geometry, not with axioms and postulates, which may be the ultimate background material of the science, but with actual concrete experiences in working with space relationships with pencil, ruler, and compass. (Incidentally, the axioms and postulates commonly given in elementary textbooks are very far from being the true foundations of mathematics—but let that pass.) Again, we have methods of teaching foreign languages which begin, not with systematic grammar, but with actually speaking the language, handled by rote. Such "direct methods" are difficult to use; but they can be made to work. And they certainly seem opposed to the idea of beginning always with the fundamental and the general.

C. Third, consider a reply which can be made to the argument that in order to comprehend the city water supply, or the issues of a political campaign, the pupils need background. One may retort: How much? And also, just what is "comprehension"? For a complete "comprehension" of anything, one needs to know—everything. Which seems a little difficult! Very well. How much less than everything must one know, in order to understand anything? From how remote a vantage point must one begin one's intellectual stalk? Through how long a novitiate must one painfully live, before one dare study the water works without mental disaster? After all, it is possible to spend such an interminable time preparing to understand something, that one dies before one comes to it. What about the high school pupil who has been led, grade by grade, through ancient, mediaeval, and modern European history, and is just about to discover America—when he quits school? You may be so long practicing the strokes on the bank, that the pond dries up before you have a chance to try to swim. The question: How much mental background is enough? cannot be answered. Nobody has "enough." And nobody ever will.

The general outcome of these arguments would seem to be that the idea of developing mental background by beginning with the general and the fundamental, is untenable. It is, in fact, a misinterpretation of the doctrine of apperception. And there is a still deeper objection than any I have stated, which points also towards a better way. Mental background is not something which can ever be handed to a person ready made. It is something which each one of us must make for himself, in his own way. It comes to us, not prior to concrete experience, but in and through concrete experience. Profound understanding, broad and sweeping vision, precise and masterly insight, living grasp of first principles—these are not the beginnings of education. They are its culmination. The wisdom of the great mind is incomprehensible to the beginner, because it is a wisdom garnered from experience, and because without experience it is a nullity. We build up our apperceptions, and our mental controls of behavior, by a progressive reinterpretation of significant experience. To try to communicate to the immature, relatively unfurnished mind, the full-panoplied wisdom of generations of great thinkers, is futility. The attempt to render meaningful to a high school student the massive logical structures of pure science or pure mathematics, is like trying to transfer a thousand year old California redwood into a small garden plot of shallow soil. The only hope is to plant the seed, and possess our souls in patience till it grows. This may be unfortunate, but we have to accept it as one of the inevitable limitations of the human mind. We must begin with the concrete, and if necessary, with the fragmentary. To be sure, we must always work towards a developed and articulated background. But too much haste, and too many short cuts will surely defeat us. The project which is no more than a project, the interest which is only a whim, is surely worthless. But so is the standardized, logically organized body of subject matter, utterly out of contact with the realities of the learner's world. We do not begin with background. We work towards it; and achieve as much of it as we may.

One further question we must raise before we have done with the notion of mental background as embodied in the doctrine of apperception. What is the content, the stuff, of mental background? When we acquire it, what do we acquire? To possess a mental background always means to possess in and for ourselves some measure of the intellectual resources of civilization. When I see a salad fork beside my plate at dinner, and use it correctly without thinking about it, my instantaneous, unconsidered, yet correct interpretation of what meets my eyes, and my line of action regarding it, are possibly only because I have made my own some of the conventional ways of doing things, some of the "folkways," which have been created by society. When the people in a community refrain from rushing to draw out all their funds from a local bank, in spite of a doubtful financial outlook, their self control depends ultimately on an intellectual foundation. It is the outward sign of a social enlightenment. It is possible because their interpretation of events, and their choice of the right thing to do, is controlled by a background comprehension of certain economic concepts and principles. When a mechanic locates and corrects some obscure trouble in your car, he is able to do so because of his general body of knowledge and skill in dealing with internal combustion engines. Such knowledge and skill is not something he invents. Rather it is something he inherits. For it is a selection from science and the techniques of industry; and a part of the intellectual accumulations of the human race. So always, when we say that a man possesses and uses mental background, we mean that he has inherited at least some of the great treasury of resources which civilization has accumulated for the ends of better living.

This is an idea well worth pondering, for it leads us to many great issues. I want to mention just three points in connection with it, which may stimulate your minds.

First notice the implication that to be wise in counsel and

action is to be socially minded. No man can live alone and be human. No man can think alone and think well, or indeed at all. The mark of the truly great mind is to possess an unusual share of the intellectual wealth amassed by the race in the past, and to concentrate this with unusual adequacy upon present problems. Without the intellectual resources of civilization, a man lacks all mental tools; he hardly has a mind at all; he has only the potentiality of a mind. The mental and the social are in this sense one and the same. We should remember this, for our great task in education is to render the racial wisdom available for current living.

Second, notice that the intellectual resources of civilization are valuable, not for their own sake, but for their effect upon human action and adjustment. This is a point on which I am concerned repeatedly to insist. Science learned merely to pass an examination in science, history studied merely for the sake of a mark, mathematics mastered just because one is told to do so, represent so many perversions of the purpose and meaning of education. We must transform these things into controlling backgrounds, which form and fashion action and comprehension, and which make living fuller and more civilized. They are not subjects to be studied. They are the intellectual foundations of our civilization. Not till they play this part in the learner's mind, have they become truly educative, genuine agencies for mental growth, or indeed things worth learning at all.

Third, notice that the great body of human intellectual resource which constitutes the stuff of our mental background, and which is the ultimate control of all social action, cannot be conveyed ready made, or assimilated in a lump. True, the movement of our minds must always be towards a more general and adequately logical grasp of intellectual materials. We must seek to develop an understanding of the logical structure of science as science, an apprehension of the detail and sweep of history, an insight into the order system of language. But these are the end points, not the beginnings of the process. Moreover, they are end points which no human being ever reaches, or ever very closely approaches. To have a complete and organized mental background would be to know everything that man has ever learned, and infinitely more besides. It would be omniscience. When the eminent scholar feels impatience at the lowly and limited processes of his students in college, or of children in high school, and when he wants to cut corners and force something upon them which they cannot yet receive, it may be a healthy thing for him to consider his own limitations. If he had to deal with some superman, endued with a more than human knowledge and insight, like Mark Twain's Mysterious Stranger, and if such a being tried impatiently to convey to him, ready made, the results of such knowledge and insight, he might well cry: "Remember that I am only human! Remember my many limitations! They are the fixed conditions under which alone my mind may grow towards the level of your own. On these terms, and these only, I can learn from you. I must be educated as I am, with all my fragmentary insights and my narrow horizons, or not at all."

6. *Is there in the individual a fixed natural order of mental growth?*

One of the most persistent, subtle, and almost-true fallacies in educational thought is the idea that there is an order or sequence of mental growth fixed by nature. It has recurred again and again in many forms. It haunts the minds of many teachers. And we are compelled to come definitely to grips with it.

The present fashionable expression of this doctrine is the theory of recapitulation. To be sure, this theory is coming to be a little out of date. But its central idea is quite sure to recur in other guises. So nothing is lost by discussing it here. The theory of recapitulation is the doctrine that every individual repeats, in his own personal development, all the stages through which the race has passed in reaching its present status. It was brought into vogue by a series of remarkable discoveries in the field of embryology. Biologists found that the human embryo does, in fact, seem to pass through a whole series of sub-human stages, so that one might say that in the period between conception and birth, we have a miniature of thousands of years of racial evolution. This was regarded, and rightly, as a very wonderful and richly significant discovery. Philosophers, and the more liberal religious thinkers, became interested in it, and discussed it widely. And psychologists and educators considered that it had important bearings on their fields of work.

The general drift of the recapitulation theory is perfectly evident. If each one of us really does repeat, each in his small way, the whole sequence of racial development, then evidently we are all pinned to a natural sequence of growth, mental and otherwise. But before we consider the doctrine in this, its most general aspect, we shall do well to study two of its most influential applications to education.

A. It used to be thought that a human being went through three stages on his pathway to maturity; an intuitive stage, where he was dominated by sense impressions; an imaginative stage; and a rational stage. Many practical conclusions were drawn from this notion. For instance, it was held that one should not try to appeal to a little child's reason, because logic had for him no natural meaning. If we ask why ordinary school work is not more effective, the believer in this form of the recapitulation theory will answer: Because its content demands the use of a faculty which is not yet present—because that content is imaginative when it should be purely sensory, or logical when it should be imaginative; because we ask the child to think too soon; because we try to appeal to something in him which is not yet there at all.

Here, indeed, is some truth. But also there is a very grave error. The truth is that a child can gather mental nourishment only from experiences which have a living appeal and seem real to him. The error lies in thinking that at certain periods of life, only certain definite kinds of experience can be real. A child hears another one play at a recital; straightway she wishes to study music. Another, rather older child, takes part in a school project to study the causes of typhoid in a home; he is aroused to a fascinated interest in certain aspects of bacteriology. Here are splendid concrete instances of what education ought to be. But what has recapitulation to do with them? Clearly, nothing at all. Reasoning, imagination, intuition, all these and many more mental powers are involved in both cases. This is true of every educative experience, and of mental growth at all stages. We cannot mark off an intuitive, and an imaginative, and a logical level. Children "reason." Adults "intuit." There is no period in the life of a child when he cannot learn science, or language, or mathematics, or music, or anything else; the one condition being that the material must be organized and presented so as to appeal to his natural interests and his present needs. The growth of the mind is not a sort of Turkish bath affair, of going from one room to another. It takes place, like the replenishing of the strength of Antaeus in the Greek myth, by contact, in any way, with the solid ground of appealing experience.

B. Another way in which the recapitulation theory has been applied to education is the famous, and once tremendously popular notion of "culture epochs." It is said that the human race has passed through a number of cultural levels—perhaps savagery, barbarism, and civilization, if we happen to like this list—and that the individual in his education must pass through them too.

This is a point of view with which, in its non-technical form, almost everyone is familiar. Who has not heard ten year old boys called little savages or young barbarians? Well, the culture-epoch theory is just a glorified form of this venerable wisdom. It has been worked out in great and logical detail. And when we apply it to education, it is supposed to tell us what kind of studies are appropriate for various age levels. Thus the proper curricular materials for young children would be built out of the materials of primitive culture, for instance the Homeric poems. The youth has perhaps climbed the tree of life as far as the Middle Ages, and can bear something rather more sophisticated. And so on through to maturity, when science bursts upon his ken.

Our criticism of this kind of educational doctrine must be far more severe than in the foregoing case. Consider how it would work out. We have taken a group of children to a political rally, and they have decided to work out the issues of the campaign. In doing this, they read newspapers about current events, and delve into social science and recent historical trends. Certainly they seem to learn a great deal, and to enjoy doing it, which should mean something. But the believer in culture epochs tells us that this is all wrong. "These children" says he "are really not civilized beings at all. They are barbarians. And they ought to be reading a good translation of Homer, and eagerly discussing the wrath of Achilles and the wicked madness of the King of Men, instead of dealing with the modern, complex, sophisticated world, which, in the nature of things, can mean nothing to them for years to come."

Obviously this is sacrificing the child on the altar of a theory. But such is exactly the effect of the doctrine of culture epochs. It deliberately limits the horizon of the child; and does so in the name of education. It says that the child must not have certain types of experience, because we know, without any direct investigation, but just by some sort of supernal insight, that he is not ready for them. "Nature" is supposed to tell us this; though how the revelation is made, deponent saith not. Now to be sure, one should never force experience or knowledge upon a child irrespective of his sense of a need for it. But on the other hand, one should never deliberately withhold it, if he does feel the need for it in his business, which is adjusting himself to life.

But behind all the things we have been saying, there looms up the general question, with which we now must deal. Is it really possible to apply the recapitulation theory to education at all? Reluctantly we answer: It is not. The theory is a theory of the embryologists. Its foundation of fact is that foetal life does seem to repeat in some fashion the long sequences of evolution. But we have no right to apply it, blanket-wise, even to physical growth after birth, still less to mental growth. The great error, the great heresy, is the idea of a sort of iron law of mental development, which will tell us in advance just what the ideal sequence of education for everyone is. Mental growth, however, is individually determined. It is a social rather than a physiological process. It depends wholly upon a person's progressive grasp of the intellectual resources of civilization, which are the controlling background of all enlightened living. And the only valid basis for education is individual significant experience, which comes when and as it may.

Still, those who have sought to apply the recapitulation theory to school work have brought to our attention certain considerations which cannot be repeated too often. This is why I spoke of the doctrine as "almost true."

First, they have reminded us that mental growth cannot be hurried. It has nothing to do with covering ground, or knowing what one "ought to know," or swallowing a measured dose of facts in a given time. It is an affair of reorientation, of readjustment. And this must take its own good time, and go its own sweet way. When we try to hurry education, so as to arrive on schedule and please the supervisory officers, we wreck it.

Second, they have reminded us that we must deal with the child as a child, and not a miniature adult. It is not true that he is destitute of certain faculties later to be his. But it is true that he lives in a child world, and has a child experience. It is worse than useless to present to the child mental content, organized on a basis of adult interest, and expect him to thrive on it. To do this is to work against rather than to use wisely the conditions of mental growth.

Chapter 4

WHAT IS THE SIGNIFICANCE OF THE THEORY OF FORMAL DISCIPLINE?

1. *What is the theory of formal discipline?*

There is an account of the nature of mental growth which differs fundamentally from the one I have presented. This is the famous theory of formal discipline. It is a theory of very ancient origin; but since the end of the seventeenth century, various historical causes have brought it into great prominence. However, the chief reason for dealing with it here is not that it has been put forward so often in the past, nor even that it has been advocated so frequently in more recent times. The reason is its surpassing importance. It is nothing less than a complete theory of the foundations of education. And it leads to a program so sharply different from that advocated in this book, that in criticizing it we shall reach a better and clearer understanding of our own educational doctrine.

What then is the theory of formal discipline? It is the theory that the business of education is the training of the mind. Certain studies are supposed to have peculiar virtues for this end. For instance, it is said that geometry will train the reason, that history will train the memory, that science will train the power to observe or the power of accuracy, that literature will train the imagination, and so on. Above all has the study of the classics been defended on the grounds of its supposed disciplinary value. Most of us have been told things of this sort by our teachers. There is no doubt that it is widely held as gospel.

So far it may seem to you that we have a doctrine not sharply different from that which we have already been proclaiming. Geometry, history, science, literature, and the classics, are all of them studies of the highest value. Their effect upon the mind and its growth can and ought to be profound and beneficial. They must have a recognized place in any ordered scheme of education. But their value lies in this, that they have a content supremely worth mastering. They are the means of intellectual enlightenment and power, the agencies for a better way of life. And it is exactly here that we part company with the believer in formal discipline. For according to him, the value of a subject does not consist in the worth, or the practicality, or the significance for life, of its content. It does not lie in the content of the subject at all. A subject is said to be educationally valuable because it provides a mental exercise. It is worth studying because, to use the clear and classic phrase, it "strengthens the mental muscles."

And just as muscles strengthened by any kind of exercise, can then be used for all purposes, so, according to the theory, mental powers developed in one kind of study can be used anywhere we like. If geometry has strengthened the reason, we can reason better about scientific matters, about the executive problems of business, about repairing the engine of a car, or about a social difficulty. If the learning of names and dates in history has improved the memory, then we can better remember the names of acquaintances, or the times of appointments, or anything else. If literature has developed the imagination, then we can use this increased ability whenever and wherever it may be needed. This is the essence of the doctrine. Such illustrations may seem to you fantastic; but many far more so are at hand. Many music supervisors in the public schools insist that learning to read the score is valuable not at all because it is a very useful or important thing to be able to do, but because it develops quickness of reaction, since children must spot notes rapidly. Many teachers of science believe that one chief value of laboratory work is merely to train children in accuracy of movement and physical coördination.

Putting it in a nutshell, the theory of formal discipline is a theory that mental growth takes place through formal exercise.

According to it, the whole business of education is to provide the right kind of exercise, and thus develop "the powers and faculties of man." It is in the sharpest contrast with our own account, which is that mental growth takes place through significant experience.

2. *What are some practical consequences of formal discipline?*

The full force of the theory of formal discipline is not to be appreciated from a general statement of it. So I wish to invite your attention to some of its most striking practical consequences.

A. It has been used to determine what subjects should be studied in school; that is, it has served as a basic theory of the content of the curriculum. Indeed, it was to defend the privileged position of certain subjects that the theory was first made prominent. Until well along after the Renaissance, there was not much question but that the classical languages and literatures should be the staple of education. But decade by decade, the claims of the modern languages and literatures, and above all of the sciences, became harder to resist. The common sense arguments for teaching these subjects were very strong. How could they be answered? What could one say when it was pointed out that Latin and Greek are much less useful in most people's lives than French and German, chemistry, biology, and physics? The reply developed was that Latin and Greek have preëminent value, in that they give far greater opportunities for the training of the mind. In other words, it was said that we must not look first and foremost to the content of what is being studied, nor ask chiefly about its significance, in determining its educational value. We must inquire mainly into its value as a mental exercise.

This argument has had a most curious and interesting history. In spite of it, modern language and science little by little gained ground. And now they are respected members of the academic family of subjects. But here is the oddity. The very arguments once used in favor of the classics alone, are now used to defend the position of the sciences and of foreign language. For it is said that they deserve their place in the scheme of education, because of their

SIGNIFICANCE OF FORMAL DISCIPLINE 77

disciplinary value. The theory once used to shut them out, is now put forward to keep them in!

What can we make of this? There is only one possible reply. Any subject can be defended equally well on disciplinary grounds. If we once admit that there is such a thing as mental training, is there any reason why it should be monopolized by Latin and Greek? Certainly not. It can surely be derived just as well from modern language and science, or for the matter of that, from chess, which in fact is actually taught as an exercise in certain German schools. Indeed, it can be derived just as well from music, manual training, and home economics. In the dark, all cows are black. Looked at from the standpoint of its capacity to yield mental training, any subject is just as good as any other. And so the attempt to choose the best material for a curriculum by means of this theory, falls to the ground. There is only one way to determine the proper make-up of a curriculum, and that is to concentrate on the actual *content* of the different studies, and ask what things are most worth knowing.

B. Another consequence of the theory is that it makes teachers indifferent to the content of what they are teaching. This of course, is natural enough, simply because it is the doctrine that exercise rather than content is important. But it is fatal. Suppose I am teaching a course in geometry in the conventional way. The pupils learn their assignments, memorize proofs of theorems, recite day by day, and write some tests which are largely *memoriter*. If I happen to think of it, I know perfectly well that, were these pupils suddenly put up against a life situation in which they had to use geometrical skill, the great majority of them would fail, simply because they have no real geometrical skill at all. If one of them were asked to calculate the area of a roof which made an isosceles right angled triangle at the peak, though he could not get a ladder long enough to reach the top, would his memory knowledge of the theorem of Pythagoras enable him to get the answer? He has the necessary intellectual tools for this particular bit of life adjustment—or at least he ought to have them. But can he really use them? Every experienced teacher knows the answer all too well.

How then do I make this right with myself? Quite likely by saying: "Ah well, they may not be learning much geometry. But going through all these proofs must surely be training them to reason." That is, my interest centers, not on giving them a geometric competence, but on training their faculties. In effect, I am not teaching them geometry at all. I am giving them a mental exercise which I think will develop reasoning power.

This, I must insist, is a very bad thing. The teacher ceases to be responsible for connecting the subject with life, or for making it significant. He does not even have to care whether the pupils really master it, or come to see what it is all about. He is simply providing them with mental calisthenics, and strengthening their mental muscles. This very thing happens all the time in school. A great deal of language teaching establishes absolutely no ability to read, write, or speak; but no one gets agitated over it, for the theory is that the pupils are learning to concentrate. Modern students of the curriculum have maintained that not much time should be given to teaching the musical score in the grades, because few will ever use it in after life, and because other aspects of music are much more valuable. But many supervisors blandly continue to place almost the entire emphasis in the first six grades on developing the notation, and do not even care when, after all their efforts, the pupils gain little independent mastery of it; for they say that the children are acquiring quick reactions and fine powers of observation. So the theory of formal discipline makes the music, or the geometry, or the French, or the Latin, quite secondary, and mental training primary.

C. The theory of formal discipline, again, gives us an entirely wrong notion of the nature of good classroom procedure. Manifestly it implies that the important thing is not how much a pupil learns, but how hard he works. The aim is not useful or significant learning, but arduous exercise. So it actually becomes a virtue to make a subject difficult. There can be no doubt that part of the older objections to curriculum revision came from the belief that the new studies were easier than Latin and Greek, and so could not possibly have the same educative value. And it is an historical fact that teachers of Latin have opposed reforms in methods of teaching, and the introduction of improved textbooks, on the ground that such things would make the subject less difficult to master.

Now this worship of difficulty is about as violent a perversion of the true aim of teaching as one can easily imagine. What would you think of a golf professional who deliberately went out of his way to make the game harder than it normally need be? Yet this has been done with school subjects. What is a teacher for, anyhow? We must insist that the sheer difficulty of a subject has absolutely no necessary relation to its educative value. The task of the really good teacher is to remove rather than increase difficulties. For the value of a subject lies, not in its effect on some mental faculty or other, but in its content. School subjects are not sets of exercises for the mental muscles. They are selections from the intellectual resources of civilization, which provide us with the means of better adjustment to the demands of life. And the more easily we can acquire them, the better.

3. *Where is the fallacy of the theory of formal discipline?*

All the educational malpractices for which the theory of formal discipline is responsible stem from a single root. For the theory offers a false account of the nature and meaning of mental growth, and a false conception of the nature of the mind. Perhaps the best way of clearly exposing the fallacy involved is by a discussion of what is known as "faculty psychology," which is the foundation of the theory of formal discipline.

According to faculty psychology, the mind is an entity made up of a large number of separate powers or faculties. To give a complete list of all that have been suggested would be quite impossible. It has been said that human beings have a faculty of reasoning, a faculty of memory, a faculty of observation, a mathematical faculty, a faculty for language, a faculty for science, a faculty for liking children, a faculty for doing well in business, and so on. These are just a few samples from an endless list. Faculty psychology thinks of the human mind as being made up of a great number of separate and special abilities, each able to operate more or less in isolation.

This theory of the faculties is the foundation of the quack science of phrenology. The phrenologist tells you that he can find out what sort of person you are, and what abilities you possess, by feeling the bumps on your skull. For he says that there is a separate bump for each faculty you possess, and that the size of the bump indicates the strength of the faculty.

But also the doctrine of faculties is the logical basis of the theory of formal discipline. For that theory proposes to set up exercises which will develop memory, and reasoning ability, and the power to observe, and what not. And our ultimate criticism, both of phrenology and formal discipline, is simply the assertion that no such faculties exist.

If you have read Kipling's *Kim,* you will remember how Kim and the little Hindu boy are given practice and tests in observation. The Hindu boy can glance for a moment at a tray of jewels, and then give a marvelous account of what he has seen. But Kim is comparatively a bungler at this game. However he can hopelessly beat the other boy at giving a detailed description of people he has watched. Now if there were a general faculty for observation, each boy should be just as good with one kind of material as with another. Practice with jewels should improve one's capacity to notice details of dress and manner; and *vice versa*. As a matter of fact, it is not so. One boy has a highly organized and efficient grasp upon one kind of material, the other upon another. One shines in dealing with one kind of experience, and the other with a quite different sort. There is no general mental capacity which can be increased by formal exercise, and then used anywhere and everywhere regardless of content. There is only an increasing efficiency in dealing with a certain kind of situation. This is universally true. It holds for reasoning, for imagination, and for any other "faculty" we may happen to name. A man may astound us by his brilliance in dealing with mathematical problems, and astound us just as much by his inept handling of social situations. Darwin was an imaginative giant in the field of biology; but he himself has told us that his feeling for poetry steadily declined to the point of complete atrophy. So one could go on.

What conclusion then must we reach? Surely this. Mental power is not something which exists separately from its applications. It is not like muscular strength which can be developed by formal exercise. It is not like electricity, which can be generated, and stored in a battery, and then used equally well in any way we like. It means neither more nor less than *the organized grasp upon a body of experience*. It is the power to deal with certain situations, to meet certain demands, to solve certain kinds of problems. To press, and perhaps slightly pervert, the electrical analogy, the mind is not like a battery made up of a number of cells, one containing imaginative force, another reasoning force, another observational force, and so on. It is not a storehouse at all. It is our capacity to react to and deal with circumstances. Its value depends precisely on what the circumstances are to which we can react, and with which we can deal. One man can deal very well with the circumstances of a chess board, while another can deal very well with those in an electrical armature. We say at once that the latter possesses by far the more significant and valuable mentality. And the fact that the former may, in a certain sense, be quite as clever, seems relatively unimportant.

So the essential thing in producing mental growth is not to strengthen certain abstract general abilities, or to bring about an increase in general mental power; for such entities do not exist. What is essential is to bring about an increasing mastery of and insight into *significant situations*. The content of education is the vital matter. And this is in sharp contrast with the theory of formal discipline, which regarded content as secondary, and formal exercise as primary. Why, for instance, is chemistry educationally valuable? Not because it is hard. Not because it provides good practice in reasoning. Simply because it is an interpretation of a whole range of human experience, and because, when we understand it, we achieve an insight into this experience, and a new power to control the situations of actual life. Why is poetry worth reading and studying? Not because it furnishes an exercise for the imagination, but because in it we make contacts with the insights of the creative mind. All the intellectual resources of civilization are tools which man has developed through experience for the interpretation of experience and the control of action. Their value in education does not consist in the opportunities they offer for the development of a fictitious mental power, or the sharpening of abstract mental faculties, but precisely in the enlightenment they bring into the affairs of everyday living. Their organized acquisition for these ends is the process of mental growth.

4. *What truth is there in the doctrine of formal discipline?*

It would seem from the argument of the last section, that we cannot entertain the theory of formal discipline. That theory involves a false notion of the nature of the mind and its growth, and leads to untenable educational principles and practices. But a doctrine so anciently and so widely held, and maintained by so many of the greatest minds, cannot lightly be brushed aside. Indeed, it represents and reminds us of a supremely important truth, which we must never forget, if we hope to think soundly concerning education, although it interprets that truth wrongly. This is the truth that *transfer of training takes place.*

Whenever an ability learned in one context or connection is used in another, what we call a transfer of training has occurred. In a course in algebra, one learns how to solve equations; and one uses this ability in a course in physics. One studies the rule for the use of the subjunctive in conditional sentences in Latin; then one applies it in the writing of Latin prose, or in making an English translation. One practices golf shots at the net; then one tries to apply one's newly acquired skill on the golf course. These are all instances of the transfer of training.

A moment's thought will show that transfer takes place very commonly indeed. It is, in fact, the normal thing for learning to yield transfer values. As I type out these words, I have probably never followed just this exact succession of hand and finger movements on the keyboard. But I do not have to learn it specially. My general skill as a typist, such as it is, transfers to this particular situation. If transfer were impossible, then each particular situation would have to be learned individually like a trick, and general skills, such as the ability to run the typewriter, or to play golf, or to do arithmetic, or to read German, could not exist. For ability to run the typewriter means the power to write on the machine any sequence of letters I may desire, without having to rehearse it specially. Ability at golf means the power to deal with situations which must often be new and strange. And arithmetical ability means the capacity to apply arithmetic when and as needed. Clearly the existence of general abilities of this kind is no more than a most obvious matter. So, in the hundred or more experiments dealing with the matter, some modicum of transfer has been found in the vast majority of cases.

Now the theory of formal discipline is in effect a recognition of the fact that without transfer of training, education itself, as we know it, would be impossible. Here lies its essential truth. We memorize dates in history, not just for the sake of knowing them, but to give us a better, more organized understanding of the temporal sequence of events. We learn lists of words in a foreign language, not to be able to recite the foreign word when challenged with its English equivalent, but rather for the sake of recognizing them when we see them in a piece of continuous discourse. We drill on the trigonometrical ratios, not just to be able fluently to recite them, but rather with a view to manipulating them in solving problems. We give children precise number work, not at all for the sake of putting on a smart, impressive recitation, but because we want them to be able to use arithmetic in all sorts of situations, in and out of school. We acquire the intellectual resources of civilization, not for their own sake, not for the sake of passing examinations or putting on a sort of educational vaudeville known as a classroom recitation, but because they will affect behavior in all kinds of ways. Everything taught in school is taught with at least the hope that it will transfer from the immediate situation in which it was learned. And when this does not happen, we have an educational failure.

All this the theory of formal discipline recognizes. It insists that content learned merely for its own sake has little or no educative value. Here we entirely agree. Where the theory goes wrong is in inferring that content is not important, and that transfer is brought about, and mental power built up, by formal practice and the sharpening of general, abstract mental abilities. This is nothing but a belief in magic. Mental faculties do not exist. The content of what we learn is essentially important; but not for its own sake. Content becomes the very stuff of education when learned in such a way that it transfers to life situations.

If transfer is not brought about by the exercise of mental faculties, and still is a fact, how is it caused? I think the best way to explain this will be to discuss some actual instances of successful transfer, and to see what is involved in them.

In a certain experiment, two groups of pupils were chosen, and one of these groups was taught the principle of the refraction of light. Both groups were then given the task of learning to hit with a dart an object under water of a certain depth. Clearly, the principle of refraction was involved; but the group which knew about it in theory showed results no better than the one which was ignorant of it. So far, there was no transfer from knowing the scientific principle to using it in a practical situation. Then the depth of the water was altered, and again the groups began practice. But now the group which understood about refraction in principle, learned the skill very much faster. Transfer did take place. Why was this? The answer is that to them, their previous practice had meant something which it had not meant to the others. They were able to comprehend it as a concrete application of a general law. What for them was enlightened practice was just routine drill to the others. The former were able to see in it the application of a generalization to a particular problem. When the situation was altered, the generalization helped them. But the latter had to go to work and learn something quite new. Transfer was brought about by the application of a general principle to a specific problematic situation.

In another experiment, three groups of subjects instead of two were used. Before any learning started, they were all given a test to show their ability to frame good definitions. Then came the practice. Group number one practiced framing definitions, and at the same time were led to discuss and think about the characteristics and requirements of good definitions. Group number two merely practiced framing of definitions, without any such discussions. Group number three had no practice at all. When it was all over, and another test on their ability with definitions was given, the second group showed very little superiority over the third; that is, their routine learning did them no particular good; they were virtually no better at making definitions afterwards than before. But the first group showed a very great advance indeed. Here again we see the importance of understanding and being able to apply a general principle, which is exactly what accounts for the success of the first group. Mere drill on defining terms leads to little or no improvement. But enlightened drill, which is perceived as the intelligent application of a principle, is highly effective. Once more, we see the commanding power of generalization.

A very similar experiment was set up to deal with memorizing. Again three groups were used. All were tested for the ability to memorize poetry. Group one then practiced memorizing, and at the same time discussed good methods of learning, and some of the controlling psychological principles of memory work. Group number two merely practiced memorizing, without any discussions or explanations or thought about psychological principles. Group number three had no practice whatsoever. When the second memory test was given, the results were strikingly like those in the foregoing case. The second group showed no particular advantage over the third. Mere drill had not improved their memories, which is quite in keeping with what we said when we insisted that there is no faculty of memory, to be strengthened by exercise. But again, the first group showed remarkable improvement. Here too their practice was enlightened. It was not just routine. It was the intelligent application of general ideas. And it succeeded.

Exactly similar results have been obtained where the content of school subjects was used as experimental material. The ordinary method of teaching Latin will bring about some improvement in a pupil's knowledge of English words derived from Latin. But if the principle of derivation receives some emphasis in the Latin course, this transfer is notably increased. Or again, we may compel pupils to be neat in their written work in arithmetic, but this will not mean an increase in neatness in written work in other subjects. But if, while insisting on neat work, we also explain to them what neatness means, and why it is desirable—if we make it an *ideal* for them—then a transfer takes place from arithmetic elsewhere. Or once again, it has been shown that while perhaps all of a group of students will be able to write down the square of $(x+y)$ some who succeed with this will fail if you ask them to write down the square of $(p+q)$. Clearly they cannot have grasped the principle involved, or the mere change of symbols would not trouble them. So in geometry it is a commonplace that a pupil may be able to give you the proof of a theorem as long as you call the triangles ABC and DEF, but will go to pieces on the job if you call them pqr and xyz. In these last two instances, we see what weakness is produced by the absence of generalization, and how this prevents transfer. If you are giving a test in algebra or geometry, one of the elementary ways of finding out whether pupils are reciting from memory, or working from a real understanding, is just to alter the symbols. Try it some time, and see.

So we are ready for our conclusion. *Transfer takes place by generalizing from a particular instance.* I practice hitting a golf ball at the net, not in order to be able to hit it better at the net, but in order to be able to do better on the course. And I succeed in transforming my golfing skill just in so far as I am able to get into my head, and also into my muscles, the general principle of the swing. I write off various exercises on my typewriter, surely not for the sake of writing exercises. Rather I want to build up a general coordination, to be used flexibly in any situation. I learn a date in history, not because it is a supremely valuable bit of information to carry round in my head, but so that I can use it as a peg on which to hang historical backgrounds. I learn a chemical formula, not to be able to reel it off in class, but because it involves a scientific law which I want to be able to use in many ways. Transfer depends on generalization. Education itself consists in learning things in such a way that their general meanings and applications are apparent.

There is another theory of transfer, which we ought to mention in passing, though it is not our purpose to engage in controversy. This is the theory of "identical elements." According to this view, skill in one situation brings about improvement elsewhere just in so far as there are certain elements in common be-

SIGNIFICANCE OF FORMAL DISCIPLINE 87

tween the two situations. For instance, I learn how to solve equations in my course in algebra; then later on I elect a course in physics, and there I find some equations to be solved. I am able to do these, and accordingly I find a transfer between algebra and physics, due to an identity of content. Or again, it has perhaps been my pleasure to memorize a good deal of poetry from time to time. I am given a part in a play, and I find I can learn it more rapidly because of my practice with poetry. According to the theory of identical elements, this may be because there is such a thing as a good memorizing mood, which I have acquired. If I were the sort of person who hated to memorize material, and who always wanted to stop and criticize it, instead of getting it into his head, this would tend to make me a "slow study" in dramatics. But I have, as it were, tuned in on the right mood in my practice with poetry. And this stands me in good stead in another connection. Here are illustrations of the account of transfer as due to identical elements.

I am well aware that this sketchy review does not do justice to the theory we are considering, which has been sponsored by one of the greatest minds ever devoted to the study of education. But briefly I want to indicate why the doctrine of identical elements does not seem to me satisfactory.

In the first place, it is possible to have glaring identities of content, without any transfer taking place. One of the very instances I offered is a case in point. For physics teachers often complain that students come to them with their algebra prerequisites all neatly docketted in the registrar's books, but seeming to be quite unable to apply the subject in a new context. Transfer is lacking, in spite of the content of the two courses being to some extent the same. Clearly, the identity of content is something which has never occurred to the pupils' minds. And if they do perceive the identity in the two situations, what does this mean? Surely that they have managed to generalize upon their original learning. For what is generalization but an ability to see how a certain principle or technique fits into many different situations?

Or suppose I say that the study of Latin helps with German, because there is an identity of procedure. The method one uses in learning to conjugate a Latin verb is very much like that which one would use in learning a German verb. And the *modus operandi* of puzzling out a Latin sentence would certainly seem applicable to German also. This may be very true. But still, can one really say that one learns a trick in Latin, and then transfers this very same trick to German? Surely there will be at least some differences? Surely the identity will not be absolute? Will it not be an identity of *principle,* rather than one of specific detail? What really seems to happen is that I acquire in the study of Latin certain skilled methods of dealing with language problems, and am able to transfer these just in so far as I grasp them *as principles,* and understand their *rationale*—that is, just in so far as I generalize them.

So one could go on. I think it could easily be shown that when we speak of an identity of mood as between memorizing poetry and learning a part in a play, we can hardly think of it as just lifting the self-same mood up from the poetry, and putting it down upon the play. What actually transfers is a generalized attitude, which applies to a whole range of situations whose details differ. In short, the theory of transfer by identical elements seems to me to transpose itself into the theory of transfer by generalization, whenever we closely examine what takes place. But does this matter? Is it not just a bit of verbal gymnastics? Is the argument of any practical importance? Indeed it is. If we take the theory of identical elements literally, it clearly means that you can learn something in a perfectly routine, unintelligent manner, and then be able to use it anywhere you wish. You can drill a pupil on equations in algebra, without helping him in the least bit to understand the principle underlying them, and then expect him to be able to use them in any situations where they may occur. You can hammer out a good old-line course in Latin, on the rule of working them hard and giving them no explanations, and then expect large improvements in English, just because many English words are derived from Latin. And so on. Now none of these things work in such a way. In practice, they represent notions about education just as indefensible and vicious as those arising from the theory of formal discipline. And the constructive essence of our criticism of the doctrine of transfer by identical elements in that transfer comes about and content is made significant by intelligent, enlightened learning—that is, by generalization.

Notice in closing that this notion of transfer by generalization is wholly in accord with the account of mental growth given in the last chapter. Mental growth does not come about by any strengthening of the mental muscles, or the training of the faculties of the mind. Nor does it come about by learning content for its own sake. Mental growth means an increasing power to generalize on significant experience, a movement of the mind in the direction of the universal. When mere fumbling gives place to rules of thumb; when rules of thumb give place to the principles of applied science; when the principles of applied science give place to the laws of pure science—then we have typical sequences of mental growth, whose ultimate end might perhaps be found in the Divine Calculator of Laplace, who apprehends the entire universe in a single infinitely complex differential equation.

5. *What are some practical applications of our account of transfer?*

Our account of transfer of training as brought about by generalization, is rich with illuminating insights for the teacher, the supervisor, the administrator, and the curriculum maker. And here I want to pick out and explain a few of its more striking applications.

A. This account shows us in a new way what is really involved in bringing education into touch with life. In dealing with mental growth, we insisted upon the importance of beginning always with actual life problems and meaningful situations. The proper and fruitful starting point for any bit of educational development is a life experience which has meaning for the pupil.

But we all know that a great many everyday life experiences have little or no educative effect. A great many people work year after year at their jobs, carry on their social relationships, look after their health and the health of their dependents, read the newspapers, vote in elections, and amuse themselves in a variety of ways, without learning very much, or becoming in any marked degree, different and superior human beings. Clearly, all these situations offer chances for learning. Our lives are full of educative opportunities. But we fail to use them. What right have we, then, to insist that such experiences are the proper and natural starting points for education, both with children and adults? What must we do to make a life situation educative?

The answer which we can make, in view of our previous discussion, is clear. We must bring about transfer. A boy has a job working at a lathe in a shop. He may make it a matter of the most unmitigated routine. He does well enough to avoid being fired, and to get some sort of promotion by seniority. But that is all. Virtually no mental enlargement is taking place. But now suppose that he begins to think and study about his job, in connection with the whole work of the shop, or as an instance of applied science. He works out, and comes more and more to understand, the general principles embodied in it. And these will serve him elsewhere. His adjustment is no longer rigid and limited. It becomes inventive, flexible. He not only learns his particular job as a routine; he uses it as a means of understanding wider problems. He generalizes it, and so gains from it attitudes, abilities, and insights, which will serve him well elsewhere. In other words, he capitalizes a life situation for transfer value.

This is exactly what ought to happen in a school project. When a group of grade school children work out a play on the landing of the Pilgrims, they are surely not just mastering the routine of play production. They are using this particular situation to broaden their mental horizons, and to see history in a new way. When a general science class in junior high school studies the city water works, they are not preparing to become hydraulic engineers, still less making a detailed documentary study of the local plant for the sake of knowing about it. They are learning science through its application to life. The educative value of the experience does not lie merely in the experience itself. It resides in the transfer which is developed. Essentially, the point is that if they come really to understand the water system, they will then be able to understand a great many other things better.

So the principle of transfer by generalization is the foundation of modern school procedures in relating education to life. We take real experiences and make them valuable by developing their implications, by deriving transfer values from them.

B. Our theory of transfer applies very directly to the problem of vocational education. Many people imagine that the great aim of vocational education must be to train young people in this or that skilled routine. Even in vocational preparation on as high a level as teacher training, this idea is current; for often one seems to run upon the assumption that what a good teacher chiefly needs is a bag of classroom tricks, or a set of rules of thumb. But this whole view about vocational education is wrong, here and everywhere else. If a man is to do really well at a job, and above all, if he is to be able to grow in his work and to adapt himself to changing conditions, he must not be trained as we would train an animal to do tricks. He needs a general insight into the principles of his work, so that he may be able to invent new and better procedures, and to avoid becoming obsolescent when working conditions change. To be sure, the education he needs will not be theoretical in the vicious sense of making no contacts with his vocational problems. But neither will it be practical in the equally vicious sense of establishing blind habitual routines. Its aim will be to set up *enlightened* routines. In other words, the ideal situation will be one where the worker generalizes his vocational experience, and in mastering one job, learns also to do others. This is merely saying that he ought to learn his job, both for its own sake, and for transfer. Here is a principle which applies to vocational education all the way from ditch digging to the practice of medicine.

C. Again, our theory of transfer throws a flood of light upon the problem of drill, and its proper management. The old-line teacher was a devout believer in drill, and was wont to insist that one should make the pupils work hard. Some very progressive teachers go to the opposite extreme, and say that there should be no drill at all. Both positions are false. The former is really based upon the theory of formal discipline, and the notion that hard work is good in itself, because it exercises the faculties. The latter simply ignores all the serious implications of a valid theory of mental growth. What stand, then, ought we to take? We find the answer in our theory of transfer.

Obviously, drill which fails to transfer is waste of time. No one practices hitting golf balls at a net, or five finger exercises on the piano, or simple applications of some mathematical operation, or the spelling of lists of words, just for their own sake. The whole point is to develop a mastery which one can use elsewhere. Drill which does not look beyond itself is mere folly. Now we have seen that mere grind, mere routine, yields a bare minimum of transfer, perhaps even none at all, because transfer is not the product of some strengthening of the faculties, and does not take place in the absence of generalization and insight. So drill must be enlightened if it is to serve its true purpose. We must establish the proper golf swing, or catch the feel of the desirable finger action, or see better the *rationale* of multiplication or subtraction, or notice the principles of construction in our list of words. We must always seek to generalize the experience.

Anyone who thinks progressive teaching is opposed to hard work, is laboring under a delusion. What it does oppose is stupid, unenlightened hard work; because there is every reason to believe this is useless. A story is told about a certain artist whose remarkable color effects mystified many critics. Someone said to him: "What do you mix your paints with, to get these effects?" And his answer was: "With brains, sir!" Here is the precise application of our account of transfer to the problem of drill. We insist that drill must be mixed with brains.

D. Our theory of transfer brings to us a new comprehension of the responsibilities of the teacher, and a new insight into what good teaching can accomplish. For the teacher chiefly determines whether transfer will take place in learning; and if so, how much, and in what direction. You will recall that we saw how the routine teaching of Latin yielded some improvement in mastering English words derived from Latin; but that an intelligent emphasis on derivation enormously increased this transfer. Exactly the same point was brought out in connection with learning to memorize poetry, and to make definitions. And it holds universally. Whether pupils in a language class are only learning grammar, or are acquiring language mastery through grammar, depends chiefly on the teacher. Whether pupils in algebra are only acquiring habitual routines of manipulation, or are building up a real mastery of mathematical processes and ways of thought, which will serve them in good stead in all sorts of different situations, depends chiefly upon the teacher. Whether pupils in science are memorizing rules and formulas, or learning the secret of scientific thinking, depends chiefly on the teacher. Whether pupils in history are simply grinding on facts which they will soon forget, or are assimilating insights and attitudes which they will use, and be influenced by, in countless life situations, depends again chiefly upon the teacher. The crucial question about any process of education is this: Is the learner going through a routine; or is he arriving at a better understanding of his task by generalizing it? And the teacher is the person in control of this vital strategy of learning.

All this should help you to appreciate, to some degree at least, how wide and vital are the bearings of the theory of transfer of training. It should also explain how important a place has been occupied in educational thought by the theory of transfer through the discipline of the faculties. Erroneous notions about transfer are highly dangerous, simply because of the central significance of the entire topic. And in order to understand education itself aright, it is necessary to grasp clearly how transfer in fact takes place.

*

Chapter 5

WHAT IS THE PLACE OF THE SCHOOL IN EDUCATION?

1. *What is the unique educative task of the school?*

The moment we define education as the process by which the individual becomes flexibly, creatively, and progressively adjusted to the institutions of society, we necessarily regard it as something far broader than schooling. Every social institution—the state, the church, the economic system, the press, the family—does far more than render certain useful services, or make available certain material goods. It alters the dispositions and tendencies of all those who come into contact with it. It moulds and changes them. In a word, it educates them. And so society itself has often been called the "great school." And many philosophic thinkers have regarded the entire historic process as the education of the human race. Man as he is today, with all his powers and limitations, with all his greatness and littleness, is to a very large degree the product of his social experience. And all our hope for a better world, and a nobler and wiser humanity, depends on the possibility of altering and improving that social experience. Only by taking this broad view, can we adequately understand the nature of education. If we think of it as schooling, we fatally limit ourselves, and shall never be able properly to comprehend the issues before us. The school must be seen as a part of a much larger whole. Of this we must constantly remind ourselves, or we shall begin talking nonsense, and imagining vain things. Yet the school is an essential part of the picture.

Indeed, it is even the center of the picture. Every social institution is an educational institution. But the school is so in a unique sense. What then is its unique task?

To be intelligent about the place of the school in the scheme of human life, the first thing to understand is that all through its history it has been forced to take over educational functions from other institutions. In the most primitive societies, there are no schools at all. Yet of course there is education. And it is carried on by a direct sharing of the various institutional activities. Girls have their appointed place in the home; boys in the hunt. Young people take a part, which grows greater with increasing age, in the doings of the tribe. And such undirected, informal sharing is all they need to adjust them to the simple requirements of their mode of life. Instead of being pupils in schools, they are apprentices to society. But as society becomes more complex, its institutions grow more specialized. The church becomes separated from the state. The means of earning a livelihood and of securing recreation, separate themselves more and more sharply from the general, undifferentiated social complex. Family life becomes more definite, and also more limited in scope. Together with this increasing specialization goes an abandonment by every institution of very important educational functions and duties. And with the rise of industrialism, the whole process is immensely speeded up. Contrast, for instance, the educational possibilities of the old time, self contained family, and those of the modern urban home. Much training in religion and morals, in literature and the fine arts, in craftsmanship and the practical arts, has gone out of the home, never to return. The same change has taken place in industry, as we can see at once by comparing the old craft system and apprenticeship, with the modern factory. As the great constructive institutions have given up ground, the school has been forced to take it over. And the end is not yet.

This, of course, explains that tendency, so well marked in all great modern societies, to increase the amount of human life spent in school. In 1870, in this country, about half the number of children between the ages of five and eighteen were attending school; while some fifty years later, the proportion was about eighty per cent. In 1870 about one in ten of all children of the appropriate age were attending high school; while now over half are in attendance. There is a universal tendency to open schools to younger and younger children, by setting up kindergartens and other institutions for the very young. And there is a similar tendency to increase the length of the school year. It has been said that in 1890 our population had, on the average, a third grade education, while now they have a sixth or seventh grade education. If such trends were peculiar to the United States, they would be striking enough. But they are world wide, though in few countries have they advanced as far as with ourselves.

It is a great mistake to think that the rapid growth of our schools is due merely to propaganda and publicity. Eloquent and persistent propaganda for more, and better, and costlier schools, we certainly have had. But it has been effective only through its harmony with a massive and irresistible social change. Underneath all the pamphleteering, and speech making, and argument pro and con, there has been the solid fact of a steady diminution of some very important kinds of general social education, which compels a steady increase of formal school education. People who argue for lessened school costs and more limited school facilities, give exactly the impression of those who plead against the economic drift of a powerful bull market. For a moment they may seem to accomplish their end, and slow up, or even reverse the movement. But the forces at work are mightier than any propaganda. They are the underlying tendencies of our civilization and of its evolution.

In view of the fact that the school takes over various functions given up by other institutions, some educational thinkers have said that its unique value lies in the performance of a *residual* service. But this is a great and critical misinterpretation. The business of the school is most certainly not to take on all kinds of educational odd jobs which nobody else will tackle. We cannot build up any constructive account of its work merely in terms of doing left-over tasks, even though the steady abandonment of educative influence by other institutions has meant its growth. Rather the point is that society, by delegating to the school more and more duties and functions, makes it increasingly able to perform what is in truth its unique service.

A. As the school has been forced to undertake more and more of the responsibility for the whole business of education, it has been brought face to face, ever more cogently, with its first great and unique task, which is the task of *choosing*. The need for selecting those things most essential to be learned has become increasingly pressing, as the range of things which might be taught has become greater. In our country's early years, the schools had little choice in their offerings. Society demanded of them that they should have all children learn to read, to write, and to master elementary arithmetic. Everything beyond this could be taken care of elsewhere. But during the nineteenth century, the scene changed. All kinds of new subjects came pressing into the curriculum, not because the school asked for them, but because they were virtually forced upon it. Navigation, stenography, typewriting, mechanical drawing, beauty culture, home economics, hygiene, to mention only a few samples from the enormous list, were introduced as school studies, often over the active protest of teachers. It has been a clear case of the delegation of educational responsibility.

Now what is the school to do about it? Simply to try to teach everything and anything, is clearly impossible. This would be the road to chaos. And as a matter of fact, we have gone dangerously far in this very direction. Our curriculum has become enormously rich. But at the same time, it presents no clear authoritative indication of just what we think an ideal education ought to be. If you have ever been puzzled to know just what courses to choose for your own best good, or how to spend a year in school for your highest advantage, this is the reason. Society has forced upon the school a richness which is highly embarrassing. It has not known what to do, or how to make a coherent scheme. Everything has been lumped together, and the responsibility for choice has been shifted to the pupil.

There is only one answer. We must choose those things which are most valuable and most fundamental. And we must organize all our processes so that those things will be made available, and indeed inescapable, to the pupils. This cannot be done over night, or in the twinkling of an eye. It calls for a rigorous sifting of materials, for deep and careful thought. What is required is the practical application of fundamental educational principles to determine what is most worth while. One of the weak points of our whole modern school system, and also of your own individual experience in the schools, is that we offer an immense wealth of alternatives, but no clear constructive philosophy of choice. Here is one of the chief lines which must and will be followed by educational evolution through the coming years. School education differs from general social education, in part at least, because it must increasingly involve intelligent and conscious choice. And the school differs from all other social institutions precisely in the fact that it is a *selective* educational environment. That is an aspect of its unique and peculiar genius, which it must find the means progressively to realize.

B. Another momentous consequence of the increasing educational responsibility which social evolution forces upon the school, is that it becomes compelled to think of, and plan for education, as aiming at a *common way of life*. Every other social institution tends to educate for a special way of life. Apprenticeship was a system which sought chiefly to train boys to be efficient in a certain definite trade or job. To be sure, it might make them better men in other relationships of life, but this was a by-product. In the same way, the state will seek to inculcate patriotism, and patriotism of a certain kind. A religious denomination seeks to inculcate certain dogmas and attitudes of mind. The home educates for home membership and family life. And the more specialized an institution becomes as it develops, the more limited and narrow its educative effects tend to grow.

Now when a whole range of our most important institutions give up many of their most necessary educational functions, and center them largely in the school, a very interesting situation is created. The school cannot possibly do just the very things which once were done elsewhere. It cannot give a little bit of apprenticeship, and a little bit of training in patriotism, and a little bit of various kinds of religious training, and a little bit of education for home membership, and so on. It is not in this sense residual. It is not a sort of catch-all. It cannot serve each separate institution, by doing the precise job of education which each institution once discharged of its own accord. Instead of serving *each,* it must plan to serve *all.* It must select those common elements which are found necessary for human adjustment to the whole range of civilized institutions, and make these its stock-in-trade.

One good illustration of this tendency is found in the peculiar problem of vocational education. The old apprenticeship system worked very well. It took care of vocational adjustment so completely that no one ever thought of advocating vocational training at public expense in the schools. The job of the school was reading, writing, and arithmetic; something with which the industrial system had no immediate concern. As industry, with its increasing specialization, gave up its major educative function, a demand arose that the school take it over. But it soon became evident that one could not simply put apprenticeship into the school, and for a very simple and final reason. An apprentice was already committed to a certain trade; but a child in school was not. Even if the school could offer training for every conceivable kind of job which its pupils might engage (a thing impossible in itself), there would still remain the problem of finding out which children should be trained for each vocation. Both educational thought and practice are still fumbling with this issue of vocational training. But the true solution is becoming more and more evident. Vocational training in the sense of a narrow apprenticeship does not belong in the school at all, or at the most has a very small place there. Nevertheless, if the school is to adjust the pupil to the demands of life, it must take cognizance of vocation. It can only do so by choosing those general elements of knowledge and skill on which any kind of vocational fitness depends, and making them available for everybody. As we shall see later, the whole sharp distinction between cultural and vocational education tends to vanish, simply because we are coming to think of vocational adjustment in terms so widely human. Here is one instance of the change brought about when a specialized educative function is abandoned by a social institution, and delegated to the school. There are many others. The best teachers of home economics, for instance, apprehend and present their subject in its very broadest aspects as a social science, and aim at far more than the mere teaching of household skills not ordinarily learned at home.

It has been found so impossible to serve the interests of each one of our numerous religious sects, that the usual attitude taken is to have nothing to do with religious training in the school. Civic training in a good school means something much broader than the sort of patriotism directly inculcated by the state. And so one might go on.

Of course our schools are very far from always succeeding in keeping the balance true, and resolutely serving the good of all, instead of the special interests of each. They are always apt to be unduly influenced by some powerful group or institution. But their genius consists, partly, in thinking of human life, not in its separate aspects, but as a whole. This is the second unique function of the school. It is, as we have seen, a selective educational environment. But also it is an environment whose primary purpose is *general* rather than special education. And I use that term, not to indicate the conventional "cultural" curriculum, but an education definitely planned to serve the social interests and needs common to all men, and to provide the basis of a common way of enlightened living.

C. A third momentous consequence of the delegation of educational responsibility to the school, is that it becomes peculiarly responsible for bringing about a social adjustment which shall be flexible, creative, and progressive, rather than rigid. The educative effect of other institutions tends towards rigidity, simply because it is special. Industry wants the recruit to acquire certain techniques, and certain folkways and mores. This looks like the practical thing. And it is enough, if all we are concerned with is to make a good machinist or tailor. Even so enlightened a body as the American Medical Association is under criticism as tending to build up a certain professional narrowness of mind and hostility towards change. The educational influence of any specialized institution is almost bound to be towards rigidity of social adjustment, towards learning only those things which the full-blown "master workman" ought to know.

Now the school stands to serve the interests, not of each but of all. It is not training some to be machinists, and others to be carpenters, and others to be physicians, and others to be home makers, and others to be politicians. It is educating human beings, so that, within the limits of their capacity, they may enter effectively into any or all the relationships of life. This cannot be done by imparting a tremendous repertoire of specialized tricks, but only by giving a broad grasp of the intellectual resources of civilization as the agencies for enlightened living. What shall it profit a business man to know mathematics? Why should an engineer study history? What is the use of art to a farmer? So long as we think only in terms of educating business men, and engineers, and farmers, there is no very good answer. What these men chiefly seem to need is an array of working techniques. But the school precisely does not think in such terms. Rather it seeks to make men better business men, and engineers, and farmers, by making them more effective human beings. One of its great tasks is to furnish an answer to these very questions. It must show that history, and science, and art, and literature, are indeed valuable for business men, and engineers, and farmers, and housewives, and physicians, and ditch diggers, because they are the agencies for flexible, creative adjustment to life. It stands, as we have seen, for a general culture in the sense of a foundation for a common way of life. But it must go one step further. It must seek to make culture practical, by having the pupil acquire it in close relationship to the great business of living.

So, in closing this rather lengthy section, let us sum up our answer to the question: What is the unique educative task of the school? The school, as we have seen, is forced to take over educational functions progressively given up by other institutions. But it is not in essence a residual institution. In taking over such functions, it assumes a constructive responsibility in three directions. First, it must select, from among the whole range of possible educative experiences, those of most worth. Second, it must think through and plan education as the foundation of a common way of life, and in this sense general rather than special. Third, it must seek to produce a flexible, creative, progressive social adjustment by rightly imparting the significant elements from the array of our intellectual resources.

2. *What is the chief danger of the school?*

The great danger which constantly besets the school is that it may forget its mission and become divorced from life. This arises from those very characteristics which we have just been discussing. When a business house organizes a class for salesmen, such a peril hardly exists. Certain techniques and conventions are taught for immediate use. Everything is perfectly and obviously practical, wholly and directly related to the needs of life. In such a situation, this is easily achieved, because we know exactly what we want. We are aiming at a specific and limited outcome, a comparatively rigid adjustment. But the school, by its very nature, is committed to something quite different, and vastly harder to accomplish. It seeks an adjustment, not to one or two definite situations, but to life in general. It must promote, not rigidity but flexibility, creativeness, progressiveness. There is only one way in which all this can be brought about. It must choose from the intellectual resources of civilization those items of most worth, and out of them build up a general curriculum. And then it must try to make this general curriculum just as practical in effect as the narrow and limited curriculum of the salesmen's class. This is a tremendously exacting task. There is an almost overwhelming temptation to treat subject matter as valuable in and of itself. To do this is so very much easier than to try earnestly to make it truly educative.

The difficulty of always relating the school to life is peculiarly great in our own country. This is because American life offers no intelligible, definite social plan. In Germany, during the nineteenth century, there arose the doctrine of the supreme state. All German institutions came to be shaped more and more to conform to the demands of the state. And we see the ultimate results of this development in the dictatorship of the National Socialist Party under Hitler. Much the same thing has taken place in Fascist Italy, and also in Communist Russia, though there, of course, the social dogma is quite different. But in these three instances, we see a planned, disciplined, highly organized society, consciously built on an intelligible pattern. And in these countries, the relationship of the schools to the whole business of life is a relatively simple matter. The schools of Germany have as their great business the production of patriotic Germans, according to plan. The schools of Italy educate in the ideology and mental attitudes required by Fascism. And the schools of Russia seek to produce young Communists. But in America we have nothing of the kind. It is, of course, possible that the ultimate outcome of Franklin Roosevelt's "New Deal" will be a planned society somewhat akin to that of the Fascist and Communist states. If this should happen, the problem of the schools will be automatically solved for them. And some educational thinkers seem to hope it will.

I think, however, that we may believe that the very difficulty of adjusting the schools to the demands of life in a free, democratic society is an inspiring challenge. If this country were organized as a vast, definite social pattern, then to be sure it would be easier to grasp the proper aims of education, and to relate what is learned in school to the life which the pupil leads outside. But such an easy solution would be purchased at a very great price. Our schools would tend in the direction of the class for salesmen. They would be dominated by one institution—the supreme state. They would achieve a certain stability, and educators could heave a sigh of relief, and stop thinking about fundamental issues. But they would become committed to producing a rigid adjustment; and they would sacrifice essential human values. For my part, I would prefer to take all the consequences of our relative planlessness in the hope and faith that, as we work and think and live together, we shall come better and better to understand the meanings of our common life, and discover how to educate a race of men able to share the common undertaking, and at the same time enjoy creative freedom. Not tomorrow, nor next year will this come about. Yet surely it is the meaning of the American dream. And it is the true solution of our problem of relating education, with its great mission of social prophecy, to American life.

Putting aside for the time being such large issues, let us ask just what happens when a school becomes divorced from life? What are the symptoms of the complaint?

A. The most notable symptom of a diseased condition in any educational system, is an excessive and perverse bookishness, a belief that the symbol is greater than the thing, and the word greater than the deed. I once went to a school which stood on one of the most famous roads in all the world, the ancient way by which the Roman legions marched up country from the southern coast of England.

Canterbury and Hastings were within easy reach; and so were Battle Abbey, and the great historic sites of the south land. Of course we studied English history. We read from our books about the Roman invasion, the landing of the Norman William, the slaughter of Beckett. But we never visited the historic spots; we were never so much as told to turn our heads and look out of the classroom window at the white road, over which, nearly two thousand years ago, the legionaries had marched.

This is a strikingly bad, but not an altogether unfair example of the meaning of bookishness in education. You can probably match it from your own experience. The symptom crops out on all sides. For instance, in many elementary schools, we see an actually reprehensible condition, because teachers have an unconscious prejudice that children are not being educated if they move about and manipulate things, but that they are being educated if they sit still and pore over printed pages. Again, if you are a teacher, and will remind your class of some principle they have learned out of a book, and then ask them to write down some illustrative applications, you will find that many of them will fail to think of the most easy, obvious, and immediate ones. School has made them so book-minded that only the remote, the unusual, the exotic, seems worthy of consideration.

The reason why the schoolmaster mind tends towards excessive bookishness is clear enough. The intellectual resources of our civilization exist very largely in printed form. And learning them necessarily means reading out of books. When this is made an end rather than a means, it is a clear case of the divorce of education from life. Still, the remedy does not consist in trying to have schools without books. It consists, first of all, in having all learning from books organized in the closest possible contact with the situations and problems of the pupil's life; and second, in choosing such reading as will be interesting, significant, inspiring, and appealing to the pupils, rather than sticking to the conventional assignment from the old fashioned textbook.

B. Another symptom which warns us that we are dealing with an institution divorced from life, and sundered from its essential purpose, is the retention of socially meaningless elements in the curriculum. Here we have the atrophy, the negation, of the selective function, the responsibility to choose what is of most worth, which we found to be one of the unique educative tasks of the school. The Renaissance movement, in its educational aspect, was a rediscovery of the classical literature. These new studies, at first, had a rich and wonderful social meaning. They inspired and inflamed men's minds with the hope of a better way of life. They profoundly affected human modes of action. But soon there came a change. The schools ceased to proclaim a new enlightenment, shining from the great writings of antiquity. They ceased to trouble about the message of the ancient literature, and concerned themselves entirely with—its grammar! To study the grammatical structure of the Latin and Greek languages came to be the central business of education. No real reason could be given for it, but it was the thing to do if you wished to be educated. The practice was continued through the vested interests of the schools, and of teachers who could handle such material, and nothing else. This kind of culture, with its pedantic effort to copy every small detail of the prose style of one great Latin author, was given a label by Erasmus which has stuck, and which one may apply to all educational formalisms. He called it "Ciceronianism."

Our present day educational practice abounds in Ciceronianisms. Latin is treated as a "dead" language, and taught with the major emphasis on a dissection of linguistic bones and sinews. Algebra and geometry are often presented as if no one could ever dream of applying them to actual situations. In English courses, we still find an extensive use of "literary" theme topics, such as the character of Ivanhoe, or the sanity of Hamlet, in preference to the use of the vernacular as an agency for conveying something a high school pupil might conceivably like to say. And in most colleges, modern foreign languages remain a fixed and bulky requirement, irrespective of the known fact that few students will ever use them, and the strong probability that much more significant material exists. Changes in these and other similar respects are being made. Forward looking teachers recognize that such things are wrong, and are determined to alter them. But the tendency still exists, and indicates clearly a separation between school and society.

C. Yet another symptom of a divorce from life, is a conception of teaching as essentially the setting of tasks and the checking of results. This often seems the obvious, inevitable, "common sense" view of teaching. If this is not the essence of the matter, what is? Now the reason why we find this notion of the function of teaching so natural, and so hard to avoid, is that unconsciously we accept the sundering of the school from life. Place children in an artificial situation, give them tasks which have no direct intrinsic appeal, and which cannot seem to them nearly as important as their social affairs and athletic interests, and of course you will have to make them work. You do not have to make them work when they are planning a dance, or practicing for a game—and yet at such things they will work far harder than you can ever make them. The clear suggestion is that curricular activities should be made just as real and powerfully appealing as so many social events or athletic practices. Notice, however, that the way to bring this about is not to accept and follow the unguided "interests" of the pupils. Capricious individualistic interests may, by chance, be educationally significant; but the probability is against it. If we can so organize our work that the pupil feels and knows he is studying things really worth while, and achieving masteries which, here and now, are transforming his living to higher levels, then we shall have an aroused, consecutive, disciplined interest, which is exactly what we need. And teaching will become guidance and stimulation rather than task-setting; for the tasks will set themselves.

D. Still another symptom of a divorce from life is the general tendency to set standards in terms of ground covered, rather than of working masteries achieved. In some school systems, teachers are supposed to cover a definite number of pages, or sequences of topics, each month, or each week, or are even held to a daily schedule. And where no such iron rule exists, the instructor often feels a secret shame if, in a semester, an adequate number of subjects have not been discussed and picked over. Such an attitude is sure evidence of a certain mental bias. If our chief interest is in subject matter rather than life, then the more of it we can cover in a given time, the better pleased with ourselves we shall be.

Now the extent to which any process of education is effective in modifying the pupil's social attitudes and dispositions, does not depend at all directly on the amount of ground he manages to cover. What really educates is significant experience, and constructive, worth while achievement. These are the ideals which the school should be organized to realize, and the terms in which all standards should be set. Any pupil has reached satisfactory standards in his real education, if he has done significant work, and entered into some significant experience—if he has really learned something, really seen its true inwardness, really come to possess it. Quantity is a minor consideration—even a dangerous consideration. One may have spent a semester very well in the study of some subject, although one has only perceived the true significance of a very small fraction of it, and although one has not "covered" it in any encyclopaedic way. But one may have wasted one's time if one has merely travelled through a large number of topics and sub-topics, and learned them as so many set lessons out of a textbook.

E. The last symptom of a divorce from life with which I wish to deal, is what has been called the "cold storage" theory of education. This is the idea that in school we store up certain items of knowledge, which will be useful later on—sometimes many years later on. Just how anyone can tell what bits of knowledge you and I and anybody else are going to need ten years from now, may seem a bit mysterious. But of course some pedagogues do seem to have second sight! Just why one cannot be trusted to look up any item in an Encyclopaedia when one wants it, may also seem a trifle hard to tell. But perhaps the notion is that soon after leaving school most pupils are to migrate to the center of the Sahara where such conveniences do not exist!

The real issue, with which we must come to grips, is that this cold storage notion, in all its subtle forms, is a complete perversion of the educational mission and meaning of the school. The school is not a place where children accumulate knowledge as bees accumulate honey. The only people who make knowledge the chief thing about education are those who are interested in a purely school-bound tradition. Our conception of the matter is absolutely the reverse. For us, education is a process by which the child comes to adjust himself more and more perfectly to social institutions and social demands. Instead of *storing* knowledge for its own sake, or for some remote and questionable use, the child needs to learn to *use* knowledge. This is the essence of becoming educated. We must have an immediate applicability, an immediately apparent significance. And the reason why the cold storage theory in one form or another, has been so popular, is that teachers are often dealing with material which has no great life value, either now or later, for the pupil, and wish to mask the uselessness of what they have to offer by references to the future and an avoidance of the present as a criterion.

Putting it in another way, education is an affair of mental growth. And it cannot be measured by the amount one remembers, either now or later. Its essential effect is a changed outlook, a changed attitude, an altered personality, a new type of adjustment and response. Here are the realities of the process. We can no more say that a growing mind stores the knowledge presented to it, than we can say that a growing body stores the food it eats. As soon as we think of education, not as schooling, but as adjustment to the problems of life, or as mental growth, then the whole cold storage doctrine utterly falls apart.

So to sum up, in so far as we divorce the school from society, it becomes formal and feeble. The schoolmaster, with his vested interests and fixed traditions, looms up in the middle of the scene. Education becomes school keeping. And subject matter loses its vitality. The way out is in two directions. We must reorganize our schools internally. And we must seek to bring them creatively into touch with other institutions.

3. *On what principles must the school be reorganized?*

The conventional school is essentially a mechanism for teaching subject matter, apparently in the hope that it will automatically transfer to life, and thus serve the ends of education. This is evident in every detail of its procedures. We see it in the way teaching is done, in the way assignments are given, in the system of examinations, marking, and credits, in the setting of standards primarily in terms of ground to be covered, and in the whole spirit and tone of the place. Many educational thinkers have recognized very clearly the unsoundness of all this. They have perceived that subject matter becomes valuable only when the learner acquires it as an agency for more effective living. And they have seen that this involves a demand for a school organized for the central purpose of bringing subject matter into touch with life, rather than for the purpose of teaching subject matter as an end in itself. The content to be learned becomes educative only when learned in a particular way, and in a particular environment. All over the world, schools organized to fulfill this condition are coming into existence. While they face manifold difficulties and problems, we know that they are practically possible. So to formulate the general principles which must control them is neither utopian nor impossible.

Fundamentally we must think of the school as an organized and ordered environment which favors mental growth, and which provides manifold opportunities for many-sided, significant contacts with life. This is suggested by the derived meaning of the word "school." It comes from the Greek *schole,* which means "leisure." That is, the school should be regarded as a place where learners are protected from the immediate, narrowing pressures of earning a livelihood, with the limited institutional adjustments which this implies, so that they may achieve a better and fuller development, and have time to secure a richer insight into the meaning of life itself. It must be an institution, provided and supported by society, where young people are granted the boon of living on a higher, a freer, and a more creative level than they otherwise could.

All the implications of this doctrine I cannot here formulate. But I will indicate three of them, which seem of immediate and central importance.[1]

A. In the first place, the school will seek to organize the pupils' learning in an environment of free and spontaneous group activity. One of the best and most obvious means of making anything an individual learns really mean something to him, is to throw him in with a group working in the same field, though not necessarily learning exactly the same thing. In this way he catches an infectious

---

[1] These points are suggested by the analysis given by Rugg and Schoemaker in their book *The Child Centered School:* World Book Company, 1928.

enthusiasm; and by the contribution which others make to him, and which he makes to them, acquires, almost unconsciously, a strong faith in the significance of what he is learning.

Such spontaneous group life will not come of its own accord. It must be deliberately organized. There must be a machinery of freedom. The conventional school organizes its group life in terms of control. The class is set up for the sake of being managed and directed by the teacher. Witness the prohibition against freely moving about, and the fixed seats which so strongly suggest the audience. This is necessary, because there is no real group concern with the learning, which is not in evident connection with the needs and intellectual appetites of the pupils. In the free group the teacher is still a necessity. But he guides rather than commands. He sustains a social situation in which the pupils may learn freely and contribute to each other. Much of his authority is used to prevent things from degenerating into a *melée,* where no one learns anything. A free group will have its routines. But they will not be those of the controlled recitation group or audience.

B. The school will regard the living interest of the child as the foundation of the program, and will organize its work with this in mind. Some people think that as soon as one speaks of building education on interest, one means building it on unregulated whim, and the cancellation of all organized direction for the sake of letting the pupil do exactly what he likes. Teachers who have the point of view of the conventional school always protest against this, and very properly. They say that there are certain things which it is supremely important for any child to learn, which is also very true. But they go on to intimate that he must learn these things, whether he is interested or not. And here arises a fallacy. For if he learns under duress and without interest, he will not learn properly. What he acquires will not become an integral part of his life development. And so the precise point of organizing school work on the basis of interest comes to this. We must handle our whole situation, from the kindergarten to the graduate school—and this also means taking into account far more than the immediate classroom situation—so that the pupil will share our own recognition of the importance and value of what he ought to learn. If it is essential that the pupil learn certain things—as indeed it is—we have not set up the proper conditions of education until that necessity is cogently apparent to him. This must be the source of his interest. Towards this everything in the school environment must point.

C. The school will organize its work to recognize the great principle that each individual must be encouraged to make his unique contribution and develop his unique point of view, without losing touch with social reality, or compromising his social adjustment. On the one hand, we do not want mere conformity. But on the other hand, we cannot approve the anti-social rebel, to whom individuality means an absolute right to do whatever he pleases.

Now the school, as a place for living on the highest possible level, and growing with the greatest possible fullness, must be an environment in which individual freedom and social adjustment are brought into a constructive unity. This is no easy problem. Certainly it is hopelessly bungled in the conventional school. Mass methods—mass standards—the primary emphasis upon competition—all such things tend strongly towards ironclad conformity. An enormous premium is put on doing what everyone else does. The pupil is discouraged from expressing what is in him, and developing his own personal tendencies.

And yet the individual in all his uniqueness, is the crux of our whole endeavor. He must be adjusted to social living; but always in his own way. The most hopeful environment for such ends will be one which fosters creative self expression, carried on in a free, interacting medium. Stimulate the child to learn in his own way and to contribute in his own way. But place him in a situation where "his own way" must be accommodated to the way of an active group. The great artist, to be sure, does his own unique work. But this is not all. The freak does this too. The artist accommodates his contribution to the mind of a social group. This must be the thought which guides us in building our new educational machinery. Upon it we must construct our class procedures, our administrative procedures, and our standards.

I cannot better sum up the characteristics of the school organized to bring learning into contact with life, than in the words of Bagley: "A good school is characterized by eager and aggressive industry, whole-hearted coöperation, a spirit of helpfulness, happiness, fine workmanship, and the ability of its product to stand alone." [2]

4. *What should be the relation of the school to other institutions?*

Education cannot be brought adequately into touch with life, and cannot fully achieve its great purpose of social adjustment, so long as it is regarded as the special preserve of the school. During his one hundred and twelve or so waking hours during a week, the child is in school for only about thirty. And his education is going on during the entire one hundred and twelve hours. So the school cannot achieve its complete purpose so long as it has nothing to say about, and no influence upon, all the other relationships and activities of the child. No internal organization, however sound and excellent, will in itself be sufficient. Indeed the very principles of reorganization which we have been discussing, imply that we must plan education in terms of total life activities.

There appeared recently in one of our national magazines, an account of how an enthusiastic and most intelligent father, living in New York, contributed to the education of his two sons and one of their friends in this very way. The four of them undertook to explore the city. They gained permission to watch the inside workings of the lighting and power systems, the sewage disposal plants, the arrangements for receiving and distributing foodstuffs, the water supply, the transportation system and so on. It was much more than a scheme of interesting sight-seeing trips, for they made it a matter of serious study, reading pamphlets and reports, and going thoroughly into the scientific principles involved. Here we see a definite attempt, and a brilliantly successful one, to capitalize the colossal educational possibilities of the most complex industrial community on earth.

What was done thus informally by this little group, is being undertaken regularly as a definite plan by progressive schools in this country and abroad. The attempt is made to educate children for social adjustment by giving them the experience of living as

[2] *Idaho Journal of Education*, 1930, vol. 11, pp. 300–302.

intelligent junior citizens. But we find this scheme carried furthest towards its logical conclusions in the schools of Soviet Russia. Nowhere else in the world has the dogma that education is life rather than preparation for life been so completely accepted. Children going to school are required to spend part of their time working in a factory, not for the sake of becoming trained artisans, but to catch something of the real meaning of machine production. Physics and chemistry are learned in their technological applications by visits to machine shops. In handling social science with little children, both teacher and pupils live for part of the summer actually as primitive human beings, seeking to understand the problems of primitive life by direct experience. The child learns much of the ancient history of his city or village through visits to museums rather than through learning out of books. The local post office is often placed in the village school, and the children learn much of their writing and arithmetic by handling the mail, such knowledge obviously being acquired in the most direct kind of social situation. Or they may have the task of sending out notices for the meeting of the local soviet. Again, we find pupils working up a report on water pollution in a district. And in another instance, the school embarked upon a study of a local agricultural problem, and staged a demonstration which had a strikingly beneficial effect upon the crops the peasants were able to raise. Going to school—being granted the boon of leisure—here means an opportunity to live a rounded social life with wide and significant contacts. One Russian educational authority exhorts the teacher in the rural school thus: "Live as the intelligent farmer lives, and may his work educate you and your children as it has educated millions of generations before you." And it is hardly a surprise to learn that in the Russian elementary school serving children from the age of eight to eleven, textbooks are almost needless.

While there are certain things in the Communist scheme to which exception may be made, it is worth noticing that no country takes education with a more desperate and whole souled seriousness. And the Russian authorities believe that if a system of education is to do its full work, it must be conceived thus in terms of the entire range of the child's social relationships. While it would be visionary to expect American education to be organized in a short time as complete, ordered social living, yet we have here a principle eminently sound. It indicates for us a clear program of advance. More specifically, it shows us an immediate task, and reveals a more remote, but still cogent ideal.

The immediate task is this. The school must constantly seek to deal with, reorganize, and rectify all the institutional contacts of its pupils. It must reach out into other institutions. It must seek to guide the child in the whole of his living. It must not be satisfied with merely teaching him lessons. It must take him by the hand, and lead him into a fuller life, where the intellectual content he learns within its walls, finds its meaning and justification.

For instance, it must maintain a constructive contact with the home. The home exercises upon the child an enormous educative influence for good or ill. And if the school takes seriously its task of adjusting him to life by raising the level of his present living, it cannot possibly remain indifferent to what he does in his family relationships. It is concerned to convey to him that part of our intellectual capital which exists under the labels of physiology and hygiene. If this is not immediately to affect his living as a whole, and his family living in particular, it will tend merely to be so much stuff learned out of books, and speedily forgotten. One rural school met this problem by having the children learn about biology through exploring the causes of typhoid on a farm. Here we have a prototype, albeit an ambitious one, of what ought to take place generally. Learning about biology, physiology, and hygiene in school must arouse in the child an interested concern over the conditions of life in the family circle. Again, the school seeks to bring the child into touch with music, and art, and literature. If these things are simply assigned tasks, with no outlet upon life, they will be sterile. They must generate in him a disposition to read, and a capacity and wish to appreciate the works of the great creative artists. If the teachings of the school do not affect the kind of books and magazines the child reads in his home, and the kind of pictures and music he desires to find there, those teachings have failed of much of their life influence and educative effect.

Again, the school must maintain constructive relationships with

SCHOOL AND EDUCATION

the political state. Social science and history become transforming forces only when brought into touch with the daily realities of political life. This shows once more the futility of the course in civics which consists largely in memorizing the Constitution of the United States. But we cannot even be content with teaching the abstract mechanisms of government, as is done, for instance in such a lesson as: How a bill becomes a law. In political campaigns with all their hurly-burly and misrepresentation, in the actual problems of municipal finance and management, of poor relief, of police activity, law enforcement, and punishment, and so forth, we have some of the situations where the content of social science becomes the agency for better living. For instance, in a certain community there was a strong move sponsored by real estate interests, to sell to the school district a certain tract of land for a high school. Surely any educational system committed to the social point of view would bring its pupils into touch with such an issue.

Again, the school must seek constructive contacts with industry. This means a great deal more than an occasional personally conducted tour through some factory. It means helping pupils to discover the truth and falsity of advertising, the facts behind a conservation program, the advantages and disadvantages of installment buying, and many other such things. So long as economics is only so many lessons learned out of books for examination purposes, it is mere subject matter and educationally dead. It does not take its true place in the scheme of human social life until it becomes the guided and enlightened exploration of actual, existing economic and industrial phenomena.

These are but a few illustrations of a great principle. They indicate the true direction of educational advance. But you may be inclined to say that what is required is impossible. Parents will resent it if children become critics of the conditions of their homes. Politicians will not tolerate a close and direct scrutiny of their operations. Industry will prohibit the investigations of even the best intentioned outsiders. This is all true enough, though persistent and tactful effort will carry things much further than we easily suppose. But it brings us to our next and final point. Our principle that social education must mean a complete ordering of life, involves not only an immediate task in which full success is hardly to be hoped. It also involves a remote but vital ideal.

The school cannot fully discharge its function in an imperfect society. The reason why every institution will, beyond a certain point, resist disinterested educational scrutiny, is simply that it has something to conceal. The reason why every institutional contact in the child's life cannot be immediately reorganized is that in all those contacts there is something perverse, something wrong. Only in a state like Soviet Russia, wholly committed to a new way of life, can we have thoroughgoing educational coöperation. And so our educational ideal cannot be satisfied short of the progressive reform of society itself.

Something of what education might mean in a reformed society is at least indicated by Macaulay's imaginative account of life in ancient Athens: "Let us, for a moment, transport ourselves in thought, to that glorious city. Let us imagine that we are entering its gates, in the time of its power and glory. A crowd is assembled round a portico. All are gazing with delight at the entablature, for Phidias is putting up the frieze. We turn to another street; a rhapsodist is reciting there; men, women, and children are thronging around him; the tears are running down their cheeks; their very breath is still; for he is telling how Priam fell at the feet of Achilles, and kissed those hands—the terrible—the murderous—which had slain so many of his sons. We enter the public place; there is a ring of youths, all leaning forward with sparkling eyes and gestures of expectation. Socrates is pitted against the famous atheist, from Ionia, and has just brought him to a contradiction in terms. But we are interrupted. The herald is crying—Room for the Prytanes. The general assembly is to meet. The people are swarming in on every side. Proclamation is made—'Who wishes to speak?' There is a shout, and a clapping of hands; Pericles is mounting the stand. Then for a play of Sophocles; and away to supper with Aspasia. I know of no modern university which has so excellent a system of instruction." [3]

Obviously, participation in such a life would be of enormous value, and profound effect. It would far better fit a young boy to

[3] *On the Athenian Orators.*

understand and share it all, than if he had been boxed up and shut away all day, in an institution whose walls and fences were an outward and visible sign of an inward and spiritual isolation. It is towards social education on this scale that we must set our hearts. In it the school will still have an essential place. Indeed, the school in an ideal society will be much more vital than the school we know. For it will be the directive center of enlightened living for the young. The ideal society will be centered on the school to a degree of which we hardly dream. For education, in its broad and final sense of the release of human quality for human ends, will be the supreme concern of that society.

Part Two

OUTCOMES

Chapter 6

HOW MAY EDUCATION ADJUST MAN TO HIS CIVIC INSTITUTIONS?

1. *Is there a recognized need for civic education?*

Every great modern state has recognized, by its practical policies, the urgent need for civic training. In France, after the revolution, one of the first matters discussed in the National Assembly was the organization of a system of schools which should promote the new civic ideas and attitudes. Germany, recovering from the crushing defeats administered by Napoleon, sought to recreate herself as a nation, largely through a system of education whose aim was to inculcate an enlightened patriotism. Throughout the nineteenth century her statesmen showed the keenest sense of what the schools could do in the way of developing desirable civic qualities. And so great was their success that it has been said: "The Prussian schoolmaster won at Sedan."

Coming to the present day, we find all the leading nations seeking to build up in their peoples a civic consciousness and a national feeling, through educational agencies. Sometimes, as in England, there is not much in the way of direct emphasis and conscious attention given to civic matters in the schools. But this is only because it is not felt necessary. The fact that England is an island, with a long and continuous political development, and a highly homogeneous population; the fact, too, that she has many most effective educational agencies quite apart from the schools, such as royalty with all its ceremonial, an aristocracy which still has much prestige as well as a long tradition of public service, and political parties of unusual integrity and intellectual quality; these things have made deliberate teaching of national ideals and behavior in the schools seem needless. In France, however, and still more in Germany, which latter has a brand new regime to support, civic training receives far more in the way of conscious emphasis. And we find this tendency carried to its height in Fascist Italy, and Communist Russia. This is no more than we might expect. For in these states, a whole new system of political ideas must be expounded and assimilated. And great efforts are being made to utilize every possible educational agency in their interest.

In the United States, the importance of civic training has been recognized from the early years of our national period. As soon as it became clear that the suffrage was to be extended, and the country governed on a democratic basis, leaders began to insist that we must have an educated electorate. And at the present time, our schools everywhere pay much attention, both in their curricular and extracurricular activities, to the claims and significance of the political state. We may certainly say that the need for civic education is universally recognized. Our question must be whether it is intelligently recognized, and whether any kind of adequate program is being built up.

2. *Is our civic adjustment adequate?*

Here is modern man, with much the same native abilities, both physical and mental, as were possessed by his ancestors of the New Stone Age. Over thousands and tens of thousands of years, he has managed to fashion for himself certain massive institutions, which, as we have seen, are really standard ways of living and acting. By means of his institutions, he has become the conquering animal type. The most complex, and, next to the home, the most ancient of these, is the state. In primitive societies, the tribe is the counterpart of the state, and its sovereignty resides in the person of the chief. Civic adjustment is a simple matter. It consists merely in being at the disposal of the hereditary chief, within the limits set by rigid custom. Contrast this with the modern state. It is the most powerful social machine ever constructed. And it is the most complex, many sided institution in history. Citizens of a modern industrial state are no braver, and no wiser, as individuals, than members of savage and barbarous societies. But even where equality of numbers exists, no society on a primitive level, or on the level of agrarian civilization, has much chance against such a state, if it puts forth all its power. Just as the pack of wild dogs is supreme over and invincible to animals stronger or braver separately than they, so the national state is the invincible aggregate of mankind.

I have developed this thought to show you the importance of the question: Is our civic adjustment adequate? Are individual human beings adjusted as well as they should be to this new, enormous, potent, and complex social organism? It dominates the life of civilized man, and its authority certainly is not likely to diminish as time goes on. Is modern man well adjusted to live within the metes and boundaries of this greatest of his institutions?

We should try to answer this question in a matter-of-fact, critical spirit. Many writers, when they deal with political and civic adjustment, seem immediately to turn into Jeremiahs, and begin pouring forth a tale of woe. According to them, all is lost, or soon will be, unless we hastily do something miraculous. But this can hardly be so. It is obvious to very casual observation that our great national structures seem to work at least fairly well. Far from being impressed with their fragility, we may well wonder at their recuperative power, and their ability to withstand the direst shocks. As one contemplates the evolution of national life since the World War, one cannot but remember a remark made by Adam Smith to a young man who assured him that England was being ruined by her debts. The father of political economy replied: "There is a great deal of ruin in a nation."

Nevertheless, we can by no means hold that the adjustment of modern man to his civic institutions is all it ought to be. Let us confine ourselves to the American scene. What do we find? Notoriously, there is a suspicion of politics among the better educated classes; and a suspicion of politics is no light matter. It indicates clearly a great defect in civic adjustment, because politics is the agency through which any state, by definition, must be run. Continuous political activity is unduly confined to certain professional and semi-professional groups. The average man is ill informed about public issues, and about all but the most prominent candidates for office. There is a fair probability of his voting in a presidential election; but much less likelihood in a local contest, and still less in a primary. The best type of citizen is apt to feel a reluctance to hold public office; and when he does so, he is often unfitted for effective work by his lack of practical political background. Most of our high school and college students have no very definite or serious political views, and give little thought or discussion to public matters. The average attitude towards the enforcement of the law, and the suppression of crime, tends to fluctuate between cynical acceptance of bad conditions, and rather hysterical and ill considered violence. And in such a matter as the payment of taxes, our people are hardly notable for fiscal patriotism.

So I might go on. But enough has been said for illustrative purposes. Notice that I am not raising the question whether our country is better or worse in these respects than others. In some ways, it is indubitably worse, but not by any means in all. Nor am I asking abstractly, whether these things are right or wrong; whether, for instance, having nothing to do with politics may or may not be morally justifiable in some sense. The only point is that here we have ways of behavior which are commonly recognized as characteristic of the American people, and which are clearly out of keeping with the requirements of the national state. They sharply and definitely indicate defects in our civic adjustment, which education must seek to remedy.

But the picture is far from wholly dark. Beyond all doubt, we find today a more effective demand than fifty years ago for a high type of man for public executive and administrative work, and for civil service, if not for legislative activity. We find, also that much public business is far more efficiently and honestly transacted than it was even comparatively few years ago. Then too, there is a better public attitude towards questions of civic honesty and dishonesty, as expressed for instance in the theft of the public domain. Recent events throughout the country have shown the immense influence which can be exerted by strong national leadership. And above all, the burst of disinterested patriotic service on which the state may count in time of war, cannot fail to impress anyone not ridden by the Jeremiah complex. We certainly cannot agree that all is lost, or that our civic adjustment is utterly futile.

The probability is that many of our civic deficiencies are more or less temporary, and due to transient and special causes. Yet no one can say that the majority of our people make the most of their civic institutions. As Sisson has put it: "Being a citizen of the United States is a highly skilled occupation: it calls for practical knowledge and special capacities far beyond the present attainments, and far beyond what our educational system, in school and out, has yet even attempted."[1]

I cannot here undertake to give a full account of all that is involved in effective adjustment to civic institutions. The reason is lack of space. If you want an exhaustive schematic outline, I refer you to Chapter Four of C. C. Peters's book, *Objectives and Procedures in Civic Education*,[2] where he presents an impressive list of the characteristics of desirable citizenship. What I propose to do is to pick out some of the most striking marks of effective civic adjustment. And my aim will be to help you to understand, concretely, what our educational agencies must attempt in this connection. I shall deal with the following points: Interest in and knowledge of public affairs: Proper balance between regionalism, patriotism, and internationalism: Political judgment of issues and personalities: Breaking down of rigid economic class distinctions. This, to repeat, is no complete account. But it will serve to show what education ought to, and can accomplish, in the way of making man more at home in his civic institutions.

3. *How may education promote interest in and knowledge of public affairs?*

Here we have the basic presupposition of any system of political democracy. Democratic government can be based on no other assumption than that the citizen has an informed and intelligent attitude

[1] *Educating for Freedom:* The Macmillan Company, 1925, p. 123.
[2] Longmans, Green and Co., 1930.

towards public business. As a matter of fact, our own government is managed on the assumption that the average man knows far more about public affairs than is at all possible. For instance, the electorate is asked to choose for office men whose work is that of expert specialists, such as engineers, or superintendents of schools; and also to decide on definitely technical matters, such as the floating of bonds, the construction of buildings, or the making of roads and the granting of franchises. Intelligent action of such matters is not to be had by popular vote, for the simple reason that few possess either the ability or the time properly to inform themselves regarding them. But at least this does show the great importance of widespread interest in and understanding of governmental business, if we hope to have that business efficiently and honestly transacted.

We all know perfectly well that the extent of such interest and knowledge leaves much to be desired. It is quite insufficient to insure reasonable efficiency, or to meet the legitimate needs of a democratic form of government. When an issue comes up for vote, most people, at the very best, make a decision on hearsay evidence. They read certain statements in the press about tariffs, or franchises, or bond issues, or about the fitness of various candidates. Or they are told about these things by word of mouth. Very rarely do they make a genuine attempt to get at the truth. In fact, in most cases, they would hardly know how to go about doing so. And therefore they make the only kind of decision they can, which is an arbitrary one. Perhaps they may not do even so well as this. Perhaps they just mark their ballots in accordance with party lines, and let it go at that. Or, still worse, they refrain from voting.

Here then, is a primary educational task of the greatest importance, and one of the chief ways in which effective adjustment to civic institutions may be promoted. There are a number of important points to consider in regard to it.

A. Notice, first of all, that it is a task for the schools. Certainly they should play a much larger part in creating interest in and knowledge about public affairs than they do at the present time. And this emphasis should be carried all the way from the grammar grades, to senior year in college. There are several reasons why the schools are peculiarly fitted for such an undertaking. The first is that they are much more disinterested than other agencies which have this work in hand. Much civic information and discussion is promoted and conveyed by the press, by the radio, and by political parties. But they all have axes to grind. Their information and discussion is pretty sure to be highly colored. Their aim is not to lead the voter to intelligent, independent conclusions, or to arouse him to a continuous, critical, constructive interest in public affairs. It is only, or chiefly, to get him to vote in a certain way, regardless. In other words, self interest leads them to desire a rigid, rather than a flexible, adjustment. The second great advantage of the schools is that of dealing with young people. These are hopeful subjects, not just because they are young, but because they are free from the urgencies of making a living, and have time to think and grow. So the schools may promote a constructive political interest that will be lifelong and continuous, rather than sporadic.

B. Then notice how proper civic adjustment requires the whole range of civilized intellectual resources. Suppose the issue before us is that of a tariff on goods manufactured in countries with depreciated currencies. Certainly this is no question to be decided on a snap judgment. It is about as broad and complex as anything could be. Wise action upon it will demand our best in the way of instructed intelligence, and will make heavy drafts upon the intellectual resources which man has accumulated to aid and enlighten him. First of all, we must have much knowledge of life conditions in our own and other countries; that is, we must utilize the human agencies for inter-communication. Second, all kinds of scientific and technological knowledge and insight are demanded. Third, we must have effective and civilized attitudes, and avoid cave-man prejudices against, or soft minded prejudices in favor of, the foreigner as such. Clearly the only agency which can possibly develop and render available all this, is an institution which deals in wide terms with the entire range of human mental capital.

So we come to see three things. First, very much more is involved than just a course in civics somewhere along the line. The whole curriculum, and the extra-curricular program as well, needs gearing to the civic issue. One of the ways in which the sum total of knowledge, insight, skill, attitude, belief, and habit which education seeks to convey, ought to be shaped up, is with respect to civic problems. Second, it is of course true, that the schools cannot immediately influence decisions upon great public problems which face us here and now. They have their effect upon the situation by raising a more public minded generation, by directing mental growth into a particular channel. And one way in which they should, and indeed must, do it, is by taking cognizance of current issues, and making them teaching opportunities. Children in school should study, and seek to comprehend, the immediate problems of politics, and should canvass its personalities, not because they are able to affect the course of events by their votes, but in order to gain generalized insights, which will transfer to other situations they will confront in adult life. Third, we see once more the futility of teaching the intellectual resources of civilization with no thought of actual application, with no relationship to actual life adjustment. A man may know—or may once have known—a great deal of history or geography, or natural or social science, and still be completely stupid when confronted with the need to decide about a complex and potentially irritating tariff issue. Intellectual content must be geared consciously to life purposes, or it is not educative at all.

C. As a third main point, it seems worth while to say that we must not make it our chief concern to stock the memories of pupils with a large selection of facts about public matters, in the hope that they will use them later. Here again is the cold storage theory. Rather what we want is to develop, in and through the study of concrete problems and the application to them of a wide range of intellectual resource, a certain attitude or disposition. This is the disposition to look for, and find out about, public questions for oneself. Here is something worth more than mere knowledge. This, far more than any possible information, is the essential and living factor in civic education in this connection.

4. *How should education develop a proper balance between regionalism, patriotism, and cosmopolitanism?*

This is the second characteristic of effective civic adjustment which I propose to consider. One of the most notable and constant characteristics of primitive tribal life, is an exceedingly sharp distinction between the "in group" and the "out group." The individual shows a most intense, unquestioning, unreasoning loyalty to the group of which he is a member. He usually has a very strong feeling, reinforced by various superstitions, for the neighborhood inhabited by his tribe, and even for the very soil on which it lives. And on the other hand, he shows a very marked hostility to all strangers. We have here a feeling which persists, though considerably modified, far above the primitive level. Thus the Greeks called all who were not Helenes, barbarians; and to the Roman, the Empire marked the boundaries of the world, and the domain of truly human life. Even today, more than traces of this primitive exclusiveness persist. We still suspect the foreigner, and look askance at him, as of other flesh than ourselves. And we still easily assume the superiority of our own clan, as a background for many of our attitudes towards life.

Now it must be clear that primitive regionalism, unmodified, has no proper place in the life of the modern state. Just as, towards the close of the Middle Ages, the rising autocracies became more and more hostile to feudalism, as a threat to their power and supremacy, so the modern national state is nearly always jealous of unduly strong regional and sectional loyalties. One of the tasks of government in France has been to establish and promote the state as against local loyalties. The old Austro-Hungarian Empire, in spite of its imposing façade, was so weakened by excessive regionalism, that it was the first great power to disintegrate during the World War. And our own history is marked by one of the most epic struggles of all time in behalf of the Great State. So, modern civic life is impossible, and the state becomes an unworkable mechanism, if the individual retains those primitive regional attachments which have played so great a part in the evolution of the human race.

But if extreme regionalism indicates bad civic adjustment, so also does extreme cosmopolitanism. There is a type of attitude which makes men behave and talk as though their own country were always in the wrong, and as though its interests should be casually disregarded. I am inclined to think that this sort of thing is a good deal more common in America than in Europe. Undoubtedly, it is produced by our general educational background and experience. Its fundamental weakness is its sentimentalism. It is a faulty adjustment, simply because it undertakes to ignore certain very prominent factors in the environment. We may, perhaps, argue that the national state is not the ultimate or ideal type of human association, or even that it has various evil aspects. But it remains one of the great realities of our world as that world exists today. So we must admit that effective action on many matters of vital concern cannot possibly be had by pretending that the state is a figment, or that its interests can safely be ignored. This is exactly what is proposed by extreme internationalists. Possibly an international society is the final word of our social evolution. But what we must strive for today, is a sound national-civic adjustment.

The argument which I have so far presented, clearly leads to the ideal of striking an effective balance between regional feeling, feeling for the state, and the sentiment of cosmopolitanism. All are necessary and important in a proper civic adjustment. So far as one can see, we obtain a proper balance between them only by educating men to take an attitude which may be expressed as follows: The community for the sake of the state; the state for the sake of cosmopolitan human society. Let us review these propositions one by one.

It will readily be granted, in theory at least, that the local community ought to subserve the wider interests of the state. When a town, by political influence, is able to modify for its local interest, projects set up for the good of the whole state, we all admit that a wrong has been done. Yet such instances are very common indeed. Moreover, there is a pretty general disposition to take them for granted. When a power franchise is granted or withheld, a transportation system planned, or public funds spent, with regard to local rather than general interests, most people are apt to think that such things are inevitable defects of the existing system. To be sure, our civic machinery continues to work fairly well, so long as these abuses are not carried too far. But this is only because, as Adam Smith remarked, there is a great deal of ruin in a nation. They are

ADJUSTMENT TO CIVIC INSTITUTIONS

perfectly definite defects. And their toleration is a clear sign of faulty adjustment to our civic institutions.

Perhaps the second proposition, that the state ought to exist ultimately for the sake of a greater social unit, may seem more questionable. Yet it has been seen as a necessity by the greatest and most enlightened minds of all ages. We find it represented at the highest point of Jewish prophetic vision, during the Babylonian Exile. And certainly it is in the purest tradition of Christianity. We have now reached a point of civic evolution where it is of crucial importance that what the choicest spirits of the past perceived as true, be built into the effective behavior patterns of the masses of mankind. And the reason for this is the enormous growth in power of the modern state. Untamed, unmodified national sovereignty has become a most perilous thing. Extreme, blind patriotism, which may be a mere extension of the primitive feeling for the "in group" and against the "out group," ceases to be a virtue, and becomes a danger, when it is implemented with weapons tremendous enough to destroy the whole structure of civilization. On the other hand, the plea is not for an abandonment of patriotism. For this the greatest minds have not contended. What we need is the sense of the mission of our country, a recognition that its greatest value lies in its power to serve. But to render full service, its own unique contribution needs to be preserved, and its interests must not be wantonly sacrificed on sentimental grounds. Perhaps the attitude of the ideal citizen in our present day civic environment can best be expressed in the pregnant lines:

> "He is the best cosmopolite
> Who loves his native country best."

You may think I have been sketching a utopian scheme. I do not agree. Such an effective balance between regionalism, patriotism, and cosmopolitanism, could be quickly and surely achieved by an educational system which really set out to do it. If you doubt this, let me ask you to remember two things. First of all, our present civic attitudes are the results of education. They are not born in us.

They are not inevitable, or part of a "human nature" which nothing is supposed to be able to change. We are brought face to face with this whenever we really become acquainted with the life of a foreign country, and find there the same human creatures, but a bewilderingly different attitude towards the state. Second, let us recall that at least one great country is definitely setting out to transform the civic adjustment of its people according to plan; that it is doing this through the agency of education; and that it is succeeding. I refer to Soviet Russia, whose schools have embarked on the enterprise of creating that portent, the "new man," in accordance with the Communist dogma. Are we to admit ourselves helpless, where Russia, with all her limitations of personnel and resources, and all her appalling obstacles, actually seems on the way towards success?

How then can the desired type of adjustment be brought about? Briefly, by gearing to the problem before us the intellectual resources of civilization. The man who, in his proper person, possesses a full measure of these resources—that is to say, the educated man—should have, as one outcome, a proper balance between regionalism, nationalism, and cosmopolitanism.

Let us try to make this still more specific, in terms of a program of teaching. First of all, the school should have its roots in the local community, and should deal with its problems and explain its phenomena. It should definitely set out to capitalize for educational ends, the local contacts and relationships of the pupils, so that the subjects they study are given a conscious bearing upon community matters. And then intellectual content should be brought into touch with the whole range of political institutions in which the individual lives and will live. The teaching of history may aim to have the pupil consider public problems from the standpoint of the larger social whole, and may seek to interpret the meaning and mission of America in the family of nations. Community civics may well build up pride and interest in the local unit; but obviously it cannot do so in the spirit of the booster, who wishes his own town to flourish no matter what happens elsewhere. Geography, properly taught, may be one of the most vital subjects, in the aid it can give to understanding the interrelationships of human life, and the bearing of all parts of human society on one another. And it can give the pupils a sense of intimacy with remote peoples, living in strange lands. Social science and economics, again, can teach the pupil how local business can subserve the common good. And certainly one great outcome of living instruction in literature ought to be to help young people to feel themselves citizens of a Great Society; not, to be sure, uprooted from the local, limited community, but through it able to adjust themselves effectively to a larger whole.

I have not tried to give any complete program of civic instruction bearing upon the problem of balance between regionalism, national feeling, and cosmopolitanism. All I have said is by way of a hint as to what may well be done. But it is enough to bring before us again two points which were mentioned in our previous section.

Again we see that civic adjustment demands a great deal more than one or two formal courses in civics. It depends upon a complete, directed, civilizing of the individual by the educational agencies. He must be equipped with knowledge, skill, insight, attitude, belief, tradition, and habit. All the intellectual resources which society has accumulated must be pointed in the desired direction.

And then once more, just a mere formal knowledge of the content of the school curriculum is not enough. Civics as a mass of facts about constitutional points, American history chiefly as a string of names and dates with a few interesting stories interspersed, economics as a series of principles to be memorized—all this is useless. What we need is a civic message in all our teaching. We must develop the intellectual background of the great current public problems, so that later on, our pupils will become enlightened citizens.

5. *How may education develop political judgment of policies and personalities?*

One of the most essential attributes of a citizen in a democratic state, is the ability to form sound judgments of policies and personalities. Obviously the whole theory of voting and popular choice depends upon it. Yet this ability is by no means so general as it ought to be. The average American business man gives only sporadic attention to problems of public policy, and usually concerns himself only with such issues as seem directly related to his narrow pursuits. And his knowledge of the personalities, tendencies, abilities, and records of those who run for public office is apt to be extremely limited. It is a noteworthy fact that the elements in the population whose interest in politics is most continuous and most intense, are not those on the whole best fitted to shape intelligent public opinion. Very often those who have the greatest educational benefits, are most completely cut off from political participation. Here we have yet another instance of poor adjustment to civic institutions. And in this matter, the schools cannot be absolved of blame. It sometimes seems as though the net actual effect of our educational system is against, rather than in favor of, the sort of political attitudes and ways of action which seem desirable and necessary to all thinking men.

What is necessary for effective political judgment of policies and personalities? In seeking to answer this question, I follow, in part, the discussion of C. C. Peters.[3] First, one must have "the habit of acquainting oneself with the local conditions that the policies are designed to meet." Then we need "a knowledge of, or the disposition and ability to investigate, the history of similar ventures in the past." Then we need "a knowledge of, and a disposition to apply, the general principles of sociology and economics, under which the special cases are to be subsumed." Then we need "the disposition and ability to ascertain what policies are pursued in other communities and countries." Then we need "the habit of studying the temper of the people as related to the matter in question, to the end that the bad effects of a shallow idealism may be avoided." Besides these things, we must have a disposition and ability to inform ourselves of the record and background of men offering themselves for election, and a capacity to pass reasonable and balanced judgment on such information.

Clearly, we have on our hands, once more, the same kind of educational task which we have discussed in the two foregoing sections. Our aim must be to help children to think about current

[3] *Objectives and Procedures in Civic Education*, pp. 45 ff.

policies and personalities, by applying to them the intellectual resources of civilization. This is the only chance we have of avoiding political prejudice, and stupidity, and of combating indifference. And it is one of the living contacts which the content of the curriculum should make with real situations and problems. If we can develop these attitudes, dispositions, and skills in school, there is every hope that they will transfer to the concerns of life later on. Again it is not a matter of giving a short course in civics, dealing with such questions in a more or less hortatory spirit, but of directing a rich and rounded education along fruitful and functional lines.

Notice, too, that this is a formidable undertaking. As soon as the school dares introduce such matters, it invites attack. In an imperfect social order, the beneficiaries of political institutions are not likely to welcome too much in the way of impartial investigation. Yet to take the bull by the horns is the obligation of a vital social education. We cannot have an education which is both living and dead, which at the same time deals with current issues, and offers a stock in trade of harmless academic generalities.

6. *How may education break up economic classes?*

In the modern state, extreme class distinctions based on lines of economic cleavage, are a source of weakness. A benevolent despotism may perhaps be able to tolerate the existence of a great mass of underprivileged toilers, whose share in the common good and the general enlightenment is exceedingly limited, and who are regarded by the more fortunate as hardly human. But there really are no benevolent despotisms of the pure type left in the western world. The machinery of representative government may have broken down in Germany, or Italy, or elsewhere. In moments of irritation and despair, we may be inclined to call both England and the United States plutocracies. But as a matter of cold fact, the dogma that government exists by the consent of the governed, rather than by divine right, is universally acknowledged, and widely effective in the modern world. No matter how poorly parliamentarianism may be faring, no matter how influential a hypothetical money power may have become, the existence of a great unenlightened proletariat is perilous as never before. The truth is, that it is sure to be fatal to our civic institutions, if it is tolerated. To paraphrase the words of Lincoln, which are just as applicable here as to the conditions of which he spoke, a modern state cannot exist part slave, part free.

In the United States, class lines are not nearly so deeply ingrained as in most of the older countries. But still, there are influences in our educational system which operate, perhaps in part unconsciously, to perpetuate, rather than to obliterate them. Secondary schools and colleges are still the preserves of the economically more favored elements of the population. When the children of small farmers or laborers enter these schools, it usually means an ambition to "rise" in the social scale. And the very idea of thus "rising" implies a hierarchy of classes fairly well defined. Contrast this with the state of affairs in Denmark, where the secondary school takes such young people, and tries to fit them more adequately *for life in the social class in which their parents move*. In other words, it offers a "cultural" education for what we would be apt to call the "lower classes," and thereby works powerfully against hard and fast class distinctions, and in favor of an enlightened civic adjustment. The real symbol of an education beyond the rudiments is, in this country, not the academic gown, but the white collar. And it hardly seems to occur to us that even those who will earn their living by physical toil, might also benefit by broad and rich cultural advantages, and might thereby become better men, and more effective citizens.

It is, of course, true that there must always be differences of economic function. But there is no necessary or valid reason why such differences should result in a system of sharply segregated social classes. When this happens, it is because those who perform certain economic functions—more particularly the functions of manual labor—are deprived of any full share of the common cultural heritage. Indeed, cultural advantages may be decisive in determining the social level of any group. The clergy, as a body, are less well paid than some of the higher ranks of skilled labor. But they enjoy a much higher social status and esteem. And this is because they enjoy a much richer and larger share of the cultural resources of our social order.

So the problem of breaking up economic classes is not in the least that of obliterating all differences of economic function. This would be utterly impossible. The real task is to mediate to all as full a share as possible of our common culture. And the crux of the problem lies with the secondary school, and to a less extent, the college. We must seek a secondary education for all; and higher education on the basis of individual capacity, rather than social rank and economic good fortune. This means planning our secondary schools to deal with pupils very different from those who now predominantly enter them. It would mean profoundly altering the curriculum, though this would remain a general and not a vocational curriculum. Also we would have to change the way in which teaching is done, and the way the school is administered; and besides this, it would cost more, simply because our high schools would come to serve greater numbers. But our expenditures would be a direct investment in efficient political and social democracy, and would probably lead to an advancing prosperity, which would more than cancel them. Can anyone doubt that, if we set out, as Denmark has done, to broaden the intellectual horizons and enrich the lives of our farming and laboring groups, the gain to our civic institutions would be prodigious? It would transform their political and social attitudes. It would make them more effectively cooperative members of society. It would lead the present favored classes to regard them, and the state as a whole, in a new and far healthier manner. This may all seem very visionary and impractical. It would seem much more so were it not being effectively achieved in the world today, though not, unfortunately, in the United States. But, after all, when great sums are being lavished on our schools, and greater ones demanded, have we not some right to require aims which are beyond the ordinary, aims which may have in them some touch of the visionary, even the utopian? What we must seek is an education committed to fashioning for all a common way of enlightened living.

7. *What are the chief dangers which confront civic education?*

I have already spoken, incidentally, of some things which ought to be avoided, if we are to do all that can be done in the way of setting up effective civic adjustment. But it seems worth while to deal with this question somewhat more formally and completely.

A. One of the most common deficiencies in civic education is lack of reality. A staple item in older courses in civics, often required by law, was the teaching of the Constitution of the United States. Inevitably, it was learned for recitation purposes. There was little chance that the children would be able effectively to understand its provisions. It could hardly make any difference in their behavior towards the state. And it was about as fine an instance as one could have, of an educationally sterile piece of learning. In more modern courses, we often find units dealing with such topics as: How a bill becomes a law. This may or may not be of some genuine value. If it calls only for memory knowledge of the abstract machinery of government, it will mean hardly more than learning the provisions of the Constitution.

So there is a certain element, if not of make-believe, at least of unreality, about much of the teaching of civics. The actual detail of political action sometimes seems too disillusioning and too crude and dangerous, for children to know about. It is very true that the schools should not emphasize, still less by implication condone or glorify, the sordid aspects of our public life. But these boys and girls with whom we deal, will have to live in the world as it is, and make shift with the actualities of politics, if they are to be effective citizens. It is this very isolation of our most fortunate classes from the actual grimy mechanisms of government, which is one of the weakest points of our civic equipment. There is no way of building up a genuinely effective civic adjustment without bringing learners into contact with realities, which are sometimes not as pretty as we could wish. Teaching them about the imaginary affairs of a utopian paper commonwealth, which never was by sea or land, and never will be, is merely dodging the issue, and gets us nowhere.

B. Another defect of much training for civic adjustment is

ADJUSTMENT TO CIVIC INSTITUTIONS

undue narrowness. I have mentioned this repeatedly, and will do no more than touch upon it here. We cannot do what needs to be done by segregating a course in civics, or even by setting up a "civics curriculum." What is needed is a general curriculum, made vital by its conscious relationship to actual civic issues, and offering a deep, broad, human interpretation of actual civic problems.

C. Another danger in civic education is propaganda. As a matter of fact, propaganda permeates a great deal of the teaching of history and social science. You may not clearly realize the fact, but it remains true that the school textbook in history which you have used or are using, is almost certain to have been written with a view to stressing certain happenings and points of view, and suppressing others. This is so in every country. The Hundred Years' War is taught with one emphasis in England, and quite another in France. The French schoolboy reads a very different story of the events of 1870-71 from that presented to the German schoolboy. One of the few, honorable examples of impartiality in historical instruction in the schools is the treatment of the American War of Independence in the United States and England. In both countries, it is presented with an almost exactly similar emphasis, though the English account is naturally much briefer.

If we look at it in one way, the intensive propaganda which has been woven into school texts in history and social science, is a testimony to the possibilities of education in influencing civic adjustment. There is no question whatsoever but that it actually does so. When anyone intimates that our schools cannot change and improve the civic attitudes of our people, he is talking nonsense. The schools have had a very great deal to do with making our attitudes what they are today. But it has not been a deliberately planned attempt. Even so, the forces of propaganda have been exceedingly strong. And if we should intelligently and deliberately set out to deal with civic training so as to produce the very best results, placing our emphasis upon impartiality and constructive reasonableness, our schools are in a position to make a commanding contribution to American life.

Of course, in a certain sense, all education is bound to have in it an element of propaganda. If we strongly believe a certain social interpretation to be true, we shall also believe that it ought to be taught in the schools. But there is a very great difference between serving the selfish, narrow interests of some one institution within the state—the Republican party, or the oil companies, let us say—and earnestly seeking to present an unbiased and prophetic vision of the whole social good.

D. Lastly, we must beware of working towards rigidity in civic adjustment as an outcome of our training. Fixed prejudices, and opinions which nothing can alter are the results of propaganda, narrowness, and divorce from reality. Such mental attitudes and tendencies are the outstanding weakness of the Soviet, and to some extent the Fascist schemes of civic education. Always we find a fixed orthodoxy, whether of Marx or Mussolini, which must not be questioned. This kind of rigidity is perhaps necessary when we are dealing with what is in essence a dictatorship, with its supporting system of ideas, and its arbitrary requirements upon conduct. For a democracy it can mean nothing but weakness, and, carried too far, failure.

This does not mean that the educated citizen will be a wild and radical critic of existing institutions, or some kind of a fanatical rebel. Quite the contrary. But it does indicate a reasoned freedom in the face of the political structure; a willingness to experiment; a hospitality to change where change seems requisite. It is often said that Americans are unduly timid when confronted with political emergency; much given to extremes of conservatism; inclined to regard any political novelty as dangerous and wrong. If this is so, it merely indicates an unfortunate rigidity of civic adjustment. The way out is not by a propaganda of radicalism, which, after all, is just another orthodoxy; but by building up a systematic insight into our political institutions, and a sense of familiarity and mastery in dealing with them.

*

Chapter 7

HOW MAY EDUCATION ADJUST MAN TO HIS ECONOMIC INSTITUTIONS?

1. *What is the fundamental educational problem of the economic order?*

One hundred and fifty years ago, the wand of science was waved above the world. Thick about us has sprung up the magic forest which we call the industrial system. And we are still wandering bewildered through its mazes, with only faint intimations of the true path. So swiftly has this come upon us, that since the close of the Napoleonic wars, the conditions of human life have changed more than during the whole preceding course of civilization. Our forefathers of the time of the American Revolution, had, in their physical circumstances, more in common with the Babylonian, the Egyptian, and the Roman, than with ourselves. Man's adjustment to these rapid and prodigious changes is yet very far from perfect. And one of the greatest tasks of modern education is to make him at home in his economic institutions.

H. G. Wells, in a recent visit to this country, made the statement that if the affairs of the world were put, without reserve, into the hands of a committee of expert economists, the causes of depression would be swiftly removed and the problem of the business cycle solved. Let us imagine that such a committee has actually been brought together, that they have formulated an adequate plan, and that they have been given the authority to execute it on the widest scale. Where would lie the greatest difficulty in giving it effect? What would be the chief obstacle to success?

Can we doubt that it would be the attitude and habit of mind which such a plan would encounter? Like guests bidden to the wedding feast in the parable, most people would, with one accord, begin to make excuse. They might say that the plan was admirable in theory; but they would be sure to cast about for plausible excuses for refusing to coöperate. What about the bankers and the great business magnates, who would have to submit to controls of which, today, we scarcely dream? Already they complain of too much government in business. Would they tolerate a radical extension of regulations which they already deem dangerous invasions of private rights, even though it might be in the interest of everybody? What about the investors in the securities of corporations whose profits might be decimated by a scientific revision of the tariff? What about the farmer, that "rugged individualist," who would have to be told how many acres to cultivate, and what kind of seed to sow? What about the small business man, whose relationships to industry and finance as a whole, would surely come up for revision? What about the skilled laborer, whose right to strike would be sacrificed, and whose union might be threatened? The National Industrial Recovery Act is of course a step in this direction. Yet it is far from representing a completely planned economy. But it probably goes as far as most people would be willing to follow.

An economic plan could surely be made, which would give us a far greater and more general prosperity than any we have yet enjoyed. The industrial system, under expert cultivation and pruning, would yield a vastly heavier harvest than it has yet produced. But such a plan would have to live, not only in the minds of a planning commission but also in the understandings, the dispositions, and the activities, of the masses of men. It would require coöperation as well as leadership. And here it would break down. For men are still far too engrossed with private interest, and the immediate assured return, for them to take the longest view, or to think and work in terms of a really complete social scheme, even for their own ultimate good. Does not this mean that they are not adequately adjusted to the demands of this new industrial institution, which has grown up so fast? What other interpretation is possible? For what we have said is that men do not yet have the mind to operate the modern economic system to their own greatest advantage.

But is the situation hopeless? There is no good reason for believing any such thing. After all, every great advance in the control of human life has been made in the face of just the same kind of difficulty. There was a time when a person living in Virginia hardly recognized any community of interest with another person living in Massachusetts. But this has been overcome, and to the great benefit of us all. If we still had the mentality of primitive mankind, we would be utterly incapable of thinking, feeling, and behaving as members of any such vast scheme as the American Union. We would be loyal citizens of Toonerville, and nothing more. And consider how far we have come, even in the industrial sphere itself. Of course, if we were to go back into the past two hundred years, the scientific knowledge and technical skill needed to create and manage such a vast business unit as the Ford Automobile Corporation, could not possibly be found. As a matter of fact, one of the chief troubles of the early inventors of the steam engine was to discover blacksmiths skilled enough to make a cylinder that would hold steam. But something else would be lacking too. This would be the managerial and financial intelligence, and the social discipline necessary to give that intelligence effect. For modern business is a social, a spiritual, as well as a technical phenomenon, and depends in the broadest way upon the mind and dispositions of mankind. We certainly have no reason to give way to despair when we survey the past. Man has learned, again and again, to postpone immediate gains for greater advantages in the future. Again and again he has risen above parochialisms, to his own great profit. He has learned a great deal, too, about how to live in an industrial civilization. The American Federation of Labor has a broader and sounder economic outlook than a mediaeval trade guild. And the American Bankers' Association has a financial insight far in advance of that of the Hanseatic League.

All this should serve to show us that an educational program for economic betterment has excellent chances of succeeding. Many radical critics of our industrial life take a view which is altogether too desperate and pessimistic. Often they give us the impression that nothing has been accomplished in the way of human readjustment to technological conditions, and that nothing is likely to be. Unwarrantably pessimistic also are those stolid conservatives who meet any scheme for basic industrial betterment with a shake of the head, and the wise comment that you can't change human nature. As a matter of fact, you can. And you may know this, because it has been done, and is being done before our very eyes. To be sure, no adequate economic plan can be imposed by fiat. It must grow up in the minds, the dispositions, the habits, the traditions, of our people. It is an undertaking, not for an expert commission with autocratic powers, but for our educational agencies, and above all, our schools.

To define sharply the educational problem set by the industrial order, it comes to this. Men need urgently to learn to think and act with respect to the system of industry as a whole, and to be willing to put aside immediate though limited advantage for the sake of an ultimate good. This is no more than the application of that practical intelligence, or, if you will, that enlightened self-interest, which has made the human species more successful than the apes and the wolves and the tigers and the buffaloes. Consider how obviously necessary is such training, and such an outlook. There are all sorts of problems which everyone knows are of the first importance, but which, being everybody's business, are at present adequately attended to by nobody. For instance, much of our future depends on the conservation of our natural resources; but few private corporations will feel justified in freezing an investment for a hundred years, while a new forest grows up; and we know how the average oil operator feels when he is told that he must not hurry to get every drop of production from his field. Or take the question of stabilizing currencies; or the problem of tariff revision on a world wide scale, which is the only possible scale for dealing with it properly; or the tragic issue of unemployment. Here are some few samples of the problems which cry aloud for solution, in terms of a wisdom wider than immediate self in-

ADJUSTMENT TO ECONOMIC INSTITUTIONS

terest, and yet whose adequate treatment will be of enormous benefit to everybody. What we must aim at is an adjustment to industrial conditions which will make their solution not only possible, but obvious and natural.

Perhaps the point of view I wish to suggest may be made clearer if we contrast it to the directly opposing philosophy of life in an economic order, the famous doctrine of *laissez faire*. According to that theory, the good of the whole is best served by unrestricted competition among individuals. Each person is supposed to be able to see his own interest, and to work towards it; and thus is to be achieved the greatest benefit of the greatest number. As we understand it today, this doctrine is a piece of the wildest optimism. What actually takes place under free competition, is that everyone sees a very immediate and narrow interest, full of antisocial dynamite. The farmer wrecks his soil for a quick return, and then moves on. The employer hires children to labor sixteen hours a day, and is indifferent to the fearful toll of impossible working conditions, and a miserable standard of living for his employes, so long as he can retire at fifty, and leave a competence to his family. Perhaps if we were all ideally wise and good—if we were all guided by what Socrates used to call "right reason"—*laissez faire* might work. But the whole difficulty of leaving the individual free to follow his own interest without restriction is, that he has not the wisdom or the insight to know what his interest really comes to.

So once more we return to our claim that the great educational task is to teach man to understand, and behave with respect to, the industrial system as a whole, if he hopes for a tithe of the benefits which can come from the scientific management of our world. Fully to explain the scope and detail of the program here implied is beyond my ability. But it may stimulate your thinking, and help you to understand more definitely the meaning of a vital social education, if I try to indicate some of the lines which such a program must follow. I shall briefly consider how education may improve man as a producer and as a consumer, how it may undertake progressively to raise his standards of living, and how it may contribute to the establishment of an industrial democracy.

2. *How may education affect man as a producer?*

We may perhaps take it that man, as a producer, was well adjusted under the craft system—that he found in the conditions of his work the means of personal satisfaction and fulfillment, and that he met with real adequacy, the social problems then presented. But now he has to deal with a very different institution. He works with machine tools, on a large scale. He is a factory producer. His adjustment is no longer what it ought to be. His occupation is apt to be a source of personal frustration. And he is out of gear with social realities.

The point of the difficulty is beautifully illustrated in a dramatic episode in Arnold Bennett's novel, *Clayhanger*. Old Clayhanger has a most unhappy boyhood as a child worker in one of the early factories. He has extremely limited educational opportunities. But when he grows up, he enters the printing business, and through his initiative and native ability, begins to succeed. But his success is almost his undoing. Bit by bit, he installs machinery in his shop. He seems, however, to entertain the notion that the joists of his floor will stand any strain; and he proceeds to load them with heavier and heavier equipment. At last comes the final straw; the floor begins to give way; and a ruinous disaster is averted only by the quick thinking of his son. The moral for us is obvious. Clayhanger's efficiency as a machine producer is limited by his practical stupidity. He refuses to take into consideration all relevant factors. And only luck saves him from paying the penalty.

Here we see exactly how education must apply itself to the problem. And we also have warning against a common error. Would it be a good plan to seek to improve man's production efficiency chiefly by teaching him superior routine skills? Would this be a wise aim? Shall we bend our efforts to teach the plumber more and better tricks of the trade; to make the farmer better at the techniques of farming; and so on? Of course, the value of doing such things will differ in different instances. If a man is a very clumsy or unskillful operator, he must have instruction here. But it is not the vital point of attack. A vocational school might have made Clayhanger more skillful at typesetting, and the other routines of the job of printing. But if his outlook remained so limited that it failed to include the joists of the floor, all this would have gone for nothing. Notice, too, that the floor joists are only symbols and samples of many other things which must also be taken into consideration. Besides the physical, there are also the social circumstances of productive work. These also are relevant; and man cannot be considered well adjusted as a producer, if he ignores them. It may be a mediaeval and pitiful stupidity to act as if a floor would hold any load. But to act as though we can operate a great industrial system in the midst of social patterns, and by means of social outlooks, appropriate to feudalism, is stupidity just as fatal.

The great educational task in making man a better producer is to teach him to use his intelligence adequately with respect to production problems, and to see his job in the widest setting, and in relationship to the industrial whole.

This point is absolutely borne out by one of the most effective studies ever made of the problem, the report of Herbert Hoover's Committee on Elimination of Waste in Industry, and of the Federated American Engineering Societies.[1] The question raised is: What are the chief causes of productive waste? It is answered by a survey of a number of important industries. Let us consider a few points in their diagnosis.

One cause the Committee finds is faulty material control. They write: "The average contractor has no calendar of operations except the dates of starting and finishing a job. He largely regulates deliveries of materials by visits to the job, or through statements received from the job superintendent. Haphazard methods of planning result in delays for want of material, or in burdening the job by an over-supply of material. The same practice results in frequent lay-offs, causing dissatisfaction, the loss of good mechanics, and a high labor turnover."[2]

Another cause of waste is faulty production control. Again I quote: "A shoe factory having a capacity of 2400 pairs of shoes a day could turn out for a considerable period only 1900 pairs of shoes because of shortage of needed racks.... It is found that at least ten

[1] *Waste in Industry.*
[2] pp. 10–11.

hours per man is thrown away on energy-wasting and time-wasting work resulting from lack of shop methods, while an additional two or three hours per man per week are wasted on unnecessary work." [3]

Yet another cause is interrupted production. It is pointed out that most industries are to some extent seasonal, so that it is very difficult to arrange for constant full time work for employes. This indicates a radical and wasteful maladjustment between man and industry. And business depressions and labor troubles still further accentuate the fluctuating character of productive activity.

Yet another cause is faulty labor control. To quote the report once again: "With perhaps two or three exceptions, shoe shops have no departments maintaining modern personnel relations with the employes. Thus the worker has no unbiassed means of approach to his employer, and the employer lacks the means for treating with his own employes. Among the plants studied, only a few have effective employment methods." [4] Again: ". . . a high labor turnover is a rough index of one of the common wastes resulting from inadequate labor management." [5]

These are but a few excerpts, yet they present a fair idea of the tenor of the whole report. Clearly, the chief thing lacking is a broad, competent, practical intelligence, which takes into consideration all the aspects and conditions of man's activity as a producer under industrial conditions. This, rather than narrow industrial skill, or mere lack of mastery of industrial techniques, is the great weakness. Ineffective workmanship is recognized as one cause of waste. The report says: "Still another loss resulting in low production arises from inefficient workmanship; for much of this the management is responsible, through failure to provide opportunities for education or special training. Management, however, cannot do more than provide these facilities, and experience has shown that it is difficult to interest workmen in training courses which are designed to increase effectiveness." [6] But this is only one cause amongst a great many—far more than I have cited here. And it is

[3] pp. 12–13.
[4] p. 13.
[5] pp. 13–14.
[6] p. 15.

not greatly emphasized, or regarded as of prime importance. We are fully justified in insisting that the great necessity for better adjustment to production tasks, is a broader industrial intelligence and outlook.

But where does the responsibility rest? Are not almost all the factors we have mentioned, within the province of management? Shall we conclude, then, that the best thing to do if we wish to educate for better production, is to have schools for industrial leaders only? This would be a great fallacy.

It is admitted that the primary immediate responsibility for poor production rests with the management to a large extent. The report says: "Planning and control should be adopted as fundamentals of good management. For the most part they have not as yet penetrated the mass of American industry." But labor also has a very large share of responsibility in the search for improvement. We read: "In discharging its responsibility for eliminating waste in industry, labor should coöperate to increase production. The need for facts instead of opinions stands out everywhere in the assay of waste from intentional restrictions of output. All concerned need to remember that science is an ally and not an enemy, and that no policy can be soundly based which ignores economic principles. Ignorance of these principles lies at the root of most of labor's restriction of output. The engineers who made the field assays unite in pointing out that this attitude is beginning to change. The change should be aggressively led; not allowed to drift." [7] So labor also should share the responsibility of calling for, and applying performance standards, of revising regulations and restrictions, of improving health and reducing accidents, and of bettering industrial relations. It is quite clear from all this, that just to educate the managers into an effective industrial outlook, will never be enough.

Then too, where do the managers come from? Many of the best are recruited from the ranks. Even if it were possible to pick out in advance those men who are to be in control of industry, to give them the necessary broad and informed outlook, and to put them into managerial positions, and to ignore everyone else, to do so would be monstrously unwise. And such a scheme is fantastic.

[7] p. 27.

Our system must produce its own leaders. Short of the hereditary principle, there is no other way. It is a vital matter to see to it that every knapsack contains a baton. And this can be done only by diffusing economic intelligence throughout the rank and file.

So what our institutions obviously need is a personnel, not just trained for the job, but educated for enlightened participation in the complex activities of production, able to see the task in its ramifications and wider settings, capable of adjusting itself flexibly to new conditions, and of creating new techniques, endowed with the power to grow in and through its work.

How can all this be brought about? By a broad education concentrated upon this specific issue. The worker in industry needs a full share of the intellectual resources of civilization, if he is to develop his full efficiency as a producer. He needs a full share in the human means of communication, through which is created an understanding of other men. He needs to be educated to the scientific outlook, both physical and social. Artistic insights may find a multitude of applications in the task of production, where beauty of design has very tangible values indeed. He cannot retain the popular beliefs and ideals appropriate to a craft system, and be efficient in an industrial system. His habitual modes of action need to be enlightened. And he must be led actively to desire and seek improvement in industrial techniques. In sum, his need is for a general education which fashions for him a common way of enlightened living, and which yet has specific reference to production problems.

This, you will admit, is quite a picture. It is the picture of industry staffed by educated men. It is an utter contrast to the all too common vision of an industrial structure directed by a few favored, god-like beings at the top, and manned by semi-human robots. But it is what we get from a report on production conditions which few will dare to call soft minded, or foolishly idealistic. A claim is made that the efficiency of the old British Regular Army depended to a considerable degree on the fact that most private soldiers were as good judges of position, tactics, and even strategy, as their officers, so that they fully comprehended, and were able to coöperate in, every military operation. This is exactly what is required of machine industry. To draw another military analogy, a type of tactics developed towards the end of the World War was attack by infiltration, in which individuals, or small groups, seeped semi-independently into the enemy's position. This required a good deal more independence, and soldierly competence, than merely acting rigidly in common with a mass. In just the same way, the conditions and requirements of modern industry have become so complex, both physically and socially, that the obvious necessity is more and more for an educated personnel.

3. *How may education seek to improve man as a consumer?*

If you will contrast our situation with that of those living two hundred years ago, with respect to the variety and complexity of available goods of all kinds, you will have some understanding of the magnitude and newness of our modern problem of consumption. With rapid transportation, scientific methods of preservation, and refrigerating machinery, the number of different kinds of food which can be had, has increased enormously. Moreover, it is offered to the purchaser in a great variety of new forms—in packages and containers, cooked and prepared in various ways. Think for a moment of how the bewildering complexity of the modern consumer's diet problem is capitalized by advertisements for various dental preparations and proprietary remedies, and you will perhaps be newly impressed with its reality. Clearly, he needs to know far more than he would if he lived in an older, simpler civilization, if his dietary choices are to be wisely made. Much the same is true of clothing. A very great variety of kinds and grades of cloth and leather are upon the market. And there has been built up a whole series of graded standards of manufacture. At the same time, it has become possible to disguise inferior workmanship and material, and to give an article of poor quality an excellent initial appearance. Comparatively few of us have the knowledge, or the training in observation required, if we are really to protect our own interests at all adequately, in the purchase and consumption of clothing. Of course, the manufacturer's brand means a great deal, and in many cases is an excellent guarantee. But one probably pays rather high for it; and it is not an adequate substitute, in any case, for better public information. In the same way, the problems which confront the purchaser of a house, have multiplied and grown more and more complex. The degrees of difference between the best obtainable product, scaling down to one that can hardly be considered satisfactory at all, have become so numerous and so fine, and so hard to distinguish, that again, most of us are simply forced to trust the expert, and buy and use what he recommends.

In the face of all this growing complexity, how does man fare as a consumer? None too well. So far as I am aware, nobody knows how adequately adjusted in this respect were our forefathers, who lived under the craft system of industry. Their problem was certainly simpler. But their knowledge was less. However this may be, there is no doubt at all that modern man is far from being as expert in matters of consumption as the conditions of his life require; and that part of the task of adjusting him to his economic institutions, is to bring about improvement here.

Henry Harap [8] has undertaken the very interesting task of determining adequate consumption standards for food, clothing, and shelter, and of comparing them with the present practice of the American people. His method has been first to assemble, from all available sources, information on what is desirable in the abstract in the matter of using food, clothing, and housing; then to bring together information relating to the actual use made of goods of these three kinds. From this he is able to derive a large number of specific instances of defective consumption. And such instances indicate just where the need for education in such matters lies. Let us select some of his conclusions, for the sake of illustration.

In regard to food consumption, his general statement is: "The selection, purchase, and use of food combine to form one of the fundamental processes of economic life. At the present stage of development of the race, this process is performed with a good deal of imperfection. The theory of proper food consumption is far ahead of present practice. We have discovered much about nutrition, but we have not really begun to convert what knowledge we

[8] *The Education of the Consumer.*

have into food habits."[9] Some of the specific educational objectives which emerge from his study of food consumption, are the following: "To know the relation in general terms between the weight of food and its nutritive value. To know roughly the amount of calories, protein and ash in the common weights and measures of food. To consume more vegetables and fruits by weight. To consume less meat, fats, and sugar by weight. To consume more dairy products." Again, in the purchase of food, we find much avoidable inefficiency. Regarding buying food in packages, Harap finds the following among desirable objectives. "To ascertain what package foods may be bought in bulk. To ascertain the actual difference between food bought in bulk and food bought in packages. To purchase milk in bulk. To buy bread by the pound. . . ." Food myths, again, militate against efficient consumption. "In New York City, consumers pay high prices for white eggs and in Boston consumers pay high prices for brown eggs. Chemical tests show that no relation exists between the quality of eggs and the color of their shells. Cold-storage products are tabooed not for their intrinsic inferiority, which they sometimes but not always show, but because of the early originally well-founded prejudice against cold-storage foods. . . . Apples are bought for their red color although some of the reddest are poor for eating purposes. The neck piece of the beef carcase is as nutritious and can be made as palatable as other cuts, yet it is considered improper to buy it. . . ." And he estimates that the average American family wastes ten per cent of its total food consumption.

Turning now to housing, he finds it desirable to set up and recognize the following aims to be achieved by education. "To know the fundamental elements which determine the quality of a home. To understand the significance of rent, number of rooms, water supply, bathtubs, ventilation, and home ownership as elements in the housing problem. To make a housing standard a part of the mental habits of the people of our nation—and that this standard shall include the following elements: rent, type of house, number of rooms, toilet, bath, gas for heating, ventilation, closet space, storage

[9] p. 19.

space, running water, lighting, drainage, laundry, and washtubs. To use these standards in the purchase and selection of a house. To know how to report illegal housing conditions to the proper government authority."[10] Similar desirable aims are set up with regard to housing materials, furniture, and fuel. And some of his objectives in regard to clothing are well worth quotation: "To consume clothing for its intrinsic worth rather than for display. To differentiate between expensiveness and real worth in clothing. To know how fashions are created. . . . To know the effect of staple fabrics and novelty fabrics on style."[11]

Confronted with a program of this kind, you may be inclined to ask: "Do you really mean to say that the schools should set up courses which will deal intensively and directly with such points? Are all these very definite 'objectives' (of which, of course, you understand, I have selected only a very few), to be regarded as a list of definite habits, which ought to be formed one by one in the course of education?" My answer to both these questions is: No. What I do mean, however, is that when the school undertakes to teach literature as a means of communication, and natural science, and social science, and to organize a social life with a view to modifying traditional controls of conduct, it should have these outcomes very clearly, and very specifically in mind. I mean that improvement of consumption skill, along such definite and literal lines as these, is one of the things pupils ought to "get out of" their studies and activities in school. I mean that such improvement is an essential and relevant item in the business of becoming educated. If we can put an intellectual background behind what a person does when he goes to market and buys some food for supper, when he purchases a suit of clothes, or arranges a contract to build a house, we have made his education a reality. Instead of his intellectual possessions being like mummies stored in a glass case, we have made them live; and we have done this by making them useful. They no longer constitute a mere decorative culture. They are applied to the improvement of his relationship to his environment, which is an intensely practical and specific matter. Recall once again the general

[10] p. 83.
[11] p. 228.

educational principles which have been elaborated in these pages. On the one hand, specific habit, and specific information based on the cold storage theory, will not serve our purpose. On the other hand, abstract general ideas and knowledge will not give us what we need. We must so arrange the pupil's education, that his intellectual resources will transfer and apply to these concrete matters. This is the basis of a living curriculum.

We may, perhaps, remark in closing that this ideal of improved consumption has something in common with the notion of large scale economic planning with which we opened the present chapter. It would not necessarily further the immediate interests of business men. It would mean a great increase in sales resistance in certain directions. And it might actually, for a time, mean a decrease in total sales in some lines. But it is hard indeed to believe that the ultimate result would not be greatly to the advantage of all concerned, and lead to a more stably prosperous community life.

4. *How is education related to the standard of living?*

Yet another way in which education should seek to adjust man to his economic institutions, is by helping to raise his standard of living. And here we come upon one of the most interesting, significant, complex, and far-reaching relationships between the individual and the industrial system.

What do we mean by the standard of living? Ross Finney, in the book I have already cited, *A Sociological Philosophy of Education,* defines it as follows: ". . . that list of goods and services which a person, family, or class has formed the habit of regarding as necessary, and for the maintenance of which persons will expend effort, make sacrifices, and practice foresight." [12] In a word, man's standard of living is his system of wants. And the main thought I wish here to present to you is that industrial progress requires that man shall be brought to want more and more, and to want with increasing wisdom.

Thus bluntly stated, the idea may seem questionable to you. Perhaps I can show you its truth best by raising a further question,

[12] p. 225.

and developing a few points in answer to it. My question will be: What is the actual effect of a living standard upon an industrial society?

First of all, the standard of living is the chief determining cause of wage levels. Often we think of this relationship as being just the other way round. We suppose that wages determine living standards. But this does not seem to be true. One of the most famous generalizations of classical economics is Ricardo's "iron law of wages," according to which the price of labor tends to be set at a level which permits the workers to subsist and to perpetuate their race, without increase or diminution. Like most other so-called "natural laws" of the dismal science, it has been used to justify all sorts of Tory practices, and more particularly, the forcing of wages down to the lowest possible levels. But the matter is by no means so simple. What is a subsistence level? Surely it differs greatly in different places, and with different people. It is one thing in an Illinois mining town, and something else again at Palm Beach. It is not determined by some group of scientists, who figure out the absolute minima of food, clothing, and shelter required to keep people from dying. It is determined by what people think they need; that is, by their wants. A Slavic immigrant will work for a certain wage. But a native born American refuses it. Or, if through ill luck he must accept it, he is never satisfied with it, and always tries to get back to a higher level, and usually succeeds more or less. Teachers are wont to complain, and very justly, of their low pay. But this depends on something more than that other great economic bogey, the "law of supply and demand"; or at least on something more than that law as ordinarily interpreted. If persons with the training required to teach, simply would not work for the pay offered, it would have to be raised, or the schools would close. Ultimate social classes, on the average and in the long run, get about what they demand. They may do some grumbling. But if their grumbles lack faith, if in their hearts they really believe that any great advance would be a dream only, their wants are not genuine wants. Our wants determine our dollars, rather than our dollars our wants. This is not so, perhaps, for the individual. But it tends to hold for the group.

Secondly, a standard of living helps greatly to determine productive efficiency. Ross Finney gives an excellent illustration here. He speaks of the method of coaling ships at various oriental ports, such as Port Said. Coal is carried on board in baskets, by an endless chain of native laborers, supervised by a foreman with a rope's end; an inefficient system made possible only by the very low pay of the workers. Such a system would be impossible at Duluth, or in the port of New York. We have no such supply of cheap and dirty labor. But does this mean that our coaling stations are less effective, and less economical, than those of Port Said and Port Sudan? On the contrary, we put in modern machinery, which actually makes our higher paid workers less expensive, unit for unit, than the natives who are glad to toil for the daily cost of a few handfuls of rice.

Thirdly, the standard of living determines markets. This is something which every advertiser ought to know, and which most of them do. Who are our best customers for manufactured goods and raw materials? Those nations where the general level of economic life is highest. Which would most American manufacturers prefer, free market access to England with her forty millions, or to India with her three hundred and fifty millions? Need one reply? We have all heard a great deal about the vast business opportunities in opening up new lands, inhabited by primitive races. No doubt much money has been made by selling them cheap cutlery, beads, and loin cloths. But the possibilities involved in increasing the wants of peoples already high in the scale of civilization, are incomparably richer.

Fourthly, the standard of living is a potent factor in determining the general level of civilization in any country. This is so, because, where the standard is low, there is little opportunity or leisure to gain enlightenment, or to pursue education in an adequate fashion. It has been said that the standard of living in France just before the revolution, was the highest in Europe. This meant that a great many people had leisure and enlightenment enough to absorb such notions as those of Rousseau. Hence came the imperious demand for a change in the form and manners of government, while countries like Austria and Spain jogged along contentedly in the mediaeval rut. One of the chief benefits of our own rising standard of life has been the extension of educational facilities, all the way from public kindergartens to public universities.

From this last consideration we may conclude that a democratic form of government, which presupposes popular enlightenment, and in fact demands a great deal more of it than we actually have, also calls for a high standard of living. Peasants, whose days are filled, from dawn to dusk, with the labor of scratching a bare living from three strips of land dotted around the communal holdings, are not the best people in the world to vote on tariffs, or to develop extensive and well considered opinions about foreign affairs. All the social influences with which our lives are engaged, then, seem to depend upon, and presuppose, high and higher standards of living. Far from following the ancient injunction of the Latin poet, and seeking happiness by limiting desire, it begins to look more and more like a virtue to keep wanting with ever growing enthusiasm.

A rising standard of living, then, is a part of man's proper adjustment to his economic institutions. What can the school do about it?

In the first place, it can do that of which we have already spoken. It can disseminate economic intelligence. Through its courses in history, social science, and natural science, and through its teaching of the means of human communication, it can spread throughout the whole population just social-economic opinions. Now this is a very great deal. One of the chief handicaps to progress, one of the chief reasons why so many people sit down and fold their hands, and believe that what is, is not only necessary, but also right and proper, lies in their acceptance of a scheme of economic mythology. The iron law of wages narrowly interpreted—the inevitable working of the law of supply and demand—the beneficial results of free competition—they may have heard of these things vaguely, but they have never been taught to think about and comprehend them critically. And their minds are overshadowed by half understood dogmas, and their wills paralyzed. We must remember that between economics as the economist understands it, and as it actually affects the popular mind, there is a great gulf. To bridge this gulf should be one of the chief undertakings of the school. Scientific economics is a gospel of social hope. It does not proclaim the inevitability of poverty, or the virtue of an abject resignation. It points straight to a world where the fruits of industrialism shall be more widely shared, and universally enjoyed, with each decade. Much popular economics is a mythology which will not stand examination, and which is no more than the orthodoxy of the god of greed.

Second, the schools can actively work to reorganize the pupil's system of wants. To take a further illustration from Ross Finney, he tells us that "The first thing that Booker T. Washington, at Tuskegee, did for the negro youth from the rural slums of the Black Belt, was to make them provide themselves with toothbrushes. The toothbrush became to them the symbol of a more decent way of living. Our public school policy should be equally wise."[13] The school, let us remember, should be regarded as essentially an environment where life may be lived at a high level. Here is the central secret of its educational influence. And simply by showing the pupil what it means to live a full life, it should inculcate discontent with inferior ways, and an active demand for something better. This is something which implies far more than the teaching of subject matter. It is an educative effect produced by the total of institutional life, and its tone.

Thirdly, the schools should relate themselves actively and constructively to vocation. I have insisted that the main purpose of the school must be general rather than special education. And, as we shall see more fully in another chapter, we cannot wisely set up a large amount of specialized vocational training in our public educational institutions. But the point is that the general curriculum must relate itself very definitely to actual life needs, and must be the basic preparation for a vocational fitness which depends on something more than a narrow mastery of some of the techniques of industry.

5. *How may education promote industrial democracy?*

The clear implication of the industrial order is a cultural democracy. To operate that order on the basis of a depressed proletarian class, sharing to but a meager extent in the wealth of the

[13] p. 239.

world, and only dimly enlightened by the available intellectual resources, is impossible. Attempts to do so lead to continuous industrial unrest, which is simply a symptom of maladjustment, and indicates that our whole industrial structure needs to be re-shaped. Education can and should be a potent agency for promoting industrial democracy, and allaying pernicious industrial unrest, by removing its fundamental causes.

According to Fitch,[14] there are three great causes of industrial unrest, which are impediments to industrial democracy. They are, conflicts of interest between capital and labor; industrial specialization and the routine job; and the inferior rights of the worker as contrasted with the investor and the manager. A vital social education will make an attack on each of these three points.

A. Between capital and labor there seems to be a fundamental conflict. To be sure, in a certain sense they are partners in a joint enterprise. But when it comes to the point of sharing the returns of industry, they turn into competitors. This conflict has only been palliated by the high wage theory of labor costs, associated with the name of Henry Ford, according to which it pays to grant to the workers a larger share of the returns than heretofore. For obviously there comes a point when increasing wages become a liability rather than an asset. But this is by no means necessarily the point at which the wishes and demands of the workers cease. Industry, after all, is carried on by two different groups, not by an association of colleagues. This is the stark reality of the situation.

What the ultimate solution will be, no one can say. But one thing is clear. Such a breach is not likely to be healed by compromise—by one side giving up a little, and then the other one making a sacrifice. What we must hope for is a new pattern of industrial relationships, not perhaps thought out and promulgated by any one individual, but evolving gradually in many minds. As a matter of fact, men of good will on both sides are constantly reaching out towards such a solution. This is a first rate illustration of what I mean by creative adjustment; the securing of satisfaction by the invention of a new mechanism, the building of a new way. And education can be a potent agent for its promotion. This conflict between capital

[14] *The Causes of Industrial Unrest*, Harper and Brothers, 1924.

ADJUSTMENT TO ECONOMIC INSTITUTIONS 161

and labor is one of the deep and tragic issues of many individual lives. It is one of the great problems with which they must wrestle. Can a scheme of education which pretends to any true vitality, afford to ignore it? We may not have any ready made solution to offer. But we have those means of enlightenment whereby a solution will be found, and which will lead to its acceptance. Simply because so many of its pupils will, in their own living, play some part in the great conflict between capital and labor, the school should make it a business to convey to them those social and economic concepts which will enable them to understand the realities with which they must deal.

B. Our industrial system has developed the routine job. Even a humble agricultural laborer may be able to take some pride, and find some personal satisfaction and fulfillment in his work. Most certainly the same was true of the mediaeval craftsman. But there is something anti-human in spending eight hours a day tightening bolt number forty-three on the assembly line. Such work lacks all personal significance, something for which good pay does not compensate. The toiler has no informing sense of vocation. And he readily becomes infected with an unrest and dissatisfaction, due to his maladjustment to the environment.

Now what can we do about it? Shall we preach the virtues of a passive resignation, and the blessedness of drudgery? This is an impossible doctrine, and a false one. A human being is right in his dissatisfaction with such a task. He is right in his demand for significant work. Shall we then preach discontent? This again is no solution. Whatever future technology holds in store, the routine job is not likely to be eliminated for a long time to come. We must find other means to deal with it. To attempt to accommodate ourselves to the environment by simply brushing it away, would be altogether too easy. Again, no one can foresee the future, but certain probabilities are already above the horizon. For instance, we may add significance to the routine job, if we give the worker an opportunity to see the process of manufacture as a whole, if we give him at least some of the training accorded to the executive and the manager. This enables him to understand his own relationship to an interesting, complex process. Or again, we may make his relationship to his work more satisfying and significant by giving him a voice in collective dealings with his employer, or even in the management of industry. Each one of these plans has at least been tried. A final solution of the problem of industrial routine will probably come from a combination of all three.

Here once again, education comes into contact with human need. What is desirable for the routine worker is a broad grasp of the industrial process. He cannot find himself in industry through craftsmanship, as did his forefathers more than a hundred years ago. That solution has become impossible. But he may find himself through intelligence. If education in the schools, and education in industry, can reveal to men's minds, broadly and yet with specific reference, the significant operations of the economic system, and their own relationship to those operations, much of the poison of industrial routine will be removed.

C. The worker has inferior rights in the industrial commonwealth, as compared with the investing and managerial classes. About all he is entitled to do, is to decide to grant or withhold his services. But if he withholds them, it makes comparatively little difference to the organization, while for him it may mean starvation. So long as he has this right, he remains above the status of the chattel slave. But its effect is strictly and narrowly limited. And beyond this he cannot go far. For instance, he has no such right to his job as the bondholder has to his interest. He is not entitled to participate in managerial decisions. And even his rights to collective bargaining have been seriously questioned. In the words of Fitch: "Consequently the wage-earners are not citizens of the industrial commonwealth. They are aliens, rather, possessed of few rights, and subject to deportation without trial." [15]

Some specific changes have taken place within recent years, due to the advance of unionization and the great shop committee movement. But the main dependence must probably be upon a changed ethical sense in general society, a feeling that the worker is entitled to a stronger position in the economic world. Such a change can be brought about largely by the steady impact of educational forces. The laboring classes have been under-privileged in

[15] p. 398.

the sense of being largely excluded from our richer educational opportunities. Above the eighth grade, the public schools have very strongly tended to select their pupils from the more favored social groups. This tendency has not been a deliberate plan, but a resultant of many forces operating more or less blindly. Still, it has had a profound effect. It has had the tendency, which I have already discussed in our last chapter, to create fixed social classes along lines of economic cleavage. It has made the withholding of an adequate status from manual workers seem proper, because of their inferior cultural position. Now what we need is secondary education for all, not for the sake of turning everybody into a white collar worker, but for the sake of a democratic distribution of cultural privilege, irrespective of differences of economic function. If we can follow in the footsteps of the great Danish educators, and create a "cultured" laboring population, "able to live like human beings," to repeat the pregnant quotation, then the common sense of society will be all in favor of granting them fuller rights in the industrial order.

6. *Why is economic enlightenment an urgent necessity?*

In this chapter I have been able to discuss only a few of the manifold aspects of human adjustment to the system of industry, and to show how education may deal with them. Many others will readily occur to us.

For instance, one of the greatest problems of American life is created by the existence and accessibility of our open markets for securities and commodities. Such open markets are probably essential for the financing of business on a large scale. But they lay us open to the great evil of speculation. There is not the slightest doubt that the unbridled speculative mania of 1928 and 1929 made the great collapse of the fall of 1929 far more disastrous than it would otherwise have been, and deepened and prolonged the depression. Equally certain is it that if that mania should gather momentum again, it will shatter our hopes of an early recovery, and drive us down still more deeply into the abyss. Such speculation is a most malignant economic ill, which must be cured if our system is to survive. But how can it be cured? Something perhaps may be done by more stringent regulations on the part of the New York Stock Exchange and the Chicago Board of Trade. But if once the public fairly takes the bit between its teeth, to stop it is like trying to stop an avalanche. There is only one possible answer—the systematic, progressive diffusion of economic enlightenment. Only so can our people be prevented from ruining themselves by the very mechanisms which they have created for their own benefit. They must learn sobriety, wisdom, and self control in the operation of their economic institutions. Otherwise the system is sure to collapse.

Another instance is the operation of the gold standard, and the management of the currency. As certain economists have insisted, the gold standard is no law of nature. We can have a perfectly valid medium of exchange without it. Its effect, after all, is largely psychological. If everyone suddenly demanded gold in exchange for paper money, it could not be worked for twenty-four hours. The effect of a gold backing is simply this; it prevents an arbitrary tampering with the currency, such as has repeatedly led to calamity in the past, as it always must. Now we can have a valid and stable "managed currency" without a gold backing, if we want it; but always on one simple but imperative condition. We must exercise intelligence and self control in dealing with it. If public opinion is so stupid and short sighted that it influences our politicians to start the printing presses, and run off untold billions of dollars to pay for anything we think we might like, there is only one end. Our medium of exchange has, as its ultimate foundation, not a pile of gold in the vaults of the government, but the economic enlightenment and sane self control of the popular mind.

So I might go on. But I think the case is clear. Such issues throng upon us. And they are the issues of happiness, and life, and death. Not a person who reads these words, not a person who goes through our schools, but is most intimately affected by them, in his dearest hopes and fondest plans. They affect our jobs, our living, our provision for our old age, our ability to support those who depend upon us. No matters in the whole world have a more urgent, a more personal importance than these.

In the face of such urgency, it is impossible not to feel the deepest impatience with the inept complacency of the academic educator. What are the pupils in our schools learning? How are they spending their time? Is it their main concern to secure a directed enlightenment, which shall make them more efficient producers, wiser consumers, better able to create for themselves a sane standard of living, more happy in their work, more self controlled in their financial dealings? They are being herded in droves to the study of foreign languages which they will never read, of mathematics which they will never use, of science valuable only as a preparation for more science, of history made up of names and dates and the provisions of ancient treaties and the intricacies of half forgotten strategy, of literature with the emphasis chiefly upon points of esoteric scholarship. Only a small proportion of them engage in learning economics. This is a kind of perverse insanity. It is fiddling while Rome burns. The educators who are responsible for such leadership have not even the poor excuse of Nero; they hardly seem aware that a conflagration is going on. And the reason given for offering these dry husks of a curriculum hopelessly out of touch with the great realities of life is, forsooth, that it will train the pupils' minds. Has the great depression taught our teachers nothing save to grumble over salary cuts?

One great lesson emerges as clearly as anything can, from the argument of this chapter, and indeed from everything in these pages. *The study of society must be the core of education.* And it must not be an academic study, a new formalism. Our pupils must secure their mental growth by grappling with those real, cogent issues with which their lives must deal. We must mediate to them a broad grasp of human intellectual resources for the sake of flexible, creative, progressive adjustment to social institutions in general, and to economic institutions in particular.

Chapter 8

HOW MAY EDUCATION ADJUST MAN TO FAMILY LIFE?

1. *How do modern conditions tend to impair family adjustment?*

The conditions of our modern industrial civilization constitute a threat to the ancient institution of the family. Much that has made life seem significant, and worth the living, has come to man through his family relationships. The home has never been a place of unalloyed ease and pleasure. Its maintenance has required sacrifice and toil. But it has repaid many times over such effort as it has demanded. For it has offered, more completely than any other institution, a sense of abiding contentment and self fulfillment. Through the agency of the family, men and women, all through the history of our race, have been made to feel themselves at home in the world.

This has come about because the family home has been a center of many-sided activities, and has offered the unique opportunity for complete and satisfying living. It has been an institution of extraordinary stability, and a source of stability in the lives of individuals. But in the course of the past one hundred and fifty years —since the beginning of the industrial revolution, that is—its functions have been steadily whittled away. The modern home in an industrial community cannot compare in institutional strength and completeness, or in prevailing and sustaining influence upon its members, to the patriarchal family.

First, and most critical of all, it has lost much of its economic significance. In colonial times, the American home was an almost completely self contained economic unit. The amount of ready cash which it needed for outside purchases seems to us incredibly small. All the members of the family worked together to provide the physical foundations of their common life and happiness. And this in itself tended to make that common life rich and significant, in a way that is hard for us to appreciate. But now the average home depends upon the pay of a wage earner, and far less upon the cooperative endeavors of husband, wife, and children. It is true that a great deal of necessary work is still done in the home, so that "housekeeping still remains one of the major industries, and home management is one of its most important occupations."[1] But the major dependence is now on outside sources and agencies. If the entire economic system were to fall in ruins about our ears, a family of the old type would be only slightly inconvenienced; but the modern family would starve.

Again, the modern family is now, in far less measure than formerly, a center and agency of protection for its members—for the young and the very old, and for the sick. The old time home might not have all the bright efficiency of a good hospital, or institution for the care of the aged. It certainly approved much on which a modern pediatrician would frown. But it accepted a major responsibility for the physical and mental welfare of its members. And this contributed enormously to the significance of the way of living it offered.

In many other ways, home life has been depleted of its traditional richness. The meat market, the delicatessen store, and the bakery, have freed it from the full responsibility once discharged for the nutritional care of its members. It is no longer a place where meat is butchered, bread baked, and stores of provision laid up for the winter. The free clinic, the child health center, and welfare work in the schools, have supplanted home remedies and home doctoring, and even undermined the position of the family physician. The fabrication, repair, and cleaning of clothes have largely ceased to be household duties. Most people no longer even shine their own shoes! Saving, too, which used to be almost wholly one

---

[1] *Recent Social Trends:* vol. 1, p. 671.

of the communal responsibilities of the thrifty, well-balanced family, is now taken care of elsewhere, with the advent and spread of systems of public allowance, great insurance companies, old-age pensions, and loan institutions of various sorts. The whole point of view regarding financing has been changed. A mortgage on the family home used to be regarded as almost a disaster. Now it is even considered an advantage, because it may help to make the place easier to sell. Can we wonder that with such vast impairments and diminutions of its activities, the significance of family life has declined? Members of families have far fewer important and necessary things to be done together. The home has become far less essential in their lives. And so they tend to value it less highly.

We may, of course, argue that many of the functions, once discharged in the family, can be handled elsewhere much more effectively. This is probably quite true. The health of children in a great city like New York is far better than in many rural regions, where there is a much closer approximation to old-time home conditions, and where they are taken care of more completely by their fathers and mothers. The meat packing industry probably insures us a better, more varied, and cleaner diet than amateur butchering on the farm. Milk from a great distributing agency in a city is more likely to be safe than milk which comes directly from the barn. This social specialization, this taking of functions out of the home and allocating them elsewhere, is not only a necessary part of our social evolution. It is, in many ways, a great benefit. But it most assuredly threatens the stability and integrity of the home.

What all this means in terms of human attitudes, I will try to show you by two actual instances. "Angelene V., an Italian girl, entered the commercial department of a high school. This girl, it was learned, had seven sisters and one brother. During the past four years, Angelene had worked every evening after school hours and all day Saturday for the amount of four dollars a week. Her work consisted of washing and drying the dishes for three meals a day, preparing the evening meal, cleaning the entire house and taking care of three small children while in the home. Her parents want to give her a high school education but are unable to send her to college, therefore she decided to take the commercial course so that she could go into the business world and not be forced to do housework all her life. At the present time she detests housework and vows that she will never do it after she has finished school and has a position in an office. Her opinion of creating a home is not an enthusiastic one as it appears to her to be only a life of drudgery." [2]

"Several years ago there was an Italian immigrant family living in Chicago. In this family was an old grandmother. She used to sit on the low doorstep and, with her head in her hands and her elbows on her knees, move her body back and forth and moan quietly. If anyone would listen to her she would say, 'Oh, why did we come to this country? We were all so happy in Italy. We were interested in the church. We knew our neighbors and helped each other when we were in need. The little girls sewed and made pretty things. The boys worked and sang and played. The children went into the fields for flowers. We had bread enough, but no, we must come to America. Now what do we have? Money—money, bah! Everybody works to earn more money. The girls don't make pretty things; the boys don't laugh and sing; nobody has time to go to church. The boys work hard to go to the big dance. The girls work in the factory to buy a store dress. Tony is cross and sore because he does not have a big house like the boss. Louis wants a big car. But nobody has time to be happy and enjoy what they have. They must earn more money. Bah!'" [3]

Here we see exactly what is apt to happen when family life becomes depleted and begins to lose significance and importance. We may agree that many family functions are better discharged elsewhere. But when this takes place, there is the risk of very great loss. Such people, extreme cases admittedly, evidently lack an anchorage in life, which the most efficient set of institutions fails to provide. The highly developed industrial civilization in which their lot is cast, has undermined the foundations of their family living, and has turned them adrift in the world, homeless.

---

[2] Manuel C. Elmer: *Family Adjustment and Social Change:* Ray Long and Richard Smith Inc. 1932, pp. 254–255.
[3] *Ibid:* pp. 279–280.

2. How is the reconstruction of family life an educational task?

To praise unintelligently a vanished past, to mourn the present state of affairs, to regard the future with dark fears, is entirely futile. The old family solidarity cannot be reconstituted. The old patriarchal home was significant in the lives of its members, largely because it was a working group. The homes of the new age can become even more significant and beneficent, by becoming groups of diverse personalities, which render to one another a mutuality of moral and spiritual support. This, of course, is something which the home has always meant. But it now becomes the keynote of the domestic symphony. Here is where education takes hold upon the situation. If we wish not merely to save the home amid all the threats of our industrial development, but to raise it to new and better levels of human value, we must educate its members to desire and sustain, one to another, relationships of mutual support, and strengthening encouragement. We must emphasize, above everything, personality relationships. This is the direction in which to set to work to make "effective and lovely the social patterns demanded by mating, parenthood, and responsibility one for another." [4]

It has been well said: "There remains little excuse for the family unless it can develop a monopoly of certain spiritual functions." [5] Those very forces which have undermined the patriarchal home have brought to the forefront just such spiritual functions, and the personality relationships which they imply.

We have seen that, whereas the family used to be a self contained, self sufficient economic unit, working together to provide the physical foundations of a common life, it now depends on the pay envelope of the wage earner. This involves a formidable insecurity. The average man has the chance of earning a much more luxurious living than was possible to his great grandfather. But he pays for it by the risk of being unable to earn any living at all. No matter how hard and well he works, he cannot be certain that

---

[4] *Education for Home and Family Life:* The Century Co., 1932.
[5] Gruenberg, S., "Family Relationships in the Changing Home": *New Era*, 1930, vol. 11, pp. 49–52.

forces quite beyond his control will not cut down his wages, or render advancement impossible, or, in times of cyclical depression, deprive him altogether of his job. This makes it increasingly difficult to maintain the conventional pattern of relationships as between husband and wife, which were current, let us say, as late as 1890, and according to which the woman was definitely the dependent partner, and it was a disgrace to the man if she made any active overt contribution to the family living. The real secret of the stronger position of the woman in the modern family is, quite largely, the weaker position of the man in the economic system. Now this does not mean that most wives are going to be forced to take jobs outside the home, and contribute directly to the economic support of the family. But it does mean that the wife is challenged to furnish a quality of moral and spiritual support and companionship, of which the man is sorely in need. I am not attempting to suggest that the wife in the old-time home did not furnish such support, or that her contribution was solely, or chiefly, physical. But the conditions of modern life are emphasizing this quality of wifehood with a unique urgency. Here we have one of the lines of tendency which are making personality relationships the center of the domestic picture.

In the same way, the fact that the mother, the wife, or the daughter, now finds it quite possible to secure employment, greatly alters the pattern of family life. It is entirely possible, of course, for a woman who is holding a position which brings her into interesting contacts with the world of large affairs to be an excellent wife and mother. The effects upon her of holding a dull routine job may be another matter; though even still those effects need not be too adverse. But it is quite clear that her wifehood and motherhood must be of a very different kind from that of the woman whose horizons were bounded entirely by her home, all her life long. If the employment of the wife, or the mother, is to have a beneficial influence in the home, it must come from the fact that she is a more interesting, varied, appealing, and understanding personality because of it. To try to combine two jobs—that of office drudge and home drudge—is hopeless. Here there is no true solution. The woman must achieve a new integration in her living. Her contribution to the home must be made in terms of spiritual understanding and moral support.

Again, the decrease in the size of the average family, forces personality relationships to the forefront. In the large, patriarchal family group, the contacts of the individual members were diluted by mere numbers. The parents had so many children to think about and attend to, that there were very marked limits upon their intimate and unassuaged dealings with one another. In the modern home, however, the couple with very few children, or perhaps none at all, must learn new, and none too easy lessons of companionship. They must be able to find spiritual and moral values in their common association; or else their whole relationship is apt to lose significance.

Then again, one of the great characteristics of an industrial society, is that children remain children much longer. The modern home is haunted by the problem of the dependent adolescent. Under the mores of the old-time home, the child was, very simply, a being to be controlled by command. By the time he showed any considerable capacity for active and full partnership in the affairs of the family, he was earning his own living, and well on the way towards independence. If we project into our modern situation, the mores of the old-time home, we court disaster. Parents still think it proper to deal with their children as children were treated a hundred years ago. But the status of the child in the home has profoundly changed, not because of some sort of pervasive idealism about his rights, but merely because he is destined to stay there until he is much older and more mature than used to be the case. We all know the results of unintelligent domestic conservatism. The high school boy whose father bullies him for his low grades, responds with a vicious and sulky resistance. The adolescent girl whose mother tries to control all her friendships, refuses to bring her intimates home with her to be criticized; and coldly refuses to appreciate the parties her well-meaning mother organizes for her. Then parents get together, and sigh about the astounding changes which have come over the younger generation. Such changes have, indeed, taken place. But they are due, not to some mysterious alteration in the personal make-up of individuals, but to a great alteration in social status. The years of dependent home membership have been greatly prolonged. The home which tries to maintain the treatment and point of view suitable for young children—a line of treatment, and a point of view, once entirely feasible—is bound to fail. The child must be dealt with, more and more, as an active partner in a spiritually and morally significant group. The lesson to be learned is one of a new pattern of personality relationships.

Moreover, those very changing conditions which, before our eyes, are destroying the social pattern of the patriarchal family, and which, as we have seen, make it more and more evident that personality relationships are the secret of the significance of the new family, are also making the achievement of such relationships more and more possible. Enormous advances have taken place in the physical facilities for the management of the home. Much time-devouring drudgery has been eliminated from the business of housekeeping. And this means that the members of the family have more time and strength for other things. Again, the intelligent planning of family life, and its conscious direction for morally and spiritually constructive ends, is possible today as never before in the whole history of the world. Means are at hand for placing considered limits upon the number of children, and for their most advantageous spacing. All kinds of expert aid for the raising and training of children, for the planning of family budgets, and for the financing of a happy home life, are now available. Again, those very economic forces which have sapped the foundations of the old-time family, are making possible for ever greater multitudes of men, the creation of a new pattern. At first it might have seemed that the transformation of the father from his status as head of an economically self sufficient group, into a wage earner, was sheer domestic disaster. But as the system has worked out its implications, it has endowed him with the great gift of increasing leisure. To be sure, he does not yet adequately know what to do with it. He needs both new techniques and new attitudes, in order to be able to spend that leisure wisely in the home circle. But these can and will be forthcoming. And we may hope to see arising a new type of fatherhood and husbandhood. Again, there has been an immense multiplication of hygienic, aesthetic, and recreational resources. The average home can be made a healthier place than it ever was before. It has within its reach the means of enjoying the best in music, art, and literature. And it can furnish a play life fuller, more varied, and potentially more satisfying than the world has ever seen. Once again, and lastly, the social and mental sciences furnish us with new insights into those very personality relationships which must become the heart of the new home. The intellectual resources of our civilization have been vastly enriched in these respects, within recent years. It is now possible to understand one another better than heretofore, and to enter into one another's problems, to comprehend the need and true nature of tolerance, to create wiser and more humane controls.

In the face of all this, how can one say that the home is doomed? Of course there are threats and difficulties. We cannot have a home life adequate to the new age in terms of the educational and cultural status of the past. The old Italian woman whose case I mentioned in the preceding section, is an example of what happens when we try. But assuredly, there is not the least need to sit down, and allow disaster to overwhelm us. The means are at hand out of which to fashion a happier, freer, more appealing, more humanely significant family life than has ever appeared upon the earth. To utilize these means is the task of education for family adjustment.

3. *What qualities must education develop for the sake of effective family adjustment?*

What does it mean to be a good wife and mother, a good husband and father? What qualities make for success in such relationships? No question can be more cogent than this. No question can appeal more strongly to the hearts and minds of men and women who hope to make something worthy out of their lives. It is a question which cannot be shirked by educators who believe that their supreme task is the adjustment of human beings to the demands of the social environment. C. C. Peters, in a study of the objectives of education for worthy home membership, has tried to answer it by an ingenious and valuable application of the questionnaire method.[6] He undertakes to present what he calls a "blueprint of the domestically efficient person." While the method he uses involves well known and admitted limitations, and while I shall not follow his list of qualities in detail, yet what I have here to suggest is in large measure based upon it.

A. In the first place, we must educate to produce an ability to meet the economic problems of family life. First and foremost, this means vocational fitness, chiefly on the part of the man, but also, to a very genuine degree, on the part of the woman. A justified confidence that one has a reasonable ability to earn a living, is one of the chief foundations of family happiness in our industrial society. Those who argue that, because education ought to be general, it should have nothing to do with vocational adjustment, should reflect well upon the formidable implications of such a position, and also upon their own grave responsibility in taking it. The vocationally unfit person, is compromised in advance, in his or her efforts to achieve domestic stability.

But the economic problems of family life are not merely problems of earning. They are also problems which relate to the administration and expenditure of the family resources. It has been estimated on good authority that efficient home management, which uses all available resources, advice, and knowledge, for planning and guidance, can increase the effective value of the wage earner's salary by as much as from forty to sixty per cent. Here is one of the great opportunities for practical intelligence on the part of the wife, in building an effective family life. It is a most impressive argument for the need of working enlightenment for the woman whose vocation is to be that of home maker. What she needs, to deal with the shifting, difficult economic problems she must face, is not a rigid set of traditional habits and customs, but a flexible ability to avail herself of the manifold resources of our civilization, and to capitalize them in the interests of her task.

Moreover, it is clear that the economic problems involved in

[6] C. C. Peters: "Objectives of Education for Worthy Home Membership": *National Society for the Study of Educational Sociology; 2nd yearbook,* 1929, pp. 136–147.

the administration of the family are not problems for the wife alone, or for the wife and husband alone, but for all the members of the family. What is desirable and necessary is not a preoccupation on the part of the parents, in which the children have absolutely no share. Rather we should seek a condition of group coöperation under parental leadership, which seeks to maintain an adequate standard of living for the group, and to free its members from the incubus of drudgery, and of lonely anxiety.

B. In the second place, we should educate to produce an ability to meet the problems of raising children. Now, by this I do not mean that we ought to set up in high school a required course on child training. I have in mind something very much more far reaching, and also more feasible and sane. One of the most revealing questions we can ask concerning any system of education is: What influence does it have upon the attitudes of young people towards children? Our conventional scheme of education has either no such influence at all, or a negative one. And to this degree, it unfits, rather than fits, young people for life. When Mussolini decided, for political and military reasons, if I am correctly informed, that the Italian state required large families, he undertook what was, in effect, an intensive campaign of education, by no means confined to the schools. Now propaganda of this kind we obviously do not want. But if we are going to teach a social science which is something more than a study of extremely theoretical blueprints of an essentially fictitious group machinery, and a psychology which is more than a schematic account of how the mind might work if it followed our prescriptions, surely part of our endeavor might be to make young people, both men and women, aware of the matchless appeal, and profound significance, of the child. Let us remember that all we can do in advance—all we can do in school—is to lay the foundations for parenthood. And one chief part of such foundations consists of a positive attitude towards, an interest in, the child and his problems and nature. Certainly it is true that even college trained mothers are woefully deficient in knowledge of the physical and mental conditions for effective child raising. We cannot supply this knowledge in advance, and expect that it will be remembered and used later on. But we can educate for an awareness of the child, an interest in the child. We can educate in such a manner, that the way to the sources of knowledge will be familiar, when that knowledge comes to be needed.

C. In the third place, we need to educate for an ability to maintain the hygienic conditions of the home. Here, as always, what is required is a capacity for intelligent, flexible, adjustment to the problems likely to arise, rather than a set of fixed rules of thumb. The Gruenbergs tell us of a mother, who, when she first heard about vitamins, asked: "Don't calories count any more?" [7] What such a person lacks is obvious enough. She had been told that calories were important in connection with nutrition. But she had no general mental background of scientific understanding. The new idea about vitamins was just a new idea. It did not fall into a place in an intelligible system. And so she found it merely bewildering. The effective maintenance of hygienic conditions is the outcome of a general scientific understanding, given point and meaning for life, by its application to a definite, significant, practical problem.

D. We need to educate for an ability to maintain the aesthetic and recreational activities and interests of the home. In the monograph on family life in *Recent Social Trends,* it is said that the home remains a center of considerable recreational pursuits. There are often to be found one or more pieces of outdoor play equipment. And indoors we find provided facilities for mechanical music, and some supply of books and magazines. The statement is made that "budgetary studies show a growing proportion of family expenditure for things other than food, household equipment, rent, fuel, and light. Much of this increase is undoubtedly for recreation." One reason for this increase seems to be the swift growth in popularity of the radio.

In view of what we have said about the growing importance of personality relationships and spiritual values, in giving constructive significance to family life, such aesthetic and recreational interests are peculiarly noteworthy. It should be understood that a man or a woman who is a recreational incompetent, and whose aesthetic interests are either very narrow and poor, or else entirely lacking,

---

[7] Gruenberg, S. and B. C.: "Education of Children for Family Life": *Annals of the American Academy of Political and Social Science,* 1932, vol. 160, pp. 205–215.

is not likely to be an effective parent. The parent well adjusted to the demands of home life in the new age, will be a person keenly alive to the values of art, and music, and literature, possessing a wide and varied range of interests, able to be a leader in the constructive use of free time, and in the choice of pursuits initiated for their own intrinsic interest. Such a person will have one of the most important qualities necessary to the building of a home life capable of holding the rising generation, and of giving balance and stability to young lives.

E. We need to educate for insight into the personality problems which arise in the home—the problems of the relationship of husband, wife, and children. The avenues of such insight now exist. They should be made available. Specifically, this means that the study of psychology should have its place in our scheme of social science as the core of a general education. Much of what is ordinarily taught in the conventional course in psychology in college is pretty dead stuff. When it is proposed to introduce the subject into high school, one feels some hesitation. If this is to mean simply a weakened and simplified version of ordinary college psychology, one rather wonders why anybody should wish to study it at all, let alone why it should be so placed in the educational scheme that large numbers of adolescents will be "exposed" to it. Psychology, like everything else, becomes educative only by making contacts with life and its problems. And surely it should be handled so as to make contacts with the problems of family life and home relationships. As a matter of fact, a great many intelligent parents, aware that important things are being said which bear upon the issue they are dealing with, undertake to read some popular psychology. What they read seems often to have little connection with any academic courses they may have taken. And all too easily, they are led astray into preposterous and dangerous errors. Now, when such a demonstrated appetite exists, it should mean something to formal education. The hint ought to be taken. We should see to it that a controlled, scientifically critical, judicious insight into the major findings of modern psychology as these relate to domestic problems, is made available in place of the crude popularizations so eagerly sought, and so easily misunderstood.

4. *How may education seek to engender the qualities needed for effective family life?*

Nothing can more strikingly reveal the impotence of the conventional scheme of education, than a serious proposal to adjust children to the demands of family life. It throws into startling relief all the fallacies, all the weaknesses, which we have been discussing in general terms. When anyone who regards education as the mastery of a standard body of subject matter, is confronted with such a proposal, he may, to be sure, admit its validity. He may confess that, somehow or other, education ought to be able to help children to lead a better and fuller home life, both now and later on. This, indeed, can hardly be denied as a general proposition; for to do so would come pretty close to saying that education is good for nothing. But when it comes to setting about such an undertaking, he is likely to feel quite helpless. "What can we do?" he asks. And he falls back upon the conventional defense, which is really nothing but an illegitimate excuse, of calling the proposition noble, idealistic, but impractical. He salves his conscience by making a sort of mental genuflection; and then he goes on with the subject matter grind.

On the other hand, nothing can better illustrate the practical force, and the working value, of the educational principles we have been trying to set forth, than an undertaking to reconstruct family life through the agencies of education. In it, all those principles are exemplified. What is necessary, is a scheme of education organized *as* living, and *for* living, in which the mastery of subject matter is never an end in itself, but always a means for flexible, creative, progressive adjustment to the demands of society.

A. The fallacy and weakness of the cold storage doctrine is nowhere more evident than here. To give little children in the elementary school, or adolescents in the high school, direct instruction on the problems of home life, as these confront a married couple, would be to the highest degree absurd. What can such things possibly mean to them? Even young men and women in college, are as yet far from ready to accept, and benefit by, much conscious education for parenthood. To give such instruction in the expectation that it will be recalled and applied later on, would strike us all as ridiculous. It has been well pointed out that between the second grade and high school, not a great deal in the way of direct education for family life is possible, beyond making an appeal to the child's sense of fairness in connection with the performance of home duties, helping him to appreciate his immediate relationships to the family group, and leading him to coöperate for the maintenance of his health.[8] Moreover, the amount of such education which can be soundly and hopefully undertaken, even to the end of college, is limited, simply because young men and women have their major domestic responsibilities still in the future, and what seems to them the remote future. Here as always, we must deal with the individual as he is, and work for the future by making the immediate present more significant.

B. Again, the purpose of educating for worthy home membership shows the fallacy and weakness of working for a limited, rigid, static adjustment. If you will review once more the list of qualities given in the preceding section, it will be quite evident that they imply a flexible, many-sided personality, with broad human interests able, above all things, to meet new situations and achieve a solution of unfamiliar problems. And there is an even more convincing reason why an effective adjustment to family life must have the qualities of flexibility, creativeness, and progressiveness. When anyone assumes the responsibilities of parenthood, he takes on the task of living and dealing with children, whose interest, activities, and relationships are likely to be very different from those of his own youth. As children remain in the home to a more and more advanced age, the challenge to the parent becomes more and more cogent and exacting. We all know the kind of parental failure who disapproves of the doings of his children, merely because "father never did those things when he was a little boy." Rigidity means failure. It makes the parent an unwholesome influence in the life of the child. It may express itself in attempts at severe repression, or in simply dropping the reins, and disclaiming all responsibility. The parent needs flexibility, so that he can accommodate himself to personal situations which cannot be foreseen. He needs creativeness, so that he can invent new patterns for the home, new solutions to its problems. He

[8] *Education for Home and Family Life:* Century Company, 1932.

needs progressiveness, so that the children will not be the only people in the home who are growing.

Even the effective physical and economic management of the home cannot be well achieved by rule of thumb. I insisted on this point in the previous section. And it is recognized by forward looking teachers of home economics, who regard their subject as dealing with far more than an assemblage of tricks of the domestic trade, and who believe that it should be treated as one of the social sciences, and made a correlating, integrating center for a rich body of intellectual content.

C. Education for worthy home membership means, fundamentally, a broad general curriculum, made real at all points by contact with the family situation. The following suggestions may serve to make the idea clear and concrete. In the kindergarten and the primary grades, we should have varied home plays and discussions. These can be made one of the significant centers of correlation and integration for the child's first guided contacts with art, music, literature, and science. In the intermediate grades, we should have social science, again informally treated, and pointed to show the child the status and relationships of his family experiences in time and space, and to the whole social mechanism. At this level also, natural science may be made significant, by revealing it to the child as the great means by which the physical environment of his home is in process of reconstruction. Arithmetic may well be applied to the problems of the family budget, and of the child's own budget. It has been found that American family life can be treated effectively from the historical point of view in the elementary school. In addition to all this, health work and instruction, which, as I have suggested elsewhere, should integrate closely with the beginnings of biology and physiology,[9] can be brought into close relationship with home experience. In one school, a great deal of subject matter learning was brought successfully to a focus in a series of group discussions, in which were considered such topics as: getting up in the morning; preparation for breakfast; breakfast; the school lunch; preparation for school; arrival home from school; doing household chores; play; preparation for supper. Always the prin-

---

[9] *Vide* Chapter 10.

ciple is perfectly clear, though its applications may be infinitely varied. We wish to raise the level of the child's immediate home and family experiences, by bringing to bear on them the intellectual resources of civilization. And always we find our familiar dual benefit—subject matter becoming educative by contact with life—life becoming enlightened by contact with subject matter.

At the level of the high school, rather more in the way of specific education for family life becomes possible. We may set up courses in home economics, which should be organized on a broad basis of technique, insight, and appreciation of human relationships. Such courses may, as I have pointed out, be broadly educative, because they bring to a focus a very wide range of subject matter. Courses dealing with family relations have been found successful in some schools, dealing chiefly with relations between parents and children, between brothers and sisters, and between children of marked differences in age. Occasionally matters are carried still further, and we find work offered in child care, and even the establishment of demonstration cottages and apartments. Nevertheless, our main reliance must still be upon a general curriculum pointed in a specific direction. Music, art, literature, natural science, and above all, social science, must be handled with the sense of a definite mission to raise the level and increase the richness of the pupil's immediate home experience. The so-called extra-curriculum should also be definitely planned with this, among other things, in view. Naturally, the arbitrary traditional subdivision of curricular material into unit courses makes the full working out of this scheme difficult. It is, indeed, a serious obstacle to most progressive educational projects. It subdivides, when what is needed above everything else is an integrated grasp. Our general aim must be to concentrate the full force of subject matter masteries upon the home situation and its problems.

Several recommendations have been made for the re-direction of college education for the sake of family life. At this level, we go still further towards conscious, specific training. We need a redirected health service, and an orientation course dealing with health problems in terms of the concepts of social and natural science, coordinated with the health service. We should have an orientation course in general social science, dealing to a considerable extent with the problems of the home and family; and a more specialized elective course on marriage, parenthood, and family life. The work in the field of psychology may be made more vital by dealing with the problems of family relationship, mental hygiene, and the observation of children. And the entire curriculum, and the extra-curricular social activities as well, need to be transfused with a sense that what the student is learning should transfer, now and here, to his home and family life, and should be the means of growth to more effective domestic relationships.

Clearly, a great deal can be done, even under the present circumstances of our school work, to secure effective family adjustment. The obstacles are the fragmentation of the curriculum into narrowly subdivided courses, the insistence upon standards set in terms of credits rather than of socially significant masteries, and the emphasis upon subject matter for its own sake. As educational reforms work themselves out, and these obstacles are progressively overcome, what can be done will rapidly increase.

D. Education for worthy home membership requires a certain orientation and interest on the part of the teacher. It is astonishing how much a determined and ingenious teacher can do, even under the handicap of a very rigid administrative system, to make subject matter function in terms of life. This, indeed, is the heart and soul of all teaching. If the instructor is aware of the bearings of what he is presenting upon the problems of the family, if he feels a living interest in the matter, he will find countless opportunities to impart his insight to his pupils. Of course we must be careful here not to load the whole responsibility upon the "personality of the teacher," which is often a mere excuse for doing nothing. No really adequate plan can be had, short of extensive administrative re-direction. But the teacher's attitude is one of the critical factors for success.

E. Lastly, education for worthy home membership calls for a close coöperation between the school and the home. Of course, neither the individual teacher, nor the school system through its officials, can push into the home and reform it out of hand. But there is no reason why the teacher and the school cannot exercise very considerable tactful influence in the home, in the interests of the child. Certainly we cannot hope for effective training for worthy home membership, so long as the school acts as an entirely isolated institution, without any constructive and positive relationships to the home. Our hope is that what the child learns in school, he will seek to apply in the home. So it is important that the parents shall understand our purposes, and feel some sympathy with them. We are educating for the future. But our only means of doing so is to raise the level of the present.

Chapter 9

HOW MAY EDUCATION PROMOTE RECREATION?

1. *What is the nature of play?*

We may define play as purposive activity engaged in for its own sake. This is a broad, and very significant notion. It is highly important for us, because it shows just what we should aim at, when we seek to educate young people for recreational living. Let us consider its meaning and implications.

First of all, it means that one cannot tell whether an activity should be classed as work or play, simply by inspecting its *content*. A member of a professional baseball team may seem to be playing, when really he is working for a money reward. The fact that he is engaged in what is conventionally called a game, does not, in itself, mean that he plays at it. On the other hand, a business man may spend sixteen hours a day in his office, and insist that he is really doing so because he likes it. That is the way he takes his pleasure. Writing a book, solving problems in mathematics, reading history, repairing one's home, managing an organization, may all of them be play activities. They cease to be such when they are carried on for ulterior motives, for some external reward, to avoid some difficulty or threat, or because someone else compels us to do them.

Then our definition enables us to see why an activity may be very difficult, and still be play. Chess and mountain climbing, for instance, are no occupations for people mentally or physically lazy. They are a good deal harder than most men's jobs. But assuredly they have their place within the realm of play. One may play oneself into a physical and mental collapse. So, whatever the value of play may be, one cannot say that it is a good thing because it gives us a chance to rest.

Again, we should notice that the presence of a money reward does not, in itself, prove that the activity concerned is not play in the true sense. Although the player is likely enough to feel pleased at the idea of his bank balance swelling, still his controlling motive may remain the game for its own sake. So the line between the amateur and the professional is certainly not that which divides the player and the non-player. An amateur may drive himself to win for the sake of collecting a bet, or impressing a lady, or doing honor to some organization. Indeed, one of the greatest stars in the firmament of college football once sent a shock through alumni nerves by flatly stating in public that he hated the game, and only continued in it from a sense of duty, and a feeling of obligation for the gate receipts. And few professionals determine the vigor of their efforts in strict proportion to the size of their salaries.

The true distinction, in fact, is not really between work and play. It is between play and drudgery; that is, between play and *unwilling* work. Thomas Alva Edison, a short time before his death, once said that he had never worked a day in his life. He had always been terrifically busy; but always he had been busy about things he wanted to do. Mark Twain, in an eloquent passage, insists that performers in a symphony orchestra, with the glorious tides of music sweeping round them, could not be called workers. I suspect that his acquaintance among hard-boiled orchestra men must have been limited. But there is a real point in the saying. For an activity may offer so much in and of itself, that even those who earn their daily bread by its discharge, may be buoyed up and inspired by its intrinsic appeal, however cynically they may talk at times.

2. *What is the importance of play?*

Psychologists have been deeply and properly impressed by the universality and tremendous persistence of the urge to play. We find it in all the higher animals. We find it in all children. They gravi-

EDUCATION AND RECREATION

tate towards play activities, as moths towards a light. If opportunities are not furnished, they invent them. And they will go on playing, until ready to drop with fatigue. In the monograph on recreational interests in *Recent Social Trends,* it has been estimated that the American people spend annually the enormous sum of ten billion dollars for recreation. This forces us to ask: Why? We are dealing, obviously, with one of the strongest tendencies of all organized living things. What is the reason for it? What is its importance, its value?

Several theories of the importance and value of play have been put forward. None of them seem entirely satisfactory; and yet all of them contain some truth. Let us review them.

A. First of all, there is the "surplus energy" theory. According to this, play is due to a bubbling over of impulse and energy which does not find adequate expression elsewhere. When one watches an energetic child amusing himself, such a notion seems not unreasonable. But it will not bear examination. In the first place, it involves a false account of the nature and origin of action. Action is a response to the environment, not a releasing of some store of energy. There is, in the organism, no such store of energy, but only mechanisms of response. In the second place, play is not mere activity. It is purposive activity. If the surplus energy theory were true, why should not a child be just as willing to do an arithmetic lesson, or split kindling, as to play baseball? If all Tom Sawyer wanted was to use up steam, why did he object to whitewashing the fence? Obviously, the whole point is the direction of the activity, not just the fact of being active. And what about the striking, pathetic behavior of children who are forced to toil in mines and factories? Surely all their surplus energy must be gone. At least it is very certain that they become pathologically weary. But when their day's work is done, instead of going straight to bed, they hurry out for a game before dark. No; the surplus energy theory will not fathom for us the mystery of play.

B. A second theory has attempted to explain play on the basis of recapitulation. When we play, it is said, we revert to an older and simpler way of living, and give ourselves up to activities which come from the childhood of our race. This, of course, would explain why play is important and valuable. The normal development of the individual is supposed to run parallel to that of the race. And so the child should be given full scope to live out his racial impulses, and should never be hurried through that stage of growth at which his chief business is to play.

But since we have decided against the recapitulation theory in general,[1] it is clear that we cannot accept its application here. The psychologists who have put forward this explanation have been men of delicate and keen perceptiveness, and broad human sympathy. They have deeply felt the great truth that play is of enormous importance. But their theory does not explain that importance. It is no more than a recognition of the fact. A certain warrant for the recapitulatory theory of play there is, since many of the games of children have, indeed, a very ancient origin, and carry us back to a remote past. But this, after all, does not mean that children are actually living through stages of racial development when they play hide-and-seek or dance around a maypole. And how can such an explanation serve, when we try to understand the play activities of adults? The appeal of contract bridge, or automobile riding, or the movies, can hardly be due to our desire to relapse into the primitive, and to live once more as our remote ancestors did in the primordial past.

C. The third, and most famous account of play, is what is known as the "practice theory." It is said that when the young creature plays, he is rehearsing and perfecting himself in activities which, later on, must be performed in dead earnest. The kitten chasing the whirling leaf, is learning to catch mice. The puppy, gnawing at a bone, or worrying a dead rabbit with infantile fierceness, is preparing himself for the hunt and the fight. The child who plays a game, is acquiring a pattern of behavior, which, later on, will stand him in good stead. Play is practice. From this comes its importance.

This theory has definitely influenced the work of our schools. In the early kindergartens, games were devised which would duplicate many of the serious work activities of adult life. Children were lured into playing cobbler, carpenter, and so forth, in the belief that by such means the true utility of games could be realized. Games

[1] *Vide* Chapter 3.

were regarded, and organized, as a preparation for real life.

The difficulty with this theory is that it is quite unable to cope with all the facts. Even with children, we find all sorts of play activities, which do not seem to have any obvious and direct preparatory value. And yet, we would surely hesitate to say that such activities are undesirable or useless, or to organize things in such a way as to shut the child off from them. And when we come to adult play interests, the case is still more obvious. What is the preparatory value of golf for a business man? For what is a teacher, or a lawyer practicing, when he plays tennis, or goes skiing, or mountaineering? How can we account, in such terms as these, for the appeal of the movies, or of automobile touring, or of reading detective stories? It seems manifestly fantastic to say that all worth while play is useful practicing.

The particular objections to each one of these theories arise from a common source. They all try to explain play on ulterior grounds. The assumption is that play is not "serious"; that it is foreign to the chief business of living; and that we must try to justify it by showing how it leads to "worth while" ends. Now this is precisely contrary to the truth. Play needs no justification. As soon as it must be justified, it ceases to be play. Here lies its very essence. It is purposive activity, engaged in for its own sake. It means precisely, doing what we want to do, because we want to do it. When a man plays, his adjustment to his environment is, for the time being, and within limits, brought to a pitch of perfection. There is no conflict of the will. He is not under constraint. He is not compelled to accommodate his purpose to something foreign to it. He does what he likes.

There recently appeared a novel called *The Fortnight in September*. It is the story of the brief vacation of a clerk and his family. The story shows how, in his business life, he was more or less frustrated and disappointed. In spite of long and faithful service and a keen sense of duty, he failed of desired promotion, and was evidently destined to spend all his years as a drudge and a subordinate. Then come his two weeks of annual release. He spends them with his family, in no very thrilling round. But he finds the keenest happiness, precisely because he has the blessed privilege of doing what he likes, instead of what he is told. Here lies the whole secret. In our play, we seek, and in so far as we are successful, find, modes of life and action, in which inner purpose can come to free and satisfying expression. And the urge to play is nothing else than the urge to live according to our nature, and to devote ourselves to doings which are, for us, intrinsically worth while.

This, for beings who have inner purposes at all, is the obvious way of happiness and fulfillment. When Edison insisted that he had never worked a day in his life, he was calling himself a most singularly fortunate and happy man. He had been able so to organize himself and his affairs, that his entire life was a life of play. It meant a perfect adjustment between himself and the world. Few can ever achieve this. For the rest of us, much that we do must be done under compulsions of various sorts. But here is the ideal way of life, the way of life open to everybody in the ideal society. In such a way of life we see, working out to its ultimate consequences, the fundamental logic of play.

Notice again, for it is important not to be led astray here, that play need not be easy. Golf, chess, mathematics, music, are none of them to be acquired, and fully enjoyed without effort, even intense and exhausting effort. But it is not effort that human beings really dread, nor laziness that they naturally seek. The ideal life for a responding, purposive organism, is not a *dolce far niente*. What it is natural for us to desire is activity which is our very own, and not imposed from without. And this is the essence of play.

3. *Why is play an educational responsibility?*

It may seem to you that if play is simply purposive activity engaged in for its own sake, and if its essential value lies in the individual's expression and satisfaction of his own inner impulse, then education has nothing to do with, or to say about it. Should we not simply turn a person loose, and give him unguided, untrammelled freedom to go his own way? Shall we not inevitably spoil everything for him, and defeat our own ends, if we begin to try to tell or show him what to do? This is a violent error. The ability to realize one's inner purpose is not something which comes by mere chance. It is something we achieve. We must find the means, and learn to use them. Watch a child who is simply turned loose with nothing at all to do. For a time he may amuse himself; but soon a shadow falls. He grows bored with too ample and undirected freedom. He comes and complains that he can think of nothing to do. Here is the precise point. It indicates the nature of our educational responsibility in the matter. People must learn to play.

It is often said that the great increase of leisure time—that is to say, time away from the job—has created a new task for education. This is quite true; but often it is rather superficially understood. When we give a man leisure, we impose upon him a responsibility, and a difficult responsibility. We make him directly responsible for finding what to do. Mere free time is nothing but an opportunity. And it may be grievously misused. If you take a man whose education, whether in school or elsewhere, has not really fitted him to live, and simply turn him loose without any duties or any prescribed round of activities, he will be helpless. What shall he do with all his time? He does not know. He alternates between bored listlessness and unsatisfactory attempts to amuse himself. He has been set a problem too hard for him, a problem he has no means of solving. And he welcomes the return to toil with a deep sigh of relief.

One of the finest illustrations of the peculiar, intimate, searching responsibility created by free time, is that of a professor on sabbatical leave. When a university grants a member of its staff the privilege of a year's freedom from teaching, it is giving him a chance to do exactly what he likes, a chance, that is, to *play*. If he does nothing but loaf, and go round the golf links occasionally, the whole purpose of the arrangement is defeated. Such a privilege is justified on one ground only. The professor is a man whose education has given him things he wants to do, things which are worth doing. He is a man who is able to take charge of himself, and to find avenues of self expression and personal fulfillment. Let us say that, on his leave, he writes a book which has long haunted him. This is a true play activity of the highest type. It justifies his leisure. And it is possible for him only because he is an educated personality.

Or, by way of further illustration, consider a case from classic fiction, the Abbé in the Chateau D'If, in *The Count of Monte*

Cristo. Here we have a man condemned to solitary confinement, as terrible a punishment as could be meted out to a human being. His whole life is to be one of absolute leisure. What a terrific responsibility! What a fearful problem! In real life, perhaps all but a very, very few would hopelessly sink under it, and within a few months become mere imbeciles. But the Abbé in Dumas's romance solves the problem. How? By virtue of his education. He acquires skill in chess; he builds up a system of ideas; he lives in the world of his mind. Perhaps this would be really impossible. But it dramatizes for us the responsibility of education in the matter of play and leisure. The increase of leisure time, which is one of the great boons of our civilization, simply means that our people, as individuals, are to be thrown more and more upon their own resources. What those resources will be, depends upon education.

So it is one of the great concerns of a vital education to create in men recreational capacities and inclinations. The fact that play essentially means doing things for the mere sake of doing them, does not mean that a person ought simply to be left alone to find his way. On the contrary, this very freedom of personal choice, which is characteristic of recreation, involves a very cogent need of guidance. For freedom is something which must be organized and directed, if it is to be genuinely realized at all. Moreover, if education shirks this duty, what will surely happen is that commercial interests will step in and dominate the scene, to the great impoverishment of our recreational life.

We must remember, too, that while all play consists of activity carried on for its own sake, this is far from meaning that every type of play is equally valuable. For instance, the National Socialists in Germany are actively encouraging children to play an elaborate war game, with the deliberate purpose of instilling into them a militarist disposition; and surely most Americans would think such play little better than pernicious. So it becomes a further responsibility of education to pick out the most desirable avenues of recreation, and make them available. How can such a selection be made? In educating a person for recreational living, what determining criteria should guide us? Let us see.

In the first place, everyone should have a wide and varied range of recreational interests. This is becoming ever more necessary as the amount of leisure grows. For it means a continual increase in the weight of responsibility for directing one's own choices. A man with only ten hours of free waking time during the week, needs only a limited recreational repertoire to be able to live as good and happy a life as his circumstances permit. But, as his free time grows longer, that repertoire must grow ever larger. He must be given more and more things to do. In the old fashioned school of the "three R's," music, art, and literature could, perhaps, be regarded as unessential fads and frills. The reason was that life was so strenuous, and the burden of drudgery so heavy, that little time and opportunity for self directed activity remained. But now the educational emphasis must change, simply because life has changed. What used to be unessential, is coming to be ever more essential. To turn out children into a world of abundant and increasing leisure, without any particular guidance in matters recreational, is clearly to shirk a great responsibility. A person who can do nothing more with his spare time than go to the movies and play cards, is clearly a misfit in modern society, and represents in himself the failure of education.

In the second place, everyone should have socially propitious and suitable recreational interests. A program of recreation well suited for the city, might be seriously out of place in the country. Moreover, there will surely be some types of play which, under any circumstances, are undesirable—gambling on horse races, for instance. In England, this particular avocation has grown to enormous proportions, which Americans always find astonishing, so that literally millions of people are constantly wagering sums of money in this way. Obviously, it is socially and economically undesirable. Obviously, too, it is something which education, in a broad sense, operating over a period of time, can control. What we want is to guide people into pursuits which will be beneficial rather than damaging. Civilization has built up an enormous range of possible occupations, which can be capitalized for recreational ends. And it is the business of any sane and humane scheme of education to make these available, not to the chosen few only, but as far as possible to everybody.

4. *How is recreation dependent on institutional adjustment?*

We may think of the great practical task of education, in promoting recreation, as securing institutional adjustment. Here, as everywhere, our formula holds. Education deals with the individual. But it cannot be properly understood in individualistic terms. It deals with the individual by enabling him to achieve his proper relationships to society. This is just as true with recreation, as with civic, economic, or family life. And the reason is simple. Play activities are those in which we engage for their own sake. But this, as we have seen, is far from implying that they have no need for organization and regulation. They can survive and flourish only if supported by social institutions. And for the individual, there can be no continuous, satisfying recreational life apart from such institutions.

Even the play activities of children depend upon, and are determined by, social institutions. When children are left entirely to their own devices, they spontaneously set up fairly definite, but still quite transient, social patterns in the interests of recreation. They club together; they behave group-wise; they formulate rules of fair play; they invent procedures. But without any direction at all, such attempts are not likely to be very successful at the best. The ephemeral, poorly conceived institution serves its purpose but haltingly. It is more or less disappointing to its members. And they soon abandon it. Very often, indeed, it may become positively pernicious. And the essence of the attempt to better things recreationally for children, consists in trying to help them to set up better institutional ways. Hence we have the provision of toys for little children; the development of guided play; and such movements as the Boy Scouts and the Campfire Girls. These are all attempts, initiated by adults, to reform the recreational institutions of the child. And they succeed just in the measure to which the social pattern created really meets his needs, and makes possible to him the free, constructive realization of his purposes.

So all recreational living, whether of children or adults, depends upon, and is supported by, a structure of institutions. Let us consider in what ways they serve it, and are necessary to it.

A. First of all, an institution adds prestige to a recreational pursuit. Not so long ago, golf and tennis were regarded askance in what Mr. Mencken is fond of calling the American hinterland. People carried golf clubs and tennis rackets through the streets, only at the risk of undesired notice, pitying smiles, and the hoots of small boys. The last ten years has seen an enormous change; and it is due largely to the fact that powerful institutions have been built up, which support and validate these once despised pursuits.

Now such prestige is sorely needed for the sake of an adequate recreational life. Few are they who will persist in some avocation, no matter how pleasing to them, if it runs steadily counter to the force of social gravity. Some members of the staff of a mid-western college were greatly interested in hiking as a sport. It was not, however, one of the recognized fashions of the community. They felt that it would be difficult, and perhaps rather unpleasant, to satisfy their harmless urge by acting as individuals, and astounding farmers by actually tramping through the woods and over the country roads. So they formed a hiking club—an institution—and the problem was solved. This factor of institutional prestige is an enormous force in our recreational life. A person is considered perfectly normal if he goes out into the woods to hunt or fish. But he would be thought rather more than queer if his expeditions were made for the sake of aesthetic dancing under the open sky, or climbing trees. Yet, to the chilly eye of reason, one occupation is just about as wise or silly as the other. The difference lies in the simple fact that one has the protection of a supporting institution while the other lacks it. Or consider how natural and normal we think it, when a worthy lady prepares a paper on Michael Angelo, and reads it to her literary club; and how very extraordinary it would seem if a person should do such a thing in an informal circle of friends, if women's clubs were unheard of. Institutions are necessary for a full recreational life, because most of us all the time, and all of us some of the time, need the support of their prestige in behalf of our ways of enjoying ourselves.

B. Another, and much more obvious way in which an institution may serve a recreational activity, is to provide the proper facilities for carrying it on. Reading, for instance, is considered one of the best types of human recreation. It is open to everybody at small cost; and it is an avenue for rich, varied, and abiding enjoyment. But its possibilities would be enormously limited, unless we had a profusion of public libraries, book stores, and publishing houses—unless, that is to say, we had an institutional machinery to furnish the needed facilities. We easily think of reading as a purely individualistic performance, involving no social relationships at all. This is only because such perfect social arrangements have come to be made that we hardly notice them. Our point of view might undergo a sudden change if we could go back to the Middle Ages, when books were kept under lock and key, or at the best, chained to a lectern, and when horrible curses against prospective thieves were written upon their fly-leaves. So it is that educating a child to find his pleasure in books is by no means merely a matter of teaching him to read. It is also a matter of teaching him to use libraries, and to select and buy books and periodicals. He must learn wisely to use the facilities which society affords. It is an affair of institutional adjustment.

And the facilities needed for recreation are by no means wholly physical. Also they are social. One cannot play tennis without balls, a racket, and a court and net. But neither can one play it without another like-minded person. Stamp collecting, were it merely a hermit-like brooding over perforations and water marks, would lose most of its charm as an avocation. There must be other collectors, whose interest, admiration, and kleptomaniac impulses we from time to time arouse, and who, as a group, determine the value of our rarities. All these necessities, physical and social, can be provided only by institutions.

C. Another great boon conferred by an institution upon a recreational activity, is that it tends to make it available throughout the whole course of one's life. Mountain climbing in the Himalayas is certainly not a highly institutionalized sport, whatever its appeal and prestige. And so it is an occupation for the few, and largely for the young. Exactly the same would be true of golf, if one had to make prodigious efforts, and devise brand new, and unheard of social expedients (like organizing droves of Sherpa porters), in order to get a game. The general trend of an institution is to make an activity easily available for everybody throughout the whole course of active life. When a person becomes too old, or too fat, for strenuous participation, a way for milder action is at hand. And even to the end, he may share the doings as a spectator.

D. Lastly, an institution tends to act as a watch-dog. It preserves the recreational activity from abuses of various kinds, and seeks to regulate it for the best interests of all concerned. Sometimes this is done unwisely. A sporting association may make foolish distinctions between amateurism and professionalism. Its decisions may at times be unduly influenced by commercial interests —those, for instance, of the sporting goods manufacturers, who would like to have a new type of equipment made standard every year. A discussion club may adopt rules which lead it to degenerate into a stiff and formal arena, in which members show off their wit and wisdom by reading deliberately unintelligible papers. But, after all, what would happen to a recreational activity, if it had no supporting and defending institution whatsoever? It would, most assuredly, disintegrate in a very short time. An institution may become infected by abuses, as witness recent bitter criticisms of college football. But an institution at least provides the hope of reform, and of better guidance. If football were just a game played by a few crazy people on muddy back lots, if it were not the center of an imposing social pattern, there would, of course, be nothing much to attack. But neither would there be anything to defend. The sport would have no significant place in our life.

5. *Why is a free adjustment to recreational institutions desirable?*

Education for recreation necessarily involves institutional adjustment. It is not enough merely to give a person a certain skill or ability. He must be fitted in disposition and capacity to take his place in a social pattern. And here, as elsewhere, the type of adjustment achieved becomes of the utmost importance. What we must seek is a creative, active adjustment, rather than one which is rigid, passive, conformist. We must try to educate participators, rather than spectators. Only so is it possible to save the institution itself from encroaching abuses, and to enable it to serve the interests of its members, and fulfill its purpose of preserving a form of pure and direct enjoyable activity. A few instances will show why this is so.

One of the great faults of collegiate athletics, and particularly of football, has been that it is organized largely for the sake of the spectator rather than the participant. It is a social pattern in which few play and many watch. And most of the grave abuses which have arisen come from this. The game tends to cease to be a game, because of an exaggerated will to win, and an uncontrollable gladiator complex. To wring our hands, and run about loudly deploring, is not the slightest use. The way in which the thing is organized has brought this upon us. A winning team becomes a commercial asset, with resulting tendencies to bootleg players, and to connive at all kinds of vicious practice. The star athlete presents us with a gratuitous educational problem, and in many ways threatens the integrity of our colleges. The alumni become obstacles to sound educational progress, instead of its natural supporters. All this is very largely due to our having permitted a wrong institutional adjustment to build itself up in our midst. What if the sport were organized chiefly on the basis of active participation? What if only the most important intercollegiate games could draw a considerable audience, because everybody was occupied with a game of his or her own? Evidently, such a state of things, partially realized in England, would be far sounder, if what we want is recreation. Players who participate chiefly for the sake of enjoyment, will not easily or tamely permit abuses which threaten the source of their pleasure. Their attitude is likely to be relatively sane and realistic. They *feel,* even if they do not consciously understand, what the institution is actually for. And they are apt to insist, pretty vigorously, that it shall not be deflected from its purpose by any kind of racketeering.

Or consider music. Here is a splendid illustration of the great importance of participation, and an active attitude, in institutional adjustment. Our musical life in the past has centered rather largely about the concert. It has been not far from ninety-five per cent spectatorship—or listener-ship, rather. What has been the result? The twilight of the concert gods, and the growing regime of the radio, which, whatever its possibilities, is a most dangerous musical medium, simply because it can be turned on and off regardless, like a faucet. The whole structure of our musical institutions would be enormously sounder, if they existed at least as much to encourage and provide chances for amateur performance, as to yield opportunities for passive listening. Many prevalent abuses—excessive commercialism, reputations inflated by publicity, a star system carried to vicious lengths—are possible chiefly because people are musically passive rather than active. Moreover, if our musical life were set up more extensively in the social pattern of performance, it would mean far more, and convey far richer pleasure, to everybody who shared in it.

So one might go on. But the point seems clear. Never in this imperfect world will all abuses be obviated, whether in recreational living, or anywhere else. Never will we have a set of institutions which directly, perfectly, and without flaw, serve the purposes of mankind. This is too much to expect. But whenever men are educated for active participation rather than passive receptivity, and, accordingly, whenever recreational institutions are organized democratically for free, creative activity, then they are safest from disease, and have in them, in the fullest measure, the spirit of life.

6. *How may the school promote an adequate recreational adjustment?*

The account here given of the place and meaning of recreation in human life shows the direction the school must take in seeking to promote an adequate recreational adjustment. Above all, it shows the futility of narrow conceptions. Education for recreation means far more than a half hearted, ill considered, poorly regulated recognition of games and sports, as a sort of addition to curricular studies which are regarded as the serious business of schooling. The school must be a place where pupils become aware of the possibilities of a wide range of significant pursuits; where chances are provided for doing all kinds of things which a person might well wish to continue doing all his life long. It must be a place where ways are opened, rather than one where preparation is made. Let us see more specifically what this means.

A. First of all, the curriculum must be organized and chosen with a view to recreational values. We have seen that play cannot be determined by its *content*. There are no human pursuits which are recreational as such, in contrast with others which are not. All the intellectual resources of civilization may be turned to recreational ends. And people who possess them, not as so much subject matter learned for its own sake, but as agencies for life adjustment and the reconstruction of behavior, will tend to use them for this very purpose. Hilaire Belloc has spoken of the writing of history as a "liberal occupation." And assuredly this should also be true of the reading of history. Dr. John Erskine, internationally known as a scholar and writer, is also celebrated as a fine amateur pianist. Louis XVI spent his leisure time mending and making clocks. Here we have instances of the means of communication, the social sciences, the fine arts, and the techniques of industry, serving recreational ends. And this holds true of the entire range of curricular studies.

What we need can be put very simply. We must have curricular studies taught to be used, instead of just to be learned. When children learn rote songs in the elementary grades, does this make them more apt to sing such songs spontaneously, in groups or alone, out of school? What effect has their school music upon musical expression at home, or on picnics, for instance? When we give a drawing lesson, are we suggesting to the pupils the possibility of finding pleasure in drawing out of school? When we teach history, are we aiming merely at a recitation knowledge, or engendering an interest in the reading of history for pleasure? Is our work in mathematics, in natural science, in foreign language, in manual arts, pointed towards any kind of recreational use of these resources? If not, why not? It certainly can be. Moreover, this will largely determine its educational value. The educational value of learning anything is not an affair of some strange and hidden magic. It can be determined on a basis of sheer common sense. It depends merely on the extent to which the person in question will actually *use* what he learns; the extent to which his learning modifies his general behavior. So a curriculum, organized and selected for recreational values, is simply a curriculum organized and selected for life values. It is a curriculum which exists for the sake of significant pursuits, rather than for the sake of passing examinations and securing credits.

B. Secondly, the extra-curricular program must be organized and selected with a view to recreational values. As a matter of fact, our whole point of view tends towards the obliteration of the distinction between the curriculum and the extra-curriculum. It is an historical fact that the extra-curriculum has been created by the students, and the curriculum by the instructors. But it is far from true that the curriculum has certain magic virtues and values which the extra-curriculum lacks. If we think of formal school education simply as the deliberate provision of opportunities to do significant things and to have significant experiences, the whole distinction collapses, in theory at least. Extra-curricular activities become just as important as curricular studies themselves.

Now the great danger of an extra-curricular program which is not wisely conceived and sympathetically administered, is precisely this, that the spirit and value of play—of activity carried on for its own sake—will vanish from it. That spirit needs to be fostered and guarded. And without careful guidance, it is apt to be lost. Competitive, and even commercial motives, enter in so strongly, that the educational possibilities of the program are more or less dissipated. We easily get an undue emphasis upon sports which advertise the school, or the community, irrespective of their effects upon the participants, and also an undue emphasis upon the desire to win. We should not, however, think so much in terms of curbing these tendencies, as of providing something better. People—and particularly young people—behave pretty much in accord with the situation in which they find themselves. If, then, we allow a situation to arise, where membership on a winning football team, or eminence in fraternity politics, carries a tremendous prestige, we need not be surprised at the consequences. Not human nature, but our arrangements for it, are at fault. What we need is an extra-curricular program which offers diversified and significant activity for everybody, taken seriously as part of his education. We need a program whose constant organized emphasis is upon activity for its own sake, rather than for any kind of ulterior motive. And we need a program which constantly favors participation rather than spectatorship.

C. It is often said, and very truly, that in educating for recreation, we should lead young people into pursuits which they will be able to carry on throughout their entire lives. What this actually seems to mean is that we must do more than simply train them in certain techniques of amusement, or even in some of the other intellectual resources of civilization for recreational ends. We must seek to induct them into some kind of definite institutional adjustment. For instance, part of learning to read should be learning to use a library, and to choose and buy books. Part of learning music should be learning to take part in ensemble performances, to play and sing for others, and to attend musical events. Part of the study of art should be learning to use picture galleries, when one has a chance. Part of learning any game should be coming into association with those who play it. One of the great difficulties of making mathematics, science, and perhaps history, agencies of recreation is precisely that they are not highly institutionalized. In such cases, the difficulty may be largely overcome, because these pursuits need but little institutional support. And what they do need can be supplied in a measure by the organization of departmental clubs. One chief reason why college football has comparatively limited educational values is that its social organization involves its discontinuance when one leaves college. We often hear a great deal from coaches about the noble virtues developed by playing on the team. And there is much truth in such claims. But if the institutional structure of the game were such that alumni kept on playing it on Saturdays till they were fifty years old, instead of making trouble because of changes since their college years, all such educational advantages could be multiplied many times. So the point is not quite that we should pick out those pursuits in which the pupil may continue to engage throughout his life, as the ones into which it will be most valuable to induct him when he is young. Rather, we should always remember that an institutional structure is a very important element in recreation, and that we must reckon with it in trying to build up an adequate recreational adjustment.

D. Fourthly, we must by no means despise the techniques of

amusement as part of a person's education. This, of course, has been implied very clearly in all that I have said. But it seems worth while to bring it out into the open in an explicit statement. To be brutal, one often feels that a good course in contract bridge would have more common sense educative value than a great many of the subjects taught in school. The techniques of amusement have their place in life; and it is an increasing place. For this reason, they ought to have their place in education. We should have nothing but approval for attempts to teach children good form and correct action in golf, in tennis, in baseball, in checkers and chess, in horseback riding, in card games, and so forth. A sane approach to education makes this seem like a very proper and desirable thing to do—far more so than concentrating on developing a virtuoso technique in football in a few highly selected athletes. On the other hand, we must not suppose that recreational adjustment begins and ends with the techniques of amusement. That adjustment is as broad as life, as comprehensive as the mind of man; and it consists in being educated to find a wealth of significant activities to be pursued for their own sake.

*

Chapter 10

HOW MAY EDUCATION PROMOTE HEALTH?

1. *Why is the promotion of health an educational responsibility?*

The answer to this question arises from the conception of the nature and aim of education already developed in this book. Education exists for the purpose of securing to each person a flexible, creative, progressive adjustment to the demands of the environment. Its central purpose is to raise the level of human living. Looked at from the standpoint of the individual, this means giving him the utmost possible opportunity to make the most of himself, now, and later on. Looked at from the standpoint of society as a whole, it means the conservation and improvement of human resources. Now no one will deny that physical well-being is the cornerstone of effective, fruitful, happy living. And so the preservation and promotion of physical health appears to be, in a way, the most basic educational responsibility. If attendance at a school does not make a pupil a healthier child now than he would otherwise be, and if it does not mould him into a healthier man for the rest of his days than he would otherwise become, then that school fails of its full, indeed of its most characteristic, purpose as an educational institution.

In view of the principles we have been discussing, this idea seems obvious. Yet it is not universally recognized in theory; still less universally put into practice. Why do our minds seem to resist it? I think we may find three reasons, which it will be helpful to consider.

A. In the first place, we are apt to think of education as concerned with the mind rather than the body. Such a notion, to be sure, has not always held sway. It certainly was not entertained by the Greeks, to whom the education of a boy had just as much to do with perfecting his bodily grace, skill and endurance, as with intellectual keenness. The Romans, too, had that often quoted proverb, *"mens sana in corpore sano,"* to describe the ideal human type. Throughout the Middle Ages, the training of the knight glorified physical prowess, even to excess. And to the greatest men of the Renaissance, an education which ignored, or made little of, the body was wholly wrong. But today we are beset with a very powerful prejudice in favor of the purely intellectual aim of education. Probably this comes from mediaeval notions about the proper training of the cleric, which was very largely bookish. Also we must remember that practically the whole educational tradition of our western civilization has been enormously influenced by an extreme, militant Protestantism, which regarded the flesh and all its works with grave suspicion at the best. To the New England Puritan, the mind was far more important than the body. And our American school system sprang from the loins of Puritanism.

In this extreme emphasis upon the intellect, we have one reason for ignoring the claims of health in education. And yet there is in it a certain truth. Education does indeed deal with the mind. But what is the mind? Not something which exists in its own right, and which can be trained in isolation from the body. Rather it is the agency for securing a complete adjustment to the environment. So here already we gain at least a glimmer of insight into our whole problem. The true task of promoting health is a task of steering the mind, of setting up intelligent controls, of making men and women "health minded."

B. The second reason for overlooking what seems like the obvious responsibility of education to promote good health, is a very faulty and partial notion of the nature of health itself, and of the real task of creating it. By good health we often mean no more than relative freedom from disabling disease. And if you talk about the promotion of health, many people will think you mean merely calling a physician in a hurry when you are sick—and perhaps only when you are sick enough to scare yourself and your family. And what has education to do with this? Very little, it would seem.

For many years, the American Medical Association, the great insurance companies, and various other agencies, have been preaching a much more adequate doctrine. They have been urging that the important thing is not so much the cure, as the prevention, of disease. If we accept this, then the business of promoting health becomes, in part at least, submitting to fairly frequent physical examinations, and following certain lines of medical advice. Here, clearly, is something very much more constructive—something, moreover, which it takes a certain amount of educational effort to achieve. But we must go a step even beyond this. We must stop thinking about health merely as the opposite of being sick, and of its promotion as either the curing or the dodging of disease. Health is a positive, not a negative state. It means, as the derivation of the word suggests, full and balanced physical functioning under the stresses of a civilized environment. This must be our aim. And we can achieve it only by the enlightened ordering of our lives.

Try this thought out on a physician, and he may agree with it "in principle," to use the diplomatic catchword. But he is apt to seem dubious. Press him, and you will force him to admit that his profession has enough resources of knowledge and skill to go a long way in this direction, and greatly to raise the level of positive physical well being in the population. But he will tell you that it is quite impracticable. People only seek his services when they have lost their health; or, if they happen to be unusually intelligent and fortunate, when they fear that they may lose it. They treat him as a healer, not as a missionary for perfect positive physical functioning. And so he can do for them, not the best possible, but only the second best. But this is just the point. It is exactly where education comes in. The physician is a representative of a great, amorphous, poorly organized social institution, which has grown up little by little, for the preservation and promotion of health. That institution cannot serve us fully because our adjustment to it is imperfect, and more or less stupid. (Incidentally, this is also why it is not yet a better institution.) What we need is to be made able and willing to take better advantage of the facilities in the way of knowledge and expertness which actually exist, and thus to achieve a better social adjustment. And as we have seen, the improvement of social adjustment is the characteristic task of education. When we think of health in a narrow and negative way, merely as the absence, or avoidance, of disease, we can see no genuine educational problem of very large proportions. But the instant we conceive of it positively, as the perfection of physical functioning, the task of promoting it is seen as one of enlightenment, that is, of education.

C. Another reason for overlooking the responsibility of education for the promotion of health, is the idea that the problem of physical well being is one for eugenics. Some people have maintained that, under modern civilized conditions, the human race is degenerating physically, so that there is no use trying to increase the general health of the population by any kind of training. The only way out, according to these pessimists, would be by controlling sexual selection, so that none but the higher types were permitted to reproduce themselves. And of course, this is not very likely to be put into practice.

As a matter of fact, however, the idea that the promotion of health presents chiefly a eugenic—which really means an impractical—problem, is false. With regard to the physical status of modern civilized man, we can say that, while he manifests many serious defects, yet these are, in general, traceable to unintelligent living rather than to racial degeneracy. Moreover, the total effect of the civilized environment upon health has certainly not been to lower it. The noble savage, with his triumphant physical fitness, is a myth. Usually, primitive man presents no such attractive picture. He is apt to live, with content, in dirty, unhygienic surroundings; to subsist on a poorly balanced ration; to be helpless before the onset of epidemic illness; and to have a poorer physique and a shorter span of life than his civilized brother. The difference between the health of civilized and primitive man is not due to eugenic measures. It is the effect of enlightenment and of developed institutional controls. Most assuredly we cannot hold for a moment that the health problem lies outside the range of human management by social agencies either already existing or well in sight.

If we give up these three ideas—that education is concerned with the mind to the exclusion of the body; that the promotion of health means the cure of disease; and that the improvement of health is possible only through eugenic measures—health takes its proper and central place in a scheme of education whose aim is to adjust human beings to the demands of life.

2. *How is the promotion of health dependent on institutional adjustment?*

Healthful living is a mode of social action. It cannot be understood on any merely individualistic plane, such as the taking of drugs, the adoption of a personal regimen, and so on. This is an absolutely essential idea, and the beginning of all wisdom in health education. Always our aim must be an improved institutional adjustment.

A splendid illustration of this statement, which may at first seem strange and hard to understand, is furnished by Warwick Deeping's novel, *The Promise of Love*. It is the story of a young physician who comes, fresh and enthusiastic from his scientific training in one of London's great hospitals, to a sleepy English country town. As he goes about among the people, he begins, little by little, to perceive that they are living in the midst of conditions which greatly lower their vitality, and which lay them open to the threat of epidemic disease on an appalling scale. He preaches, and argues, and bullies, but accomplishes little. His efforts are met either with stolid indifference to what are considered the newfangled fads of an inexperienced youth, or with active hostility from vested interests. At last the place is gripped by an epidemic of typhoid; and the population is terrified into some willingness to consider new ways. Even then it is difficult to do much. Obstacles are placed in the way of segregating the sick and protecting the children. It is impossible to persuade people to discontinue drinking water from a polluted well. But gradually, under great pressure, the community mobilizes itself, and the disease is overcome. Essentially, the young physician goes to work by creating for these people a new social institution, a new mode of social action, with reference to which they may re-direct their living. He himself furnishes the key point of the institution; and about him everything arranges itself—segregation of the sick, hospitalization, rebuilding of infected tenements, avoidance of pollution, and so forth. His success depends, not on administering drugs, but on bringing about a new and better pattern of social adjustment.

Yet another illustration, this time not from fiction, but from fact, is the control of health conditions in the zone of the Panama Canal. Under the direction of Goethals, the whole life of the working community was so organized that it protected itself against the scourge of yellow fever, which, ever before that time, had devastated the region. Contrast this with the construction of the Suez Canal, where men died literally in multitudes. Where was the difference? In one case we see a health-promoting and preserving institution consciously planned and set up, and a control established over social behavior. In the other case, the only problem was the removal of the dirt and the building of the canal structures; and health was not considered in any comprehensive manner.

Improvement of just this kind explains the enormous advance of general health over the past two hundred years. "As late as the seventeenth century, smallpox was so common in England, that the police considered the apprehension of a missing criminal in large measure assured if to his description could be added the phrase 'not pockmarked.' In New York in the early part of the nineteenth century, 644 cases were recorded in 2 days, and as many more were believed to have escaped the official count. Today, a pockmarked face is almost a curiosity. From 1800 to 1879, the United States was swept every year except two by a yellow fever epidemic. In 1878 the year's bill for this one disease was over $10,000,000 for New Orleans, and more than $100,000,000 for the entire country. Yellow fever has now disappeared as completely from the United States as have laws against bathtubs. Only thirty years ago typhoid fever contributed heavily to the death rate; 35.9 persons per 100,000 succumbed to it. In 1930 it was responsible for only 4.8 deaths per 100,000, and even this minimum percentage is reducible by the use of measures already proved effective. We have been able virtually to bar our national door against cholera, typhus, and bubonic plague, scourges which have destroyed millions of Europeans and Asiatics. In the south, modern medicine has brought about the restoration to useful activity of multitudes whose energies had been depleted by malaria and hookworm. Whole communities have been transformed economically by the elimination of hookworm disease alone. The increasing use of diphtheria antitoxin has reduced the death rate from this most dreaded of all diseases of childhood from 43.3 per 100,000 in 1900 to 4.9 in 1930, and has brought within the range of possibility its final extinction."[1] And elsewhere in the same report, it is shown that, for a long time, there has been a downward trend in the rates of morbidity and mortality, as well as other evidences of gains in physical vigor and well being in the population.

If we ask how this enormous advance has come about, our first inclination may be to answer: "By advancing skill and knowledge." We think of the laborious and selfless researches of men like Pasteur, Koch, and Lister; of the revolutionary improvement of surgical techniques; of the discovery of vaccination, of anaesthesia, of insulin; of a thousand other such triumphs of the human mind. But while such things are indeed essential, they are not enough. So far, we have only half the story of the war. Knowledge kept secret in the research laboratory and the scientific monograph, is of no service to mankind. Skill, which is only the private possession of the expert, has no more social significance than excellence at solving crossword puzzles or juggling billiard balls. It is necessary to translate knowledge and skill into a pattern of social action; to make our new intellectual resources serve their true end in enlightened living. And this means the creative evolution of new institutional types. Here we have the second, and equally necessary, chapter of the table. There has been a steady advance in the trained competence of physicians, dentists, nurses, hospital workers, and pharmacists; and a discovery of better and better ways of making their services available to the public. There has been increasingly effec-

[1] From *Recent Social Trends,* report of the President's Research Committee on Social Trends; by permission of the publishers, McGraw-Hill Book Company, Inc., vol. 1, pp. 1061–1062.

tive mobilization against such diseases as tuberculosis, smallpox, and syphilis. Improved organization has been sought in connection with hospital work, clinics, and industrial medicine; and the idea of establishing community health centers has been proposed by responsible authorities. Federal, state, and local governments have steadily increased their activities in the way of health service. And various plans for spreading and carrying the costs of promoting health and overcoming disease have been discussed, and to some extent tried out—including the idea of compulsory sickness insurance.

All this has been very aptly called the distribution, in contrast with the production, of knowledge and skill regarding physical well being. Notice particularly that what is happening is the creation of new modes of social action. The picture of the finely trained, broad-minded physician is incomplete if we omit the intelligently coöperative patient. The community health center which is just a beautiful building to which nobody comes, and an expert staff with nothing to do, is a mere monument to the folly of impractical idealism. The anti-tuberculosis campaign which is all posters, and radio talks, and bustling publicity, and no popular coöperation, is fit only for the musical comedy stage. Such things mean new patterns, new ways of social action, or nothing at all. Here we have the very essence of that institutional readjustment which is the medium of all progress, and the great end of all education.

I have explained and illustrated at length this idea of the promotion of health as a type of institutional adjustment, partly because it is both important and at first sight strange; but much more because it is so very often overlooked in discussions of health education. Progressive workers and writers who deal with the problems of teaching health in our schools are fond of insisting that information is not enough, and that we must aim at forming health habits in the children. As far as they go, they are entirely right. Merely to have the pupils learn various facts about calories and vitamins and sleep and exercise and the conquest of disease, is certainly not enough. We are back once more to the level of teaching subject matter for its own sake. And all experience, and educational research, warns us that such book knowledge transfers most meagerly to practice. But neither is it enough merely to make a drive for better habits. Yet some of our most forward-looking programs of health education concentrate their chief energies here. For instance, in one school system, procedures were devised by which the teacher, in coöperation with the homes, sought to build in the pupils such habits as going to bed earlier, spending more time out of doors, brushing teeth, drinking more milk, eating more vegetables, standing and sitting in better posture, and avoiding nail biting. Most of these things are, no doubt, admirable. But so far, we seem to be thinking of the individual, outside his social relationships and contacts. And we fail to strike down to the heart of our problem. The real task of teaching a child how to promote his physical well being under the stresses of civilized life does not turn on setting up a number of habits, however desirable. It turns on teaching him to coöperate intelligently and effectively with the social institution which exists for the conservation and up-building of health. We want him to be able to collaborate effectively with physicians, dentists, nurses, public health officers, pharmacists, and so forth; to take his part, either as leader or follower, in campaigns against epidemic disease and for better general health; to avail himself intelligently of existing resources in the way of clinics, health centers, industrial medical programs, sickness insurance plans; to have an intelligent interest in, and a willingness and ability to seek and find, further information regarding his physical welfare, if and when he may need it. The specific health habits I mentioned above have, indeed, a very important place in the program. But they are not its center. The great aim of health education must be to secure a flexible, creative, progressive adjustment to the evolving social institution devoted to the cause of physical well being.

In closing this section, I will call your attention to two points. First, the securing of a better institutional adjustment is the way towards the progressive improvement of our health-supporting, health-promoting institution. Ross Finney has interestingly dubbed this institution the "therapeuton." At the present time, in spite of great advances, it is poorly organized. Medical service is based on the principle of free competition and *laissez faire,* so that it is not distributed in accordance with social needs. (178 physicians per 100,000 of population in California, and only 74 per 100,000 in South

Carolina, for instance). Adequate medical and hospital treatment for certain diseases is hard to find outside the great centers. Inferior types of treatment are in wide use. There is undue toleration of worthless, or even harmful, proprietary and patent medicines. Much commercial advertising bearing on health is undesirable in tone, and false, and even destructive, in the suggestions it conveys. There is very inadequate emphasis upon the prevention of disease. And the costs of medical care are badly distributed. None of these things can be cured by fiat. They are beyond the power of experts to alter abruptly. Like any other institution, our "therapeuton" can be improved only by intelligent collaboration between leaders and followers—by men with vision to show the way, and other men with sense enough to follow it. It is a matter of improving institutional adjustment—and this means, specifically, a task for education.

Secondly, notice that an improved adjustment to the health-preserving, health-promoting agencies means a transformation which must radiate through the whole structure of society. If our population can be educated to more enlightened standards of thought and action in regard to physical well being, it will more and more decisively refuse to tolerate certain conditions of work, of home life, of recreation. A fully health-conscious community would almost certainly insist upon a drastic change of regime in the local jail. The only reason why our food supplies are now handled so much better than they once were, is that the social mind has come to demand it. A distinguished writer has suggested that in an ideal society illness would be punished as a crime. Of course he was uttering a paradox; but it helps us to imagine what would happen in the way of social advance, if the work of health education could be fully performed. A president of the American Medical Association once said: "If doctors could apply all they know to all the people, not only would life be prolonged and human happiness increased, but the whole aspect and order of life would be altered." [2] To open the way for the expert, to make his path plain, to transmute knowledge into power, is here as everywhere the task of education.

[2] Quoted by Chapman and Counts: *Principles of Education:* The Houghton Mifflin Company, 1924, p. 202.

3. *How is the promotion of health dependent on enlightenment?*

A short time ago, the press gave considerable space to a story of dramatically inadequate adjustment to the social agencies for the promotion and preservation of health. It was discovered that one of the children of a poor immigrant family urgently needed a major operation. The parents were frantic with fear. They barricaded the house; defied all comers; and kept pots of boiling water on the stove for the benefit of health officers and social workers interested in the case. After standing a siege for several days, the family decamped in the dead of night. This well illustrates the principles we have been developing. Their trouble was a sheer refusal to coöperate, a violently negative line of social action, an antagonism rather than a mere indifference towards a beneficent institution. It shows us with fresh force how completely the promotion of health depends upon certain modes of social behavior. So much is clear. But what ought to be done about such an affair? Of course, the police might have broken in the door, flooded the house with tear gas, and carried the child off to hospital. But such a solution, even if it were legal, could hardly be considered humane or constructive. One could not be content with forcibly dragooning these poor people. One must try to do something to their mental attitudes; to change their minds, in the most literal sense of the phrase. These people did not *understand*. What they lacked was a certain background of social and scientific insight, and certain ideals and conventions, which have become part of American life. They needed something which cannot be conveyed to them all in a moment; and that is, enlightenment, which is the product of education.

We must always remember that the controls of human action are mental. A man may be *in* a highly civilized society; but he is not *of* it unless he possesses those intellectual resources which are the agencies of civilized behavior. The pathetic figure of the frightened immigrant father shows us, in a sharp and shocking contrary instance, how completely we are made the people that we are by our mental inheritance. If we want to develop in anyone a better adjustment to any social institution, including that which is concerned with the promotion of health, there is but a single way to do it. We must seek to build up in their minds an appropriate background of knowledge, insights, skills, wants, ideals, and conventions. If a man is to care adequately for his physical well being, he must do far more than refrain from resisting expert advice and direction. He must do even more than tamely submit to such advice and direction. He must be wise enough to seek it where it can be had, to judge and understand it when it is given, and to follow it intelligently afterwards. He must, in fact, collaborate with, rather than blindly follow, the expert. There must be a meeting of minds, a mutuality of understanding; not a mere giving and receiving of orders. This is the only kind of institutional adjustment which will work out to success. And it is possible only by the creation of a mental background through which social behavior can be flexibly and creatively controlled.

This shows us what to seek on the mental side of a program of health education. That program must endeavor to build up in the mind of the child a growing core of knowledge and insight, by means of which his behavior may become more and more intelligent. But this does not mean simply teaching various items of "health information." In the first place, if we rest satisfied with nothing more, we shall find ourselves teaching knowledge for the sake of knowledge, rather than for the sake of life. The children will learn the information, because we compel them to do so. But it will not become educative, since it lacks the vital interpretive contact with action. In the second place, the bits of knowledge which are often lumped together under the heading of health information are apt to be mere unrelated facts. One may, for example, tell the children that sugar has a high caloric value; that tea and coffee are not nutritive substances; that tobacco has a deleterious effect on young people; that it is desirable to have eight hours sleep each night; that vaccination is a preventive of smallpox. These things are true enough. But just as so many unrelated chunks of fact, they have a minimal value for the educative process and the effective control of conduct. What we want is to have the pupils not merely believe such statements, but, little by little, understand them in their broad relationships. In other words, we cannot be content unless their minds are steadily moving towards a grasp of the scientific principles upon which healthy living depends.

Health information needs to be coördinated, rather than encyclopaedic. The reason for this is obvious enough, as an illustration will show. Within the last few years, there have been very rapid changes in point of view on the subject of nutrition. Now what chance has the layman, who has merely had some items of information handed out to him, to cope intelligently with such problems? He will either stick blindly to what he has been told; or else he will rush after each new fad as it appears; or he will say that the whole scientific treatment of nutrition is bunk. He can be saved in one way only. He must gain some organized insight into the scientific principles of nutrition, rather than just some information about it. How far he can go in this direction depends upon his native ability and his circumstances. But it is the aim towards which health education should move.

Modern programs for teaching health often are defective here. They may avoid the gross error of information for the sake of information. But they fall into the subtler mistake of supposing that the only practical knowledge is an *ad hoc* array of unrelated facts. And so we have what is sometimes called a "health curriculum," which may be correlated with the general curriculum, but is not *integrated* with it. This is certainly an error. Intelligent and effective adjustment to the health promoting institution, is a product of the general growth of the mind from the fragmentary towards the complete, from the piecemeal towards the unified, from the empirical towards the scientific. What I would suggest, then, is that instead of setting up a sort of subject matter subdivision labelled "health information," we develop the essential, controlling intellectual background in conjunction with the general curriculum, and more particularly in conjunction with the study of general science, biological science, social science, and history. If we do this, we make these subjects more significant by connecting them to a great and vital issue. We handle our general science, and our biological science, in such a way that the pupil sees they have a personal message for him, dealing with his own physical well being. We handle our social science so that the pupil is aroused to an understanding of those social agencies and structures designed to promote health. And part of the content of a living course in history may well be the fight against disease and death, and the triumphs of medical science. Of course, all these studies must begin in the lower grades in a very informal way. Perhaps the natural starting point will be nothing more portentous than a discussion of the value of drinking milk, or of spending time in the open air, closely in conjunction with a program designed to inculcate actual milk drinking and open air activities. But we must not think we have done enough when we stay on this level. Always there must be a movement of the mind towards a systematic grasp of fundamental principles. This is the meaning of the mental enlightenment which is the controlling force in human action. We must mediate to the pupil an increasing grasp of the intellectual resources of civilization, focussed, among other things, upon the problems of adjusting himself to the institution designed for the preservation and promotion of his health, the evolving "therapeuton."

4. *What should the school seek to do in educating for health?*

We are now ready to see how the controlling principles of health education may be applied in school work. We must always remember that our aim is the improvement of a mode of social action through enlightenment and the development of mental background. This will show us what we ought to try to do.

A. First of all, we must organize a comprehensive program of health activities. Without activities, we cannot even make a proper start, because our aim is to raise the level of a type of human behavior, not to convey knowledge. Without comprehensive activities, we cannot go either far or fast, because we shall lack some of our best opportunities. Turner has pointed out how inadequately conceived the health activity program may often be. He tells us that "one man spoke to me of a dental clinic as a 'health education program.' A teacher once said that she was sorry she could not show me her health education program, because she had loaned it to the teacher across the hall. She referred to a set of health posters."[3]

[3] C. E. Turner: *Principles of Health Education:* D. C. Heath, 1932, p. 17.

The basic activities should include, first of all, certain routine procedures. We should have monthly weighing and measuring. This should be carried out carefully and accurately, and a cumulative record should be kept for each child. Second, it is desirable to devote a few minutes at the opening of school to a daily health review, taking account of some, or all, of the following items: "Cleanliness of hands and nails; biting of nails; cleanliness of face, neck, and ears; cleanliness of teeth; neatness of hair; cleanliness and neatness of clothing; carrying clean handkerchief; removal of rubbers, overshoes, rubber boots, and extra sweaters. The number of items will be few at first and will be increased or changed as the pupils become able to meet the standards set." [4] Part of the morning health review may also be devoted to checking up on health habits in out-of-school living, and to observing symptoms of illness. Third, the mid-morning lunch of milk and crackers should be considered an integral part of the whole program of health activities. Fourth, the work of the elementary school should be planned to secure properly arranged relaxation periods.

But also the planned program of health activities should reach far beyond the school. This will involve active coöperation with other institutions. For instance, it is found possible for the school to work with the home in promoting proper standards of nutrition, rest, and ventilation. The children should be made conscious of what is desirable in these directions, and encouraged to set up the right kind of activities in the way of eating, sleeping, and out-of-door play. Then we should have physical examinations and follow-up work for the correction of defects, including, of course, the proper care of the teeth, the removal of diseased tonsils and adenoids, the rectification of defective vision and hearing, and so on. Teacher and pupils should seek consciously to coöperate with the public health authorities, in the prevention and control of communicable diseases. There should be a sense of joint responsibility for maintaining hygienic conditions in the school building, including the ventilation and temperature control of the classroom, the regulation of lighting by means of window shades, the proper adjustment of the desks and chairs to the size of the pupils, and the gen-

---

[4] Turner, *op. cit.* p. 137.

eral cleanliness and order of the whole building and grounds. Lastly, the physical education program, and also athletics, should be considered as a part of the activity basis for the teaching of health.

Notice always that health education, like every other kind of education, must begin with what the child is actually doing. Our starting point must be the control of the pupil's behavior, both in and out of school.

B. In the second place, the whole program of health activities must be carried on in a spirit of active social participation and cooperation. We are not training athletes, or fattening stock. We are trying to bring about a better adjustment of human beings to their environment. Our purpose is not physical, but educational improvement. Unless we remember this, the best planned and most comprehensive program will fail of much of its effect.

Primarily this means that every health activity must be so carried on as to enlist the active, increasingly intelligent interest of the children. The changes, month by month, in a child's height and weight are facts of great importance for the pediatrician. But they do not become educative till they mean something to the child himself. The school lunch, as an item in the day's routine, is just so much stoking, necessary and valuable for its own sake, no doubt, but nothing more. But if the pupils are brought to discuss the reasons for it, or, in a rural school, to help in preparing it, then it becomes also an educative opportunity. Turner gives us an illustration of just what we should desire. He tells about a class which became much interested in the diet habits of a girl who showed many signs of malnutrition. They were all concerned with getting Sally to drink more milk and much pleased when they succeeded. This was good for Sally's physique, no doubt. But more than this, it was also good for Sally's mind, and for the minds of her classmates. To do such things as this requires tact and discretion. But it is within the realm of proved and practical possibility. And it is a part of the essence of health education.

But the use of health activities as educational opportunities means more than this. They give us our chance to secure a definite adjustment of the pupil to the health promoting agencies, which are to serve him during the whole of his life. The visit of the school nurse, or the school dentist, or the school physician, should provide a point of social contact between the child and all nurses, all dentists, all physicians. The task of such officials is not physical only, but also educational. In the same way, the establishment of quarantine in cases of communicable disease should not be just a brute fact. It should have a meaning in the lives, and minds, and attitudes of the pupils. It should be one starting point for their life adjustment to the organization of public health.

C. In the third place, we must have an integration between the health activities and the subject matter of the general curriculum. When a pupil needs some dental work, or has to be fitted to glasses, this surely is an opportunity for the teacher of physiology. When children are vaccinated against smallpox, surely one may hope that they will be permitted to hear the name of Jenner, and to learn something of those profound social changes which have issued in the control of *variola minor*. When the pupils report that the home of one of their classmates has been placarded for measles, is it fantastic to think that social and general science may find something apposite and relevant in the situation? I have already protested against the idea of setting up health information, simply as a separate curricular subdivision or subject, and nothing more. Rather it would seem best to relate health activities to the general curriculum, and in this way seek to render them enlightened, and bring them under intellectual controls. Notice again our familiar reciprocal effect. Activities carried on purely for their own sake, and without any relationship to intellectual background, may have an immediate value. But they gain educative effect when they become luminous as applications of fundamental principles, and as expressions of man's intellectual control of his environment. And on the other hand, subject matter taught for itself is dead. It comes to life when it is integrated with, and grasped as an interpretation of, significant situations. Notice, too, that mental growth always begins with the rendering intelligible and meaningful of such concrete undertakings as drinking more milk, consuming more vegetables, having a decayed tooth filled, or defective vision corrected. Its progress is away from such fragmentary origins, and towards a complete logical grasp. That progress, when properly made, means increasing capacity for flexible, creative, adjustment, and for efficient living. And here we have another reason against teaching health information in isolation from the whole range of mental content, just as so many factual items immediately connected with various activities.

5. *How may the school promote healthy living throughout life?*

The great test of any plan of education is its effect upon life, now and later. If our pupils cease to develop, the moment they go out into the work-a-day world, then the school is not succeeding. Human adjustment must be not only flexible and creative, but also progressive. We cannot be content unless children become increasingly effective human beings year by year throughout their whole lives, because of the influence of our work. To tell whether a school is really rendering its proper service, we must not only ask whether boys and girls are able to live better when they leave than when they enter; we must also ask whether they are able to live better at thirty than they could at twenty, and better at sixty than they could at fifty. This is universally true. But it has peculiar force in connection with health. We have seen how health, understood as the perfection and balance of physical functioning in a civilized environment, depends upon an adjustment to an institution, and how it is brought about by enlightenment and controlled by understanding. Health is one kind of practical wisdom. As a man grows wiser, he should be able to live a more and more healthful life. Perfect health is something that we never fully gain or hold; rather it is something towards which we continuously move, as we grow in self knowlege, self reverence, and self control. And the great aim of health education is to foster this life-long growth, and to make it more possible than it would otherwise have been. Here lies the importance of the opening question of this section: How may the school promote health living *throughout life?*

A. First of all, it must give up the notion of preparation for life, in the sense of storing up something to be used later. As we have seen, education can never be properly understood as serving such an end. And assuredly, the preparatory dogma is a pestilent heresy in connection with education for health. Yet even here, where its error seems most obvious, the spectre haunts our discussions and casts a baleful influence upon our practice. I think you will find it illuminating to lay this ghost; for not only does it mean nailing certain serious and important mistakes about health education; but also it will perhaps help us to see more clearly, through a concrete illustration, the meaning of our general educational point of view.

(i) Health education cannot improve health later on by laying up in the pupil a store of health and strength, on which he can draw later in life. You go off on a summer vacation; and almost at once you feel better and stronger. Why is this? It is simply because you begin immediately to live a better adjusted physical life, and because certain weakening strains are removed. "But," you may say, "this benefit seems to continue for a time after my vacation is over." This is quite true. There is a certain carry-over. Perhaps the weeks in the country, or at the sea-side, have improved the condition of your blood, increasing the number of its red corpuscles, and building up its disease-resisting powers. But notice particularly that these benefits, real and desirable though they may be, do not last very long. All too soon, the old routines and pressures do their work; and you are no better off than you were before, save for a delightful experience, which is something—and indeed, very much. You certainly would not expect a summer vacation greatly to affect your health ten years hence. Even a year in a sanitarium will not do this, save on one condition. It will do so if, and only if, such experience leads you to reorganize your way of life. Now it is just this long-time effect that we wish to achieve in health education. If our only boast can be that a pupil is stronger, less subject to illness, a more complete and adequate physical being, for a few months after we have finished with him, we are not able to say very much. Nor can we really justify our work on such grounds. Yet, if we conceive of our purpose as the storing up of health and strength, are we not dominated by what might be called the summer vacation theory of health education? There is no such thing as a store of health and vitality. Health and vitality cannot be stored. They must be used. They depend upon the way we live—that is to say, upon the mode of social action we adopt. Of course there is some lag between a way of living and its full organic effect. When you come back from your vacation, you do not at once lose all you gained. But the loss of physical benefits gained by wise and healthy living is not long postponed when we change our way of life for the worse. Here, as always, the cold storage theory proves a deceitful guide.

(ii) Health education cannot improve health simply by laying up a store of habits to be used later on. We know very well that certain ways of living are desirable—for instance, eating certain foods, taking outdoor exercise, and so on. It is our duty to try to have children adopt such ways. But we should not think of them as fixed, routine habits. It is all-important for one to understand why he does certain things, as well as doing them. And the reason is simple. When one comes up against a problem in later life, one may not be able to follow one's custom literally. What one needs is to be able to apply the principle of right action to the new situation. Often and often one must be able to invent a new way, which is consistent with the good old way, but not exactly the same. Think of Steffansson, living for months on a straight meat diet, knowing how contrary it was to all our normal nutritional routines, but perfectly confident that he would come to no harm because of his understanding of the principles of dietetics. We cannot possibly provide in advance a habit against every contingency which life may bring. This is the fatal weakness of the idea of specific preparation in education. Perhaps if we knew that our pupils would always be in circumstances exactly like those surrounding them now, we could map out a feasible set of routines in healthful living, which would cover most emergencies. But so far from knowing this, we know the exact contrary. By all means we must try to have children lead healthful lives here and now; but our idea must never be that what they do here and now, they will also do elsewhere and later. Flexibility, not rigidity, must be our aim. Our health education must make them able and willing to seek the guidance of experts when they need it; able and willing to gather new information as it becomes available. What we must wish for them is a growing, an improving, a flexible, a continuously wiser health adjustment, not a stock of ready made routines, suitable for all occasions.

(iii) Health education cannot improve health later on, by seeking to give the pupil a store of knowledge to be applied in the future. Once more, this does not mean that knowledge is not important, or that it has no place in our program. But the point is, that knowledge unapplied here and now is knowledge destined to be largely lost. The readings and lessons in general science, biological science, social science, and history, integrated with our health program, as I have suggested, must always be planned to help the pupil to understand his immediate problems and to enlighten his immediate action.

B. Again, if the school is to promote healthy living throughout life, it must, in and of itself, foster and improve the pupil's health. Is the school itself an environment propitious to health? Does a child's health tend to improve when he enters school? Is it likely to be better if he stays in school, than if he does not? Does it tend to grow better and better, as his school career grows longer? These are searching questions indeed. Yet they are very necessary ones. If we cannot say yes to them, it spells, in letters a foot high, the failure of our school program of health education. If the school does not work a benefit upon the pupil's health during the years when he is immediately under its care, is it likely that he will gain much from it ten years, or twenty years, after he leaves?

Can we, then, give an affirmative answer to such questions? Does going to school improve a child's health? Alas, our answer must be: No! The facts of the case, which are some of the most formidable confronting modern education, are clear and incontestable. All investigations of health conditions in our schools tell essentially the same story. School life is inimical to health.

When children enter the first grade, their physical well being almost always becomes impaired. Not only do they become more liable to colds, and measles, and other communicable diseases, which we might readily understand; but their appetites suffer, they begin to have headaches and to show other signs of fatigue, their blood becomes impoverished, their metabolism grows slower, and their rate of growth is probably retarded. If the famous observer from Mars could come and examine these children after six months in school, with a vision unclouded by our common prejudices, he would certainly say that they had been placed in an environment hostile to their physical living. Moreover, these health conditions do not improve as school life goes on. Just the opposite —they grow worse. More and more sickness, more and more fatigue, more and more of the ill effects of anxiety, more and more eye strain and eye troubles, more and more malnutrition due to lack of appetite and decrease of assimilative efficiency—this is the toll which the school levies upon our children. It is found that, as the school year progresses, fatigue becomes cumulative; that when the school day is long, we have more sickness of all kinds, and not communicable sickness only; and that year by year, the child suffers in his body more and more, by staying in school. In spite of all that is said about our American emphasis upon athletics, the net effect of the school is not physical improvement, but physical impairment.

Clearly, this means that our schools have not made themselves over into an environment which brings about a better and better adjustment in health. The case is made still stronger when we see very similar effects produced in the teacher, as well as in the pupil. Our teachers are recruited, in the main, from physically excellent native stock. But their work lays them open to a progressive impairment of bodily well being. They become increasingly liable to the diseases of physical and nervous degeneration, such as anaemia, neurasthenia, and tuberculosis. And one distinguished authority has said that few survive ten years of professional activity, without falling a victim to one of these complaints. Hence, premature superannuation. Hence, too, the typical picture of the cranky, difficult, elderly teacher. The calling which, above all others, should keep one human, and which should turn one into a better and more complete person, too often has exactly the opposite effect, largely because of the unnatural physical conditions of the work.

What then shall we say to these things? Clearly, schools which have such immediate effects upon health, cannot produce any long-time betterment. The reason is not that they fail to give the pupils a good preparation, or to store up a fund of vitality, or habits, or knowledge. The future is not prepared for in such ways. The failure lies in not providing an immediate environment for healthy living, out of which may grow still better and healthier living.

"But," you may ask, "what can be done? Children must go to school, mustn't they? And when they are there, surely they must study. Perhaps we can alleviate things here a little, and there a little. But, while we have schools at all, is not this the price we must pay?"

Indeed we often hear about the physical impairment which comes from schooling spoken of as the *price* of education. But this is a very faulty way of thinking. It is really the *failure* of education; for exactly, it means, a failure to achieve that physical adjustment which is the foundation of a well-lived, happy life.

Moreover, the questions raised above strike at the very root of education for health. If our schools are to be, in the full sense, agencies for the promotion of health—and this only means agencies for the improvement of life—they must, indeed, be reorganized in a far reaching manner. The solution is simply to put into practice that conception of education which has been developed in these pages. For the basic reason why the schools are physically injurious is their devotion to the aim of teaching subject matter. And the facts of school hygiene, some of which I have very briefly summarized, may be cited in evidence to demonstrate the falsity of that aim.

Let us see how a change of aim from the teaching of subject matter to the achievement of life adjustment, when applied in concrete detail, will relieve the strains which the school places upon the pupil's physique, and transform it from an environment hostile to health, into one that is definitely propitious.

First, we shall regard the physical setting of school work as a point of major importance. This does not mean exceedingly expensive, luxurious buildings and equipment. But it does mean a structure fully adequate from the standpoint of heating, lighting, and ventilation. It is interesting to remark that even this much really implies going beyond the pure subject matter conception of education, with its emphasis upon the intellect and its tendency to ignore the body. The average school classroom is, rather obviously, a place where children will sit still and acquire knowledge out of books; and if hygienic conditions are fairly satisfactory, it is by way of a bonus. What we need is a classroom—and indeed a whole building—planned as an environment for the healthy activities of a healthy life.

Second, we shall seek an extension and application of the outdoor school idea. Out-door schools have been set up even in the northern parts of the country, especially for tubercular children. It is found that they remove some of the worst effects of schooling. Whether this is due merely to the open air environment in which the pupils do their work, or to the freer spirit of the classes, I am unable to say. Clearly, there may be many subtle differences created when school work is carried on not in a classroom, however well equipped, but under the open sky. And it is proposed that this plan, so beneficial for physically inferior children, shall be extended as far as possible.

Third, we shall endeavor to reduce seat work to a minimum, and to encourage far more freedom in the way of moving about, than is ordinarily permitted. The conventional routine of school management, which requires pupils to remain seated and silent for considerable periods of time, is clearly based on the assumption of subject matter learning and recitation as the primary business of education. When we substitute the conception of adjustment to life, a much more active class regime is likely to be instituted.

Fourth, we shall seek to build up a new conception regarding the whole matter of discipline. So long as the subject matter dogma holds sway, the teacher must play the part of a policeman, to check up on the pupil's assigned work. This demands a repressive discipline and a demand for conformity. Much school strain is due to anxiety produced in the child by this kind of regime.

Fifth, we shall eliminate all home study below the seventh grade, and rigidly limit it to one, or, at the most, two hours *per diem* after that. If instruction is efficient, and the teacher knows his job, it is quite possible to have all necessary learning done in school, at least below the seventh grade—and done under better supervision, and more favorable conditions than the average home will afford. The idea of piling on home work comes partly from inefficiency in instruction, which cannot economically achieve what is desired; and partly from the idea that the more subject matter material the pupil assimilates, the better.

Sixth, we shall seek to plan our whole school day on other than the conventional lines, with much more free activity, much better motivation, a much more continuous sense of dealing with genuine problems. A six hour school day, devoted chiefly to learning and reciting upon content which has no particular meaning or appeal, is one certain cause of unhygienic strain and the lowering of vitality. The moment we notice this situation, such a conclusion is obvious. No labor is more deadly than that of the treadmill.

Seventh, and lastly, we shall build into our school work the scheme of health activities which has been discussed already in the present chapter.

There is nothing impossible about such a program. It will be fought by those who think that the school exists to grind into the pupil's head the maximum amount of reading, writing, arithmetic, history, science, English, foreign language, and so on. In one sense, these suggestions, though far from impracticable, are revolutionary, because they involve a breach with this conventional notion of the aim of education. Always our conception is of the school as a favored, carefully planned environment, in which human life at the child's level can be lived with the utmost fullness, enjoyment, and present and future benefit. The school should be a place where it is obviously good to be—good physically as well as mentally. This is how it fulfills its educational mission in general, and in respect to health in particular. The child who has spent his most formative years in such an environment, and who has been brought, little by little, to understand the why of things about him, which at first he merely accepts, will not only grow more healthy year by year while there, and emerge a physically better adjusted being for his stay; but also he will be equipped as well as it is possible for him to be to achieve a better and better adaptation to the agencies for healthy living, and to grow towards a steadily superior physical balance as his life goes on.

Part Three

PROBLEMS

*

Chapter 11

HOW MAY WE DEAL WITH THE PROBLEM OF EDUCATIONAL OPPORTUNITY?

1. *What is the problem of educational opportunity?*

The great concern of the early apostles of American education was to secure for all children ample, and fairly equal, opportunities to go to school. These men had a vision of something new in human affairs—a universal system of schools, going far beyond the elementary level. They believed, and most truly, that on this the future of the commonwealth largely depended. They were under the necessity of impressing their vision upon the popular mind and of showing to people to whom the idea was strange, how important it was that such a great school system should be brought into being. So they concentrated their argument on the most obvious and most essential point, which was that a great deal more schooling ought to be provided than actually existed.

The desire to provide extensive educational opportunities has been, and still is, one of the great impelling forces in American life. It has been achieved to an amazing and unparalleled degree. Yet the problem is with us still; and we remain far from the goal of ample, and fairly equal, educational chances for every child. In most states, children who live in the country, have much more limited facilities for education than their brothers and sisters in the cities. While legally and nominally open to all, the schools are, in fact, much less accessible to certain social classes than to others. There are still millions of children who do not possess educational privileges which can be considered adequate on any reasonable standards. And while these things are so, we must still press for an increase in the amount of educational opportunity, in the name of the common good.

But recent years have brought us to see this problem in a somewhat different light. Educational thinkers are aware, of course, that our system of schools, magnificent social achievement though it be, is not yet adequate to the needs of a democratic society. They still wish for an extension of school facilities and services. But they are coming to raise a new question. They are asking this: How can we organize education so that each person receives the opportunity for which he is most fitted? A mere increase in the amount of schooling is now seen to be an inadequate ideal. We also want to know how to distribute this increased, and increasing amount, for the best advantage of the individual child, and the greatest good of the social order. This is the problem of educational opportunity with which I shall deal in the present chapter.

This problem, of course, has always existed. But two influences have forced it upon our minds with a peculiar urgency at the present time. The first of these has been a recognition of the large costs of our educational system. And this has brought an increasing feeling of responsibility for seeing that an adequate return is made, and that public expenditures are administered wisely and with selective insight. The second has been the new recognition of the extent of individual differences in educability, which has made it very obvious that different people will benefit to different degrees from educational opportunity.

2. *What determines how long children stay in school?*

Length of stay in school is probably the most obvious and immediately essential point to consider in connection with the proper distribution of educational opportunity. For it seems self evident that, if children differ greatly in educability, they should not all continue in school equally long.

Now, continuance in school is not determined by any sort of intelligent planning, but rather by the operation of blind, mass forces. Social status has a great deal to do with it. If a child's father is a professional man, or a successful business man, then, unless he is very stupid indeed, that child is likely to stay on at least through high school, and probably through college. But the child of working class parents, though exactly equal in ability to the child from the professional family, is apt to drop out much sooner. Neighborhood, again, has a great deal to do with it. The accident of living in a locality where schools are easily accessible— for instance, in one of the "better" wards of a city—strongly favors continuance in school, independently of individual ability. And above all, the potent, diffuse, permeating propaganda for education will be a major determining factor.

This propaganda for education is a terrific force in American life. Most people are all too well aware that high school graduates earn more than those with only an eighth grade education; and college graduates more than either. To become eligible for the most desirable jobs, the right series of diplomas is becoming more and more necessary. And going to school carries with it a reward of social prestige which amounts to little less than a social menace. The result is that an enormous army of youth is marching through our schools, an army perhaps not directly conscripted, yet pretty nearly so. This involves a very heavy responsibility. The schools have hung out immense welcome signs. They have gone out into the highways and hedges; and their houses are rather more than comfortably filled. What are they going to do with each individual among these multitudes? For it is the individual who counts.

A short time ago, the papers carried a story of a girl student at one of our western universities, who was discovered to be rooming under a railroad culvert, so great was her desire to go on with her education and so limited her resources. I suppose many people saw in this only something rather funny. But it would seem to me that an act of faith so pathetic and passionate, constituted a really appalling challenge to the university in question. Was it justified in attracting this girl so strongly? Could it offer enough to fulfill the hope it had aroused? What reason had it for believing her able to take advantage of its opportunities? These, surely, are the issues involved. I say again, that the force of this educational propaganda, and its almost frightening success, impose on us a solemn duty to see to it that educational opportunity is directed to the right people, and not thrust, hit or miss, upon everybody; and that the idealistic aspirations we have aroused are not aroused in the breasts of those sure to be confounded.

"But," it may be asked, "do not these blind mass forces, which drive children into, and out of our schools, on the whole work fairly well? We know that pupils in high school are far more educable, on any index that has ever been applied, than pupils in the elementary school; and that college students stand still higher. We know that the average level of intelligence rises with each year beyond the ninth grade, because the less intelligent drop out. We know that our educational system tends strongly to select the highly educable individual, and to eliminate the less educable. Is not this proof that, after all, everything is pretty much all right?"

Certainly these trends are reassuring as far as they go. If they were reversed—if the schools tended to retain the less educable, and to eliminate the fit and the bright—it would be unanswerable evidence that something was catastrophically wrong. But still, we cannot rest satisfied. How little reason we have to be content with the situation has been strikingly shown in a recent article by Professor Thorndike.[1] He undertook to investigate the actual number of years spent in school, by about 800 fourteen year old boys in New York City. And he found that there was absolutely no tendency for the pupil of high educability to spend more years in school than the pupil whose educability was low. How then can we explain the fact that the schools "select intelligence"—that is to say, the fact that as we advance, grade by grade, the average level of intelligence rises, and the less intelligent begin to drop out? The answer is that a bright child moves through the schools much faster than a dull child. Indeed, the brightest of Thorndike's group of children, were actually four whole grades ahead of the dullest, at the age of fourteen. Fit and unfit stay an equal term of years. But the fit move along faster, and so reach the higher grade levels. This is exactly what I mean by handling the matter of selection and the dissemination of opportunity by the operation of blind, mass forces.

[1] "The Distribution of Education": *School Review*, 1932, vol. 40, pp. 335–345.

Everyone is thrown into the same hopper. A sifting process is set up. On the average, the abler individuals emerge. But there is not any planning on an individual basis, in terms of individual capacity.

Now our present method of rationing educational opportunity is wasteful and ill judged. The able pupil is capable of accepting in full measure what the schools have to offer. Surely, on any grounds of reason, he should spend the longest possible time in the school environment. Living there for a good term of years is just what he needs; and society needs it for him. But what actually happens is that he is speeded up. Instead of his brains being a reason for his staying longer in school, where he might have a favorable chance to use them, they are simply an agency for shortening his time there. And what happens to the unfit child? He is kept marking time; doing, over and over again, routine studies which have, perhaps, a minimum of social and educational significance. Such a system is manifestly wrong. Blind forces, acting upon averages, cannot give us a sane distribution of educational opportunity. We cannot be at ease in Zion, until the amount of schooling a person shall receive is determined, primarily and directly by his own character and capacities, innate and acquired.

3. *What should determine how long a pupil ought to stay in school?*

The proper general principle on which to decide how long any individual ought to stay in school emerged directly from the discussion of our previous section, with its criticism of the present regime of blind, mass forces. The only sane basis for such a decision must be the character and abilities of the person involved. But this sets up a difficult practical problem. If the length of time a person is to continue in school is to be determined by his character and capacities, we must have some way of finding out what these may be. How can this be done? Where shall we look for the information necessary to the making of a wise choice?

It may be helpful to discuss this in connection with a very concrete illustration. Let us imagine that we have been appointed guardians to two boys, Bill and Dick. They are both six years old, standing at the threshold of their school careers. We want to do the very best for them that can be done, and no difficulties, financial or otherwise, bar the way. Since, as a general proposition, individuals differ, it would not be very intelligent to think that the very best we could do would be to keep them both in school just as long as we could manage it. But how long? Shall we look forward to one or both of them going on to graduate study; or dropping out after four years of college; or at the end of high school; or after the eighth grade? How can we tell?

Perhaps we may think we can decide, if we know the hereditary abilities of the pair. And we have heard of various mental tests, which are supposed to reveal such abilities. So we have them tested. Bill turns out with an intelligence quotient of 85, and Dick with one of 125. This is an important piece of information. It means that while eighty-five per cent of all children do as well as, or better than, Bill, only three per cent equal or exceed the performance of Dick. Clearly, Dick's achievement is unusually good, while Bill's is rather less than mediocre. We begin to think of Dick as the future doctor of philosophy, and to suspect that the eighth grade will be about the limit of Bill's climb. And we may feel that destiny, masquerading under its modern scientific name of heredity, has conveniently solved our problem, and shown us how to plan the future.

But this is a rash belief. Things are not so easy as all that. Whenever we have a fact so clear cut as a person's intelligence quotient to go upon, it is always tempting to rush in and play the part of an arbitrary providence. And to do so is very dangerous. In the first place, psychologists are not nearly so sure as they used to be that any mental test is able to reveal pure native capacity. The evidence for this has always been circumstantial, rather than direct, as I have taken occasion to point out elsewhere.[2] And facts are accumulating which make it more and more probable that such tests measure the effects both of hereditary and environmental influences, mixed in what proportions, nobody knows. Intelligence may well be defined as the capacity to use past ex-

[2] Mursell, James L: *The Psychology of Secondary School Teaching,* W. W. Norton Company, 1932, ch. 10.

perience. Without adequate past experience, intelligence fails to operate. And it may quite possibly happen that, as Bill's experience accumulates in the splendid environment we are able to provide, his intelligence, as revealed by tests, will improve. So it would be very hasty and ill advised to regard his intelligence quotient, at the age of six, as an infallible gauge-reading, so to speak, of the mental pressure which his inheritance has given him. I do not mean to say that we have been silly to have our boys tested. We have on hand certain warnings, certain indicated probabilities. The folly would consist in taking the test results as a sort of oracular utterance, determining with infallible certainty their future fate.

Moreover, all kinds of things besides those which our mental tests reveal will be important in determining how much Bill and Dick can get out of school. Their seriousness of purpose, their stability of character, their power of work, their physical health, the interests they develop, surely cannot be ignored. In spite of many attempts, the brutal truth is that psychologists have not managed to devise tests to measure most of these things. They are certainly not pure inborn dispositions. We cannot tell how Bill and Dick will shape up in these respects later on. Yet all of them are momentous causes of success and failure in school. Even if it were possible to read off the measure of a person's unmixed hereditary mental ability from a test score, still this would not finally determine how long he should stay in school. Charles Darwin, for instance, seems to have gotten very little value out of his formal education, probably because his intellectual interests were so very individual and unique. Perhaps Dick will be this kind of person; and if we are thinking of education, rather than of diplomas, it might be an excellent idea to take him out of school very young. Or, it may be that Bill will turn out the kind of boy who is very anxious to do his best, and remarkably able to benefit by the kind of experiences a good school would offer him. Then the wise thing would be to have him stay on much longer than his intelligence quotient at the age of six would seem to indicate.

But these difficulties should not discourage us. It still remains true that the length of time Bill and Dick ought to stay in school must depend on their characters and capacities. But our method of trying to determine those capacities has been wrong. This should have been obvious from the start. We have to do with a complex, many-sided problem of human adjustment. Is it not obviously foolish to think we can solve it by sixty minutes of mental testing? Or to say to ourselves "hereditary ability will give us the answer," when inborn and acquired abilities are both important, and when they are so interfused with one another that nobody can tell for certain where one begins and the other ceases? Clearly, we have been attacking our problem in the wrong way. What is the right one?

The great guiding principle to which our minds should turn in deciding how much schooling a person ought to have, is one with which we are already familiar. We must remember that, whatever is true of *schooling,* education ought to be a life-long process. Will our brilliant Dick have finished his education, when he steps forward to receive his doctor's diploma with its accompanying benediction? Certainly not. If the schools have done at all what they ought to do for him, they will have made it possible for him to go on growing and developing indefinitely. He ought to be a far bigger and abler man twenty years after his official debut into the ranks of scholars, than when he graduated. If not, his schooling is, at least in part, an *educational* failure. And the same is true with Bill. His education, too, must not stop when he leaves school. He will never go so fast, nor so far, as Dick. But the very essence of the matter, even for him, is to keep on going as long as he lives.

Now we may be told that this is all very fine, and perhaps very true, but pretty far-fetched and philosophical; that we are dealing with a concrete, practical problem, and must come down to cases. It may seem that our noble idea about education as a life-long process will not help us much, since the hard fact remains that Dick can go on, with benefit to all concerned, much farther than Bill; and that what we have said is not practical. Is it not? Let us see.

As we are told to be practical, let us forget, for the moment, about education in general, and concentrate on schooling. Let us ask how long Bill ought to stay in school, for he looks like the "problem case" of our two boys. But practical though this question may be, we must still look at it in a broad way. So let us, even at the risk of irritating our critics still more, insist on asking: What is a school for? What is it that Bill and Dick—and more particularly Bill—ought to get out of school? This I have already tried to answer in an earlier chapter. The school stands for opportunity, for freedom from the immediate grind of earning a living; and this in the interest of a better general adjustment to social institutions. It exists to make possible to its pupils a better level of civic, economic, family, recreational, and hygienic activity; to fashion along these, and other lines, a common way of enlightened living. This is the essence of its service, both to pupil and community. So, when we face the question of how long Bill should stay in school, let us understand it in this specific sense: For how many years can he benefit from the services of such an institution? How much service of this kind does he need for his best adjustment to society, and his maximum possible development?

There are just two rules by which we can decide how long Bill, or Dick, or anyone else, ought to stay in school. The first is this. *A child ought to stay in school until he is able to go on growing socially and mentally, after he leaves.* Think of the analogy of a home for convalescents. Such a home provides a special environment. But, if a patient leaves too soon, his health suffers, and he may die. A few weeks more or less, may make all the difference. So with the school. If we take Bill out too soon, his essential education—his growth towards a better and better adjustment to life, his trend towards the achievement of a community of enlightenment—may stop right there. When this happens, we frustrate the very purpose of sending him to school at all. If we can give him two or three years of the right kind of school beyond the sixth grade, we may easily multiply many times the value to him of his whole school experience. And we may make him a far more useful member of society than he could otherwise become.

The second rule is this. *A child should stay in school just as long as he will develop better, and adjust himself to life better, there than out of school.* This means at once that Bill should not be sent to a liberal arts college, and perhaps not to the conventional senior high school. In such an environment, he will be just as much out of place as a man with an income of seventy-five dollars a month in Cartier's jewelry store. He will only fail; and that is bad business all round. But to say that he should not go to school at all beyond the sixth grade is quite another matter. There may be every argument in the world for sending him to a humanely managed school of junior high school type, and letting him spend three or four or more years there, not caring very much whether he graduates or not.

And of course these two rules apply to Dick. They explain why he should continue on to college and graduate school. Of course he might drop out early, and still continue to grow mentally. But his growth would very likely be hampered and hindered. Moreover, the higher institutions are designed for such as he. They are, in a unique sense, *his* environment. They furnish opportunity for doing just those unique things for which nature has fitted him—that is, for dealing with problems of an intellectual and relational kind, and for handling abstract ideas.

So our notions about education as a life-long process do not seem so impractical after all. They give us a clue we need for making up our minds what to do about Bill's schooling, regarded as a part of his education. And here is another idea they suggest for dealing with him. Suppose he stays in school four years beyond the sixth grade, and then goes to work; it may be tremendously beneficial if the school can still keep in touch with him. It can teach him many things he needs to learn, in order to prosper in his vocational, domestic, civic, recreational, and hygienic pursuits and doings. It can stimulate him to wider growth and more intelligent attitudes. Surely to think that, once full time schooling ends, the mission of the school ends too, is a great error. Indeed, it may be able to render him unique and valuable service, chiefly because he has taken his full place in the world and is actually dealing with the real problems of vocation, home life, and so on. This is precisely the idea behind the adult education movement in many countries. And much of the success of the Danish Folk High Schools is due to the fact that the student enters them several years after leaving the elementary school—years usually spent in working on the farm.

"But," we shall be asked, "how do you propose to tell just when the psychological moment has arrived for taking Bill out of school, and putting him to work?" The answer is simple and direct. Only by watching him, and studying his individual reactions to his school environments. *What cannot be done is to tell in advance.* So much has been made of mental tests that many people think they give us far more insight than is actually the case. An intelligence quotient of eighty-five indicates probabilities, but never certainties. It warns us of limitations, and puts us on our guard. But it does not tell us in advance just where these limitations are. Tests are not, and never will be, an adequate substitute for observing, and getting personally to know and understand, human beings. And the ultimate factors of guidance in education, in spite of all the pretentious developments of educational science, still remain the wisdom of parents and teachers.

I have already insisted that our knowledge of Bill's intelligence quotient is very valuable information. It gives us insight into the best means of dealing with him, and warns us what to expect. We have good reason to believe that he will be ready to drop out of full time schooling long before Dick. But we have absolutely no reason for deliberately and arbitrarily limiting his educational opportunities from the start.

Have we now touched bottom in our discussion, and adequately clarified all our ideas? No, there is still another matter of great importance to consider. If we hope that Bill will be educated best by continuing in school some years beyond the sixth grade, we shall have to choose the right kind of school. It must be a school which deliberately and sincerely dedicates itself to creating for its pupils a significant common life; which consistently seeks to foster a dynamic social adjustment, and to develop each individual to the limit of his possibilities. We must think always in terms of his needs, not in terms of preconceived average standards. The ordinary seventh and eighth grades, of the old fashioned kind, will not do at all. Bill has no need of square and cube root and long dreary reviews on formal grammar. He has no need of subject matter at all for its own sake. He ought to be in the kind of school environment of which I have already spoken so often in these pages, where he does all kinds of interesting and stimulating things; where he has contact with art, and music, and literature; where he learns, by direct experience, at least a little of the scientific attitude towards life, even though he cannot grasp the scientific techniques; where his social and civic horizons are broadened; where he finds manifold opportunities for growth which will never be his, if he is condemned to the tender mercies of a blind alley job and the association of pool-room loafers.

It should be expressly pointed out that what Bill needs is not a school where the conventional subject matter standards are deliberately cut. The solution of his problem does not lie in teaching easy algebra, easy Latin, easy science, easy history, and so forth. Nothing can really be gained by denaturing the academic curriculum. What is wanted is a school where the primary emphasis is not upon subject matter learning for examination purposes; a school where he will find a wide variety of stimulating and worth while experiences, and where he will be free to proceed at his own pace; a school where there will not be too great an anxiety about his standing relative to others, so long as he continues to grow; in a word, a school which seeks to educate and develop him, rather than to mark and grade and regiment him.

4. *What determines the kind of education a child should have?*

Another step we must take in organizing a better distribution of educational opportunity, is to give each child the *kind* of education he needs. And again, this must depend on the sort of person he is. Since individuals differ, it would seem unwise to plan an exactly similar education for all of them. But once more, blind mass forces cannot give us a satisfactory solution. For instance, it often happens that a boy attends a vocational high school, simply because he happens to live near it. This is clearly wrong. Everything should depend on his genuine needs as an individual. What then are those needs? And how may they differ with different people? Let us discuss our problem again in connection with our plans for our two charges, Bill and Dick.

At the outset, it is clear that they can, and probably will, lead very different lives. All through their years on this earth, they may be expected to do very different things. And the difference will be that the bright boy will concern himself far more with abstract ideas, and relationships, and what we call intellectual interests of all kinds. This will probably express itself in the sort of job he undertakes. Dick may become a research scientist, or a teacher, or a clergyman, or may deal with the managerial or financial problems of industry. Bill will perhaps become a common laborer or a routine clerk. And the difference in the two lives will go far beyond the realm of vocation. Dick may, later on, be summoned to Washington to advise on complex issues of governmental policy, while Bill is limited in civic matters to discussing candidates for office, and canvassing local affairs in a humble way. They will differ in the things they read, and in how they read them. They will tend towards different recreational interests, even though both have the same amount of money to spend. Their home lives are likely to present quite diverse pictures. And so one might go on. Always the trend of the one will be towards intellectual activities of all sorts—towards the manipulation of ideas and the solution of problems. This is the difference which nature has made between them.

Nevertheless, there will still be great and fundamental similarities. For both of them, successful living means an adjustment to the same range of institutions. Both of them must sustain relationships towards the economic system, towards the state, towards the family, towards the institutions of recreation and the preservation of health. The flexibility, the creativeness, of their relationships will, presumably, be different. Dick may make a far greater contribution than Bill. Dick may be a leader in many realms, and Bill a follower. But in so far as their adjustment to society is satisfactory at all, the identical elements in their lives will bulk much larger than those in which they differ.

Now, these similarities and divergencies need to be reflected in their education, which, remember, is not a preparation for, but a part of, their living. We take them at the age of six, an arbitrary point. Immediately the divergencies begin to show up. One learns to read quickly, and enjoys reading more and more; the other does not. One is keenly interested in the numerical aspects of existence, and loves to count and calculate; the other finds even the simplest mathematics troublesome. One grows fascinated by the general principles of science; the other hardly delves beneath the obvious surface. When one is dealing with beings so different—and practical teachers must do so—it is very tempting to say that they should be segregated in special environments, and each given a different sequence of education.

Yet we must never forget that their resemblances are greater than their differences; that their common humanity and common need is far more significant than their idiosyncrasy. Both need to live in an environment specially adapted to favor their full, rounded, social adjustment. To be sure, within that environment, they will not move at precisely the same speed, or do precisely the same things. Dick will accomplish far more in a year, and be much further ahead by the end of six, or ten, or twelve years of schooling, than Bill. Their education must not be identical, in the sense of being a lock-step affair. But it should be identical in that the general range of material studied, and above all, the purpose for which that material is taught, will be the same for both. For each of them, the core of education must be a grasp upon the meanings of our social structures, an understanding of and adjustment to the institutions of society in the midst of which their lot is cast.

The great error to avoid is that of supposing we can get a better distribution of educational opportunity by organizing our schools in some sort of water-tight compartments; and, on the basis perhaps of mental tests, or some other simple index, put Bill into one compartment, and Dick into another. Proposals of this kind are constantly being made. They look very practical and sensible, until we remember that human beings have similarities much more important than their diversities, and that human life is much the same for all of us. When we analyze such proposals with this thought in mind, their practicality and wisdom begin to seem much more dubious. Let us consider three of them.

A. It might seem obvious to send Bill and Dick to two quite different kinds of school, where they would be segregated with others like themselves and taught what might be considered an appropriate and special curriculum. But here we must hesitate. To do this will certainly involve great risks, and may defeat our educational benevolence. For both of them, the ultimate goal of education is precisely the same. Both need to achieve a working, and—so far as possible—an enlightened adjustment to the problems of the social environment. And each one faces a peculiar danger. The danger for the bright boy is that he may grow up into a pure and unmitigated intellectual, so fascinated with the techniques of reason that he loses all touch with reality. If this happens, his education has failed. He turns into a pedant, not an educated man. For we cannot too often recall that education is not the same thing as the acquisition of intellectual facility. A person may be born a mental dynamo; but this does no real good to others or to him, unless he is connected up to the social mechanism. The danger for the dull boy is that he may never achieve any enlightenment at all. If he is just taught subject matter in a routine way, he may make some kind of a showing—that is, he may scrape through his courses. But he is apt not to become educated. What he needs is to be placed in an environment where his social horizons are widened, where he learns by actual experience what it means to live an enlightened life. Moreover, such an environment is exactly what the bright boy needs. Somehow we must try to get him to hitch his intellect to the actual problems of living. There is only one evident and hopeful way of doing this. Put him in a significant social environment, where he carries an active part. And encourage him to do his thinking about the problems he finds there.

So, as we argue the matter through, there seem cogent reasons for sending both our boys to the same school. Of course, it must be the right kind of school. It must not be a place where children are expected to master standardized subject matter in standard time, and flunked if they fail. This will be unfortunate for both our charges, breeding in one a sterile pride of intellect, in the other an unwarranted sense of inferiority. It must be a place where diversified opportunities for experience are provided, and where these experiences are rendered luminous by being brought into touch with, and interpreted in terms of, the intellectual resources of civilization. Later on, it may be, our boys will specialize. One may go out to a job, while the other continues in college. But at first, and for a long time, a common educational environment, leading them into a common way of enlightened living, will be our choice for both.

B. Someone who knows our experiment may tell us that we should give the bright boy a "cultural" education and the dull boy a "vocational" education. What are we to think of this idea? Certainly it seems to fit in with many prejudices and preconceptions. Our friend speaks to us with what appears to be the voice of sweet reason. "This dull boy," he says, "perhaps will not even become a white collar worker. He may spend his life as a street sweeper, or a hod carrier, or a farm laborer. Why give him a taste for music, and art, and literature? What should he have to do with science and mathematics? The best thing for him is to teach him a trade, and then to find him a job. As for the bright boy, why should he learn to run a lathe, or fix a system of electric wiring? He should spend his time on mathematics, pure science, foreign language, literature, and other such studies."

How reasonable this sounds! And how entirely wrong it is! To be sure, a cultured farm laborer, or an educated ditch digger may seem to us like an oddity. But this only proves the falsity of our ideas about culture and education. If culture only means conventional ornamentation, then we cannot desire it for our dull boy. *But we cannot desire it for anyone else.* If, on the other hand, it means the enlightenment of action through the intellectual resources of civilization, then everyone should have it, including farm laborers and ditch diggers, and, in their own limited measure, low grade morons. We cannot possibly agree that there is one kind of education—"cultural" education—suitable for the naturally bright; and another kind—"vocational" education—suitable for the naturally dull.

Just as no education is purely cultural, so no genuine education can be purely vocational. A purely vocational education would be one wholly confined to some of the techniques of industry—for instance, those of the machinist's trade. If we teach our dull boy some of these skills, we have indeed served, and genuinely educated him, by opening to him new vistas of living. But this should most certainly not be the chief, or only, content of his education. Even if he becomes a machinist, his life will not be all job. He will also sustain civic, economic, and family relationships, and recreational and hygienic interests. To ignore them is surely to do violence to his essential humanity, and needlessly to limit his horizons.

Furthermore, these techniques of industry should certainly have a place in the education of the bright boy. He may be moving in the direction of white collar employment. Industrial skills may not have the same place in his life that they do in the life of the dull boy. Nevertheless, to have had the experience of working cooperatively in a shop, of assembling and disassembling and repairing equipment, of making and mending, will almost certainly be of lasting significance to him. It will tend to make him a different sort of person, to broaden his sympathies, and to give him a better understanding of the true meanings of life, and the ways in which human beings behave.

So our conclusion must be that to differentiate between a cultural and a vocational education for our two boys is vicious. Education is always both cultural and vocational. Its aim is a flexible adjustment to the problems of life, among which is the problem of earning a living.

C. Another piece of advice might be to educate the dull boy to be a follower, and the bright boy to be a leader. What looks like a strong argument can be presented here. The dull boy, it will be said, is bound to be the sort of person who takes orders, rather than gives them; who carries through the plans of others, rather than initiating plans of his own. His virtue is that of obedience and conformity. And it is contended that this calls for a kind of education markedly different from that of a person destined to create and to lead. He should be taught, of course, to read and write and handle numbers. But beyond that, our chief effort should be to give him sound ideas and docile attitudes. Only safe notions should fill his head. No effort should be made to get him to think for himself. Dangerous thoughts should be carefully avoided. Much should be made of imitation and passive absorption. Above all, he should not be educated "above his station." This will be our best and kindest plan for him.

Certainly, if we believe the educational gospel of the nineteenth century philanthropists, this will seem wise to us. They definitely held that, while the "common man" must receive some education, he ought not to have too much. The great aim, as they saw it, should be to make him a conforming person, amenable to the direction of his betters. He should be educated for that walk in life to which God—or, as we might put it today, heredity—had manifestly called him. And this is by no means unpopular doctrine at the present time. In essence, it is the claim that there must be one kind of education for followership, and another for leadership.

The trouble with this theory is that it has never seemed to work very well. During the nineteenth century, when the most serious effort was made to apply it, experience quickly showed that the barely literate proletariat was ideal stuff for incendiary movements of the machine-smashing type. Instantly the high tories began pointing the finger of scorn. "This," said they, "is what comes of educating the common people at all!" In a way, they were quite right. If we really want to keep the "lower orders" in their places, and to make them conform to a fixed social pattern, the thing to do is not to educate them at all. The very idea of indoctrinating people with a set of convenient notions, hoping that these will last a lifetime, is most questionable. As soon as you give a person *any* notions, to that extent you lose control of him. For notions are things with which he can do just what he pleases. Once a person begins to think, no matter how dimly, you cannot tell what will happen. He may stop quite soon, to be sure. But he may not. If you try to stop him, you only make him angry. And if you go on trying, and do it hard enough, he will probably try to kill you!

Moreover, the idea of followership as mere conformity is not sound. Unless one is a chattel slave, one must pick one's leaders in order to follow well. Merely to make a man docile, is positively not enough. For he may be docile to the suggestions of the veriest charlatan. And the only way to guard against this is to encourage him to form independent judgments. Moreover, when one has picked a leader, one must understand him in some measure, if one is to be his effective disciple. Following is not just being led by the nose. It is not doing exactly what one is told, without knowing or caring why. It is coöperating. The ideal member of a team is not the blind robot, but the man who could also lead the team. The ideal education for followership in society is precisely the education most suitable for leaders. Between leader and follower there must be a community of understanding, or both will be in a vacuum, and neither can play his part. *Educating people to be leaders and followers means precisely the fashioning for them of a common mode of enlightened action.* The playing fields of Eton were an ideal place for producing the higher commanding officers at Waterloo. But they would also have been an ideal place for the training of the rank and file.

My argument so far has been against planning education in any sort of rigid, water-tight compartments. This is in harmony with the doctrine earlier set forth, that the genius of the school, as a social institution, is to provide a general education. And the reason is simply the essential and substantial identity of human needs. We are, all of us, men first, and different kinds of men afterwards. Notice that I have not for a moment argued that human beings are all alike, or that individual differences are anything but exceedingly important. We must certainly recognize and deal with these individual differences; otherwise we can never have a well conceived and constructive distribution of educational opportunity. But we must not do so by sacrificing the paramount claims of that common way of enlightened living, which is the greatest of our common necessities.

Let me try concretely to say what I think we ought to do. It will not be done all in a moment, for a great deal more is involved than introducing some new administrative device or technique. It is something towards which we must work with hope, and faith, and achieve little by little. We must seek to create a common system of schools which shall have three outstanding characteristics.

1. First, our schools will be organized about a common curriculum designed to fashion a common way of life. All children will study this curriculum. Its central element will be, I believe, the social sciences, broadly understood as a direct interpretation of human society, and the place of the individual in it. This, above all, is what we should desire for everybody. Music, art, literature, the natural

sciences—each will have its definite relationship to the scheme and its place in the educational core. For notice again, our conception of the sphere of social science will be exceedingly broad. The industrial and recreational techniques, too, will be relevant to the scheme. And our central endeavor will be to produce socially minded men and women. Contrast this with the conventional program of studies, organized essentially about a linguistic core, which is of value to the few rather than to the many. Many of the problems which arise in connection with school opportunities for the duller pupils—and many of the suggestions that they do not belong in the "academic" schools—are simply due to the fact that our schools are, in this respect, seriously out of touch with life. To put it bluntly, there is no good reason for advocating a highly linguistic education for everybody. But there is an excellent reason for advocating a vital social education for everybody.

Second, our schools will be organized to permit an increasing latitude of choice, as the pupils pass on to higher and higher levels. At first, the core curriculum will be the whole story. Until the end of high school, or even the second year of college, it will be the chief part of the story. Specialization will come little by little. It will never be determined in advance. The pupil must learn, and reveal, his own interests and tendencies, before specialization can be educationally significant. His special interest must not be a mere arbitrary whim. He must see it in relationship to the grand business of living, if it is to be educationally constructive. He must grow into his choices, by a growth of mind which essentially means a social insight ever broader and deeper; he must not be arbitrarily pushed, or allowed to fall, into them.

Third, our schools must be organized to permit the individual child to move at his own pace, and to achieve whatever he achieves. He must not either be retarded or accelerated for the sake of keeping with the mass. Whenever this happens, his unique and precious individuality is sacrificed. But his free educational tempo must not mean mere individualism or any lack of social opportunity and contact. In the next chapter, I shall discuss some of the practical problems of school organization which this involves.

5. *Are there hereditary special abilities?*

A most important question, which lurks behind the discussions of our previous sections, is that of the existence and nature of special abilities. Are there people who are born linguists, or mathematicians, or artists, or musicians, or scientists, or actors, or executives? Are there definite special abilities, which derive from heredity? This is a question of immense moment for education. If we want to help a child to make the most of himself, if we want to give him the utmost educational opportunity, few things could be more significant than to know that he was born with some special talent. His whole adjustment to life, his whole contribution to society, may well depend on discovering it early, and bringing it to full fruition.

Our question seems to turn upon a matter of fact. So indeed it should. But, if we put it bluntly to psychologists and anthropologists, just the people who ought to know about it, we are likely to get disappointingly vague answers. A great deal of quite complicated research has been done on the psychology of special abilities. But we certainly cannot say that the existence of such abilities, and their dependence upon heredity, has been established clearly as a general proposition. The position which it seems wise for those interested in education to take is that, while special abilities may exist and may be innate, they do not play a great part in the lives of the vast majority of people, and are not nearly so important practically as we might suppose.

Let us consider the case which seems strongest of all in favor of hereditary special ability, the case of the great genius. Surely a Händel, or a Mozart, must be a born musician; a Michael Angelo a born sculptor; a Napoleon a born general; an Abraham Lincoln a born leader and governor of men. This seems very plausible. And yet—what we actually know about the mental processes of such men, and how they acquired them, is extraordinarily limited. The great creative genius seems to be a man to whom ideas come, he knows not how. Shortly after the Battle of the Aisne, when the Western Front had become immobile, Joffre was asked what he thought Napoleon might have done with the situation. His reply was, "He would probably have thought of something." This puts it perfectly. Michael Angelo was a man who was constantly thinking of things in terms of plastic form. Mozart was a man who thought of things in terms of tonal patterns. According to the legend of the falling apple, Newton's whole system of physics sprang from a bright idea. Lincoln was, at least in his later years, a clairvoyant in government. But how this strange, and seemingly chance ability comes about—how much is due to heredity, and how much to environment—nobody seems to know. In some cases, long years of discipline seem absolutely necessary before any distinguished work can be done. In others, the ability seems to spring up fully, or almost fully developed. We do not know what makes the genius —the man of special ability *par excellence*. And no inference can be drawn from ignorance.

The greatest difficulty in the way of believing in hereditary special abilities is that it seems very much like a return to the old faculty psychology, with nothing more than a change of name. Every argument against faculty psychology can be turned against this newer doctrine of special abilities.

A. In the first place, it should be clear that whenever a person sets out to do something, he uses, not some special subdivision of his mind, but the whole of it. Consider, for example, such seemingly diversified activities as musical creation, mathematical investigation, and the use of a foreign language. Psychologically speaking, they are not nearly so different as they seem. Every one of them involves reasoning, analysis, and the perception of relationships. Feeling and emotion play a tremendous part in the experience of the working mathematician, who finds the purest joy in a beautiful demonstration or a striking discovery. Purpose and aim must be present in all three. What we seem to see is not the operation of three quite different mechanisms, but the integral human mind, bringing to bear all its varied and intricate capacities in three different situations.

B. In the second place, we know beyond a doubt that if a man is able to do very well in one kind of task, he will almost always be able to do well in many others. If a child succeeds in algebra, you may be pretty sure that he is able also to succeed in Latin. If he does very well in science, there is no inner necessity for him to fail in English. Versatility, rather than specialization, is most certainly the general rule. To be sure, we must not push this to wild extremes. It is not in the least likely that Beethoven could have duplicated his musical achievement if he had become a surgeon; or that Scott would have been as famous a lawyer as he was a novelist. But we must remember that first rate fame is a very complex thing, and depends on many factors. A man who becomes a great and immortal figure in some field, might be no more than an ordinary respectable success, if he were born at the wrong time, or failed to make connections with the right opportunity. Again, to come back to the more ordinary case of the child in school, the fact that a pupil succeeds in Latin does not make it certain that he will succeed equally in mathematics. He may be badly taught, or his interests may be elsewhere. In a college where there is a conservatory of music, it usually happens that the music students do worse in their academic courses than the college students. This, however, proves nothing about their actual abilities. For the difference probably depends on the way they prefer to spend their time, and the interests they have developed and sustained over a period of years.

C. If it is difficult to believe in definite hereditary abilities, like the old-time faculties, to think of such abilities as corresponding to the structure of the conventional curriculum is a downright absurdity. Yet this is one of the most general of our educational superstitions. One person is supposed to have a special inborn ability in mathematics, another in English, another in foreign language, another in science, and another in history. This is a wild *non sequitur*. The curriculum is an administrative scheme for the convenient handling of subject matter, not a blueprint of the human mind. The way the subjects are divided in your school catalog corresponds not at all with the lay-out of anybody's mental abilities. No such pretty pre-established harmony as this exists. Possibly there are some arguments in favor of hereditary special abilities. But there is no argument, in science or in common sense, for an array of such abilities corresponding one by one to the departmental offerings of a high school or a college.

This very beautifully explains the *impasse* encountered when we try to predict in advance a pupil's success in some particular subject in high school or college. Suppose we want to foretell whether a given person is likely to do well in Latin. We look around for a set of so-called prognosis tests. A few years ago, a battery of these tests was in fact put together. It did predict success in Latin fairly well. But then the investigator found that it predicted success in other subjects still better! There is, to be sure, one way in which probable success in such a subject as Latin can be foretold with a good deal of certainty. We can put together a test made up of simple problems, exactly similar to those which the pupil will have to face in our Latin course. This will reveal the future pretty well. But while it is practically useful, psychologically it is a *reductio ad absurdum*. What it really means is that a person who does well in a Latin course, does well in it, and *vice versa*. For our test does not deal at all with general abilities, but is a sort of preface to the course itself. And if we changed our teaching methods—say by using the direct method—our test would cease to help us.

D. Finally, the belief in hereditary special abilities, like the belief in faculties, really explains nothing that we need to know. A child does well in algebra. Why? Because he has good mathematical ability. Another one fails in foreign language. Once more: Why? Because he has little linguistic capacity. Are such statements explanations at all? Certainly not. They are the merest camouflage for ignorance. They are just ways of saying in new words what we already know—namely, that the students succeed and fail in these subjects. They do not begin to tell us why.

And the ideas underlying such explanations are dangerous. Pupils and teachers constantly use them to alibi failure, and to justify lack of enterprise. An enormous number of able students graduate from high school, and enter college, quite convinced that they have no mathematical ability; which belief simply inhibits them from ever trying to master mathematics. But, as a matter of fact, there is probably no such thing as innate mathematical ability at all; and at least ninety-five out of every hundred people bright enough to get through college, could master the subject up to differential equations, given a reasonable chance. Many a student specializing in science, rather prides himself on lacking "historical" or "literary" ability, and takes a low grade in courses in history and English as right and proper. Musicians, artists, and scientists are often regarded (and sometimes regard themselves) as beings possessing some strange power not common to humanity in general. This is all superstition, all mythology. It all illustrates the tremendous power of mere names over human thought and action.

Squarely stated, then, our position is that hereditary special abilities, if they exist at all, are not particularly important in connection with education. If a pupil does extremely well in science, and very badly in English, this is probably not because he was born that way. It is much more likely to be due to differences in preparation, interest, and response to the kind of teaching provided. For education and for life, the really important hereditary differences are those in general ability, in the general power to learn, and to adapt oneself to new situations.

By and large, all men have pretty much the same kind of minds. But they differ in degree, or altitude, of mental ability. So again we see how strong are the claims of general education. If people had definite special abilities and disabilities about which nothing could be done, the argument for segregating them would be far stronger than it is. If the human mind were divided into faculties, perhaps human education could well be divided into compartments. But the mind is the agency for social adjustment. The great need of life is a better social adjustment shared by all men. The great aim of education is the up-building of the common mind in the interests of the common life.

Chapter 12

HOW MAY WE DEAL WITH THE PROBLEM OF THE INDIVIDUAL?

1. *What is the problem of the individual?*

Education has to do, first and foremost, with the individual—with his mental growth—with his adjustment to the demands of social living. But the educational mechanism, that is to say, the school, as it commonly exists, is designed to deal with the mass. Here arises the practical problem of the individual.

A great many schools are operated, not for the sake of developing the individual, nor for securing his best and most complete growth, but in the interests of a smoothly running administrative scheme. The administrative staff, perhaps in conspiracy with some group of school surveyors, draws a line. Then the job consists in hewing to it, and letting the chips fall where they may—the chips being the pupils! In a great many schools, pupils are treated in the precise spirit in which a California fruit grower deals with his oranges. Uniform conditions of fertilization, watering, air, light, and heat are provided. Then, after an appropriate interval, the fruit is harvested the product sorted and graded, and the culls thrown away. A mass of subject matter is blocked out. It is parcelled into subdivisions, supposed to be fairly suitable to each grade. The processing is carried a step farther by the teachers, who work it up into specific daily assignments. These are applied to the pupils, who assimilate whatever they assimilate. Recitations and tests are set up to find out how much has soaked in. And certificates of competency, of various degrees of value, are issued on the basis of the results. This is supposed to be education.

If you have followed the argument I have tried to present in these pages so far, you will be aware of the many weaknesses of such a way of doing things. But its absurdity becomes nothing less than glaring when we ask about its effect on the individual. Here it completely fails; for it is a system devised for obtaining mass results, rather than for promoting to the uttermost the personal growth of unique human beings, each with his own peculiarities, possibilities, and needs. Whenever the system touches the individual human life, which is the very stuff of education, it fumbles the issue more or less disastrously.

Consider what the conventionally managed school does with the dull pupil—the pupil who, perhaps, fails to assimilate the right amount of knowledge at the right time. Does it ask whether the subject matter it supplies is suited to the aptitudes and needs of such a pupil? Certainly not. It works on the assumption that education consists in learning set tasks in a given time to a given level of mastery. The pupil who does not do this is labelled a failure; and if such failure is often enough repeated, the machine either throws him out or edges him out. Now the task of the school is to adjust this person to life, and to develop his powers to a maximum. Has it done so by presenting him with a bouquet of failing grades? If it can manage nothing better than this, then we are bound to say that the school, rather than the pupil, has failed.

Nor does its treatment of the unusually bright pupil show much more rhyme or reason. If such a pupil receives any exceptional treatment at all, it is likely to be one of two kinds; either he is allowed to progress more rapidly than usual through the school, or he is given what is known as an "enriched curriculum" of studies. And, under the system, neither method is satisfactory. Suppose that a very bright pupil is allowed to complete the twelve grades of work in eight years. We know that this can be done, and that, in spite of the shorter time he spends, he may still assimilate as much, or even more subject matter than the average. But is it sound and sane education? I do not think so. The bright pupil is just the one for whom the school should do most; to whom the opportunity to live, and to work, in a selected educational environment should mean most; who has the most impressive possibilities for wide and splendid growth. But all the school actually does is to speed his way over the hurdles, and give him its blessing. Clearly, it has lost a great opportunity for human service, in its preoccupation with a standard performance.

Would it, then, be wiser to "enrich" his studies, and hold him in school for the full twelve years? Yes, indubitably, if the enrichment were real. What such a person needs above all, is freedom to develop and follow out his own interests under constructive guidance, to enter upon and enjoy new experiences, to live creatively. A school which offers this, confers upon him a priceless, a life-long boon. But, under the conventional system, nothing of the sort takes place. All that is done is to give the bright child more set tasks, to keep him occupied, and prevent him from becoming a nuisance. Anything more radical would tend instantly to disrupt the smooth administrative scheme. And such enrichment is not real at all, but spurious.

Let me drive home again our central thought by repeating it. The conventionally organized school makes itself ridiculous, when it has to deal with the unique individual, for the very good reason that it is designed to deal with the mass. It is the case of the fruit grower all over again. Such a school sets up uniform standards, nicely adjusted in such a way that the great majority of pupils can meet them without too much trouble. It does not bother unduly about the freaks and the culls. Indeed, a certain amount of judicious flunking may not be considered a bad thing. Like decimation in the army, it may encourage the others. So long as the great majority ripen nicely in the given time, and show up at commencement with shining faces and appropriate garments, such a school counts itself a success. These are they who have gone through the great and standardized tribulation, who have swallowed the dose, and passed the examination. To what degree the school has in any true sense educated them, might be too cruel a question for so festive an occasion.

It is abundantly clear that, if we want a system of education which shall adjust each individual pupil to the needs of life, all this must be changed. You may even be inclined to ask whether I would recommend giving up school education altogether, and resorting to some tutorial scheme. But this is far from desirable. The school can most certainly deal with the individual, and can do it better than any other educational mechanism of which we are now aware. But it must give up the ideals of mass procedure, in gross and in detail. It must rethink and reorganize its processes. In the balance of this chapter, I shall try to show at least the general direction in which it must move. I hope that this discussion may lead to a new understanding of our entire account of education. For there is no point at which a really functional educational theory more sharply challenges the preconceptions, and established procedures of the conventional school, than this one of dealing adequately with the individual.

2. *How may class teaching meet individual needs?*

The demands and necessities of the individual can be met in the class, only when we think of it, and operate it, as an opportunity for social experiences of an educative type. This is the true meaning and value of class organization as an educational instrument. Certainly it is very different from the practice we commonly find in the conventional school.

Class organization, as it exists almost universally today, is a comparatively new thing. Before the nineteenth century, most teaching used an individual method. Pupils of various ages and degrees of attainment, were huddled together in a sort of mob, under the supervision of the teacher. Each child worked at his own task. From time to time he was called on to recite. He went to the teacher's desk; deposited his book on it; turned his back; and proceeded to repeat his lesson. The teacher's job was to check upon each pupil in this way, and, at the same time, keep order in the room. Clearly, it was a most inefficient procedure. There could be little or no real teaching, in the sense of helping the child to learn better. The task of keeping the unclassified drove of pupils reasonably quiet was a very difficult one. And this explains, in part at least, why discipline was so very severe, and why physical strength was an important part of a teacher's qualifications.

An educational movement which did much to reorganize instruction, and to bring about class work as we now understand it, was the celebrated Monitorial School Plan already described, which was put into operation, in this country and in Europe, by Bell and Lancaster. The essence of the plan was a grouping of the pupils to render possible their instruction by the monitors. It was a highly business-like scheme for one purpose, and one only; to get a certain amount of material into the heads of the pupils in a given time. The plan attracted considerable favorable attention when it first appeared. Certainly it gave the school a much more civilized appearance than that of the tumultuous bear gardens of an earlier and rougher day. And, above all, it was cheap. Lancaster's ideal was a system by which one teacher could deal with a thousand pupils. In practice, it proved possible to handle groups of several hundred. And the expense for thus "educating" one pupil, for a school year, might be almost as low as a dollar.

The time has certainly gone by when many people would feel much enthusiasm for such a scheme for educating their children. One might almost be tempted to call it a *reductio ad absurdum* of a certain conception of class instruction. Yet, are not a great many schools doing pretty much the same kind of thing in a more sophisticated way? We certainly would not be willing to give groups of younger children over to the tender mercies of their older comrades, who could, at best, act only as animated phonograph records. Yet what shall we say of plans in some of our great school systems, where each day's work for every class is laid down in advance by the administrative staff, and where everything is supposed to move forward with the ruthless precision of a factory assembly line? What shall we say of supervisory regulations which make the teacher unwilling to follow up any side lines, however interesting, or to entertain any suggestions or contributions from pupils, because to do so may make it difficult to stick to the schedule of subject matter to be covered? And even though a great many schools are not organized down to the last button with such devastating efficiency, is not the class very commonly treated as a group of pupils conveniently arranged for the covering of a given amount of ground in a given time? Are not many of our practices in regard to assignments, recitations, tests, and grading, obviously based on this conception? While these things are so, the worst of the spirit of Bell and Lancaster still lives in our public schools.

Now this is the abuse, rather than the use, of the class opportunity. It makes provision for the individual impossible, except by "flunking" the dull, and keeping the brighter ones quiet till the average has caught up. This is so, because any such scheme simply does not envisage education as the developing of the individual child. It is dominated by the false idea that education consists in assimilating certain things in a certain order. It glorifies the machine, instead of the child.

When we try to think of education realistically, the use of the class as a convenience for driving everybody through the same stint in lock-step, seems nothing short of crazy. Suppose I happen to be reading the public prints rather widely with a genuine interest in modern political or economic movements; it will mean a great deal to me to get together with a few other people likewise interested, and talk things over. Or suppose two or three children are having the Idylls of the King read to them at home; before we know it, they will be playing games in which one will be Launcelot, another one Arthur, another Merlin, and so on. Such a group experience has unique possibilities in bringing their reading to life. Now whenever we visit a school, and see the familiar spectacle of children brought together in classes, we have before us just so many ready-made, golden opportunities for undertakings of this kind. The only reason why we fail to recognize them is that the eyes of our imagination are blinded by the conventions of routine school keeping. When the best thing we can think of to do with a group of children is to assign them uniform daily tasks, and then check up to find out how well those tasks have been accomplished, we miss a splendid and obvious chance for genuine education. The essential meaning of the class should be an opportunity for such social experiences.

Let me try to illustrate a little more in detail how this conception of the class may be, and in fact is being worked out and applied. A fifth or sixth grade group has been reading about the Vikings in their work in history. They have been collating and discussing source material, making maps, collecting pictures, and so on. Then they decide to organize a "Viking Day." This takes much planning. The room is rearranged to represent a banqueting hall. Properties are assembled. Parts are written up and assigned. And at last the time comes for the occasion, and all participate, each one according to his ability and interest, in an experience of obvious educative appeal and value. Contrast this use of the class opportunity with the common practice of concluding a unit of content with a conventional test.

Again, we have a junior high school class in English composition. We know that the greatest single problem in connection with this subject is to get the pupil really to want to say *something* to *somebody*. A mere routine composition, written for the teacher to read and mark, has a minimal value. Here again, the class furnishes opportunity ready-made. We require a considerable amount of oral composition, in which the pupil must present a topic briefly to the group before writing it up. At once we have created the vitally needed "audience situation." Here is a far better use of class time, than merely lecturing and reciting on grammatical principles, coaching laggards, scolding the lazy, and commending the industrious.

Again, we have a senior high school class in English literature. Probably one of our chief ambitions will be to develop a taste for the great masterpieces and an inclination to read more widely. And group experience is a powerful and natural agency for the achievement of such aims. Let us stimulate and encourage pupils to tell the others about what they have read, and why they have enjoyed or disliked it. Let us have frequent and well-planned contributions from pupils. Let us do considerable reading aloud of choice items, for the sake of appreciation, followed by discussions of their meaning and excellencies. In a word, let us treat our class as an opportunity for a *literature hour,* rather than as a chance to probe into the pupil's mastery of the footnotes.

Here is a class in mathematics. Some of the pupils have been reading collateral about the great mathematicians, or the applications of mathematics to astronomy and physics. Others have been trying to find different ways of developing a proof or solving a problem. We run our class as a sort of mathematics club, where all these matters, and many others like them, may be talked over as between reasonable and interested human beings. What a blessed relief from the deadly tyranny of "seat work" and "board work," and the daily stint of mangled problems and faulty computations! And how infinitely more educative!

So I might go on; for we have a conception here which applies to almost all phases of school work. Practically all learning benefits by such social opportunities. All really interested learners tend to seek them, and enjoy, and benefit by them. And the class organization offers them to us all the time. Notice in particular how this bears upon the individual and his uniqueness. No longer is he forced into an arbitrary mould and blamed when it does not fit him. No longer is he just one of a mass, all receiving uniform treatment. But neither is he dealt with in isolation, or on the basis of his solitary whims and tendencies. On the contrary, he is a sharer of a group enterprise. He contributes according to his powers. And he benefits by the contributions of others. He has a responsibility to his fellows. And they have one to him. What he does may be, and will be, different in some degree, and perhaps greatly different, from what anyone else in the group will, or can do. And this becomes a benefit rather than a misfortune. He is able to be uniquely himself, to realize himself fully in his school work, precisely because he is a contributor to a genuine social situation, rather than a mere unit going through the mill. His individuality becomes significant through its social relationships.

It is in this sense that we must rethink and reconstruct class work, if we wish to do a real job of education and to deal adequately with the individual. Instead of classes, set up as mechanisms for the orderly mastery of a sequence of subject matter, we must have constructively active social groups.

3. *How may individual instruction meet individual needs?*

You must not suppose that thoughtful teachers, principals, and superintendents are insensitive to the need for beginning always with the individual child, and giving him the amplest opportunities to develop in his own way and at his own pace. On the contrary, they are keenly aware of it, and are anxiously searching for ways and means of meeting it. One piece of good evidence for this is that a great many schools are turning away, either partially or altogether, from the old fashioned class, with its lock-step uniformity of timed assignments, and are substituting various schemes of individual work.

Perhaps the most widely known of all these schemes is that organized by Miss Helen Parkhurst, at Dalton, Massachusetts, and called the "Dalton Laboratory Plan." In a "Dalton school" there is almost no class work at all. Each pupil is given a month's assignment in every subject he is studying, laid out in detail on a mimeographed sheet. Instead of the ordinary classrooms, we find study rooms, set aside for each subject offered by the school, and known as "laboratories." Each room is furnished with a departmental library and with various implements and conveniences for study. And a teacher is in charge of each one. The pupils go individually to these study rooms, or laboratories, just as they please, and put through their assignments, calling on the teachers for help as they find they need it. They are free to organize their work, and "budget their time" just as they like. If a boy wants to do so, he may work at nothing but algebra for the whole first week of the month, and complete his entire assignment in the subject. Or he may space his algebra throughout the month, in whatever way seems best to him. The only general requirements are that the pupils shall work during school hours, and that they shall show up with completed assignments at the end of each month. Of course, this is not a complete and detailed account of the plan. Its administration is quite a complicated matter; and not all schools which have adopted it handle matters in just the same way. But its essential idea is what I have described.

The Dalton Plan has been put into operation in a good many American schools. And it has had an enthusiastic reception abroad, particularly in England. But it involves such a very complete upheaval and reconstruction that many people sympathetic with its underlying purpose hardly feel able to undertake it, And there are other schemes of individual work, which do not call for such radical and sweeping changes in the whole structure of the school.

Typical among these is the plan put into effect at Detroit. Here the children in the grades meet together in groups which outwardly look much like ordinary classes. But the work is planned in such a way that each pupil is occupied with his own task, so that, while all of them may start at the same point at the beginning of the term, yet within six or eight weeks, there may be as many as twenty or thirty quite different study jobs going on in the same room, under the supervision of a single teacher. This is made possible by the way in which the assignments are given. For instance, the work in arithmetic is arranged in a series of definite unit tasks, each dealing with a single new element. The pupils are supplied with printed or mimeographed sheets, on which these units are laid out, with very complete instructions. In this way, they all do their own studying, without any general class recitation at all. Moreover, the assignment sheets contain tests which the pupil can tackle whenever he is ready. So it is made possible for him not only to carry through his own study, but to check his own progress. He finds out for himself when he has mastered each unit. Or, if he fails in the first attempt, the assignment material is so laid out that he is able to locate his error, and to find additional drill material for putting it right. He goes on to a new unit only when he has mastered the previous one. There is no such thing as failure. But everyone moves at his own pace. The teacher is in attendance, not to hear lessons, but to assist the learners when they need help, and to time, and otherwise organize, their work. This plan has been put into operation in many parts of America, and also in foreign countries. It has been applied to a considerable number of school subjects. Experience with it has shown that an expert teacher can supervise the individual work of as many as forty children in a group, though this seems too many for ideal efficiency.

Just as the arrival of the automobile showed a doubting world that a vehicle can move over the road without a horse, so these plans for individual work are a practical demonstration that a school can be run without classes working under the doom of uniform assignments and a rigid time schedule. And, like all authentic inventions, once developed, they seem like no more than applications of common sense. After all, any kind of learning from books is naturally a private affair, though having many social outcomes and deriving benefit from social situations. If you want to master the calculus, there is no obvious necessity for attending a class. All you need is a set of instructions clear enough to follow, some tests which you can apply to yourself, and, if possible, a convenient expert to whom you can appeal when in difficulties. If you are anxious to learn the history of China, there is no need to have someone tell you to read so much by the day after tomorrow, and to threaten you with a test at the end of next week. You look for a good book; you study it at your convenience; and you take whatever measures seem necessary to make sure that you really know what you have read. In any learning of this kind, the fact that some people may go faster, and others slower, than yourself, has nothing to do with the matter. The job is your job, and no one else's. And you do it best if you treat it in this way. This is the working idea back of every worth while correspondence course. And the plans for individual work simply take it over, and make it practically applicable to large numbers of children in a school, at the same time adapting it to the limitations of young children, who need more steering than you. The conventional system of uniform assignments is really quite an absurd procedure for getting people to learn things by reading. And the plans for individual work undertake to substitute something better, and far more natural.

Moreover, it is obvious that these plans of individual work take care of the individual in a way quite impossible in the ordinary class. The bright child moves forward at his own natural pace. The child who is encouraged at home to do a great deal of reading is not held to a sequence of reading assignments, suited perhaps to the average of the group, but quite preposterous for him. The boy who is developing a mathematical mastery by studying the trajectory of rifle bullets, is not made a slave to any lock-step. And the child who needs to take more time than others to master something, is free to do so without humiliation or anxiety. These are very great advantages.

But the besetting weakness of the schemes lies very close to their highest excellence. Individual work is an admirable and natural way of learning subjects from books. But education is precisely not a mere affair of learning subjects from books. It is a growth to a better and better adjustment to the actual problems of life. It is the acquisition of the power to do. The intellectual resources of civilization are, to a large measure, contained within the covers of books. And new books can be written in such a way that children can read and master them with only the incidental tutorial help of teachers. But those intellectual resources are the means of education, not its ends. They exist for one reason only—to render action and adjustment more flexible, more creative, more human. And unless they are acquired in such a way as to bring this about, their acquisition is simply not education at all. Reading, writing, arithmetic, algebra, French, history—these things have no value in and of themselves. Their value is social. The very meaning of their existence lies in the fact that they are the necessities for an adequate adjustment to life.

Here is the great potential weakness of individual work in the schools. It is so efficient a method of organizing book learning and the mastery of subject matter, and it may easily arouse so much enthusiasm in the breasts of teachers, that it may tempt them into forgetting that there is something else, and something much more important, to be done. The Dalton Plan, in particular, has been severely criticized as no more than a tricky device for inducing pupils to learn subject matter faster and better than they will under the regime of class instruction. Certainly this is an ever-present danger. All these schemes can become nothing more than a relapse into the old, vicious individual system, rendered more efficient by the agency of the mimeograph.

What, then, needs to be done? Another forward step needs to be taken. Individual book learning needs to be closely associated with social experience and social undertakings. As Courtis has said, in his comment upon the work at Detroit: ". . . it is apparent that an ideal course of study would consist of two parts: (1) a series of social projects in which there would be need for the use of fundamental skills in meaningful situations, and (2) a series of self-instructive, self-corrective practice exercises, so closely correlated with the project work that children could avail themselves of drill exercises as they became conscious of the need." In short, the needs of the individual will best be served by allowing him to work alone at book learning, and at the same time keeping him in touch with active, coöperative group situations.

4. *What is the value of homogeneous grouping?*

One way in which our schools often try to deal with the problem of the individual is by introducing what is known as homogeneous grouping. The attempt is made to subdivide classes in such a way that pupils will work with those who are of approximately equal ability. The number of sections set up will, of course, differ according to the number of children involved. It may be as few as two, or as many as five. Sometimes a pupil will be assigned to a section merely on the basis of an intelligence test. Sometimes the results of a great many tests are taken into consideration, and much weight given to the personal estimates made by teachers.

Is this scheme a good thing? Does it involve any dangers? Can such dangers be avoided? Does it give both teacher and pupil a better chance for doing a real job of education? These are the questions which we must raise. In trying to answer them it may help us to begin by reminding ourselves of the reason for inventing and introducing the plan of homogeneous grouping. That reason is not at all hard to understand. No one will deny that if we have children in a class who differ very greatly in ability, it will make ordinary teaching very difficult in many ways. In the second grade, we may have some children who can read almost as well as sixth graders, and others who can hardly read at all. What can we do about it? If we try to teach them all in the same way, can we possibly avoid trouble? Indeed, we set out to make it. The bright ones will be bored; the dull ones will be mystified; neither will get what they really need. In ninth grade algebra, we are pretty sure to have some pupils who are really interested in the subject, and who learn fast and well, and others who seem to make virtually no progress and find constant difficulties. Once more, what can we do? If we undertake to teach them all alike, and to "put them through" the same

[1] *National Society for the Study of Education: 24th Yearbook*, p. 112.

lessons in the same time, we simply close our eyes to obvious and vital facts. If we apply any kind of uniform marking, then either we shall have an enormous crop of failures, or we shall have to award passing marks to a great many pupils who are really not acquiring any mastery of the subject. And there is the constant problem of management and discipline—the problem of knowing what to do with the bright pupils who have finished their work, while the duller and slower pupils are still at it.

In the face of such difficulties, it seemed like a good idea to divide classes in such a way that the bright would hive with the bright, and the dull with the dull. The development and wide use of standardized tests provided a ready means of carrying out such sectioning. And the plan has been very widely adopted. But we must certainly not say that homogeneous grouping is desirable, or that it is a real solution of the problem of the individual, just because it is extensively in use. It must not be swallowed whole. Indeed, its very popularity should make us critical and suspicious. Often in education, the easy and obvious way is not the right one. This may be the case here.

Just how have we actually improved matters, when we have divided pupils into sections on the basis of ability? Well, it is evident that we have given the teacher an easier job. If he is working with a "C" section, he no longer has to keep ten per cent of the class marking time, while the others catch up. If he has an "A" section, he is freed, at least to some extent, from the need of doing something about "laggards." But is this really an educational improvement? At least two considerations may make us hesitate to believe it. In the first place, the whole assumption so far clearly is, that education consists in making pupils learn a stint of subject matter in a given time. It is much easier to do this with a group of pupils who do not differ from one another too widely. At least, such a situation will suffice to get rid of some of the most trying difficulties. Indeed, an ideal condition would be one where all the children were exactly alike, so that the entire problem of individuality was eliminated! But, if our primary interest is not in the uniform administration of subject matter—if we no longer care so very much about this—then at any rate some of the advantages of homogeneous grouping will tend to disappear. Then, in the second place, we should notice that what homogeneous grouping does, is to make the teacher's work easier, to relieve him of various awkward problems. But this is assuredly no reason for thinking it educationally advantageous. What if we are dodging the very problems which we ought to tackle? If we ran our schools on the Monitorial Plan, the work of the teacher would be very much simplified; but its effect on the pupil would be very much worse. The real question about homogeneous grouping is: What does it do for the pupil? not: How much does it relieve the teacher?

Have we really helped pupils by classing them with others who resemble them more or less? It is clear at the outset that we *may* have actually hindered them. Suppose we have a boy who is placed in a "C" section. This may be just where he "belongs" in reading. But perhaps, in other studies, he really ought to be in an "A" section. Such a state of affairs is perfectly possible. Indeed, it occurs all the time. Just because a pupil is properly classified in one subject is no reason for thinking he is bound to be properly classified in others. But, in a great many schools where homogeneous grouping is used, the pupil must stay in the same section—slow, medium, or fast—in all his studies. Is this helping him? Of course not. On the contrary, it is hindering him. It is at best a silly, and at the worst, a wicked thing to do. A principal or superintendent who hears that homogeneous grouping is supposed to be a good thing, and then works it in this way, shows a most amazing lack of ordinary intelligence. What would we think of a farmer who learned that ensilage is fine for cows, and then proceeded to feed it to the horses? Yet this is exactly what is done, when homogeneous grouping is rigidly administered, so that the pupil cannot, by any means, budge from that section to which he is assigned. In reading he may be a truck horse, and in arithmetic a racehorse; but always he has the same pabulum. This means a great deal more than ignoring the individual and his uniqueness. It means deliberately working in such a way that he cannot be recognized.

But suppose we avoid this kind of Alice in Wonderland administration. Suppose we have a flexible system, which makes it possible to place the same pupil in one section in English, in another in mathematics, and another in science, and another in music, according to his real abilities. A crass and flagrant error has been avoided. But have we really helped him to learn better? This is a question of fact, not opinion. Does a pupil learn better, when all his classmates are of about equal ability? Or does he learn better if he is in a class where some are much brighter, or much duller, than others? Notice that the point is not the convenience of the teacher, but the performance of the learner. Investigations clearly indicate that there is very little difference. Sometimes learning in a "homogeneous" group seems to go a little better for some pupils. But on the other hand, sometimes learning seems to go better in a "heterogeneous" group. In any case, the difference is not great enough to be decisive. Just grouping as such seems to have very little effect on learning.

So far, the case for homogeneous grouping seems very dark. It is a convenience for the teacher who wants to impart standard doses of subject matter. But if it is rigidly administered, it becomes absurd. And even when carefully handled, it does not greatly or certainly help the child. Shall we then recommend that it be given up? No. What we ought to do is to regard it, not as good in itself, nor as an end in itself, but as a means to an end. When we have sectioned pupils, we have not, by that act, improved their education. But we have created a condition whereby their education may be improved. Homogeneous grouping should be regarded as one way in which the teacher may be helped in his attempt to deal with the individual pupil.

First of all, homogeneous grouping may aid in carrying on individual work of the kind described in the preceding section. It is so used, in fact, in many schools. Obviously, if we arrange to have pupils learn as individuals instead of assigning standard doses of subject matter, we can do a better job if the range of variation in our groups is limited. It is harder to deal with a roomful of individual workers who differ very greatly in speed and ability, than with a roomful where such differences are relatively small. And this is far more than a mere matter of convenience. In individual work, the teacher becomes a coach and a helper. The vital thing is his contact with each separate child. And if he must have on his mind the needs of thirty or forty children, strung out very widely in achievement and capacity, that contact is likely to be diluted. In this way, homogeneous grouping may assist a genuinely educative enterprise.

There is also another way in which homogeneous grouping can be of constructive value. In many kinds of group undertakings, it is natural to pick out people who more or less resemble one another in ability. If one wants to put on a play, one chooses people who can act. If one wants to organize a ball team, one does not grab the first nine human beings one can find. There is a perfect naturalness about this kind of homogeneity. And it should be recognized in many group undertakings, through which the modern school seeks to educate its pupils. I do not mean that every group project, or undertaking, should be carried on by a homogeneous group. Indeed, it is often very valuable and important that they shall not be. For instance, a school assembly may be turned into a business meeting for the discussion of some point of student government. This is as heterogeneous as any group in the school can be. In the same way, part of the value of a "Viking Day" may be exactly the diverse contributions of diverse individuals. The guiding principle ought to be common sense. If we have before us some joint task which calls for somewhat similar powers in all concerned, then this is what we ought to have. Otherwise not. You will notice that this involves carrying the principle of homogeneous grouping much farther than it ordinarily goes in the schools, and above all, making it far more flexible and easily altered than is usual.

Within the last few years, a barrage of criticism has been laid down on homogeneous grouping. Its defenders often ask the critics: What would you substitute for it? But this is not really an intelligent question. The point is not to find some substitute device, some specialized administrative trick, which will do the business better. For this we shall certainly look in vain. We must recognize, first of all, that homogeneous grouping is a perfectly sensible idea. Second, we must understand that, in and of itself, it has no value at all. In this it resembles every other educational device. Thirdly, we must see that it becomes a factor of great and genuine constructive value when properly used. It is improperly used when it is made a convenient way of shirking the problems of class teaching, which are individual problems, and of setting up a more efficient mass procedure. It is improperly used when it becomes a fetish, so that we insist on sectioning pupils, though the heavens fall. It is improperly used when it is made an agency for still more routine teaching of subject matter. It is used properly when it enables the teacher to make a more constructive contact with the individual problems of the individual child, and when it promotes more effective, and more natural group activities.

5. *How shall we administer standards with regard to the individual?*

If education must deal with the individual rather than the mass; if it is an affair of individual growth, the enrichment of individual experience, and progressively enlightened adjustment to the problems of living, how can the schools carry on their highly important function of setting and enforcing standards? How shall we know whether such and such a pupil ought to move from the fourth to the fifth grade? How shall we decide whether he is ready to enter high school? How shall we determine whether he ought to graduate? How shall we make up our minds if he ought to be recommended to college, and permitted to enter? If we really follow our logic to the bitter end, do not all these questions become unanswerable? Must we not simply let each individual do whatever he happens to do, and be content with that? Shall we not reduce the whole educational system to chaos? These are matters which it is vital to discuss. Some constructive answer must be found; or all our implied recommendations will fall to the ground. We must understand how to administer educational standards in the light of the great fact that education is essentially an individual, not a mass, process.

I shall begin discussing the problem before us by presenting three actual cases, a method which has been found instructive and helpful elsewhere.

The first is that of a boy in one of the secondary schools of the British Empire. For certain reasons, over which he had no control and which reflected no discredit upon him, he was not doing very well in his school work. However, he did develop a somewhat remarkable power as a writer. He entered an essay competition, open to all secondary schools throughout the Empire. And, although he had to meet formidable competitors from all parts of the world, he won. Yet, so far as his official school record was concerned, this did him no good. He barely scraped through his college entrance requirements. But his undergraduate career was a brilliant one. And he graduated with highest honors, as the best student of his year. Clearly, there was a great inconsistency between his high school achievement, as registered by the official standards, and the realities of his secondary education. Clearly, too, there is something very far wrong with any administration of standards which can yield such a result.

My second instance is that of a young man in college, who was under consideration, in his senior year, for election to Phi Beta Kappa. He had shown cumulative intellectual achievement and leadership, and a marked growth in initiative and creative ability. But he failed of election, because he had a low grade in a course in French, taken as a requirement during his freshman year. Is not this also a great falsification? Does it not indicate that the fraternity chapter was working in terms of quite a wrong notion of what educational standards really are? In refusing to honor this student for such a reason, it revealed something none too flattering about its own point of view.

My third instance is one I have already mentioned in another connection.[2] It is that of the famous English soldier and adventurer, T. E. Lawrence. While a student at the university, he spent his summers in the near east. Passing as a native, he visited all the military fortifications left by the Crusaders. And he wrote a treatise on the subject. His university waived all conditions and requirements of every kind, and granted him his degree on the strength of it. Here we see just the opposite of our two former instances—the full, free recognition of genuine achievement, as more important than any record produced by standardized drudgery.

[2] *Vide* Chapter 3.

What can we learn from such instances as these? Several very important things, I think.

In the first place, we see the downright futility of uniform standards, based upon the sequential mastery of subject matter. Each case is one of an individual who had proved, beyond any reasonable doubt, that he was a growing personality, intellectually alive, able to use knowledge for the only thing in the world it is good for, namely, the enlightenment of action. Every one of them was using the opportunity of his school years to become genuinely educated. Every one of them was learning in the best and most real way anyone can learn—which is his own way. Yet only one of them received "credit" for it; and that is a case so surprising that it almost calls for banner headlines. Does not this suggest that there is something pretty far wrong with our schools, and our educators?

The real question about any person in school is not: Has he managed to learn something at a given time? The real question is: Is this person growing; is he developing; is he learning to do worth while things? Until we concentrate on this, to the exclusion of everything else, we have not begun to administer our standards with reference to the individual. If a child in school, or a student in college, is doing worth while things and broadening his horizons; if he is trying his wings as a writer; if he is widening his historical and social outlooks; if he is exploring science or applying mathematics to some significant problems; if he is reading the world's great literature or taking part in the production of fine plays; then anybody who pulls a long face because, on the 17th of March, he does more poorly on a memory test than nine tenths of the rest of the candidates, is extremely foolish. He is becoming educated. What else matters? What else are schools for?

So much for the first lesson which we glean from our case material. Now let us turn to the second. One of the arguments likely to be advanced about every one of the persons involved is, that their education was really defective, because they were not properly prepared for further study. Suppose, it will be said, that our Phi Beta Kappa candidate goes on to graduate school; will not his deficiency in French prove very awkward? In the same way, the boy who writes a first rate English essay on a theme of profound importance, is supposed not to have offered presumptive proof of his fitness for the experience of a university environment, because he shows up poorly in mathematics and Latin. This is a contention which applies all up and down the line. A child is supposed not to be ready for algebra unless he has gone through the mill of standardized arithmetic. He ought to be deprived of the opportunities of the junior high school until he has fulfilled every jot and tittle of the sixth grade standards. And no one can be a first rate "college risk" unless he has had several years of a foreign language.

This whole argument is simply another form of that fallacy, beloved of pedants, according to which education is essentially preparatory. The boy who won the essay prize, later on wrote a treatise which involved much reading of mediaeval Latin, and built up a considerable mathematical skill when he needed it in dealing with certain problems. His weakness in those subjects in his entrance examinations, meant less than nothing. If the Phi Beta Kappa candidate enters graduate school, the intellectual enterprise which he has abundantly shown will enable him to master the necessary languages in short order. A child who has gained some genuine mathematical insight, though he has not the routine techniques of arithmetic all perfect, will have at least as good a chance to make something of ninth grade algebra, as he who has learned all the tricks of compound interest, cube root, and present value. It is no use saying that these peoples' education is defective. Where is the man whose education is not defective? Certainly a dray-horse plod through a curriculum laid out in terms of uniform standards is no guarantee against the most glaring deficiencies. Again, the important thing is that a person is being really educated. If so, he is a worthy candidate for honors and a "good risk" for promotion. This does not mean that all high school students ought to go on to college, whether they know anything or not. Just the reverse. Show me the boy who is reading and thinking; who has enterprise and initiative; who is finding out things for himself; who seeks humane and civilizing experiences and undertakings; and I will show you a boy who is making the most of his educational chances, and who ought to be welcome in any university in the world, no matter what his marks may be, or what subjects he is studying, or missing. The best and surest kind of preparation for the future is a rich and adequate present. If a person is becoming progressively enlightened, this is the very best that anyone can ask. If the immediate present is full of vital and enlarging experience, the future will take care of itself. And when one needs some ability, be it in mathematics, or science, or language, one acquires it.

The third thing which we can learn from the cases I have presented, is the real meaning and nature of high standards in education. One of the most familiar criticisms of our American schools is that their standards are much lower than those of European schools. It is said that the American high school graduate is about two years behind his brothers of the French *Lycée,* and the German *Gymnasium* in actual mastery of the subjects of the academic curriculum. And this is probably, on the whole, quite true. But, like any other mere fact, however startling, it means nothing until we interpret it. Our attitude towards it is the important thing. And we would be very hasty, to say the least, and, I believe, quite unjustified, in inferring that our schools must therefore be inferior as educational agencies compared with those abroad, or that the best thing we could do would be to increase the pressure upon our pupils, and to insist that they measure up to European levels of subject matter mastery.

For educational standards cannot be determined solely, or indeed chiefly, in terms of the mastery of conventional subject matter. The real excellence of a school is not to be measured by the degree to which it enables its pupils to do well in difficult examinations, or to pass standardized tests with a high score. It depends upon the richness, variety, and value of the life experiences which the school provides.

Consider again the case of the boy who won the essay prize. Here we have a pupil who has had a really splendid educational experience. But it is something which does not show up at all on the regulation measuring scales provided by the school. This boy certainly did not know various things which he was supposed to know, nearly as well as he should, according to the ordinary and mechanical educational standards. But considered realistically, his education was a great success. Here is the true way to raise standards. We need to have the courage to believe—and to practice the belief—that what develops human power is free, significant, creative experience, rather than rigid routine. When we think that the way to improve our schools is to model them more and more closely on the European type, and to insist more and more on regulation mastery of subject matter, we are following a will o' the wisp into educational morasses. I have not the least hesitation in saying, and with all emphasis, that I hope our schools will not come to approximate more and more closely those of Europe. Standards in education are not effectively raised just by having more and harder examinations, longer and more difficult assignments, and a larger crop of failures. They are raised by so reorganizing our schools that they provide a greater wealth of worth while experiences and undertakings, and so that pupils, during the years when they are free from vocational pressures, will lead fuller, and better directed lives.

One last question must be discussed before I turn away from this topic. Very likely you have been wondering how standards such as I have been describing can possibly be codified, measured, and reduced to some kind of bookkeeping record. Clearly, the ordinary credit and marking system, based on subject matter mastery demonstrated under test conditions, will not be what we need. If we persistently and consistently think of education as depending upon a wide variety of genuine, creative experiences, both individual and social, then it becomes obvious that there are all sorts of important things in it, which cannot possibly be measured and expressed in terms of marks. What mark shall we give a group of pupils who have gone to work and made a collection of the local flora, or put on a play; or to an individual pupil who has read and enjoyed some great masterpiece of literature, or written a fine essay, or an excellent short story? Such things are the very essence of education; and yet to try to give them all a cash value in marks is to stultify them, and to kill much of their value. It is a kind of slap in the face, an insult, to undertake to mark creative effort.

A substitute is needed. And as a matter of fact, it has been found. Our principle must simply be that we shall build up a record of achievement, not in marks at all, but simply as a straightforward, intimate account of what the pupil has actually done while in school. How this is worked out I shall explain more fully in a later chapter, dealing with measurement in education. But such a change in "pupil accounting" is necessary, and is directly demanded by our new conception of the nature of educational standards.

Chapter 13

HOW MAY WE DEAL WITH THE PROBLEM OF INTEREST?

1. *What is the dilemma of interest?*

When we ask what the proper place of interest in education may be, we raise a problem so exceedingly clean cut, and involving what appears to be so definite a contradiction, that it may properly be called a dilemma. It can be put very tersely. On the one hand, there can be no good and effective learning without interest. On the other, children must learn certain things, irrespective of interest. The evidence behind each statement may fairly be called conclusive.

Without interest, without the active will to learn, we are sure to have ineffective learning, wasteful learning, half learning, learning which fails to educate. All kinds of experimental testimony converges to prove the point. Without interest and the will to learn, innumerable repetitions hardly serve to fix a skill, even for the moment; material is retained only very briefly; reading is badly done; lengthy drills fail to register; and the entire teaching process tends towards futility. A pupil who is not interested is not being educated. But to follow what seems the simple logic of this truth, and permit everyone to study exactly what he likes, is entirely impossible. A child may not be interested in acquiring the ability to read, or learning the multiplication tables. But we would hesitate to use this as an argument that he ought not to be taught them. Indeed, the more clearly do we come to see the social meaning and contribution of education, the more keenly we feel the essential importance of certain things, and the more anxious we are that everyone should learn them. To argue that the child's immediate interest must determine what he ought to learn, is to go to the extreme limit of individualism. Everyone's education would tend to be different from that of anybody else. But if education aims at social adjustment, and the building of a common way of life, then, far from being different in each individual case, it must be, to a large degree, the same for all. Several times already we have intimated that a core of social science, broadly understood, should be the organizing center of every man's education. This claim is not put forward because social science is considered to a unique degree interesting, but because it is considered particularly important as an agency for social adjustment, and mutual understanding. Hence we find the dilemma of motivation exceedingly cogent. On the one hand, we cannot have a valid educative process without interest; while on the other, interest cannot determine the content proper to education.

2. *Why is interest from purely extrinsic sources undesirable?*

Every school, and every practical teacher, recognizes the need for motivation. There is always some organized scheme for taking care of it. Most of the plans which we find in the schools for setting up and directing a will to learn, are seriously defective. In no sense can they be considered constructive solutions of the problem of interest. And their weakness always comes to this. They are schemes for what is called "extrinsic" motivation; that is to say, for arousing an interest which does not derive directly from the learning itself. The credit system, with its machinery for examining and marking, is the great instance of an elaborately organized plan for securing extrinsic motivation. While a few murmurs of criticism are begining to be heard, it very largely dominates our schools. The subject matter to be learned is subdivided into various courses, or "units." Success in each one of them counts towards a total score, on which the degree or diploma, or other honor or privilege, is granted. It is carried to a stage of great elaboration by the introduction of various systems of grade points. It is used to decide questions of social and athletic eligibility; though just why a student with an insufficient treasury of educational merits, should be deprived of some of his most valuable educational opportunities, is not wholly clear. It is the foundation of schemes for regulating attendance at class, and deciding upon examination policies. Though obviously not at all well suited to the elementary school, where young pupils should be informally introduced to the intellectual resources of civilization, and where all, or nearly all, subjects are taught by one teacher, it still has a firm hold here; and little children are assigned marks or ratings on a subject matter basis. And of course, whenever a student wishes to transfer from one institution to another, the cloud of credits that he trails is a most important element in the transaction.

The credit system began largely as an administrative and bookkeeping device. From this small seed, it has grown into a large and healthy Upas tree. And it is now by far the most important single device in our American schools for putting a drive behind study. But it organizes the dynamics of learning in the wrong way. A potent drive is indeed developed. But it is not a will to learn. And hence it is not truly educative. It offers a standing temptation to students to think far more of the credit record they will obtain than of anything else in a course of study. When teachers advise pupils not to work for marks, they are guilty of a serious, even though unconscious, hypocrisy. For if pupils are not to work for marks, then certainly marks ought not to be made very important in the scheme of things, and perhaps ought to be abandoned altogether. Here, at once, we see the evil of extrinsic interest. The impulse to work is determined by something outside the work itself. And naturally, the tendency is to lead people to work for the external and artificial reward, rather than for the growth in skill, knowledge, or insight itself. Every teacher will piously advocate the love of learning for its own sake. But nearly every school systematically tempts its pupils to love marks.

Let us try to enumerate some of the chief evils which result from any scheme of extrinsic motivation.

A. In the first place, it will certainly not tend to produce effective learning. There is, in all schools, a tacit but ironclad agreement that the great majority of students must receive passing marks. Any school which operated on a contrary policy would simply go out of business. Even where general standards are quite high, this makes it possible to meet requirements without any very thorough learning, or the definite establishment of very competent masteries. So it is a fair guess that well over half the pupils in nearly all courses will not achieve very adequate learning. And there is nothing at all in the credit system to make them dissatisfied with such mediocrity. The effect of that system on the average student is to intimate to him that, if he does not do too badly, he will obtain his reward. Now contrast this with a situation where no question exists of any mark, passing or otherwise. We have this, for instance, on a golf course. There the question is not, "Can I manage to make a C?" but, "Can I go round in bogey or better?" We may remain satisfied with mediocrity still. But we do not mistake it for excellence.

And what of the effect of extrinsic motivation on the first rate, ambitious student? Here again, it is anything but favorable. He is sure to use a good deal of his ingenuity in trying, directly or otherwise, to please the teacher, who is the dispenser of all good gifts. Moreover, a competitive standard of excellence is set before him. He is incited to do, not as well as he can, but well enough to get an A, which merely means better than most.

This is all in the sharpest possible contrast with the effects of direct interest. Suppose I wish to learn enough mathematics to deal with some statistical problem which confronts me. What do I care about marks or the passing of tests? All I want is the mathematics; and anything which helps me with it, is all to the good. Suppose I am on the 'varsity football squad; do I work for an A or a B or a C? I may have my worries, but they will not be of this kind. My concern is to play the game well enough to help defeat rival teams. Or, if I am a noble savage, member of some primitive band, the important thing in my life is not to have a diploma which proves I have passed a test in scoutcraft. The big issue is whether I can go into the woods without starving or freezing to death, and bring home the venison.

B. Then consider the sort of personal attitudes which schemes of extrinsic motivation tend to produce in the pupils. When a student cheats in an examination, or copies somebody else's collateral notes, can we absolve the system of all blame? Why was this examination, or this notebook, so important? Certainly not for its own sake, or because the pupil recognized a personal benefit in doing well. If the learning itself had been made the chief thing, cheating would have been utterly out of the picture. Try to drive a golf ball two hundred and fifty yards by cheating. See if you can diagnose the troubles of a Ford car by copying somebody's notes. When we put the learning itself in the center of things, cheating loses its whole point. The way to take care of it is neither by doubling the number of proctors, nor by setting up an honor system which shifts the responsibility to the honest students, but by altering the basic conditions which encourage cheating.

Another symptom of the same disease is seen whenever a student tries in any way to coax a teacher into giving him a good mark. The thing is fundamentally preposterous. If you are being coached by a golf professional, it does not enter your head to try to conciliate the man in the hope that he will give you a B instead of a C. You do not think of it, just because no extrinsic motivation is involved. Better golf, not a record on the registrar's books, is your reward. Your attitude is apt to be quite different from that of a student in school, who treats his teacher as an autocrat, divinely appointed as a fountain of credits.

C. In the third place, extrinsic motivation is bad for the teacher. The only real reason for the teacher's existence is to direct and facilitate the learning of the pupils. His chief task is to make subject matter meaningful, important, educative—to "sell" his subject on its educational merits. But an instrument like the credit system turns him, even against his will, into a taskmaster. It enables him to force the performance of set tasks. It frees him from the necessity of making these tasks seem significant, and so, in their own right, appealing. Marking is one of the very important activities of the "practical" teacher on the "firing line." And it is a perilous thing for him, deadening to his educational conscience. It gives him the power to force his pupils to do something which looks like learning, without making a move to arouse a single scintilla of interest. And so he becomes a sceptic towards any serious proposal for interest aroused through the significance of the task itself. He regards it as visionary and "impractical"; and remains blandly oblivious to the fact that his own practice is anti-educational.

D. In the fourth place, extraneous motivation is bad for the school. One of the most essential tasks of the school is to select from the intellectual resources of civilization those items which are of primary importance for the pupil to acquire. Now suppose that some kind of a selection has been made, which, of course, is always the case. For the chosen material to become educative, it cannot merely be imposed upon the pupil from above. He must himself be a party to the choice, at least to the extent of consciously recognizing its validity. He must come to see the point and value of learning what we want him to learn. Our intellectual bill of fare cannot be rammed down his throat if it is to be digested. It must be made to seem worth consuming. It is our obligation to choose for him that which is of most worth. But he must concur in our choices.

Now this cannot be done, unless the curriculum is selected and constructed on valid lines. We want to sell the program of studies on its merits, and because of its patent and undeniable importance. We want to be able to come to the student, and say: "Here are the studies we have chosen for you. Reflection will show you that they are worth mastering." But obviously, we cannot do this unless the studies we have chosen really are worth mastering.

Consider, however, what happens when we use a great engine of extrinsic motivation, like the credit system. Learning ceases to be an end in itself and becomes a means to an external end. We are no longer forced to care whether we have a valid curriculum or not—a curriculum with a powerful and manifest appeal in its own right. For we have an instrument by which we can make the pupil learn whatever we like, whether *he* likes or not—or at least go through the motions of doing so. And so the school is under constant temptation to tolerate an inherently unsaleable curriculum. Subject matter can be forced upon the pupil. The school is not put on its mettle to perform the vital function of selection as wisely as possible. It is enabled lazily to continue all sorts of outworn and indefensible requirements, such, for instance, as that in modern foreign language. So long as its chief reliance is upon extrinsic motivation, it can dodge educational realities, just as a country whose currency is being inflated without control may be able to dodge economic realities—for a while.

3. Why is interest from purely intrinsic sources not desirable?

Having seen a few of the disasters which befall us if we are impaled on one horn of the dilemma of interest by using some scheme of organizing extrinsic motivation, let us consider the other alternative. If we direct our educational policy and practice wholly along lines of intrinsic interest, what then? One of the retorts often made to anyone who insists that learning, to be effective, must be interested, is: "Ah yes, you believe that children in school should be allowed to do anything they please!" Allowing children to do anything they please would be the extreme application of the idea of intrinsic interest. This very plan has been proposed now and then by very radical educational thinkers. And from time to time, attempts have been made to put it into effect. But always the results are disastrous. For the idea of pure intrinsic interest offers just as poor an organizing principle for education, and is just as surely destructive of essential values as a scheme of extrinsic motivation.

A. It means, first of all, a virtual refusal on the part of the school to exercise its great responsibility for the selection of those things most important to be learned. Just what this actually involves is well illustrated in the breakdown of the free elective system, introduced some time ago at Harvard by President Eliot. The curriculum of the early American college was so limited that all students took virtually every study offered. As more and more courses became available, Harvard College tried the very radical experiment of permitting the student to choose what he would take, with an absolute minimum of requirements, prerequisites, and limitations of any kind. The plan completely failed and had to be profoundly modified. It was found that even the most serious and earnest-minded students would select very injudicious sequences, omitting various studies of obvious importance, and choosing others which had little relationship to any intelligible plan. And the tendency of the academic *hoi polloi* was to run after the unlaborious course in large numbers, and with much enthusiasm. The obvious central weakness lay in the student's inability to make wise choices. One might say, of course, that under a free elective system, a selected curriculum still exists, simply because not even the world's largest university can teach everything. But the point is that a curriculum must become selective in terms of the actual choices of the students. A program of studies is not something which exists merely in a catalog; it is a working plan, realized in the activities of human beings. And our true problem is always to lead the student himself to a wise choice of studies. If college students cannot regulate their studies to fruitful ends, what chance have high school pupils or children in an elementary school? As a matter of fact, the problem of selection is one of the most difficult and exacting, one which requires the highest and most mature wisdom of all those with which education has to do. When we virtually shift the responsibility for it upon the pupil and justify ourselves by saying that he must work at whatever interests him, we are converting his education into a farce, and turning aside from the plain path of duty.

B. Then, if we guide ourselves wholly by the idea of intrinsic interest, we ignore the doctrine that education exists to secure flexible, creative, progressive adjustment to society, and to fashion a common way of enlightened living. College teachers sometimes come across students who insist that they have developed their own personal intellectual interests, and that they ought to be allowed to follow them, irrespective of anything else. Such students are often very able. And it is frequently quite true that they have built up a very definite slant in some particular direction. What ought to be done about such people? If we believe in intrinsic interest as the foundation of education, our reply will be: Give them our blessing, and clear the way for them. But is this wise? Here is a student who is fascinated with natural science, and cares for nothing else which the school offers. Here is another, who is extremely fond of English literature, and will have nothing to do with natural science or economics. What about such cases? Which is right, the student, or the school? Surely, if we believe that education exists for social ends, we shall have to say that, while a strong positive interest is a blessing and an advantage, yet a definitely limited interest is an educational weakness. There are many things in which our science student *ought* to be interested, besides his science. Our student of literature *ought* to be interested in science and economics. We have a right to say this, simply because an education limited to science, or to English literature, or to economics, is also greatly limited in its social significance. So we cannot, with a clear conscience, organize the work of our school to give the clearest possible right of way to any kind of individual interest a pupil may have. It is our obligation to seek to interest him *in the right things*.

C. There can be no manner of doubt that the extreme doctrine of intrinsic interest is a menace to intellectual continuity. This is the peculiar nemesis of the procedures found in some progressive schools. Mental enlargement, and growth, is initiated very properly with attractive, interesting, immediate experience. Projects, problems, concrete situations, are provided in abundance. A socially stimulating environment is set up. And indeed, a good deal more may actually be achieved than in the conventional school, with its mass preoccupations and artificial incentives. But the educative process goes astray because mental growth well begun is not well continued. There fails to be a steady progress towards generalization, and a steady elaboration of intellectual background. For this we require something more than merely intrinsic interest in the sense of whim.

The great weakness of the doctrine of intrinsic interest, from which all the failures attendant upon its applications flow, is that it regards interest as something we *find* instead of as something we *build*. Children do not come, either into the world or into the school, with significant ready-made interests. Rather it is our task to create in them such interests; to help them to discover, little by little, what is of concern to them, and to learn their own capacities by educative experience. Certainly we cannot, abandoning the doctrine of extrinsic interest, place our reliance on the child's untutored whim.

4. How shall we organize school work for the sake of interest?

We have been discussing two ways in which the schools have attempted to organize their work to secure that drive in learning which everyone knows is necessary. Both are failures; and the reason is that they depend on false notions. In one case we see the error of holding that educationally valuable content can be assembled and taught, irrespective of its interests; in the other case, the mistake consists in supposing that unguided interest alone can be a sufficient criterion of educational values. Now a school must have what I might call a *dynamic organization*. I mean that it must set up and maintain a machinery for putting a drive behind learning, for inducing interest. This is practically a necessity. When we try to do it either in terms of purely extrinsic, or purely intrinsic motivation, we fail. On what principles does success depend?

The great natural source of interest in any piece of learning is its relationship to an actual life need. When I am conscious of moving towards some understanding, or some skill, which has direct applicability in the social situation round me, I am interested. I am interested, because such an intellectual achievement appears to me important. If, on the other hand, I am set to master some material which has no apparent relationship or applicability anywhere, except to the passing of an examination, everything is against the arousal of interest. My teacher may tell me that this material is very significant and important. I may believe him and may have faith enough to study hard. As I progress, I may come to be interested. But this will happen because I come to see the subject somewhat as he sees it, and to appreciate for myself its bearings upon the problems of life. We sometimes hear about something called "purely intellectual interest," which is supposed to be the characteristic of mathematicians, and historians, and research workers generally. If by this we mean that such workers are fascinated by their work, absolutely apart from its social significance, we certainly err. Almost always they are sustained by the sense that they are investigating important things, not just solving puzzles. The research scientist has a very different attitude towards his undertakings from that of the person who solves chess problems or does crossword puzzles.

A mere puzzle interest, indeed, is barely possible. But it is sophisticated rather than normal. It is a limiting case. Human beings are not curious about things in general; nor do they have a universal, instinctive lust to solve any and every problem they encounter. They are curious about things which strike them as important. *So, the central source of interest in intellectual material is to be sought and found in its relationship to life, and its value as an agency for social adjustment.* This is the principle which must control us in trying to organize the course of education properly to recognize the factor of interest.

A. First of all, it means that we must have a properly selected, genuinely vital curriculum. And the reason for studying a particular subject at a particular time, must be just as evident to the learner as it is to the teacher or to the curriculum builder. In certain high school courses—geometry is an excellent illustration—one sometimes finds pupils asking: "Why do we have to learn these things?" The question is usually brushed aside, or answered with a few lies about the training of the mind. It is really a serious question indeed; and the mere fact that pupils raise it, should give us furiously to think. Evidently the subject is not "selling itself" to them. This means one of two things. Either it does not really belong in the program of studies at all. Or else it is being handled in such a way that its true values are obscured from, rather than revealed to, the minds of the pupils. When "exposure" to a subject forces into the naturally submissive mind of the pupil a fundamental doubt as to its value, something is very far wrong. Most certainly we shall be at a loss to interest the pupil in it. He will work at it reluctantly and dubiously, without any inner urge. And just because its educational purpose is not evident to him, it will lack educational value for him.

If we can construct a curriculum which deals, through and through, with vital issues, and which patently teaches the pupil how to live, we shall not find him asking, either in his thoughts or openly, what use it all is. If his work in art is really teaching him to express himself graphically with paper and pencil; if his work in music is really enabling him to sing and play to and with others; if his work in literature is really broadening and deepening his zeal for reading; and if, above all, his work in social science, history, and natural science, which should be the core of the curriculum, is opening his eyes to the present, clamant issues of the modern world—then, indeed, we shall be working towards the achievement of properly balanced interest. Such studies as these he will not find dull and forbidding. Their reason for existence will be obvious from the first, and will grow more obvious as he continues. His intellectual interest will arise from the contact established between culture and life.

B. We shall be led to invent new patterns for the presentation of curricular material. The old fashioned unit course is very far from being an educational device well suited to the proper management of interest and motivation. Essentially, it is part of the machinery of the credit system. It is set up as something to be "passed" or "failed"; as something for which one receives a mark. Thus it deals with a limited and narrow range of material, which is likely to be organized in terms of its internal logic, rather than in terms of its social significance. It is integrated about a series of oral or written quizzes and examinations. It tends, on the one hand, to emphasize subject matter learned for its own sake; and on the other, to involve the use of purely extrinsic motivation in the shape of grades. I do not mean to say that in the hands of an enlightened and skillful teacher, the conventionally organized unit course cannot be used for educationally very valuable ends, or that many of its difficulties cannot be, in some real measure, overcome. But I do say that its trend and tidal influence is towards subject matter for its own sake, and extrinsic motivation, rather than towards a satisfactory solution of the problem of interest. And I emphatically believe that enlightened teachers will not be well content with it, but will seek other patterns for the presentation of material.

Many of these have been tried. For instance, we have the exploratory course, in which the pupil is brought successively into contact with many aspects of experience, and many kinds of intellectual content, the aim being to help him to discover his interests, and to build them up. Or, we have what are known as orientation courses, in which the "situation technique" is used, and which are made up of actual problems from the social environment, blocked out for study. This verges upon the pure project curriculum, where the very term "course" may wholly disappear, and the work of the school be organized as a series of significant undertakings. The variations of procedure are already very numerous; and the technical terms which have been enthusiastically invented for the different plans, somewhat confusing. But the idea is very simple. If one has a certain amount of important curricular material to convey, and if one believes that its value to the learner depends on his ability to perceive its relationship to life problems, then one will probably not subdivide it into formal unit courses, but rather break it into large sub-divisions, determined by its applications, which are seen to be all-important. This is what our schools are seeking to do in many different ways.

C. Our attempt to organize school work for the proper management of interest, will lead us to seek for new procedures in the classroom. Notice, however, that the problem of interest cannot be solved by teaching procedures alone. We often hear discussions which imply that this is possible. But they involve a great mistake. The teacher is only the last link in the chain between those who construct the blueprint of the curriculum, and those in whose mental processes it transforms itself into reality. He cannot sell something which he has not got to sell. He cannot sell the unsaleable. He cannot bring to life a curriculum already dead. His work is to extract the educative value from a certain range of material—to show the pupil why it is worth mastering. So organization for interest begins with the planning of the curriculum, not with the work of the classroom teacher.

Still, teaching procedures have a very essential place in the process. And here again our formula holds. What is required is a consistent effort to reveal to the pupils the life meanings of what they learn.

This simply calls for the teaching of curricular content in close association with those life situations to which it applies. "Life situations" are attainable in many ways. Sometimes this may mean setting up an elaborate project, such as the investigation of the causes of typhoid in the farm home. Sometimes it may mean the organization of the class group to provide an "audience situation" for the reading of a paper, or an oral composition, or a dramatization, or the performance of music. Sometimes, too, it may simply mean the careful assignment of certain types of reading. The ordinary textbook is dull, and more or less anti-educational, because its whole idea is the parcelling out of subject matter in suitable doses without any concern for its significance or applicability. Very frequently indeed, a subject may be literally brought to life by the assignment of collateral material of genuinely human value. Such reading will often reveal to the pupil, with startling force, that the things he learns about in school, have a place and a value in the affairs of men.

The term "life situation," which has become almost a cant phrase in educational discussion, is both useful and dangerous. It is dangerous because it includes so much. We should understand it to mean a situation to which subject matter to be learned actually and directly applies. To learn mathematics for the sake of passing an examination is not to learn it in a "life situation." The reason is that mathematics is not an agency of enlightenment in the social situation of writing an examination. But to study mathematics for the sake of checking upon some advertising copy, is to learn it in a "life situation," because mathematics does indeed provide the means for a better adjustment to this problem. Here is the principle to apply in organizing our teaching procedures for the proper arousal of interest.

In the three points just presented, I have tried to show concretely how our conception of the nature of interest applies to school work. Now I want to call your attention to three further considerations of a somewhat more general sort.

First of all, there is a question which it may be illuminating to discuss. You may perhaps ask this: "If some piece of learning can be shown to connect with life, not when it is learned, but much later on—if its life value is prospective and preparatory, rather than immediate—will this furnish a sufficient source of interest?" Our answer must be that it will not. Perhaps in some very definite vocational courses, interest may be derived from the preparatory value of a bit of learning. If you positively know that six months hence you will be offered a job as a private secretary, for which you will need stenography and typewriting, then drilling on these skills may take on a very strong and driving interest indeed. But such cases are the exception, not the rule. For one thing, very few pupils in school are anything like so definite as this about their prospects. For another thing, even if they knew beyond a doubt just what their vocational destiny was to be, it would still be hard to show them exactly how each item learned now could benefit them some years later on. Investigations have shown beyond question that the "career motive," or the sense of a school study as "practical" in the narrow and prospective sense, is not an important source of interest.

In order to secure proper interest, we must have immediate, not prospective contacts with life situations. I know very well that this calls for a really profound reorganization of our educational system. A great many things will have to be torn up by the roots, and a great many other things established in their place. Our schools have succumbed far too extensively to the temptation to cut themselves off from life, to run on traditional lines, and to teach the accepted curriculum for its own sake alone. This has profoundly weakened them as educational institutions. Hence their reliance on extrinsic motivation. Hence, too, our feeling that to try for interest by teaching curricular content in close touch with life situations where it is needed, is something revolutionary and very difficult. Yet it is being done. It is being done in the Danish Folk High Schools, where there is no system at all of extrinsic motivation, and where pupils come to learn for the sake of living. It is being done in the schools of Soviet Russia, where they face the great task of creating the "new man." It is being done in the most forward looking American schools. And wherever it happens, learning is illuminated, and education brought to new life.

2. The second of the three general considerations which I want to discuss is concerned with what is often called "sugar coating." Suppose you are responsible for directing any job of learning you like to mention—reading, writing, arithmetical computation, the grammar of a foreign language, a chemical formula, the technique of the golf swing. And suppose you wish to "make it interesting." What will be the most hopeful and constructive mode of procedure? If you are a believer in "sugar coating," you will probably say: "By making the learning as pleasant as possible; by avoiding

all its painful features to the limit." For instance, you will perhaps try to teach multiplication in arithmetic by some kind of round game. Or you will personify the moods and tenses and cases of your grammar, and have them act out a little play. Or you will talk about Mr. and Mrs. Oxygen Hydrogen and their little baby, Water. Some quite surprisingly clever schemes of this kind have been thought out; and the originators of some of them have made convenient sums of money.

Now, from our standpoint, this sugar coating is for many reasons objectionable. In the first place, we are obviously dealing once more with extrinsic motivation. The idea is not to generate interest actually from the content to be learned, but to add it to, or superimpose it upon, that content. In the second place, such schemes involve a very wrong-headed approach to, and treatment of, educational content. When you hear of someone talking about "sugar-coating the pill of knowledge," you are probably engrossed in the first part of the notion—the sugar-coating. But I would like to call it to your attention also, that this person has, by implication, called knowledge a pill. This is a very great and serious heresy. Surely one cannot believe that a teacher does well to admit, in any way, that valuable and serious learning is an evil. As a practical matter, this point of view nearly always leads to teachers minimizing, or reducing the actual hard, definite learning required, on the pretext that it cannot be handled. What they mean is that they do not know how to spread it with sufficient sugar. But for us, this whole theory of interest is wrong. Interest must arise from the content learned. It must arise from the learner's perception that this content is important. It must not depend on tricking him into acquiring something we think good for him. It must depend on the conscious, explicit relationship between what is to be learned, and the life purpose of the pupil.

My third general point can be disposed of quite briefly, for it is involved in all that has been said in this section. I want to point out with explicit clearness that the account we have been presenting offers a constructive solution of the dilemma of interest. We fully recognize that interest is essential. We fully recognize that certain items of curricular content are essential. And we argue that interest must be generated by revealing to the pupil the importance of the content which we have chosen for him. Interest is not purely extrinsic, in the sense of coming from an artificial source, irrelevant to what is to be mastered. It is not purely intrinsic, in the sense of being a mere whim. It is a feeling of the importance of what actually is important.

5. *What is the relation of interest to effort?*

Our discussion of "sugar coating" which means trying for interest by making learning palatable and easy, leads us immediately to the question of the place of effort in the educative process. A criticism frequently made against the theory that interest is essential to education is that this means abandoning "good hard work," and allowing the pupils to learn only what can be mastered easily. Nothing, as a matter of fact, could be farther from the truth. The following out of a purpose which grips the learner with the utmost power, which arouses in him the most intense interest, may easily call for effort far greater than any teacher could conceivably impose. Anyone who has had much to do with a creative mathematician, knows very well that this is so. Such a person is capable of becoming so absorbed with a problem that it lives with him, and dominates him, day and night. From the moment of wakening to the moment of falling asleep, he wrestles with it. His labors are of the most exhausting kind, and quite possibly may bring on a nervous collapse. But they are imposed by his own free will. They are, in fact, the outcome of his potent interest.

Whenever we hear anyone drawing a sharp dividing line between interest and effort, we may know that he is thinking of education in mechanical terms. We are in the presence of that theory which, in one form or another we have so often characterized, and so often repudiated—the idea of a mass of inert content on the one hand, and the impressionable mind of the pupil on the other. The duty of the school and the teacher then comes to be to compel the pupil, irrespective of his will, to assimilate curricular content. That is, effort must be aroused, and interest neglected. But this is not really education at all. Education is essentially an affair of mental growth; of acquiring an ever widening background and perspective in dealing with the issues of life; of gaining a flexible and creative adjustment. Subject matter is its means only, never its end. Curricular content is no more than the raw material of education, just as food is the raw material of body-tissue.

Sometimes the dilemma between interest and effort is put in some such way as this. We have, let us say, the job of teaching a grammar rule in a foreign language. Would it be better to try to fix it up in such a way that the pupil will find himself in an entertaining situation as he learns it—perhaps by inventing a game? Or would it be better to intimate to him that he is under stringent orders, and must get busy and learn what we tell him to learn, or the consequences will be drastically unpleasant? This seems like a common sense alternative. But really it is not. Neither way is the good and proper way. For a grammar rule in a foreign language to be properly learned and made an actual working part of the mentality of the pupil, must be learned in a situation which, whether "intriguing" and entertaining or not, demands the use of this rule. We require actual contact with reality, not for the sake of sugar coating unpleasant content, but because only in this way can curricular material come to possess its true meaning, and play its true part in the upbuilding of mental life.

And as soon as we have before us an actual situation, a real life need, the distinction between interest and effort vanishes. We are not forced to choose one or the other, simply because we have both. If I am thrown into a French speaking social environment, I have a very powerful interest in learning to use and understand the new language. And just because of this, I am likely to make a far greater and more continuous effort than the most "hard boiled" teacher could ever get out of me. No human taskmaster can be so unremittingly severe, so intimately exacting, so remorseless, and so thorough, as an actual life situation. Failure there is so patently by own fault and so lamentable. Success is so evidently rewarding. And education is so unmistakably self education.

So once more, the proper arousal of interest, and the proper stimulation of effort, both ultimately depend upon one thing—bringing education more closely into touch with life. It is just when education is most exclusively a matter of schooling and tradition, of learning things whose applications we cannot see, perhaps for the good reason that they have none, that we find the choice between interest and effort, as principles of motivation, most bewildering and insoluble. On the one hand, the arguments of the drill masters for a good hard push and no nonsense, seem exceedingly reasonable. On the other, the psychologists warn us that for effective learning, a will to learn must be present. Which shall we choose? The reply is, neither. We must shift the whole ground of the discussion. We must seek to stimulate pupils, neither by driving or by coaxing them, but by revealing the dynamic contact between subject matter and life. In so far as they actively recognize that, in school, they are acquiring, not dead subject matter, but living adjustments, the demands of the real situation will provide both interest and effort.

6. *What is the relation of interest to educational outcomes?*

The full importance of interest in education can hardly be appreciated, until we understand its relationship to ultimate outcomes. It is very truly said that education, to be worth anything, must look toward the future. But if by this we mean that pupils are to learn here and now, various things which seem to them devoid of all rhyme and reason, so that later on they will be able to apply them, we fall into a profound error. As a matter of positive fact, education so conceived has a bare minimum of preparatory value. What I learn now cannot prepare me for something later, unless I retain it. And if I learn merely under duress, with no other motive than to avoid penalties, and to secure rewards, then the moment my immediate end is achieved—the moment I have passed my examination and secured my mark—I begin busily and successfully, to forget. But more than mere retention is involved. How can a school best give a pupil the kind of mathematical training he will need later on, to become an engineer? By teaching him certain fundamentals of the science, and then letting the matter rest until he enters college, or some technical institution? Surely not. It will be far better if he cannot only be taught a certain amount of mathematics, but also acquire a disposition to go on and learn more on his own account. In other words, the very best service a teacher of high school algebra or geometry can render to a prospective engineer, cannot be expressed in terms of the actual amount of mathematics the pupil knows when he leaves the teacher's hands. The best possible service the teacher can render is to create an abiding interest in mathematics, which will insure further learning independently.

Many teachers are apt to lament that pupils will just barely fulfill the requirements of their courses, and then happily let the subjects lapse. If so, it is a most serious indictment of education. The greatest gift I can carry away from a course in history, or science, or literature, or anything else, is a permanent disposition to read, learn, and think more about these matters. Indeed, if my dispositions are not in any way affected along these lines, I am justified in suspecting that my courses gave me nothing much worth having, educationally speaking. The supreme task of all education is to arouse, intensify, and organize the pupil's own interests. The great difference between the educated and the uneducated person is not one of knowledge, but of disposition. The contrast lies in the interest of the two people.

Now we may be perfectly certain that effective interests will never be built on any system of either compulsion or anarchic freedom. One must be led to perceive and understand the importance of the subjects one is learning. One must recognize the many fascinating ways in which mastering them is broadening one's life's horizons. One must generate a true interest in them in school by learning them in close contact with their life meanings; or the chance is excellent that their significance will never be apparent. We all know how easy it is for a person to go to school for sixteen years, to study all kinds of subject matter, and to come away almost completely uneducated. Many a college graduate does little reading, and less thinking, and has the point of view of a Babbitt or a yokel, concerning the things of the mind. This means failure on the part of the schools. And it is a failure of motivation. When the schools fail to develop interests, they fail to educate.

One peculiar notion entertained by many persons, about the

place of interest in education, deserves passing notice here. You may have heard it said that school studies should not be made "too interesting," because pupils will have to carry out many routine, dull tasks in after life, and should be adjusted early to the grim and tasteless grind. One obvious line of reply would be to say that on such an argument, pupils should not be protected from disease, because most of them are apt to be ill from time to time; or even that they should all commit suicide, for the sake of getting used to dying. But this point I will not press.

The essential issue is that here we have a complete misconception of the real place, nature, and value of educational interest. Interest, as we have come to understand it, is not something extra, something extraneous the condiment upon the dish, the sugar on the pill. On the contrary, we never learn anything well unless we are interested in it. And we never learn anything for the most permanent values, unless we are interested in it. Uninterested learning is learning not worth the trouble it takes. One would be better advised to go and play ball. Education does not prepare us for the tasks of life by storing up material for later use. It prepares us by producing certain active tendencies, certain directions of growth. There is, in the human mind, no storehouse of knowledge. The best we can do is progressively to readjust ourselves to higher and higher levels. If we fail to do this, we do nothing at all.

Chapter 14

HOW MAY EDUCATION SERVE THE ENDS OF CULTURE AND VOCATION?

1. *What is the social significance of culture?*

A very great man once spoke of "culture" as the most terrible of words. Certainly there are few more generally abused in educational discussions. It is supposed to indicate the superficially elegant, the merely ornamental, in contrast with the useful and the practical. Utter it, and you will arouse in many minds visions of airs and graces, of trivial little artistic and literary pursuits, of "parlor tricks," of anything which may contrast with a man's work in a work-a-day world and the job of earning a living. So long as our thoughts run in such channels, we have no chance of understanding it, or grasping its true place in human life and education, and its connection with the problem of vocation. This entire conception is wrong. We must give it up, and find another. And there is no better way of ridding ourselves of the error, and turning towards a true interpretation, than to ask the question which stands at the head of this section: What is the social meaning of culture?

Every great culture has been, and must be, the expression and interpretation of a way of social living. Each age has produced great men, who have caught the current atmosphere of opinion and belief, and expressed it in literature, or art, or music, or in the creative reform of institutions. Such men are like reflectors, catching the diffused rays of the sun, and bringing them to a dazzling focus. They grow like trees, deeply rooted in a common life, uniquely embodying and expressing the native soil, and air, and sunshine. Their creative work is the culture of the age in which they live. In it, the meaning of life, as understood in that age, comes to clear expression. Here is the secret of their power, the greatness of their work. They belong to all ages because of their unique association with one age. They are interpreters of the hearts and minds of their contemporaries; and they live for succeeding generations, because their message speaks of that which must always be the chief concern of men—the human drama itself. As Goethe has said: "The man who has been of his own time, has really been of all time."

When we turn the pages of Saint Thomas, or stand before the façade of Chartres, we hear the voice, and gaze upon the vision, of the Middle Ages. Here is far more than a wise logic or an impersonal beauty. Only once in all history has there been, upon this earth, a way of life which could produce these things. And in coming into touch with them, we begin to understand a little of how life must have seemed to the men of the thirteenth century. Or again, what social order save that of Imperial Rome could have given birth to the literature of the age of Augustus, or to the great legal system, or the magnificent network of communications, which was the body of the Roman Peace? Homer could not have made the Aeneid. Pindar could not have written the odes of Horace. Neither the Greek spirit with its subtlety, nor the Hebrew spirit with its moral fire, were able to achieve the massive and enduring architecture of a universal state. Such things, like the Virgilian rhythm, "sound forever of Imperial Rome." Again, who but a Greek of the great age, could have done the work of a Sophocles? Where, in all the world, could the Parthenon stand but on the Acropolis and in the midst of the city whose vision of life it crystallized in stone? Would not Confucius be a stranger indeed in any other land than China? Would it not seem monstrously unnatural if we should take to building, out of reinforced concrete, pyramids to rival that of Geza? For us, surely, the skyscraper is the truer expression. What country but India could nurture a Buddha; what land but Palestine, an Isaiah; what social order but that of eighteenth century Germany, a Bach? Where but in Russia could a Dostoievsky find his home? In such utterances, and in the work of such spirits, a society comes to understand itself. Men read the word, hear the music, gaze upon the building or the picture, live in and with the institution—and, consciously or unconsciously, they say to themselves, "this is what it all means." The culture of any age is an integral interpretation of its life.

How futile, how silly, does this make the conventional understanding of culture appear. We must enter a violent protest against the thought that immortal verse was made, or profound wisdom etched in luminous prose, or the inner vision of beauty transmuted into an abiding reality, simply to amuse us in those moments when we have nothing better to do. Not for this did great men utter the word given them to speak. We must convey culture to our children, not as a luxury, but as a necessity; not as an ornament of life, but as the interpretation of living.

In America, this task, which is the central task of what is called a "cultural education," faces certain peculiar difficulties. The first comes from the tradition of our schools. Until quite recently, our curriculum has been derived, far too exclusively, from European, and far too little from American, sources. One of the standing reproaches of our scheme of education has been its reluctance to recognize and use the cultural materials created in this country and constituting an interpretation of its way of life. Lull tells us that: "The lag between the publication of the works of the following authors, and their adoption into the high schools, has ranged from 17 to 77 years with a mode of 40 years: Irving, Bryant, Cooper, Everett, Webster, Prescott, Bancroft, Lincoln, Poe, Longfellow, Hawthorne, Holmes, Thoreau, and Whitman."[1] This is just a part of our national inferiority complex. The European stamp has been necessary, before we dare believe work good. Whistler and Poe were recognized abroad long before we began to feel proud of them. The spiritual home of too many of our ablest teachers has been beyond the seas.

This explains a very great deal. It is one great reason for the scorn felt by the "practical" American for culture. A native culture, a living culture, is obviously practical, in a large but genuine sense.

[1] *Secondary Education:* W. W. Norton Company, p. 88, 1932.

It deals with, and illuminates, the issues of pedestrian living. There is a story of a rather crude though successful business man, who read Walter Lippmann's *Preface to Politics,* and said that, while he was a hard-headed practical person who didn't know anything about tariffs and gold standards, and suchlike high-falutin' junk, this fellow Lippmann made it all real. Whether or no we agree with Lippmann's interpretation, is not the point. The point is that here we see culture fulfilling its mission as an interpretation of life. And just here, a derived, conventional culture fails. Moreover, this preoccupation with alien sources also shows us why the materials of our "cultural" curriculum so often do not grip and mould the minds of young people. They feel, somehow, that here is something which may be all right in its way, if one has time for it, but which is not of the most imperative moment. For us to try to convert them is useless. We need to convert ourselves. For they are right. I would urge every teacher of literature, or history, or language, or music, or art, to ponder well the profound influence of the movies upon young life in America. To my mind, this is proof positive, if proof be needed, that young people are not indifferent to culture, just so long as they feel in it a reference to life as they must live it, and an interpretation of the social order. The movies are a culture product of a sort, which succeeds precisely because it serves this very end. The pity is that its interpretation of life is often base. How can we rival such a potent influence? Not by preaching a lily-handed, celibate-minded adoration of the expurgated masterpieces of the past, mummified in textbooks, and imported in the holds of westward faring ships. Only by conveying to young people a culture whose cogent applicability they must recognize, and whose authority they must respect—a culture made in America, for Americans, and by Americans.

But here we come upon another difficulty. Not until within comparatively recent years has a unique and adequate American culture begun to exist. Only recently has the American way of life begun to express itself with authority and power in literature, and art, and music, and social science, and historical writing, and architecture. So long as we were a frontier nation, spiritually a colony of Europe, there was a good enough excuse for our school culture being a pale replica of the culture of Europe. But the point is, that such an excuse exists no longer. In a score of fields, men are at work interpreting American life. To an increasing degree, their product should constitute the core of our cultural curriculum. This does not mean an insular contempt for the great utterances of other nations and other ages. But neither does it mean an awful worship of them, and a humble belief that what little we have is of little worth. What we have of our very own is worth more to us than anything else, just because it is our own, and just because life in the age of Victoria, or Elizabeth, or Julius Caesar, or Pericles, or Sargon, is of less pressing moment than life in the age of Herbert Hoover and Franklin Roosevelt.

What an American culture must mean, I can show you by quoting from an address by William Arms Fisher, in which he imaginatively describes the "Great American Symphony," as yet unwritten. "That symphony will be American, not because its composer was born in Oskaloosa or San Jose, but because at last a great creative genius, himself an embodiment of all that is best in distinctive American life, can as poet, seer, and musician infuse his symphony with the robust, smiling spirit of true Americanism. His masterpiece will synthesize in a glorious multi-colored flood of sound those elusive elements so difficult to name, which, fused together, make up the rich composite of our national life; a composite that is growing richer and more significant with each generation.[2]

One thing an American culture will surely do; and indeed is even now achieving before our eyes. It will convert the mighty industrial system from an alien fact, hostile to man, into a "significant habit of mind," to use John Dewey's phrase. It must interpret for us all the meaning of life in a civilization dominated in its every aspect by the stupendous fact of a successful technology, a triumphantly applied science. This is the peculiar characteristic of the age in which our lives are cast. And it is why all the ancient cultures, though they may teach us many things, still leave unsaid a word we need to hear. "The content of the school must be

[2] "The Great American Symphony": *Proceedings of the Music Teachers' National Association*, vol. 24, 1929, p. 66.

constructed out of the very materials of American life—not from academic relics of Victorian precedents. The curriculum must bring children to close grips with the roar and steely clang of industry, with the great integrated structure of American business and must prepare them in sympathy and tolerance to confront the underlying forces of political and economic life. America must awake to the newly emerging culture of industrialism, and she must become articulate." [3]

In so far as we achieve a culture which is thus a fructifying interpretation of our way of social life, it will cease seeming to people like a toy or an ornament. Literary insight will no longer be rated as rather less desirable than tap dancing. Music will not be something we endure with what polite fortitude we may, as a necessary prelude to contract bridge. History will be transformed into something one actually reads and discusses. We shall begin to lead cultured lives, not in spots or on special occasions, but all over and all the time—in the home, in the office, in the factory, on the farm, in the political campaign. And we shall lead such lives, not because we think we ought to, but because we really want to; because this seems to us the obviously best possible way of living. For culture will be to us a progressive interpretation of the social environment.

2. *What is the meaning of culture for the individual?*

For the individual, culture means enlightened living. It expresses itself in the ability to deal, as a human being should, with the practical problems of life. It is, precisely, a flexible, creative adjustment to the institutions of society. This must have been just what it meant to the best type of Greek citizen of the great age. His culture was not something remote from everyday concerns. It meant a sharing in the fullness of Greek citizenship. It meant being a Greek, and not a barbarian, in all the relationships of life. As a soldier, he was conscious of serving the state, and strong in an inner discipline. This was the spirit of the men of

[3] Harold Rugg, in *National Society for the Study of Education, Yearbook 26*, p. 149.

Marathon. As a politician, if he could not initiate action, he could understand it and collaborate in it. Such informed and enlightened living was the very essence of his culture. And what was true three and twenty centuries ago, is true today. Culture, if it is worth while and genuine, expresses itself in life—in adjustment to civic institutions, to economic institutions, to the home, to all modes of human activity. To see what culture really means, contrast the Russian peasant with the Danish farmer. On the Russian plains, you see a being who clings to ancient ways of life; whose agricultural practice it is almost impossible to reform; whose use of the land is to the last degree inefficient; who has no understanding of, and therefore can develop no effective action towards, the mechanisms of distribution and exchange on which he must depend for his living. So he is condemned to poverty, and stands a victim of recurrent famine and epidemic disease. On the sandy soil of Denmark you see a man who has triumphed over adverse physical circumstances; who has learned the lesson of constructive coöperation; who knows his way about in an industrial civilization; and who has achieved that modern miracle, a stable agricultural prosperity. What is the secret of such a difference? In one word, culture. Danish agricultural well being is the work of one institution above all others—the Folk High School. This is universally admitted. And notice that this school is not an agricultural college. Its curriculum consists of philosophy, art, literature, science—just those subjects which we, in America, think impractical. But in Denmark they seem to have a very practical outcome. This is because they are taught in such a way that young people can perceive their bearing on life; because they teach the lesson of how to be a Dane, and how to be a man. The boy or girl who goes through such a school, has done very much more than study certain recognized and standardized subjects, supposed to be the marks of elegance, and the passports to polite circles. He has learned the greatest of all lessons—how to be a human being, not a clod. He succeeds, because his adjustment to life's problems is humanized, flexible, creative, ever advancing. He succeeds as a farmer, because he is a cultured man.

Contrast all this with that common misinterpretation, which

treats culture as an affair of mere luxury and ornament—an error whose end is sure futility. I know a community where there are a great many women's discussion clubs. Month by month, these organizations meet to hear and talk about reports and papers dealing with great books, and important literary and artistic movements. Judging by the announcements in the local paper, one would say that the women of the community are literally bathed in the choicest culture of our civilization. But one discovers, with a shock, that they are perfectly capable of rallying to the support of an arrant demagogue; of housing their maids in tiny attic rooms without a thought of social or personal consequences; of unlimited stupidity in the relationships of their homes; and of acquiescing in educational abuses, which they more or less recognize, but to which they tamely submit. Their culture, so called, has little or no elevating effect on their daily living. Its value, in the way of making them more effective human creatures, is probably quite small. Can one blame the male portion of the population, treated to such a spectacle, for tacitly regarding the whole business of culture as no better than an amiable and harmless game? It is said that some of the great Flemish merchants of the seventeenth and eighteenth centuries used to assemble priceless galleries of pictures in their homes, and retire into them, to escape the drabness and grayness of their everyday surroundings. This is exactly what happens when we treat culture as a way of escape rather than a means of elevating life. To enjoy and possess the fruits of culture, is not to turn one's back on the rough world, and pace the aisles of some remotely beautiful classic temple of the mind. Rather is it to live a life of increasing enlightenment and deepening perception of human values.

Let us further work out our conception of the true meaning of culture for the individual, as the enlightenment of life, by four clarifying statements.

A. There is a fallacy in thinking of culture as leisure time activity. Often we find this interpretation in modern educational discussions. It is pointed out, quite truly, that the number of hours per week absorbed by the job is steadily diminishing, so that men have more and more time for other things. It is urged that the mod-

modern school must prepare children for the worthy use of this increased leisure, which is also true. And it is asserted or assumed that a cultural activity must be an activity appropriate for leisure time, which is misleading.

After all, why should we lump together as "leisure," all the time a person can save from his job? There are occupations just as important for a well lived life as earning a living. And what the steady decrease in the time demanded by the job really means, is more opportunity for all these other important things. If a man must toil seventy-two hours a week, he has not much energy or time left to develop any kind of effective home life, or to inform himself on civic issues, or to read the news, or to follow up lines of recreational interest, or to care for his health, or, for that matter, to achieve a broad economic adjustment. A very exigent vocation makes him less completely human than he should be. One set of claims swamps all the rest. And when these claims are relaxed, it is his opportunity to live a more complete, civilized life. What he needs is not a cultural education in the narrow sense of learning how to while away his spare time. Rather it is a more effective basic adjustment to the whole circle of social institutions—an education which will help him to be a better husband and father, a wiser and more coöperative citizen, a more effective consumer, a healthier human animal. These are his new opportunities. And here lies the challenge to education of the new vocational order of things. If you wish to call this fundamental and broad adjustment to human life by the name of culture, well and good. But culture, so understood, is more than preparation for the harmless use of "leisure time."

B. Culture is an individual possession. We speak of a man as "cultured" when he has his own developed quality, his own unique way of acting and thinking; when he makes his own inimitable contribution to social living. To be cultured is not to know certain things which are regarded as conventionally respectable, or to possess certain skills which are the badges of class distinction. It is the very opposite of being standardized, even as a "gentleman and a scholar." It means the discovery and realization of oneself, the achievement of one's own personal attitude towards, and view of, life. Such individuality is the product, not of heredity, but of education. As a person grows mentally, his controlling background becomes more and more unique; the integrated pattern of his knowledge, and skill, and insight, takes on a more and more characteristic aspect. He comes to differ more and more profoundly from everybody else, and to be more and more distinctive.

C. But then, culture means the power of making a social contribution. The uniqueness of the cultured person has its public as well as its private aspect. It is not an affair of encouraging fads and fancies; of indulging in the "artistic temperament," just to show that one is different. The aesthete, who cherishes his personal peculiarities, to prove to himself and to others how wonderful, how sensitive he is, possesses a decadent culture at the best— culture which exists for looks rather than for use. And his is a spurious individuality a uniqueness existing for itself alone, and having no place of value in the world. Our education must seek to help children to be, and to become, themselves. But also, it must seek to help them thus, for the sake of a social value, a social contribution, a social richness otherwise unobtainable.

D. Culture is not a state, but a process. It is not a list of accomplishments and a catalog of knowledge. It is not something we achieve and then display. As a matter of fact, nobody ever does achieve it. There is no such being as a completely "cultured" man, simply because culture means enlightenment, and one insight always opens up others, just as one invention paves the way for more. So we must remember once again that the school is the starting point only. If it does not so deal with the individual, that after leaving it, he continues to learn and to grow, then it has failed in its mission, so far as he is concerned.

3. *Are some school studies cultural in contrast to others which are practical?*

One of the most persistent fallacies in educational thought and practice, is to draw a sharp line of distinction between studies, as on the one hand, cultural, and on the other, practical or useful. It is a fallacy against which most of the great educational thinkers

ENDS OF CULTURE AND VOCATION

have protested. But lesser men have continually fallen into it. Consider, for instance, the educational doctrine of Plato in this matter. For him there was a living synthesis of the practical and the theoretical. He sought for the wide general meanings, the fundamental ideas, of such commonplace pursuits as those of the potter and the silversmith. And he wished the most abstract of all disciplines, pure philosophy, to be studied, not for its own sake, but to fit a man for the service of the state. But his followers, the neo-Platonists, had a trend towards snobbery, which made them despise the mechanical arts, and worship traditionally intellectual pursuits as valuable in themselves. In the Middle Ages, the content of a liberal education was very precisely defined as consisting of grammar, rhetoric, dialectic, arithmetic, geometry, astronomy, and music. During the seventeenth century, the scope of this curriculum was greatly limited, and it became largely confined to the classical languages, with chief emphasis upon their grammar. When Benjamin Franklin established the Philadelphia Academy, about the middle of the eighteenth century, he set up a Latin School, an English School, and a Mathematical School. But he had to fight the strong tendency amongst his supporters to narrow the work of the institution down to that of the Latin School alone. Due to its traditional setting, Latin was regarded as belonging distinctively to culture in contrast with mere practicality.

This idea of a distinction between the practical on the one hand and the liberal or cultural on the other, is with us still. We find it in our high school practice, when we have an academic, a commercial, and an industrial curriculum. We find it in that intensely conservative list of subjects which count for credit towards entrance into college—a list which excludes many fields whose educational possibilities are obviously great. We find it in such complaints as those recently expressed by Abraham Flexner in his *Universities,* when he attacks American institutions of higher learning for admitting such subjects as journalism and business, though here indeed, there is a further issue. Always the distinction is vicious. Always its tendency is to emasculate education, and to reduce the value both of subjects called practical, and those called cultural.

Its inconsistency with the conception of culture here presented—as an enlightened attitude towards the practical problems of life—is perfectly obvious. And it is fundamentally at variance with the entire thought of this book. Subject matter exists for one purpose and one only—to furnish an intellectual resource for the improvement of human adjustment. This is the only justification for every study in the curriculum, from Greek to stenography. If a study is not practical, it should be thrown out. By the same token, if a study is not enlightening, it should be thrown out. Between the practical and the cultural, there is no true distinction at all.

To understand how destructive of educational values this false distinction is, let us draw up a bill of particulars. Let us consider a number of studies taught in the schools. Always we shall find that if a subject is treated as cultural, but not practical, or as practical, but not cultural, it tends to become sterile, and to be divested of its true genius and meaning.

First take Latin. Why did Latin as a language ever exist? It was the chief means of communication of a great civilization; and long after that civilization collapsed, it still furnished a common tongue. This is its obvious place in the intellectual economy of mankind—exactly the same place as that of Greek, or Sanskrit, or the Mandarin dialect of Chinese. The clear inference would seem to be that, if taught at all, it should be taught as an agency of human communication. But is this done? By no manner of means. Latin teachers themselves admit as much, as you may see by referring to the *Classical Investigation*.[4] Instead of making much of the ability to read, and of spoken and written expression, the schools use the most highly formal methods, with emphasis on a kind of decoding called construing, and on the minute detail of the language structure. It is taught, in other words, as a purely theoretical, a deliberately impractical subject, a subject which very few who learn it are ever expected to use. The very expression, "dead language," is highly suggestive of the kind of educative value it is thought to possess. And what is the result? An excessively small minority of the multitudes of pupils who study Latin ever attain a working mastery of it. A mere handful become able to read

[4] Princeton University Press, 1924.

it freely, and of these again, only a few gain the power to write, still less speak it. Its claim to a place in the program of studies has to be maintained by a mass of excuses which, to speak quite bluntly, are preposterous, and which would not stand for a moment if urged on behalf of most other subjects. Its position is really supported not by its educative value, but by curricular requirements. If these were withdrawn, it would behave instantly like a currency which goes off the gold standard. And all this comes from just one thing—from treating Latin as theoretical and not also practical. Such an attitude is the greatest possible disservice to the subject itself. And it means the infliction of planned, deliberate uselessness upon large numbers of pupils, in the name of a false conception of culture and education. What should be done is to teach Latin for its intrinsic worth as an agency for communication and take the consequences, which would probably be that comparatively few would study it, but that these few would gain an educational benefit from it.

Next take science. Here the conventional emphasis is upon pure science, presented and learned as a self contained body of theory, whose only contact with concrete reality is in formal laboratory work—and a pretty emasculated contact it is. Ask the average chemistry teacher if he thinks his course makes the girls better cooks; and having made him understand that you really mean what you say, run away as fast as you can, for he will probably try to kill you! He is not teaching a base, mechanic art of pots and pans—not he; but a noble discipline of virgin theory. And this is just what blights his work. Better cooking is one small but by no means unreasonable manifestation of that better and more enlightened adjustment which it is the opportunity, and supreme duty of science, to inculcate. But he will have none of it. He wants his pupils to know the difference between an element and a compound, to remember the atomic weight of oxygen, to be able to express in symbols what takes place when one drops iron filings into hydrochloric acid and to be competent manipulators of borax beads. His imagination is limited to the cycle of such ideas and achievements. And then he is astounded to discover that his pupils are just as likely to believe in charlatans, or to oppose vivisection and vaccination, or to regard a research worker as a sort of amusing magician, as if they never had any contact with science at all. Science does not become educative until taught and learned for its social values.

Next take manual training. Here we have a subject with just the opposite trouble, a subject rendered sterile by a too brutal, too narrow practicality. Up to very recently, it concentrated chiefly on skill in the use of tools, without any consideration of the social meaning, and wider implications of such skill. Now to be able to use a chisel has exactly the same sort of place in the economy of human life, as to be able to solve an equation with one variable. It is one item from the intellectual resources of civilization. Its value lies in helping the individual to make a better total adjustment to life situations. It should be taught in a life setting, in connection with projects demanding initiative, foresight, and organizing power. It should be regarded as part of the child's development, perhaps towards becoming a carpenter, but perhaps not. Most of us can probably remember doing some kind of shop work in the schools, which seems to have had upon us very little educative effect of any kind. Almost certainly the reason was that it was taught too narrowly on the basis of direct, limited, practical skill alone. When the Russians insist that a part of every child's education must be active work in a factory, they do not fall into this kind of error, at least. The aim is not merely to convey a manipulative ability, but to produce an indelible mental attitude, which remains forever, and affects the individual, even though he may become a teacher or a clerk in a government bureau.

Home economics furnishes us with a most interesting contrary illustration. Surely one might suppose that this would be a severely, narrowly "practical" subject, dealing only with cake recipes, the washing of dishes, the cleaning of rugs and clothes, and such matters. But those who teach it have vastly expanded its scope and broadened it to include aesthetic, psychological, and even moral considerations. It has been made both practical and cultural; and thereby it has become educationally significant.

Our conclusion then must be, that no subjects are exclusively cultural, or exclusively practical. The distinction is fundamentally false. When pressed, it greatly weakens both the alleged culture, and the alleged practicality. All subjects studied have but one common end, the enlightenment of living and the improvement of adjustment.

One of the early American academies for girls furnished a curriculum which is no less than a museum piece in the way of a cultural program. The studies offered were as follows: "Petit Point in Flowers, Fruit, Landscapes, and Sculpture, Nun's Work, Embroidery in Silk, Gold, Silver, Pearls or embossed, Shading of all kinds in the Various Works in Vogue, Dresden Point Work, Lace Ditto, Catgut in different Modes, flourishing Muslin, after the newest Taste, and most elegant pattern Waxwork in Figure, Fruit or Flowers, Shell Ditto, or grotesque, Painting in Water Colours and Mezzotinto; also the Art of Taking off Foliage, with several other Embellishments necessary for the Amusement of Persons of Fortune who have Taste." [5] The clear counterpart of this appalling schedule, would be a scheme of narrow, direct practicality, without human value or vital interest.

When we push the distinction between the cultural and the practical to the extreme limit, we have just such a *reductio ad absurdum* of all education. Our common sense shrinks from this violent logic, and it is right. All education is general. All education is practical. The reciprocal effect between theory and experience is essential. And to establish it, is one of our persistent problems in school work.

4. *How may education serve the end of vocational adjustment?*

To fit a person for a vocation, the ideal education will be broad and general, and at the same time, closely and definitely connected with the real issues and problems of life. The great error to avoid is that vocational education is not cultural, and cultural education not vocational. Such a conception is disastrous in two directions. It leads us to treat culture as a mere ornament or amusement, out of relationship with the needs of adjustment to society; and vocation

[5] Quoted from Inglis, A. *Principles of Secondary Education:* Houghton Mifflin Company, 1916, p. 182.

as mere drudgery for pay, lacking in human values, and offering no opportunities for personal satisfaction and growth. This means, at once, a dead culture and a false vocationalism. What we must have is not either one or the other, as mutually exclusive alternatives, but a living, creative fusion of both. I will first try to develop a number of points on which this position depends and then try to show, briefly and in outline, the kind of educational scheme we would have, should we apply it in practice.

A. First of all, what is vocation? When we say that a person is a tailor, or a tinsmith, or a carpenter, or a nurse, or a social worker, or a teacher, or a lawyer, what we mean is that he organizes his life in a certain manner. A person's job is not so much his way of earning as his way of living. His salary check is really less important to him than the kind of things he must do to receive it. If his work is very confining and uninteresting, if it is socially obnoxious, or dangerous to his health, he will not be compensated simply by being well paid. As a matter of fact, the most desired vocations are not by any means always those which offer the most money, but rather those which furnish the best opportunities for happiness and personal well being. Your own best chance of making a vocational success, which is a most important part of your whole life success, is not to find out which job offers the most money, and then to make a bee line for it. Rather you should seek to learn the things you most like to do, and can do best, and follow this for your clue. If you know anything of life, you know that high pay simply does not compensate for cramping conditions, and generally ineffective adjustment. This is not a piece of idealism. It is a plain fact. If we forget it, if we allow ourselves to think of a vocation chiefly as a chance to earn money, rather than a chance to live a certain kind of life, we shall not achieve even the beginnings of wisdom about the proper vocational emphasis in education. The very word "vocation" itself suggests as much. In its derived meaning, it stands for "calling."

We see in this the profound importance of vocation in the life of every person, an importance broader than the need for earning. When we say that a man *is* a garage mechanic, or a salesman, or a preacher, or a physician, we exaggerate only a little. For his whole adjustment to the world is involved in his calling. His domestic and civic, his recreational and health problems, his whole attitude towards the economic system, are determined by the way he earns his living, and that apart from the size of his wage. His vocation is bound to be one of the great, organizing points of his life. This is why we say, and very truly, that each vocation tends to develop its own type, and that physicians, and teachers, and lawyers, and mechanics and farmers, are all apt to grow into a sort of family resemblance to one another.

So, for education to ignore vocational adjustment, on the ground that it should deal only with culture, is simply to ignore life itself. If we were all guaranteed an independent income of five thousand dollars a year, then, perhaps, there would be an argument for a purely non-vocational education, since the great fact of vocational specialization would be removed from human affairs. But, as things are, a man must be adjusted to his vocation if he is to be adjusted to life. And so one of the primary, universal obligations of education is to work towards an effective vocational adjustment for every pupil.

But is not this in conflict with the idea that education ought to be cultural? Only in so far as we misconceive the meaning and place of culture in life. If we think of culture as an ornament, or a toy, or a palliative, then indeed education for culture is out of touch with education for vocation. This often happens. One of the most common criticisms of our schools is that their aim is "merely" cultural. And there is no doubt at all that multitudes of children drop out of school too soon for their own and the common good, because they do not find there definite means of adjustment to their work in life. To some extent, of course, such criticisms are due to misunderstanding, but not altogether. The culture conveyed by our schools is too often, and too complacently, sterile; too much an affair of parlor tricks and the reading of nice papers at ladylike gatherings; too little directed to the ends of strong living in a real and practical world. If you will ask yourself just what life value is found in many things you studied at school, and force yourself to a stringent and candid reply, you will be compelled to admit that this is so. But, if we understand culture as the enlightenment of action through insight, then the whole conflict with vocationalism vanishes. Only a spurious culture is at odds with vocation, either in life in general, or in school life in particular. A man's true culture—and this means his enlightened activity as a citizen, as a member of a family, as a producer and consumer, and so forth—must be rooted in his vocation, not divorced from it. He cannot just be enlightened in general. He must be an enlightened physician, or teacher, or salesman, or farmer, or mechanic, or ditch digger.

Education, then, must be vocational in its deliberately planned, conscious intention, and in its outcomes. This is true, simply because life is vocational. But also it must be cultural, simply because life must be enlightened. We are not facing an alternative, but a synthesis. Until we have integrated a man's total outlook upon the world, which is his culture, about the vocational core of his living, that culture is superficial and sterile.

B. How does one make one's vocational decision? Like every other great choice in life, this decision for a certain vocation takes place by way of mental growth. For a few, it is dramatic, sudden. Like a flash, it comes to them that there is only one way of life in which they can ever be content; and from that moment, all their energies are bent in a single direction. But even such rare, conversion-like experiences, are always the outcome of long, subconscious incubation. A few people, too, make up their minds very early in life, and never change them. But all this means is that they become increasingly sure of the significance and rightness of their childish guess. Many of us, as we look back, can hardly trace the winding way which has led us to our work in life. We were directed by circumstances, reacted upon by increasing experience and self knowledge. We could not tell with certainty whither we were bound, till we arrived. This is perfectly characteristic of any kind of mental growth.

Here we have an idea of profound significance and value. I want to call your attention to some of its implications. First, it means that we must always seek to educate a child *towards* a wise vocational choice, which is one of the most crucial decisions he will ever make. Now it is clear that the best way to do this is to impart to him a wide, many-sided vision of life. When a child is in school, this is his golden chance to recognize alternatives, to consider possibilities, to come to a broader and deeper understanding of himself and the world, to be made aware of the infinite variety of living. He should precisely not be put into any groove. He should be given a wide grasp of the intellectual resources of civilization, taught and learned as agencies for more effective adjustment. He should be moving towards an adjustment to the whole range of social institutions. His education should be cultural, as we have come to understand the term. And out of this vital culture should arise the vocational decision.

"But," you may ask, "when should this vocational decision be made?" No one can tell. But there are three ideas which show us what to hope and work for here. First, the vocational decision should be postponed as long as possible. It is a choice which calls for wisdom, and which should depend on views as comprehensive and experience as varied as may be. The older a person is, the more able he is apt to be to make such a choice. And another reason for postponing it is that it has a certain limiting effect, like any other momentous choice. It is the selection of one determinate way of living, as against others; and it may have a tendency to reduce the individual's flexibility, which is also his educability, and his power to grow. Second, the vocational choice should not be put off, merely because of lackadaisical indifference, or a preoccupation with the idea that education is "purely cultural." It should be the culmination of a vocational *concern,* penetrating all education from the kindergarten onwards. The practical danger for many people is putting it off so long that the best opportunities for specific vocational adjustment have been lost. Third, the vocational decision must not be expected to come all in a moment, with perfect clarity and certitude. It is the outcome of experimentation, experience, and doubt. It is one of the slowly evolving results of an education which is a process of self discovery.

Then there is a very concrete question which you may raise. "Here," you may say, "is a fourteen year old boy. Should he go on with his general school education? Or should he be directed into some intermediate trade school with a vocational outlet? How can we tell which is best?" Bluntly, there is no magic means of deciding. Each individual case is a special problem. We cannot, for instance give him some sort of a battery of tests, and read off his fate from the results. It is a matter of getting to know him, and helping him to get to know himself. For a vocational choice must be coöperative, and the person who makes it must play the principal rôle. If he shows any reasonable intellectual aptitude at all, then school is surely the place, and general education the thing for him for some time to come. If not—if it seems to all concerned, including the boy, that immersion in an environment which is inevitably impregnated more and more with theory, would be futile —then our best wisdom will be to guide him towards a vocation immediately.

Notice, finally, how this idea of a postponed, and evolving vocational decision, makes it impossible to tell whether a given subject in school is, or is not, vocational. Is Latin a vocational study? Yes—if one becomes a Latin teacher or an archeologist, or a Roman Catholic priest; but otherwise, perhaps not. Is manual training vocational? Yes—if one becomes a carpenter; no—if one becomes a preacher. Education does not serve the ends of vocation by setting up some studies called cultural and others called vocational; but rather by making all studies vital, and giving the pupil a vision of the fullness of human life, whereby he may be guided to his own living, and enabled to determine his own plan. We have here, of course, a splendid illustration of the futility of fixed aims in education, and of the notion of specific preparation in advance. The outcomes of education are the outcomes of growth. They cannot be determined in advance. We cannot look over our sixth grade pupils, and classify them— tinker, tailor, soldier, sailor—and then educate them accordingly. Education, whether for vocation or not, must be treated as a process of growth, through which the individual comes to discover himself, and be himself.

C. What is necessary for effective vocational adjustment? For a man to make the most of himself in his job, what he needs is the fullest possible possession of the intellectual resources of civilization. To think we serve him best here, by teaching him a few routines, is a most mistaken notion. The humblest drudge, so limited by hereditary endowment that he can never rise above his menial round, will gain something by seeing, however dimly, the wider social relationships and meanings of his work. He is not a robot, but a human being; and education should seek to make the utmost of the human part of him. Vocational education does not aim merely at making the man with the hoe better at hoeing. It also seeks to alleviate and illumine the tragic darkness of his mind. And for every man above this status, adjustment to the job means assuredly the power to grow in the job, and perhaps beyond it. A worker in a bicycle shop does not become the perfecter and promoter of the cheap car, merely by knowing the tricks of his trade, but by social insight and intellectual enterprise. Fortunately or unfortunately, education cannot make every boy a Henry Ford. But it can recognize in such a life that the pattern of a triumphant vocational adjustment is not narrow but broad. It can recognize that there is more practical value in the general than in the particular.

We often hear about something called a "narrow vocationalism." Just what does this mean? As I understand the matter, it would mean a training wholly concerned with certain specific industrial techniques. Now these are necessary. But they are not enough. When we think to train a man for a job, simply by communicating to him its special techniques—the so-called tricks of the trade—we are on the road to failure. You will remember that we saw how the Hoover Commission on Waste in Industry recognized many things as more important causes of industrial waste than lack of operative skill in the workers. To succeed in every and any job, one needs to have much more than the power to go through the necessary motions. The means of communication, the sciences, the fine arts, the prevailing wants and beliefs, all of these can have a constructive value somewhere, somehow, in almost every job. They stand for creativeness and flexibility; for the power to raise the level of one's work, and to make it count for more. And conversely, the techniques of industry have other than vocational uses and meanings. So, a "narrow vocationalism" is a false vocationalism. What is necessary for effective vocational adjustment is just what is necessary for culture—action rendered enlightened by the possession, in full measure, of the intellectual resources of civilization.

D. How much specific vocational training should the schools offer? It is always a matter of doubt just how far the public schools ought to go, in trying to teach the specific techniques of industry. Should we have courses in carpentry, or plumbing, or tinsmithing, or office management, or accountancy, or stenography? Our answers to questions like these will depend, to some degree, on particular conditions. What may be suitable in one community, may not be in another. What can be done well in a large city, may be impossible in a small town. But still, there are some general, guiding principles to hold in mind.

(i) First, it should be understood that the schools cannot, by any possibility, offer specific preparation for the whole range of vocations, or anything like it. Even to try to do this, would be fantastic, and would fatally interfere with the general program. (ii) Second, it should be clear that many industrial techniques can be learned much better in industry than in the school. In a great many cases, the schools should open avenues into apprenticeship, rather than try to take over the whole job of vocational training. To teach, let us say, the machinist's trade, calls for very costly equipment of a highly specialized kind, if it is to be done in a worth while manner. And the same thing is true of other callings. The schools should limit their efforts to those things which they can do better than any other institution. And this, in the main, means concentrating on general education. (iii) Those techniques of industry should be taught in the schools, which will be of some service, whether vocational or not, to the greatest possible number of pupils. I will venture to predict that the education of the future will not be carried on in schools which emphasize specialization to the limit, and which plan their work so that small groups of pupils are learning entirely different sets of trade skills. Some contact with the techniques of industry is valuable for everybody, partly as a means of exploration and self discovery, partly as a genuine element in general culture for which there is no substitute, and which does something to and for a person which nothing else can do. But our idea should be to convey industrial techniques in the interest of general mental growth and social enlightenment, rather than for specific vocational fitness. We see the schools leading towards

ENDS OF CULTURE AND VOCATION 323

specialization, as one of the necessary consequences of mental growth, which must always be in some direction. But also, we see their services coming to an end, as soon as specialization goes beyond a certain point.

So we conclude again that there is no conflict between vocation and culture, when both are properly understood. When we separate the one from the other, in our thought, and in our practice, we become false servants of each.

5. *What kind of educational organization will achieve these ends?*

In the first place, we should seek an elementary education, lasting for at least six years, aiming at fundamental and broad social adjustment, without even the beginnings of specialized vocational emphasis, though not inconsistent with such an emphasis later on. At the junior high school level, the first alternatives, the first beginnings of specialization, may begin to emerge, though only for comparatively few pupils. That is to say, we may set up intermediate trade schools as a possible choice, instead of the general junior high school. Such trade schools would lead naturally towards apprenticeship, which would parallel the senior high school education of the vast majority of children. Specialization may proceed a step farther at the level of the senior high school, with a larger number drafted off from the main stem of general schooling, destined to more exacting and repaying vocations than those who go out from the seventh grade. At the level of the college, we should have institutions giving special training, and directed definitely towards the semi-professional occupations, though still the core of general education should be preserved. And graduate school education should be almost wholly vocational. In addition to this fundamental system, we should have adult continuation schools, which, once more, should have as their main emphasis general rather than special education.

There are several things to notice about this outline scheme. (i) It provides for the effective recognition of a valid vocational choice, at several different levels. This is as it should be. The amount of general education a person ought to receive under an ideal system, must be determined by the intellectual, emotional, social, and moral qualities that he manifests. It cannot be decided in advance by tests which purport to measure pure native ability. Everyone should go just as far as he can with general education. But as soon as it becomes evident that continued living in an environment which is concerned more and more with general matters, more and more with intellectual techniques, is a mistake, the time has come to help the pupil to find himself outside school, in the interests of a well lived life. Moreover, once a vocational choice which is valid and wise has been made, it should become the organizing point of his mental, moral, and personal growth.

(ii) It provides systematically for the postponement of the vocational choice as long as possible; and yet not too long for the pupil to secure the kind of help and training he needs to achieve his aim. Whether to enter an intermediate trade school, or a general junior high school; whether to continue on to senior high school or college, or, on the other hand, to enter some school leading outwards towards a skilled trade, or a semi-professional occupation, is a decision to be made on the basis of cumulative experience. Everybody must try himself out, and discover little by little, what is best.

(iii) It fully recognizes the idea that, once a true vocational choice has been made, education ought to take it into account. The vocational choice is a dramatic moment in an individual's personal growth. His education has brought him to it. And now it must be recognized and respected in the fullest possible manner. Otherwise we deliberately stultify the very process of growth which, so far, we have been fostering. If a boy of seventeen has come to know, with surety, that he wishes to be a machinist; and if his teachers, advisers, friends, and parents have reason to believe that his choice is wise, there is not the very slightest point in continuing to train him as though he were headed towards professional life. To do so, is to work an injury upon him. His ideal adjustment to life is not secured by making him into a second rate, half hearted, discontented white collar worker, which is just what is apt to happen, if we use undue suasion to keep him in school. Rather, his well being, and his contribution to society, are best promoted by training him to be as good, and as successful a machinist as possible, and by fully and effectively recognizing the dignity of such a vocation, and such a choice.

(iv) Notice particularly, that the whole scheme presupposes a cultural, or general education, which is vital rather than traditional. When we talk about education as general, we do not mean that it is direction-less. We must seek always an effective adjustment to life, and to the world; a close and intimate contact with reality. Only so can culture truly serve the ends of life, including those of vocation. The plan presented thus in outline, immediately falls to pieces, as does any conceivable plan, if culture is taken to mean ornamentation, and its acquisition, induction into intellectual and social snobbery.

*

Chapter 15

HOW MAY EDUCATION STIMULATE THINKING?

1. *What is the importance of thinking in education?*

There is no question you can ask a teacher, which is more searching than this: "Does your scheme of education tend to produce thinking men and women? When boys and girls have lived for a while under the influence of your school, are they forever afterwards apt to accept what is just because it is, to believe without a qualm anything they happen to read in the newspapers, to take present ways as the only ways, to mould themselves undoubtingly to current standards, to do whatever their neighbors do and be content? On the other hand, do they gain some inner strength to resist fads, and whims, and fancies; and to rise above the level of a sophomoric, wise-cracking cynicism? Are they made permanently more ready to stop and consider before the issues of life?" That wonderful vision in stone, Rodin's statue of *The Thinker,* should have a central place in the mental landscape of every teacher. Here is what we seek. To pause from unconsidered action, to stop, to weigh alternatives, to look deeply into problems, to ponder—this is the supreme human characteristic, the ability, above all others, which separates man from brute. It is the final mark of the educated man.

But is not this quite contrary to the idea which, in these pages, has been proclaimed again and again, and elaborated from so many points of view; the idea that education seeks to adjust people to social institutions, and deals, above everything, with action? If you suppose so, it is because you allow yourself two great errors, which you should, here and now, forever extirpate from your mind. You have a wrong notion of what thinking really is. And you forget the true nature of human adjustment.

First of all, let us ask what thinking really is. A few years ago, a cartoonist published a long series of comic strips, dealing with what various people were supposed to be thinking about. The taxi driver, waiting for a fare, meditates about the crowded traffic, the cop who bawled him out, the hot day, and what he will have for his supper. The pullman porter on a night run considers the large boots of the gentleman in lower ten, the chance of a good tip from upper five, the speed of another train. And so on. These cartoons, as so often happens, showed much satiric insight into human nature. What are these people thinking about? They are not thinking at all. They are only day dreaming. Like the immortal Br'er Rabbit, they are "letting their minds run on." And whatever label you may give to this proceeding, you should keep the term "thinking" for something very different. I say that the heroes of the comic strip are not really thinking for this reason; the stream of images and ideas passing through their minds has no influence upon their action. And here we see the distinguishing mark, the essential meaning, of genuine thought. Consider again Rodin's statue. What is *The Thinker* thinking about? We cannot tell. It may be a system of philosophy which occupies him; or only the scheme he has made for snaring a squirrel. Of this the master artist gives no hint. Nor need he. For every line of the figure he has created powerfully suggests the very essence of thinking, whatever its subject. Note the attitude of concentration; the set pose of one who wrestles inwardly. Whatever he is considering, it is something that matters, something momentous. Life has confronted him with a problem, either great or small. A way of action has been blocked. Behavior needs to be organized on a new plane. A routine has broken down; and something better must be discovered. This is what we must seek to have people do, when we seek to educate them to think. There is no conflict between saying that, on the one hand, thought, and on the other, adjustment to life, is the great aim of education; because thinking, truly understood, as distinguished from other uses of the mind, is the means of such adjustment, and the controlling and directing of action.

Then, do not forget our discussion of the characteristics of human adjustment. First, that adjustment is *flexible*. When a lion is trained to perform—that is to say, when he is adjusted to the circus—all that it means is that he will follow certain routines exactly, when the cue is given. But the adjustment of the trainer is altogether different. No routine is enough for him. He must be ready to adapt himself to the mood of his animals, to the size and temper of the audience, to the rest of the performance, to half a hundred other things which may vary endlessly. He must *consider*. For the animal, adjustment means conforming. For the human being, it means readiness and ability to meet, and cope with, problems. Second, human adjustment is *inventive* or *creative*. It is a finding of new ways. Civilized man in the far north discovers a wholly new dietary regime, which enables him to use the resources of the region to go where no native has dared to go, and to live better than the native. Primitive man sticks to his routine; and if his routine fails him, he dies.

Now when I say that human adjustment is not a matter of routine and conformity, but that it is flexible and creative, am I not really describing the process of thought? Thinking is exploring. It is a considering of alternatives, a rejection of many, and a choice, at last, of one. It is the exact opposite of routine action. Moreover, it is more than a canvassing of alternatives already before one. The thinker often solves his problem and achieves a better way of behavior by invention. None of the familiar pathways seem to lead out of the morass in which he finds himself. So he blazes a new trail.

We begin to see that, so far from the account of education as adjustment being inconsistent with the statement that thinking is the final mark of an educated man, it really renders that statement inevitable. And there is yet a third characteristic of human adjustment, which makes the connection still clearer. Human adjustment is *progressive*. It carries one on endlessly. As soon as the pioneer has cleared the forest, he is ready to put in his crop. As soon as he has reaped and sold his first harvest, he is ready to build a bigger barn and buy more stock. As soon as he obtains more equipment, he is ready to clear more land, and diversify his planting. The time when the work is finished, the time of ultimate finality, never comes. This is a parable of education. One mastery continually leads to others. The higher we climb, the more we see ahead of us, and the more deeply we comprehend what is behind. When this does not happen, education itself has failed.

Here again, we see the characteristic nature of thinking. To solve a problem by thought is indeed, in a sense, to have done with it. But also it is to become conscious of other problems in a new way. Only idle dreaming, like that of the persons of the comic strip drama, can come to an end with perfect satisfaction. The more one really thinks, the more one wants to think.

John Dewey has written: "Deliberation is a dramatic rehearsal (in imagination) of various competing possible lines of action. It starts from the blocking of efficient overt action . . . Then each habit, each impulse involved in the temporary suspense of overt action takes its turn in being tried out. Deliberation is an experiment in finding out what the various lines of possible action are really like. It is an experiment in making various combinations of selected elements of habits and impulses, to see what the resultant action would be like if it were entered upon."[1] Thought, in other words, is the companion and guide of action, if it really deserves its name. This is why I say that the thinker is the fine flower of an education whose aim is better adjustment to the demands of life, and whose great concern is the improvement and enlightenment of behavior. How then, may we, with good hope of success, set about the great and delicate task of producing thinking men and women? The school must be made, above everything else, the home of thought. How can we make it so?

2. *What principles must guide our effort to produce thinking?*

To induce anyone to think is a very difficult and delicate undertaking. Notice the verb in that last sentence—the verb "induce." You can never force a person to think. You can incite him, and help him,

[1] *Human Nature and Conduct*, p. 100.

and encourage him. But compulsion is not possible. This is why the task is so difficult. You can make a child recite something to you. But you cannot make him really reflect upon it.

Yet you must do your best. If you, as a teacher, feel an inward uneasiness over just going through the conventional motions of school keeping; if you cannot rid yourself of the belief that there should be more to education than hearing lessons and preserving order; then your only way towards a better adjustment for yourself is to try to induce your pupils to think. And, indeed, there is much that you can do. You know the old saying that one can lead a horse to water, but one cannot make him drink. This is very true. Yet, if you never lead him to the water, he will never drink. And if you lead him there tactfully, choosing well your moment, he very probably will. So do not leave the inculcation of thinking to pure chance. Do not suppose that the ordinary round of subject matter exhausts the possibilities of teaching, and that anything further comes unsought, like fire from heaven; for this is not true. And do not give up in despair, because the task is hard, and frequent failure certain. For it is, beyond measure, rewarding. Plan definitely and purposefully to stimulate thinking in your pupils. Learn how to do it in the only way we humans learn anything—by understanding the principles involved, and slowly working out their full application to suit your need.

A. The first step in inciting the pupil to think, is to plan his education in such a way that he is beset with things worth thinking about. Thought always begins in one way—the sense of a problem arising out of experience. Both the problem and the experience are necessary. A great deal of school work is managed in such a way that numerous problems are indeed presented. Courses in algebra and geometry, in science, in history, in literature, all teem with what, in the abstract, seem splendid opportunities and challenges for thinking. But somehow, the stimulus does not seem to affect the pupil. He is capable of maintaining a stolid composure in the face of issues to which an expert will address himself with the keenest interest. Why is this? Simply because the problems involved in his studies do not touch his experience. In a course in educational psychology, or the technique of instruction, given to undergraduate students, it is an easy matter to make statements which would start a riot in most teachers' meetings, but which provoke not so much as a ripple in the undergraduate group. A professor of economics may proclaim doctrines which would rouse the excitement of bankers, and give business men an attack of high blood pressure; but his class passively absorbs them, and continues to decorate the furniture, and chew the cud. Again, why is this? Surely not because the challenges are absent; nor because there is no opportunity for thinking. Yet somehow, the problems are not felt. The students remind one of people who are being challenged and insulted in an unknown tongue, and who show exactly the kind of mild and benevolent interest characteristic of tourists in certain oriental countries, when this very thing happens to them. And, as I say, the reason is that we are presenting to them problems which are verbal only, not experiential.

So our very starting point, in teaching pupils to think, is to give them something to think about—something which arises out of their own experience, and confronts them with the inescapable feeling of a genuine problem. If we fail to do this, there is no way of saving the situation. And this is exactly why so much very well meant effort proves so worthless. Thinking is by no means a process of empty mental manipulation. You do not make a pupil thoughtful by giving him a series of intellectual calisthenics in the shape of problems in geometry, algebra, science, sociology, economics, and what not. Notice most particularly that I have not advised organizing the content and materials of these courses in problematic form. This is not the first step. Doing so may have some value, but only after a prior condition has been fulfilled. Always we must bring our problems into contact with the pupil's actual living. Otherwise, we are condemning ourselves to certain failure in the enterprise of educating for thought. Physical education has pretty well done away with the idea that one can build up a healthy, skillful, well-coördinated, well-adjusted physique, by dint of formal exercise. Rather it insists upon the importance of physical undertakings which have some genuine interest and significance. Exactly the same principle holds if we wish to produce a healthy, active mentality. The reason why the study of economics, and science, and history, and literature, and mathematics, does so extremely and amazingly little to stimulate really active thought, is not that there are too few problems involved in what the student reads and learns. On the contrary, every page and every exercise bristles with problems. But the pupil goes past them, like a man in a trance. Much work in school is really done in a dream world. And there is a good reason—and an unavoidable reason—for this intellectual insensitiveness. The problems make no contact with the pupil's actual experience. Between what he learns in school, and what he does in life, there is a great gulf fixed.

This discussion makes it possible for us to anticipate a certain question quite likely to be asked. Is not every problem worth while? Is not every curricular field—history, social science, economics, physics, chemistry, mathematics, literature, manual training—filled with splendid opportunities for thinking? Can we then say that what is needed is to choose and organize problems, if we wish to stimulate thought? Are not all problems important and valuable? This indeed is so. But our point is that the child does not, and cannot, learn to think by taking problems, which, however valuable and important for other reasons and in the lives of other people, actually mean nothing to him. Education is the reconstruction of experience, the putting of more and more meaning into the concerns and activities of everyday living. Hence, it must not start with the remote, the strange, the unfamiliar. Our starting point in inciting the pupil to think, must be an experience which has the hall mark of genuineness. Let us build our introduction to economics about the neighborhood store. Let us make contact with natural science through the experiences of the home and the local community. Let us, like Pestalozzi, start geography from the crack on the blackboard. Thinking at such levels may be humble. To the academic highbrow it may seem trivial and worthless—beneath the dignity of formal education. But what is of supreme importance is that thinking be real, and not spurious; a grappling with a felt problem, rather than a half hearted manipulation of verbal symbols.

Another question which may be raised in this connection is the following: When we try to incite children to think in school, should they think about subject matter, or about life experience? Which is the more desirable, a careful consideration of the inventory problem

HOW TO STIMULATE THINKING

of the neighborhood store, or a reflection about the underlying economic principles which it exemplifies? Which should we have, an analysis of the possible sources of typhoid infection on a farm, or a concentration upon the laws of physiology and hygiene? Should the pupils devote their minds to the city water supply or the problems of natural science? Such questions present a false dilemma. When we think as we should, there is not a choice between subject matter and life. Thinking means the interpretation and control of experience, in the light of a mastery of subject matter; and reciprocally, an advancing mastery of subject matter is possible only as we come to understand its applications. When the child in school is taught to think as he should, he learns to deal with the cogent, genuine problems thrown up by experience, through the use of the intellectual resources of civilization.

So much for the first step to be taken, if we wish to influence the pupil to think as a result of his school life.

B. The second step must be this: When the child has sensed a problem, we must incite him to follow it up. Always bear in mind that it is not enough to start the thinking process. Also we must take definite measures to provide for its continuance. The saying, "Well begun is half done," may perhaps be true here. Certainly we shall never succeed in inciting thought, unless we take the first step, and deliberately plan to make the pupil conscious of genuine problems. But, however good our beginning, it is surely not more than half our task, if even so much. Following the pupil up, helping him to organize his processes, steering his mind, and keeping his activities relevant, is also essential.

It is just here that so many teachers fail in the task of helping pupils to think. They seem to suppose that thought is an absolutely free process which cannot be guided, and that all one can do is to present a stimulating problem and hope for the best. This may, perhaps, be true for the mature, highly individual, relatively expert thinker, whose mental processes are so uniquely his own that no one can give him very much help. When an author is writing a book, or a research worker is carrying on an investigation, no one can give very much guidance. Of course, conversation and discussion will often be most helpful. But if an outsider should undertake to lay out the work to be done, or plan in detail for the mature and accomplished worker, the whole task would be frustrated. This, however, is not true of the child. You must remember that by the time a man has become capable of consecutive, self initiated, self disciplined effort such as is necessary for authorship or research, he has learned a very great deal. He may be very far from any goal of final perfection and competence; but also he is very far from his crude beginnings. He has learned, by long and hard bought experience, what it means to sense a problem, and then follow it, as a clue, through innumerable windings and confusions, to some sort of finality and solution. The pupil in school does not, and probably cannot with any fullness, know what all this means. His idea of the way to deal with a problem which strikes him as real and interesting, is to think about it a little, perhaps to write a short theme about it, and then let it drop. And this is exactly what we want to train him away from. Having sensed a problem, he must now learn how to follow it out, and develop it consecutively.

Can this be done? Can a teacher directly educate a child in these subtle processes of consecutive reflection? Why not? I am not going to try to persuade you that you can do it with every pupil; or that you can succeed every time you try. But I am going to try to persuade you that the effort is entirely worth making, and wholly sane and sensible. You may have in your mind a fixed idea, held, perhaps not quite consciously, by a great many teachers, that the only mental undertakings which you can control directly in the pupil are the routines. That is, you can assign a chapter in the textbook; and then you can check up to see whether the assignment has been mastered. Or you can tell your class to work out a certain number of examples in arithmetic, and bring them to school next day; or to translate a certain number of Latin sentences into English. And so on. Things like this, you may say to yourself, a teacher can really do. But a teacher cannot make a child wrestle mentally with a problem, or organize an adventure in thinking. Routines are teachable; free, constructive activities are not.

This is a proposition with which I violently disagree. It seems like saying that real education is impossible, and that the only things which can be done in school, are the things least worth doing at all.

HOW TO STIMULATE THINKING   335

Violent disagreement, however, is not a sufficient reply; particularly to a doctrine quite widely held. So let us take it to pieces for minute inspection.

Consider, first of all, the claim that a teacher can compel the pupils to achieve the routine learnings. All one can say about this is that if he really can, he seldom does. Let your mind dwell on the routine tasks which are being assigned today in a large city high school, or, for that matter, in a college or university. And then ask yourself what total proportion of all these tasks will really be done by tomorrow, or on the date set or, indeed, at all? It is quite clear that, as a matter of fact, teachers may assign the study of chapters in history texts, the memorizing of chemical formulae, the solving of ten algebra examples, or the translation of ten Latin sentences; but this does not compel or guarantee the actual learning. But, you say, it could be done. If the teacher were put in a stronger position, so that he need not fear the complaints of the pupil, or the resentment of his parents—if he could use the kind of threats and pressure available to the instructor in a German *Gymnasium,* then indeed, the routine learning would really be done. Even of this, I am not very sure. There is no doubt that the pupils would tend to recite better, if very strenuous measures were taken to coerce them. But how much better they would really learn, seems more doubtful. Some of them would almost certainly learn much worse. For instance, I know of a boy in a European school, who was violently bullied in class, because he had not properly memorized a passage from *The Excursion.* After that, he prepared much more carefully and seriously. But he acquired a life-long hatred of Wordsworth, for which, I am perfectly sure, his improved recitations in no way, shape, or manner compensated. Even routine learning has a certain quicksilver-like quality about it when we try to control it. A teacher says to himself: "I will force my pupils to do the tasks I set. I will 'mark hard', and penalize them when they fail. I will be hard-boiled in class. They may hate me now, but later they will appreciate me. I will compel them to recite adequately on the history or the grammar rules I assign, or to bring to class the mathematical examples, or the translations I set, and to do so on time. This, at least, I can accomplish." Perhaps he is right. But a day may come when he will be astounded to find how very little all this learning and reciting seems to mean to most of his pupils; how inept they are in interpreting modern happenings in the light of the history they are supposed to have studied; how hard they find it to apply the grammar rules on which they were so glib; how swiftly the mathematical techniques demonstrated under pressure slip away from them. This is all because a teacher can indeed compel certain external actions, but cannot force the pupil, by direct means, to achieve even the simplest routine learning.

If you have agreed with this discussion, you should at least be free of a prejudice which is enough to wreck any effort you may ever make to teach pupils to think—quite enough, indeed, even to stop you from making any such effort at all—the prejudice, namely, that only routine activities are teachable. Now we are ready for a positive proposition. I say that consecutive reflective activity can be taught, and can be assigned. I say, moreover, that it is utterly absurd for teachers to talk about the desirability of thinking, and then do nothing but set, and check up on, routine tasks. What you cannot do is to *compel* thinking. But you cannot compel any learning. All you can do is to set up conditions which greatly favor the kind of learning you want, and hope that it will come. But this is doing a very great deal.

Let me try to make my meaning clearer by a concrete illustration. A boy in junior high school becomes interested in an issue up for vote by referendum, dealing with the state conservation program. As his social science teacher, I see in this an opportunity opening up many possibilities. There is a chance for a little missionary work in favor of what I consider a sound solution. There is a readymade, Heaven-sent illustration for certain points I have been developing in my course. But what interests me above all, is the chance presented by my pupil's feeling for a real problem, of stimulating him to do his own thinking. How can I take advantage of it? When he comes to me with his question, I must not give him a brief, cut-and-dried answer, for this will prevent the very outcome I most desire. Furthermore, I must not send him off with some vague advice to think the matter over, or even with one or two casual references. I must treat his problem with all respect, as an educational opportunity. I must make it just as important, both for him and for myself, as any assignment I have ever given. I must sit down with him, and discuss the question. I must assign or suggest a sequence of readings, and set times for him to do them, not as a police measure, but to help him organize himself. I must indicate a way of making notes, and criticize some of the notes he takes. And I shall be wise if I definitely and frequently advise him, not to read or annotate or do any of the conventional research tricks, but *just to ponder about what he is accumulating.* Is there any possible reason why we should not make a direct drive for meditation, for silent thinking, in our school work? Is it absurd to suggest this, frequently and emphatically, to an individual, or to a class, when there is work being done on a problem? I will venture the statement that, if we made half as much direct fuss about silent problematic thought and analysis, about assuming the mental attitude represented in the physical pose of *The Thinker,* as we do about routine memorizing, our education would mean much more than it actually does.

C. The third essential step in teaching a pupil to think, is to call for a definite outcome. The process of reflection must arrive somewhere; it must culminate in some tangible result; or it is mere dreaming. If the pupil is carrying through a scientific experiment, he must not only feel the need for it, plan it, and perform it; he must also write it up. If he is at work on an individual project, such as the making of a map, or the collecting of newspaper and magazine references, he must carry his task through to a completed issue. If he is coöperating in a group project, he must feel a definite responsibility for his definite share. If he is investigating the wisdom of some conservation problem, or finding out how learning was preserved in the mediaeval monasteries, the making of some report, oral or written, is an essential part of the process. True thinking, as contrasted with a passive movement of the mind from one thing to another, begins with the sense of a problem, is dominated throughout by that problem, which becomes more and more sharply understood, and culminates in some kind of solution.

At this point many teachers make a capital mistake, which can kill the effects of their best efforts to promote thinking. The mistake consists in treating the *results* of the pupil's learning as valuable and important for their own sake. If you submit a story to the *Saturday Evening Post,* the editor will ask only one question: Is it a good and suitable story? If so, he accepts it: if not, he rejects it. He does not care whether you learned a great deal in working it out and writing it. He is not interested in guiding your thought processes. His one concern is with results. Now, only too often, a teacher takes exactly the attitude of a magazine editor. He thinks only, or chiefly, of the product, and hardly at all of the process. This happens, for instance, when a pupil's work in mathematics is marked entirely on getting the right answer, and not at all on using an interesting and intelligent method; or when the whole emphasis in a laboratory experiment is placed on writing up the results in a standard form, rather than on the fumbling trial and error processes through which the pupil learns scientific thinking; or when an English teacher concerns himself wholly with reading, criticizing, and marking a theme, and not at all with helping the pupil to organize a better one; or when everything in a course is made to depend on what a pupil can put down on paper in an examination, with little or no attention given to the way he prepared for that examination. All this is wrong. Our interest, in education, is not so much on what the pupil does, as on how he comes to be able to do it. Results we want, and must have; not, however, for their own sake, but for their valuable effect upon the processes which go on in the mind of the pupil.

All this means three things. (i) First, the result of a course of reflection should always be planned to reflect back upon, and organize, the process of reflection itself. When you assign a theme, you should not be assigning sixty minutes of writing, but a good many hours of searching and meditating, culminating in a definite, terminal activity with pen and paper. When you tell pupils that they must report on their experiments in the laboratory, the aim should be to get them to organize their work, to plan, to observe, and to note down what they do, so that everything is felt as a coördinated reflective attack upon a problem. When you tell the boy who comes to you with the conservation problem that in two weeks you will ask him to report the matter in class, this is far more than a mere test. It should

HOW TO STIMULATE THINKING

give purpose, point, and educative value, to all his reading, and questioning, and note-taking, and meditating.

(ii) Second, the result of thinking should be in a form significant and valuable for the pupil, rather than fixed and standardized by the teacher. One reason why the average laboratory course fails to stimulate scientific thinking, lies in the kind of reports which are required. Instead of encouraging the pupil to give an account of the difficulties he has met, the ways he has found of solving them, and the ideas which have occurred to him, as well as the results he has achieved, he is required to turn in a notebook on a pattern arbitrarily prescribed in advance. How much better a general, freely organized theme dealing with the experiment might be. In mathematics, again, the pupil is expected to produce neat demonstrations, and tidily arranged sequences of computations, imitating as far as possible the elegant models given in the textbook. All the fumbling, all the false starts, all the mistakes, are treated as unimportant. The good student throws them away; and the student who submits them inadvertently is heavily penalized. Now I say that these fumblings and false starts and errors and vagrant ideas, are of extreme importance. It would be far better to give fewer problems, and have the pupil write down everything that occurred to him as he worked on them, than to insist always on clean and clear results for their own sake. It is the process of mathematical thinking, not the standardized form of a conventional demonstration or calculation, that we should be after. Why would it not be a good plan to have pupils write up their problems often in the form of essays, and read and discuss them together in class, instead of having assignments completed in the ordinary way?

(iii) Third, the definite outcome of any process of thought should be regarded both as a stopping place and a starting point, both as a result and a stepping stone. Thinking must be brought to a definite terminus, because only in this way can the mind be freed for new masteries and deeper insights. Mental grasp and power is not increased by vagrant wandering without goal or direction. We finish. We achieve. And we find the end of one undertaking is simply a vantage point for perceiving further challenges.

3. *What obstacles must be overcome in teaching people to think?*

I am going to mention, and briefly discuss, six obstacles which confront us, in trying to incite thinking. These obstacles arise partly in ourselves, partly in our situation. We need to understand them, to be on our guard against them, and to see how they may be overcome.

A. First there is the danger of routine. I have no doubt that the greatest reason why the school is not more fully the home of thought, is that it is far too engrossed with routine learning. Let us take a concrete illustration. Suppose that you are teaching a course in American history, and that you come to a lesson dealing with the effect of the international situation on the Revolutionary War. The conventional way of handling this would be to assign passages in the textbook, which would tell the pupil about the tension between France and England, the loss of Canada by France, and the state of affairs with the Indians. These international influences are listed and discussed in a well organized, highly condensed series of paragraphs. The pupil is required to memorize the gist of what the book says, and to be able to recite on it in class, or prove the thoroughness of his work in a written test. And the teacher's job is to make the assignment clearly and definitely, and then see to it that the work has been done. Now, you may ask, what is wrong with this? The topic of the lesson is important; it is something which ought to have a place in our course; we would be ashamed to teach American history without at least one lesson on the international situation as bearing on the Revolutionary War. All this is so. But still something is lacking. There is absolutely no direct, deliberately planned stimulus to thought. And this goes far towards frustrating our good intentions. The pupils learn their lesson. But it is very apt not to become a real, permanent part of their mental lives. Somehow, they fail to grasp its significance. It does not alter their backgrounds, or change their attitudes with regard to their country and its foreign relationships. And the extreme probability is that many of them will forget a great deal of what they have memorized, soon after the course is over, and the threat of final examinations no longer impends.

What, then, ought we to do? Somehow, we must try to have the pupils really *think* about the topic. This may be accomplished in many ways; but for the sake of illustration, here would be one possible procedure. First of all, set the lesson up, not as an assignment to be learned, but as a problem to be considered. Instead of ordering the class to study for tomorrow chapter six, dealing with the influence of international affairs upon the war, announce that the next undertaking will be to consider the question: How did the action of other nations help the colonies to win their liberty? Do not think, however, that the mere formal statement of a problem is enough to stimulate thought. Read them the ferocious little poem by Kipling, in which he taunts the colonials with remaining safe and passive until England had removed many surrounding dangers and had her hands tied elsewhere, when they remembered "the name of freedom, and were brave." If it startles and shocks them, that is splendid. It is just what you want. The problem is not then just a form of words, but a challenge. It has struck down into their life attitudes and prejudices. Then, do not be content with textbook assignments. Try to have members of the class read some interesting and striking material dealing with the period under consideration. Use fiction and romance, as well as formal historical material. Introduce the passages in Kipling's *History of England,* where he most unamiably dilates on the thought of his poem, greatly to the disadvantage of America. Do not require the same reading of everybody. Use the social opportunity of the class to have the pupils make reports of their reading. Stimulate an active discussion. Keep back the textbooks summary until the very end. Have the pupils enter in their notebooks their own final conclusions on the material put before them. Or else have them turn in papers dealing with the subject.

Notice the principles illustrated in this example. First, we have just the opposite of a routine lesson. One cannot, for instance, time it in advance. Nor do all the pupils cover exactly the same ground. But neither of these things are educational disadvantages. Second, notice that we have a problem as a starting point. Third, we have this problem brought definitely into touch with the lives of the pupils. For this purpose the Kipling poem is used. Many other devices might be available—dramatization, collection of current periodical references, comment on present American attitudes to

France and England, and so forth. The point is that this connectic *must be made*. Fourth, a deliberate plan of work is followed. Th fact that our aim is a thought process does not lead us to make entirely free, or to give up all responsibility for careful guidanc Fifth, a definite outcome is indicated, and required.

B. A second obstacle in the way of teaching pupils to think found in the aims with which subject matter is organized. Scho studies are sometimes classified as those which aim at skills, tho which aim at information, and those which aim at discipline. L us consider each of these separately.

(i) Arithmetic and reading are two typical "skill" studies. The belong to the good old curriculum of the three R's. Usually in tl past, and sometimes still, they have been taught wholly for the sal of giving the child a facility in certain techniques. Now these tecl niques are indeed necessary and important. But their importanc lies in their use, and particularly in their use as tools of thought. Fc instance, when a child is taught to read, it is all-important that l learn something far more than, and something far different from, tl mere ability to identify words and sentences, or to move his eyes i a certain manner over the printed page. We wish to create a di position to read; or, when he reads aloud, a tendency to do so e: pressively. This requires us to teach the skill in its life setting rath(than for its own sake. It means giving the child things he will wa to read, and furnishing him with tempting opportunities to do som thing with his reading. In the same way, arithmetic should not b handled merely as the mastery of arithmetical skills, but as the a plication of those skills. When a child learns nothing more than th rules for addition, subtraction, multiplication, and division, he ha not really learned arithmetic at all. Notice how easily he can mak the most stupid and obvious mistakes, and work out a sum to a utterly impossible result, without the least qualm except such as ma be produced by a rebuke from a teacher. But, if he learns to use th techniques of arithmetic in dealing with some situation which actu ally concerns him—for instance, keeping his accounts—then erro take on a very different complexion, because we now have realit instead of dreams. So always, the danger we must avoid, if we wis to train thinking men and women, is teaching a skill merely for th sake of meeting a school requirement rather than solving a life problem.

(ii) Geography is a typical "information" study. This subject, which may be one of the most vital and fascinating to which the human mind can devote itself, is often made one of the most deadly and sterile. The missionary explorer Livingstone has told us that, as a boy, he would gaze and gaze at the map of Africa, haunted by its blank spaces, wondering what could be there. Does this not suggest that geography ought to deal with something more than lists of rivers flowing into the Pacific ocean, or the products of Burmah? Facts never take their true place in the scheme of education until they become challenges to the mind. And they are not made so, by being learned for their own sake. Information is never valuable for its own sake, and should never be taught as though it were. No one can think well who is not well informed. But knowledge comes to us, and lives in and with us, only when mastered in the very act and article of thought.

(iii) Latin, algebra, and geometry are commonly considered "disciplinary" studies. Their content is almost wholly made up of intellectual manipulation. They deal, very largely, with relationships, either in language structures, or space forms, or symbolisms. They are, in a sense, the "pure thought" studies. And here lies the difficulty in using them to promote thinking at all. Will anyone dare seriously to say that the average course in geometry, even when it contains a great many problems, in any degree tends to make pupils more thoughtful in their actual lives, or more intelligent and reflective in dealing with their social environment? Thinking is not promoted by any kind of abstract drill, but by applying intellectual techniques to concrete and appealing issues. The difficulty involved in teaching the disciplinary studies for educative issues is precisely their remoteness from experience.

C. A third obstacle in the way of inciting thought in education is the danger of triviality. Some twenty years ago a monograph was published, which analysed a large number of lessons, stenographically recorded. It was strikingly shown that teachers tended very strongly to ask "fact questions" rather than "thought questions" in their recitations. The monograph attracted wide attention, and was instrumental in bringing about a marked change. Probably if you were to visit a dozen of our best schools, you would find that many teachers asked excellent thought questions in class. This is all to the good. But it is not enough. A routine lesson cannot be transformed into an effective plan for the stimulation of thought, merely by asking a few "thought questions." Where does the main emphasis of the lesson lie? This is the crucial point. Is the total gravitational pull of our work towards thinking, or towards skill, and information, and problem solving, for their own sake? We shall not succeed in inciting thought by casually raising a problematic issue here and there, and then letting it pass; by bringing in some occasional striking instance; or suggesting, here and there, a challenging reading. We must go about a task of this magnitude by a fundamental reorganization of our whole work, which, though very radical, is also perfectly practical.

D. The Abbé Dimnet, in his admirable little book, *The Art of Thinking*,[2] has said that one of the chief hindrances to thought is a feeling of personal inferiority. Many people never try to write, because they are sure in advance that they can write nothing worth while. Many of us take a fleeting, frightened glance at the great problems of economic reconstruction, and hastily dismiss them from our minds as too deep and difficult. We are willing to accept authority not because we coöperatively recognize its validity, but because we are timid of our own opinions. Now there is in this a certain element of wisdom. The true thinker is always keenly aware of his own ignorance, and of the possibility that his ideas may be wrong. But there is a great difference between such wise humility, and a shrinking sense of inferiority which makes us unwilling to have any opinions of our own. Even a wrong and ignorant opinion is better than none at all, because the man who holds it is, at least, interested, and may learn better.

The way our schools are managed is certainly responsible for making people distrust their own minds. The children are required always to conform, to assimilate what they are told, rather than to explore and to think for themselves. They are not, from their entry into the first grade, deliberately and planfully urged to develop originality and intellectual initiative, as the most essential gift of educa-

[2] Simon and Schuster, 1929.

tion. The whole setting of the school is apt to convey to them the assumption that they are feeble and foolish creatures, who can know but little, and who should accept a wisdom handed down from above. Now it is, of course, very true that there are a great many things which a child *must* learn, and *must* believe. He must believe that two and two make four, and any educational scheme which encouraged him to insist that they make five, in the name of originality, would be preposterous. But there are very different ways of conveying intellectual content. The greatest single lesson our teachers can convey, is that to have opinions and ideas of one's very own is the most praiseworthy achievement for any child in school. Notice that these opinions and ideas need not be original in the sense of being new, but must be so in the sense of being the pupil's own personal discovery and possession. There is all the difference in the world between learning that the Civil War was, in part, the outcome of a clash of economic interests by reading it in a textbook, and by discovering it for oneself through collating material and discussing it with others. In one case, the idea is foreign to the mind, and mechanically imposed upon it; in the other, it is the product of the mind's own activity.

In this sense, all school study should be carried forward in the spirit of research. As a matter of fact, the word research is coming more and more into use in connection with school work. We are beginning to hear about research projects in junior high school social science, in ninth grade history, and even in the elementary school. Some people are apt to treat such a notion with a good deal of more or less indulgent contempt. "How can children carry on research?" they ask. "Research is hardly possible, even for unusually bright undergraduates in college. In the true sense, it belongs at least to the level of the graduate school. To talk about research in the junior high school, is a piece of silly boastfulness, another fad of educationists, who like to give big names to little things." This, I believe, is a profound mistake, and indicates a wholly false attitude. Why not give the biggest possible name to a little thing, if that little thing is living and significant? Dewey has well said: "We sometimes talk as if 'original research' were a peculiar prerogative of scientists or at least of advanced students. But all thinking is research, and all research is native, original with him who carries it on, even if everybody in the world already is sure of what he is still looking for."[3] When a third grade child discovers for himself the inwardness of multiplication; when a junior high school pupil is electrified by perceiving the relationship of the westward movement of our people to his home community; when a senior high school student masters the difference between direct and alternating electric current in a significant practical situation—then, in all such cases, the essential process of research is found. By all means encourage every child to respect his own ideas, even while you warn him that they are not final. This is the way to help him towards becoming a thinking man.

E. A fifth obstacle in the pathway of those who wish to incite thinking among children in school, is the danger of wrongly directed learning. Whenever a teacher creates a situation where pupils work simply because he tells them to do so, and simply as he tells them, he has created a situation inimical to thought. As a matter of fact, some of the very best thinking done by pupils in school is devoted to the problem of how to dodge requirements and meet the teacher's demands with a minimum of effort and inconvenience. Our first impulse may be to say that something is wrong with the pupils. But is it not likely, too, that something must be wrong with the directions? Is it not evident that when this happens—and as everyone knows, it very often does—we have posed the wrong sort of problem? The problem before the pupils—the problem about which they are really concerned to do something—is how to please the teacher. Direction, in other words, is personal. Now what we need is to create problems with their own challenge, and to handle them so objectively that the pupil is just as well aware of his own success or failure as we are. The teacher who wishes to stimulate thinking, will make himself the collaborator, the helper, the more experienced guide, rather than the taskmaster.

F. The last obstacle in the way of teaching pupils to think is one I have commented on already. It is placing an emphasis upon results rather than upon processes. The true outcomes of education are changes in the individual. What is important, is not so much the theme the pupil writes, but how he writes it; not so much the correct

[3] *How We Think:* D. C. Heath and Co.; 1910: pp. 173-174.

HOW TO STIMULATE THINKING

nswer to the algebra problem, but the organized attack upon the difficulty; not so much the formal report upon the laboratory experiment, but the planning and achieving of the work itself.

4. Can everyone think?

It is likely that this question may have come to your mind, as you read this chapter. We talk about the need of teaching pupils to think. But are there not many who cannot think at all? What of the little child? What of the person of low native endowment? Will not the attempt to get such persons to think be hopeless from the start?

Let me try to approach this question very concretely. It was once my good fortune to sit in on a meeting of the staff of Dr. Goddard's home for defectives at Columbus, Ohio. The group had before them, amongst other matters, the problem of a boy about seventeen years old, who had made himself a serious disciplinary case. He had refused to obey some directions; had attacked one of the officials; and then had fled, and crawled under a porch, where for a long time he resisted all efforts to get him out. The boy was brought into the room. He was like a scared wild animal, ready at a moment's notice to fly to pieces. A word of reproof or menace, and he would have become hysterical and violent. But no such word was spoken. Nothing at all was said about rules and penalties. Dr. Goddard calmly talked things over with him, in the most reasonable and considerate spirit, pointing out the folly of what he had done, and the difficulties it had caused, both for himself and others. The effect was remarkable. The boy calmed down as the discussion went on, and finally left the room satisfied. Here we have a case of a feeble-minded person—a type above all others to whom one might think that the only possible appeal was force and rigid routine—readjusted by being helped to think. He was given his chance to use his mind; that is to say, the regulations of the institution were put to him in such terms as he could understand, by being brought into direct touch with his experience. And the issue was enormously more constructive than if he had been dragooned and punished, and told that he must obey, whether he agreed with the rules or not. Since that day, I have never been in great doubt as to whether everybody above the level of the human vegetable was capable of thought.

Can a little child in the kindergarten or the first grade, really think? If you never encourage him to do so; if you just subject him to endless, unmitigated routine; if all you can do is to give him literal and detailed instructions—you will then find little power of thought in him. But when you say that he cannot think, and that his education should be chiefly routine, you are really inventing an excuse for your own failure. Watch a kindergarten group who are really being stimulated to think. They are building a toy village. Must they be told exactly what to do, and when to do it? Not at all. There is the most active discussion, and the most unceasing experimentation. Their thinking may be childish. But perhaps your own does not seem so very impressive to the arch-angels! The point is, that it is real. Or again, watch a rather older child, using materials planned for individual study in mastering arithmetic. He is learning how to use decimals. He reads the instructions through with great care, and then tries to apply them. After he has worked out a few sums, he checks himself against the list of answers, and finds out that he has done three of them wrong. His book refers him back to the exact point in the instructions which will show him the cause of his mistake. He checks back, and works the sums over again; and this time he gets them right. Is this not thinking? Has it not about it the authentic quality of research? Is it not, on a very small scale, a process similar in kind to that used by Faraday to discover electric induction or by Edison to make the first incandescent bulb? Will not decimals so mastered, be mastered better, and understood better, than if the pupil were merely told to do some examples, and hand them in for correction and marking? Of course children can think. But you must organize their chances for them. You must set up problems which have some meaning in their lives. And you must steer them through

An excellent way to turn the tables on anyone who insists that dull people, and young people, are incapable of thought and should be taught by routine, is to ask this question: How much thinking is actually done by those who are bright? We may admit that if anyone can show an intelligence quotient of 120, it is proof presumptive of his thinking capacity. But how much will he use it? This is quite another question. And for education, it is the essential question. We need not concern ourselves so very much over the abstract ability to think. But we must concern ourselves greatly with producing a disposition to think. If this can be done, the rest will follow. And it is accomplished by providing things worth thinking about, and by wise, sympathetic, organized guidance and stimulation.

Chapter 16

HOW MAY EDUCATION DEAL WITH THE PROBLEM OF MORALITY?

1. *What is the problem of morality?*

Moral behavior means the application of standards of conduct accepted by a social group as necessary for its institutional living. But, in our swiftly moving, swiftly changing, enormously complex industrial society, many of the standards of conduct once accepted, are questioned in theory, and denied in practice. This is the problem of morality.

In a relatively simple society, whose essential patterns do not change much from generation to generation, or even from century to century, every one knows pretty well what is right, and what is wrong. People may transgress the code; but few doubt it. But the situation of modern man is altogether different. One finds it dramatized in the common experience of immigrant families settling in New York. The parents have usually been brought up under a code of morals and manners suitable to a very much simpler social order. They believe, for instance, that the girls should be at home at an early hour each evening, and that it would be outrageous for them to associate freely with young men. Such standards of conduct may be suitable to a state of things where there are no motion pictures, or cheap automobiles, where the family home provides adequate space and reasonable seclusion, where the men earn the money and the women keep the house, and where marriage is largely decided by negotiations between parents. We all know what happens when the mores of such a social order are projected into the hurly-burly of New York. They simply collapse, often to the infinite pain and distress, and the very great harm, of all concerned. The new situation demands a new set of morals, and new standards of right and wrong. All too often, the parents are irrevocably fixed in traditional ways; and after a few devastating and pathetic conflicts, the young people break away, like ducklings from a hen, and insist on swimming, leaving the old folks clucking on the bank.

Moral education in the past was no more than an affair of imparting, largely by example and casual precept, the universally accepted mores. This is no longer enough. Of course, the break with the past is not absolute. A great body of the immemorial mores still exist, and influence us; and the child acquires many of his moral standards indirectly, and informally, as of yore. But in many of the most important relationships of life the old guides fail us. And this has come about through the vast social changes incident upon the development and application of machinery in the service of humanity. In an age of fast-moving transport, the use of alcohol involves questions which never entered the mind of mediaeval man. In an age of factory production, an employe may find himself with a loyalty critically divided between a union delegate who commands him to strike, and a just and considerate employer. What are the rights and wrongs of stock market speculation, or of commercial advertising? To what extent does the old principle of business morality, *caveat emptor,* apply when the buyer cannot possibly have full knowledge, or the basis for a really instructed judgment? What becomes of the traditional place and duty of a wife, when her home narrows down to a four room, steam-heated flat, with most of the family meals taken in a restaurant? Does a high school boy owe his parents the same kind of unquestioning obedience required of the little child in the patriarchal home? And, if not, what new attitude should he have? Where does the distinction lie, as between professional and amateur sport? Is it right for a world's champion tennis player to prepare syndicated articles for pay? To what degree is the institution of monogamous marriage modified by the increasing number of small families, and of childless married couples? These are but a few samples of the moral problems of the modern world. Fiction abounds with their elaboration. They cannot be solved by a return to the traditional mores.

Yet their solution is essential. We must have a common way of enlightened living. We must have standards of conduct which are recognized by everyone. This is just as essential for us as for the tribesman in some island of the South Seas. If we fail here, it is obvious that our civilization also fails. Quite literally, the machine will have destroyed us. Therefore, our hope consists in working towards a morality, not of social conformity, but of social enlightenment. And we must have an education whose supreme aim is to make men aware of the essence and meaning of those changing social patterns in the midst of which they live.

Some people say that human action cannot be controlled by reason. If by reason you mean merely a verbal explanation, this is true enough. A mother may kindly explain to Johnny why it is that she wants him to go to bed at seven o'clock. Her argument is unanswerable. But Johnny continues to whine and protest. And we are tempted to say that reason has failed. So, too, one may construct a beautiful argument in favor of the League of Nations. One may even silence objectors. And still, at the first provocation, national fury boils up in the crater and erupts into war. And again, wiseacres shake their heads and remind the world that man is not rational. But is this really giving reason a chance? Are we applying, so to speak, the proper mechanisms of rational conduct? Why do inhabitants of Massachusetts never even think of declaring war against South Carolina? Not because they have been persuaded by argument that to do so would be foolish; but because they are governed by an awareness of the realities of our national unity. This is a perfect instance of how we actually create moral controls. Man first learned a common way of tribal life. Then he learned a common way of national life. In the United States, he learned the public and social morality of a continental organization. Now his problem is to acquire the enlightened moral controls demanded by the industrial order.

No better instance of what enlightenment can accomplish in the way of setting up a constructive social morality can be found than the behavior of our people at the time of the banking moratorium in February and March, 1933. As all who lived through those times will recall, every bank in the United States closed its doors for over a week. There was an astounding absence of panic and disorder. People waited calmly, in patience and faith and hope. The boat proceeded on an incredibly even keel. Was it not a superb display of the finest kind of group morality? What made it possible? Certainly not the traditional mores, according to which every man has an absolute and immediate right to what is "his," surely including his bank deposits. If that had been the key to action, where would we be today? Our national behavior was possible only because of a very general appreciation of the nature of the crisis. President Roosevelt, it is true, addressed the country in most memorable words. But it was no mere piece of preaching. There was no attempt to argue people into something. The whole effect of what he said was due to a recognition that he was exposing and expounding the realities of the situation. Here, on a small scale, and in a specific instance, we see what must be the program of education for morality. We must seek to produce in man, not a rigid conformity dependent on a traditional set of notions about right and wrong, but a flexible, creative, and progressive social attitude, dependent upon insight into the essence of those institutional problems which surround us.

2. *Why does the school offer a valuable opportunity for moral training?*

The school is the greatest potential moral force in the community. It is a force greater even than the church. For one thing, it deals with *all* the children of the community. And this means something more than that it has a universal patronage, and an opportunity to reach everybody; though, of course, this in itself is exceedingly valuable. For when *all* are brought together—rich and poor, bright and dull, fortunate and unfortunate—there is a chance which nowhere else exists, for developing social outlook and understanding, and fashioning a way of life in which everyone may share. This is one great reason why the school can never express its true genius as an agency for human service, until it becomes a public school. The moral and social opportunities of the finest private school are bound to be limited, simply for the reason that it appeals to a limited class, and tends to take pupils only of certain types. An environment where all the differences of the community are represented offers a unique and inspiring chance for the development of the moral outlook, and the sympathetic social consciousness.

Then, the school is potentially the greatest moral force in society because it deals with *children*. Children are not more malleable than grown up persons, in the sense that they can learn more rapidly and better. But they are more malleable because they have time and opportunity to make fundamental readjustments, because they are not yet in a rut, because being moulded is, as it were, the main business of their lives. The very word school, as I have pointed out, means leisure—freedom from immediate worries and pressures, freedom to grow and to develop. And an institution with such an essence is clearly an ideal place for the creation of the social conscience and the moral outlook.

And once again, the school is potentially the greatest moral force in the community precisely because it deals with, and conveys to each individual, that great body of intellectual resource which is the substance of our culture. Moral conduct, as I have insisted, depends upon creative social enlightenment, upon an understanding of the whole life of society. Now any human institution, all the way from a country club to a sweatshop, tends to affect the moral outlook of its members. It is a way of living together, whether well or ill; and just because of this, it moulds the conduct and the ideals of all concerned. It influences them in the direction of fairness or unfairness, honesty or dishonesty, consideration or merciless hardness, desire to do a good job for the well being of all or selfish skrimshanking. The school, of course, shares this characteristic with every other institution simply because, like all the rest, it has a private internal life of its own, whether that life resembles the condition of a country club or a sweatshop. But also it has a unique aspect and value. For, unlike other institutions, it possesses and embodies a *curriculum*. Its deliberate and central aim is to convey to its members the body of culture, the corpus of intellectual resource, which makes enlightened social living possible. And here, perhaps, we shall come to recognize its most characteristic and unique moral contribution.

Now what we want to know is this: How may the school use,

to the fullest and best possible degree, its unique moral opportunity? Very often it fails as a moral agency. It breeds liars, cheats, tattle-tales, boodlers, grafters, racketeers, selfish individualists generally. When it does this, it fails not only as a moral, but also as an educational agency. It fails as a school. Why does this happen? How may it be corrected? The rest of this chapter will be devoted to sketching an answer to these questions.

3. *How may the social life of the school promote moral development?*

The first great moral influence in the life of the school is the direct experience which it offers of living together and working together, in a diversified, yet united social group. Better than any other institution, it offers young people the chance to manage their own affairs, and to conduct their own social relationships, and to do so under enlightened guidance. Guidance they must have, or the trend of their group experience is apt to become destructive: witness the neighborhood gang, that seminary of lawlessness. Educators have discovered the dangers of unguided association in the high school fraternity, which has been found to release tendencies so undesirable that it is almost universally frowned upon. But on the other hand, the experience of living together, and mutually acting upon and dealing with one another, is an essential part of the personal and social development of young people. It is an obvious and potent force in creating for them a common way of enlightened living, an awareness and understanding of the needs and rights of others. A necessary element of the total educative influence of the school is the education which pupils gain from one another.

How, then, may the opportunities which the school provides for direct social experience be made to serve the most desirable ends? How may it be fashioned into a moral influence of the right sort? Always the principle to be applied is this: Free social self direction under sympathetic and enlightened guidance. The constant temptation in administering the social life of the school is to regulate and regiment everything by order. The reason is quite clear. It is not that teachers, principals, and superintendents are natural born autocrats with a passion for dictatorship. Such a passion some of them may have; but surely it is not universal, nor even very strong. The simple reason why we find in any school a tendency to regulate everything by fiat, is that this makes for an obvious efficiency. It is the easiest and least risky way to manage any institution, and particularly one that is large and complex. We have, for instance, a case of discipline. If this goes to a student self government board, principals and teachers may be on tenterhooks as to what will happen. Bungling and delay are very possible. How much simpler to deal with it in the office, and settle the matter once for all! There may be some protest and ill feeling; but if the principal is a tactician, he can usually manage it, for he holds all the inner lines of communication. Or again, we may have the question of setting up some necessary rule regarding passing to and fro in the corridors. How much easier to work it out in some small faculty committee, or, still better, in the individualistic solitude of the principal's sanctum, and then post it on the bulletin board, instead of going to the trouble, and running all the chances, of trying to secure mutual consent.

Here, as is so often the case, we need to recall a very simple truism. The social life of the school should not be thought of and guided from the standpoint of efficiency, but from the standpoint of education. The school is not like a Ford assembly line, whose sole purpose is the creation of a product. It is a way of living and a place for securing personal growth. And no matter how reasonable our rules, and how smooth our operation, they will surely fail of their educative and moral value, if they are ours rather than the pupils'. Consider some of the obvious moral ills generated by regimentation and autocratic regulation in the social life of a school. Perhaps French secondary education offers as fine an illustration as can be had of the defects of this mode of school keeping. The lives of the pupils are regulated in every detail. Incoming and outgoing mail is scanned by the authorities. The pupils are under observation all the time. And there exists a well recognized spy system. Such a regime operates precisely against the kind of social morality we have been discussing. Do we find any trace of it in our American schools? I fear we do. Rules of an arbitrary kind are constantly imposed. Discipline is merely handed down from above. And as a perfectly logical consequence, there are many teachers who quite deliberately encourage pupils to tattle on their fellows when anything displeases them instead of learning to deal directly and personally with a social problem. Most assuredly, this does not make for the kind of enlightened social feeling which is the essence of morality. Imposed rules are rules to be obeyed if one must, and dodged if one can, rather than expressions of a common way of living in which it is one's pleasure and privilege to share. Examinations become incentives and invitations for cheating, since one is working in a system which one feels a desire to "beat," because it is in no sense one's very own. The child who is teased on the playground runs whimpering to tell teacher, to the instant disintegration of dynamic group morale. And if a teacher offends a pupil, the chances are that the pupil hastens whining to the principal's office, like a little yellow dog who has been kicked, instead of acting like an upstanding human being and adjusting the social situation as best he may, so gaining courage and moral insight.

So what we must have is a control of the social life of the school which the pupils will feel is their very own, and yet which must be guided and moulded and guarded from excess, and youthful, inexperienced perversion. Now I want you to see that this means a great deal more than setting up a student self government board to take care of "extra-curricular" offences, side by side with another government established by the faculty and administration. It means organizing the life of the school, through and through, in terms of social integrity. For instance, we may be troubled with the problem of cheating in examinations. What should we do? Shall we install an "honor system," which may mean merely a system of motivated tattling, and hope that the thing will work? This has often been tried; and often, though not always, it fails. Rather we may come to believe that the conventional examination creates a social pattern in which it is inherently impossible for the students actively and whole-heartedly to concur; that it is imposing something fundamentally wrong and demoralizing upon them; that it ought to be altered, root and branch; and that no mollification by sanctifying the tell-tale-tit will do the trick. This does not mean that we should give up tests and standards. But it does mean that we should stop administering them on a preposterous basis, as so many incentives to slickness and cheating.

Or we may have on our hands the problem of the eligibility of some athlete for the football team. We look up his grades, find that they are low, and issue our ukase that he cannot play. What happens? The student body, the alumni, and very probably the coach, rise up in arms, and use all sorts of expedients to get him under the line. We may talk about intellectual standards till we are black in the face. If we talk cleverly enough, we may be able to silence complaints, or at least muffle them down to a faint grumble. But we will not convince and convert the persons concerned. They will not become our whole-hearted collaborators. And the moral effect upon them, like that of any foreign and imposed regulation, is bad. What is the way out? There is no one simple answer, because here we are dealing with one of the most difficult and far-reaching defects of our whole system. Such a problem cannot be solved over night. But the direction in which to work for a solution is evident. We must work for a saner valuation of athletics in our school commonwealth. The advantage of this will not lie in having a student body which cares little about athletic success, and so is willing to gulp down almost any regulations we like to impose. The insanity is by no means all on the part of the students. Rather what we must have is a consensus by students and teachers that athletics offers an educative experience of great value, and that any person who is participating to his full capacity in the general life and interests of the school, ought to have a chance to share it. The demoralizing troubles which occur so continually in the management of school athletics, arise from a clash between an artificial, arbitrarily imposed credit system on the one hand, and a preposterous gladiatorial motivation, and a childish deification of victory, on the other. The social picture is out of perspective. In this instance, the school has failed to make itself an ideal place for the living of young people. A demoralizing influence is set going. The answer is not, again, by creating a student self government board, which can be argued and manipulated into conformity with the wishes of the faculty, acting behind a careful smoke-screen, but a reorganization of the social pattern in terms of social integrity.

These are instances of what I mean by opportunities for self government under guidance. I suggest that you try to bring together and analyze others. I believe you will come to feel, as I do, that what we want cannot be brought about by any artificial or external plan, such as merely creating a student self government board. Whether or not such a board can work effectively will depend on the total organization of the life of the school. Teachers and students must collaborate in the creation of a common way of living, in which everyone can feel a genuine and responsible share. Kinks must be ironed out. Many conventional social patterns, which are hangovers from autocratic regulation, must be done away. The school must be organized for an integral social life.

Before I leave this point, there are two matters which I want to put before you. First, notice that every teacher has an obvious responsibility outside his classroom. He is not a teacher of a subject, but a member of a commonweal. It is quite true that he is neither a nurse nor a policeman. But he has a very genuine responsibility in the way of constructive social thinking and action for the well being of the educational society in which he lives.

Second, notice that the social purpose of the school may quite possibly be impeded if it becomes too large. If we think of a school as an assemblage of classrooms where subject matter courses are taught, then who cares how large it becomes? But if we regard its inner social life as one of its major educational assets, then size beyond a certain point becomes dangerous, even destructive; for it can frustrate that inner social life. What the ideal size for a school should be, no one can say. But clearly, it is not "as big as possible."

4. *How are high educational standards an agency for moral development?*

The second great moral influence in the life of the school is constituted by the standards of achievement which it sets up. But standards must be properly understood and properly administered, if they are to issue in the development of character and the elevation of ideals. Standards become demoralizing in three ways—when they are low—when they are externally imposed—when they are arbitrary and personal.

A. Low standards are an influence directly contrary to moral integrity. By this I do not mean that the school should demand the impossible. The powers of the pupils must always be taken into account. But when the school permits a situation in which pupils may do less than the best that is in them, and still achieve satisfaction, it undermines character. Let us see why this is so.

I know of one of America's greatest educational institutions which retains on its faculty a man whose work is known to be worthless. It keeps him on, simply because he is supposed to have considerable political influence in certain directions. The students who take his courses need do no work at all. So far as the teacher is concerned, they learn nothing. This is no over-statement. What is the result? His courses are elected for two reasons; first, because they are very easy; second, because he is thought to be able to place people in advantageous positions. One feels instantly that this is wrong—more than wrong, highly culpable. But just what moral evil is involved? It comes to this. The school is a place where students go to learn, to achieve, to grow, to share significant experience. On this its whole life and meaning absolutely depend. And when it tolerates the work of such a teacher, it is striking at the very roots of its own being. It is disseminating a poison throughout every fibre of its institutional organism. The great trouble with this particular teacher's work, and with "cinch courses" in general, is not that the school cheats the student by taking his money and selling him a gold brick, though that is bad enough. The trouble is that the school deliberately, and of its own motion, frustrates the integrity of the student's purpose, and in effect, parades the cynical attitude that nothing matters except getting by. The really lamentable thing about easy courses and easy standards is that students so often tolerate them, and even like them. And this directly acts towards the breaking up of any healthy, significant, social life. Consider the kind of advice often passed round fraternity houses on many a university campus. "Don't take that course with Professor A. It's awfully hard. Can't you fix up your schedule to get some work with Professor B? You won't have to crack a book. And he hands out lots of A's." And quite possibly, Professor B prides himself on his popularity, and thinks, heaven forgive him, that he must be a splendid teacher, because his classes resemble mob scenes! There is only one word for this—educational racketeering. It amounts to cheating for credits with the connivance of the faculty. And it not only dilutes the intellectual contribution of the school. It does something worse. It poisons and demoralizes the whole social organism, by frustrating the very purpose it exists to serve.

B. But the way out is not by arbitrarily imposing a uniformly high standard, or using some scheme to "make pupils work." There are a number of methods by which this is done. For instance, we may have a requirement that for each hour of class time, a certain number of hours of preparation shall be expected. This, of course, is very artificial indeed, and really is not practical; but it is often tried. Or, the pupils may be required to complete a certain stated amount of work, or to cover a certain amount of ground, in a given time; the thought being that this will keep them busy. Or the higher and more desirable marks may be made very hard to get, by giving only a few of them. These are some common ways of setting up imposed standards. They will serve to show you just what I am talking about.

"But," you may say, "what is wrong with all this? Schools and teachers constantly do such things. They seem almost like a necessary and inescapable part of the business of keeping school. Moreover, the pupils are quite likely to accept them as right and proper. Unless some teacher runs amuck, and sets up impossible requirements, there is not apt to be any general complaint of unfairness, although some grumbles may be audible. Is it not a pretty serious matter to condemn, on moral grounds, procedures so generally used, and so readily accepted?" I quite agree that it is. Moreover, I also believe that exacting imposed standards are far better, in every way, than very low and easy ones. A school without any standards at all, or with standards contemptibly low, is a far more demoralizing influence than one where high standards are autocratically imposed. In what respect, then, is this latter situation morally bad?

The evil lies in this, that the pupils are led to work for an extrinsic and artificial reward, rather than for the sake of the work itself. Marks, grades, conformity with a requirement set up by another person, are made the goals of effort. After all, if there is any point at all in my learning about a certain period in history, or mastering a certain mathematical technique, or writing an English theme, the value lies in the achievement itself. This seems very ordinary common sense. So the only reasonable, and proper, and ultimately defensible motive for learning anything, is the feeling that it is worth learning. But if I am put in a situation where I learn something for the sake of getting a mark, or avoiding a scolding, or just doing what I am told, what happens? I learn it well enough to get the mark, or avoid the scolding, or register obedience; not as well as I can, or well enough to do me some lasting good. Here is the inevitable tendency, whenever we have standards and requirements imposed from outside, instead of arising directly from the pupil's own sense of the worthwhileness of the undertaking.

This, as I have said, leads to unfortunate moral consequences, in addition to unfortunate intellectual consequences. For instance, a serious and interested student will often feel inclined to follow up various side lines in connection with his work—to read more widely about an historical period, to experiment with some mathematical technique, to try for some new effect in his writing—in general, to work for the sake of achievement. But the steady, though unexpressed influence of the school, is simply towards doing his assignment in the required way, and treating everything else as perhaps very nice, but really secondary. This amounts to a perversion of the essential purpose for which a pupil is in school. He is there to learn and to grow, not to follow an imposed routine. But the school tends always to make him into an examination passer, and a performer of assignments.

Again, one of the most important characteristics of a school, regarded simply as a place for group learning, group experience, and group achievement, should be the recognition of, and admiration for, good work, for its own sake. If such a group is working and living on a healthy and natural basis, there will be an eager interest in, and appreciation of, achievement of high quality—an interest and appreciation shared by both pupils and teachers. But, as soon as we have imposed rather than direct standards, admiration and emulation both become concentrated on good marks, rather than good work. And, since good marks depend on competitive success, we have a system nicely calculated to engender envy, hatred, and bitterness.

Once again, imposed standards are demoralizing, because they tend to poison the relationship between pupil and teacher. Teachers exist for only one reason; and that is to help the learner learn. Notice that I do not say that the teacher exists to help the learner learn *his lessons*. Rather the purpose must be to shape up the sum total of the school as a society, in such a way that better all-around adjustment takes place. The teacher needs to act as counsellor, guide, friend, and coöperator. But how can he do this, if his chief job is the imposition of arbitrary standards and the meting out of rewards and penalties?

As a final illustration of the unfortunate effects of imposed standards, consider how they work out when it comes to accommodating so-called "extra-curricular" and "curricular" interests. Teachers often feel that extra-curricular pursuits unduly distract pupils from what is regarded as the great business of education, namely, working at their lessons. Various devices are used to deal with this. Sometimes extra-curricular activities are limited by statute. Sometimes various plans of eligibility, based on marks, are tried. But sometimes you will hear a teacher say that all such schemes are artificial, and more or less bad, and that the true way out is by making curricular requirements and standards so high that the pupils haven't much time for anything else. This is a half truth. If such a teacher said that curricular pursuits should be made so *engrossing* that pupils would take the time to see them through in spite of all counter-attractions, then we could entirely agree. The point is, that in extra-curricular activities, we have natural and direct standards, due to a desire to perform as well as possible irrespective of any formal requirements. And the only way to organize curricular activities to compete with them is to introduce the same principle. Incidentally, this will really dissolve the whole distinction between curricular and extra-curricular pursuits, and so do away with one of the most weakening defects in the social life of the school.

In such ways as these, imposed standards tend to weaken the

moral influence of the school. If you have understood the principle involved, and will look around you carefully, you will probably recognize many people in school with you, whose ideals and integrity and standards of what is right and wrong are being sapped, or at least threatened, by the system. Perhaps you will recognize yourself among this company!

C. The evils of arbitrary and personal standards should need but little explanation. I know of a teacher who openly threatens that, unless students take a certain sequence of courses not laid down by the school, and unless they meet his quite unreasonable demands, he will use his influence against them in the matter of securing jobs. The proper moral reaction of his pupils would be to throw him out of the window. I regret to say that most of them sing small, and hasten to conform, though not without heart-burnings. And I think they are morally diminished by so doing.

Now it is evident that when a teacher acts like an unleashed tyrant, he will tend to produce in his pupils the slave mentality and the slave morale. The good teacher will, indeed, be exacting; but never arbitrarily so. He will look for and desire excellence. He will blame work below the level of the pupil's best. But his standards will be objective, not subjective. They will arise from his feeling for the job itself, and his desire to see it well done, not from his personal inclinations and prejudices. The teacher who is exacting in his advocacy and pursuit of objective excellence, will maintain the proper social relationship with his pupils, and will exercise upon them a profoundly moralizing influence. In order to avoid being an autocrat, one need not become a softy.

So the school should be a place where standards are high, but not arbitrarily imposed; where interest centers upon worth while achievement for its own sake, rather than for the sake of reward; where excellence of all kinds is encouraged and appreciated; where the teachers constantly point towards higher levels of achievement as objectively authentic, rather than insisting upon them as the unintelligible demands of tyrants. Such a school is a good place for any young person to live in. Its influence will be strongly towards the building of a personal integrity and a social morality, which will serve the individual in all the relationships of life.

5. *How may the curriculum be an agency for moral development?*

So far, we have been dealing with those moral influences which the school has in common with other social institutions. Not until we see how the curriculum itself can be an agency for moral development, shall we come to the unique and special contribution which the school is fitted to make, and because of which it is different from every other institution.

Now you may ask what possible moral values there can be in the curriculum. What moral effect is there in learning reading, writing, arithmetic, history, English, French, Latin, history, algebra, science? If you put it in this way, the only answer I can make is: None. One is not learning morality; one is learning subject matter. And ethical personality becomes a by-product. But I have argued again and again that to think of the curriculum in terms of subject matter is to think of it wrongly. The curriculum consists of the intellectual resources of our civilization. Only the individual who possesses these resources is capable of enlightened social action and of a social adjustment, which, instead of being rigid and blindly conformist, is flexible and creative. The whole aim of the curriculum is the creation in the individual of social enlightenment and insight. And this is the touchstone for every detail and segment in it. So every course, every subject, and the program of studies as a whole, must be understood as a moral agent, when understood aright. For essentially, it is a means of integrating the individual with society through intelligence. Let us try to see, a little more specifically, how the curriculum works out as an agency for moral development.

A. The intellectual resources of civilization serve each and every one of us by making possible a broad understanding of our immediate experience. In this way, they furnish guides for enlightened action. A young Englishman decided to enlist during the early months of the World War. After he had been in camp for some time and was about to go to France, he was granted leave to visit his family. He went to say good-by to his grandmother, and the old lady was much distressed. Seeing this, he remarked: "You know, Granny, we're fighting to end war." You may say that, in the light of what has happened since 1918, this was an error. But it is a good example of a moral choice based upon enlightenment. He was in the presence of a very poignant personal experience. His country was at war. Should he enlist, or stay at home? He made his choice, not merely in terms of conformity, but on the basis of an intellectual interpretation. History and geography contributed to the shaping of that choice. And in it, we see their moral significance.

Now, a great many of our choices are determined precisely in this way. They depend upon a certain understanding of an immediate situation and immediate experience. Shall I vote? For whom shall I vote? Shall I support or attack prohibition? Shall I attend church or spend my Sunday playing golf? Shall I go out on strike? Shall I raise the wages of my employes? A thousand such questions are really settled by the way we interpret immediate situations. We have *acquired* our ways of interpreting and responding to such situations. They are the outcomes of a long and elaborate sophistication; but it has become so much a part of us that it operates almost unconsciously. In this manner, the school curriculum exercises a profound and pervasive moral influence. When the Frenchman finds virtue in hating the German, and the German in hating the Frenchman; when the business man fulminates against the I.W.W.; when an appeal to patriotic motives succeeds; when a political reform wins or loses; we see the potent influence of acquired ways of thinking and understanding. Both the greatness and the littleness of men are due, far more than they easily perceive, to the effect of certain concepts generated in their school studies.

B. The intellectual resources of civilization serve each and every one of us by revealing to us the factors of control in our immediate experience. We live in a world which is increasingly dependent upon the services and uses of exact science. And science should have a place in the education of every man, not chiefly for the sake of making him a scientist or a research worker, but to help him understand the conditions which surround his life. Suppose, for instance, that I call a doctor, and that he hesitates somewhat in his diagnosis. What my understanding of science ought to do for me is not in the least to enable me to take his place, and make a better and surer diagnosis, but rather to lead me to comprehend the limitations under which he works, so that I do not lose confidence, but am willing to trust him while he looks closely into the facts of my case. If I have no tincture of scientific understanding, the doctor is just a medicine man; and if he appears in the least dubious, I look for somebody with a stronger magic, and so become the easy victim of the quack. In a world of railway trains, automobiles, aeroplanes, factories, radio, and television, it is not necessary that everyone shall have an expert knowledge of all these marvels. But it is very important that everyone shall have an insight into the techniques, procedures, and attitudes of what we call the scientific mind; because only so can he understand in any adequate way, under what limitations, and with what possibilities, our industrial civilization operates, and shape his choices accordingly. It has been said, and with much truth, that all science is social science, since it is the agency through which man controls the conditions of his living. And science becomes educative and moralizing in its force, when apprehended in its social context and use.

C. The intellectual resources of civilization serve each and every one of us by furnishing the techniques and procedures necessary for the conduct of life. For instance, a civilized person should feel it morally wrong to refuse to segregate a child with an active contagious disease. The uncivilized, the uneducated person—the person who has no hold on human intellectual resources—will perhaps feel nothing fundamentally at fault in letting such a child roam the streets. Here is an ethical control, set up quite largely by the scientific consciousness and the scientific background. In the same way, our reaction to much advertising (toasted cigarettes, halitosis, pyorrhoea, etc., etc.) will ultimately depend, to quite a large extent, on our functioning scientific background. Science, both natural and social, hygiene, civics, economics—all these subjects—come to life in the form of controls and techniques for better action.

D. Lastly, the intellectual resources of civilization serve each and every one of us by creating standards of value. A feeling for art and music, and a respect for the spirit of science, are all parts of a civilized morality; because on such things depend some of the best and most fruitful forms of human social action. Without them, the individual is, to some extent at least, a barbarian with the moral outlook of a barbarian.

This, I hope, will make clear in what sense a vital curriculum is a potent moral agency. What it actually does is to render the individual at home in the Great Society. It is a guide to the business of living in the modern world. Without it, the best social action we can achieve is mere conformity. What it essentially supplies is the means of social enlightenment. Of course this implies that our curriculum must not be thought of as consisting in subject matter for its own sake. As soon as we fall into this error, we deprive it of its essential relationship to action; and so it loses all its moral potency. Moreover, since it then comes to appear foreign, and intrinsically worthless to the learner, it can only be forced upon him by arbitrarily imposed standards; and so the entire social life of the school suffers and becomes morally impoverished.

6. *What is the value of direct moral instruction?*

You may have noticed that, in trying to explain how the school may, and should, play the part of a moral agency, I have said nothing at all about direct ethical instruction. Should instruction of this kind have any place? Would it be advisable to offer lessons dealing with ideals, or a course in manners and morals? Most of our American educational philosophers have expressed themselves as opposed to the idea. And yet it is being tried out in many places, apparently with fairly hopeful results. Where is the truth of the matter?

Direct moral instruction usually means the teaching of ideals, such as honesty, kindness, courage, loyalty, truthfulness, and so on. So our question really comes to this: What is the relation of ideals to conduct? Would it be a sound and hopeful enterprise to give young people some sort of lessons in ideals, as we give them lessons, perhaps, in social science or grammar? Or would it be better simply to create in the school a socially significant environment, and trust to this as a sufficient moral influence, without any kind of direct preaching or teaching?

I have said that many of our greatest educational thinkers believe that the direct teaching of morality is a mistake. And it must be admitted that their reasons are excellent. Before we rush in with an eager and reforming zeal, and attempt to make young people good by preachments, we should understand these reasons, and recognize the difficulties and dangers of such a course. Otherwise we shall defeat our own ends.

The first great objection to the direct teaching of morality is that it so easily involves a very false and limited understanding of the nature of moral behavior. Morally desirable conduct is socially determined. This we must always remember. But the enthusiastic preacher is constantly apt to talk as if certain acts were good or bad, right or wrong, in and of themselves, without reference to their social consequences. So morality becomes the following of a standardized code, for the requirements of which no final reason can be given. Certain things are wrong; others are right. Moral instruction consists merely in pointing out which are which. It is instruction in a set of rules. This is a fallacy very easily committed. That it is indeed a fallacy, we have already seen. All the traditional rules of good behavior are true and reasonable, only in so far as they indicate socially determined ways of action. And what we want to create in any individual is not just a knowledge of the rule, but that social spirit which the rule expresses, and which constitutes its force. There is a great deal more here than a theoretical objection. When we proclaim a morality of rules and precepts, a morality which simply condemns certain actions and commends others, we become futile. The mentor may gain a respectful hearing; but he is soon lamenting that those who listen to him go blithely away to sin. And the reason is, that his fixed rules will not apply to a changing world. The only thing that will apply is a constructive, enlightened, flexible, creative social vision and insight. So we must agree that, in so far as direct moral instruction means telling people that certain acts are right and others wrong, rather than helping them to analyze the social consequences of their behavior, it is sure to fail.

The second objection to direct moral instruction is that ideals taught in words alone are worthless. Take occasion, some time, to look through the Rotary code of ethics. Then ask yourself how much that code affects the actual behavior of various business men of your acquaintance. It has, perhaps, some influence; but hardly a great deal. And what effect it has, comes from its appeal to something in the man's make-up, rather than to its sheer force as a scheme of words. So, clearly, if moral instruction is to be no more than the verbal teaching of moral ideals, it will not be worth the trouble it takes. But neither is any other purely verbal teaching. And we shall find our saving, constructive consideration in this— that direct moral instruction by no means must be purely a matter of words.

The third objection to direct moral instruction is that ideals have no meaning whatever, except in terms of experience. Suppose you wish to teach the ideal of honesty. One of your great difficulties will be that honesty actually means many different things. Consider just a few of its possible significations. What should you do if you borrow money, and later disagree as to the amount? Would it be right to borrow money temporarily from your little brother's bank? What should you do if you find money but do not know the owner? What should you do if you see money lying about in your home? What should you do when you take gate receipts where tickets are not used? What should you do if you are travelling in a bus or a street car, and the conductor fails to ask for your fare? What should you do when you discover that you have short-changed a customer? What should you do when you buy a paper when the boy is away from the stand? What should you do if you have kept a library book out so long that the fine is more than the value of the book? What should you do if you are offered pay before the work you are being paid for is finished? Here are just a few of the problems of conduct to which the ideal of honesty must apply. And unless we can teach it in such a way that it really does apply to them, we had better let the whole business alone. But, once again, this problem is in no way peculiar to moral instruction. When we teach a formula in mathematics, or a grammar rule in a foreign language, we are up against exactly the same difficulty. The learner must be made able to apply it to specific instances, and to use it in solving specific problems, or we have our labor for nothing.

These three objections really amount to cautions about what to avoid in trying to give direct moral instruction, rather than to condemnations of such instruction. Ideals, expressed in words, and even abstractly taught, have a genuine place in moral education. The thing to remember is that they are *generalizations,* and that they have all the value, and carry all the risks, of generalizations anywhere else. When we say that men should be honest, we sum up a great mass of social experience; just as when we say that supply tends to equate itself to demand, we sum up a great mass of economic experience; or just as when we say that $(x+y)^2 = x^2 + 2xy + y^2$, we sum up a great mass of algebraical experience. Now, of course, we cannot create experience by teaching any formula. Nor can anyone really understand a generalization without having had some of the experience to which it has reference. But that is surely a very different thing from saying that the generalization is not worth making, or discussing, or teaching at all.

If we will stick to these ideas, they will show us pretty well what we ought to do, and avoid doing, in the matter of direct moral instruction. Here the following considerations should guide us:

A. Ideals should always be taught as generalizations from the learner's own personal experience. In elementary school work, this is often brought about by what is known as a "conduct assignment." A certain ideal—honesty, truthfulness, kindness—is set up for study. The essence of the assignment consists in having the children observe the details of their own daily living, over a given period, to notice instances to which the ideal under consideration would apply. Above the elementary school level, it might be possible to draw more and more upon vicarious experience—that is, upon the materials of reading, and of the curriculum generally; and at the same time, to set up more interesting problematic moral situations for analysis. The social life of the school will always provide ample and fascinating concrete instances, in terms of which to deal with any moral concept we wish to present.

B. The same point may be put somewhat differently if we say that ideals should always be taught for transfer. When we criticize a man for moral inconsistencies, or the lack of a fully integrated character, what we mean is that his system of ideals applies in certain situations, but not in others. As Charters puts it: "All of us have different 'selves.' The keen hard business man may be kind and pliant in his home; the man who is a good spender among his business associates may be morose with his family; a youth may count his pennies for a month and spend all his savings in one evening in a cabaret; a man may be self-confident in his relationships with other men and with his subordinates and yet be shy with women; a woman may be neat in her personal appearance and slovenly in her bedroom; a boy may be courteous to strangers and extremely discourteous to his sisters; a mother may be courageous with burglars and afraid of mice; and a professor may be logical in his own field and at the same time be governed by prejudices in practical affairs." [1]

Now, of course a fully integrated personality cannot be created by the preaching of verbal ideals. But you will remember that transfer depends on conscious generalization. And I think it not unreasonable to believe that the integration of character through transfer of ideals, may be much helped by direct moral instruction which makes those ideals explicit and conscious.

C. We must always remember that the best of moral instruction will lose its force, if it is carried on in a perverted moral environment. This is why the direct teaching of ideals becomes futile and worse, save in a school whose whole spirit and atmosphere favors right action and the healthy growth of character. In such a school—one whose social life is dynamic and inspiring, whose standards are at the same time exacting and appealing, whose curriculum is socially significant—direct moral instruction, in which the ideals presented are kept always in close touch with the experience of the pupil, has a very real and valuable place.

[1] W. W. Charters: *The Teaching of Ideals;* Macmillan Company, 1927, pp. 337-8.

Part Four

INSTRUMENTALITIES

Chapter 17

HOW SHALL WE PLAN THE CURRICULUM?

1. *What are the defects of our present curriculum?*

The curriculum—the organized program of studies—is the first great educational instrumentality which we must discuss. If we fail to plan this on sound principles, then nothing—not the most expert teaching, or the most careful marking, or the finest administrative plans—will save our scheme of education from failure. For the curriculum is the heart of the educational system.

If you wish to understand the true principles on which a curriculum should be constructed, you will find it a very good point of departure to consider your own school experience. Why were you constrained or persuaded to study the subjects you actually undertook? On what grounds was it decided that these were the best subjects for you, if you wished to become properly educated? How much of what you were required to learn was truly educative? Could your program of work have been arranged to yield greater values?

A simple answer to such queries is not easy to give. To a considerable extent, it would depend on what schools you happened to attend; for some schools construct their curricula with much greater care and success than others. Moreover, we could not give quite the same replies regarding your work in the elementary school, the junior high school, the senior high school, and the college. There is good reason to hold that a modern elementary school, or a first rate junior high school, carries a more consistently valuable stock-in-trade than the average senior high school or college. Into such details and differences one can hardly enter here. But certain broad answers can be given to the questions I have suggested. And their general outcome must be that the present day curriculum, as a whole, has many very serious defects; that you were far from receiving the highest possible educational dividends for your time and effort; and that there is urgent need for reform.

The first great point to understand is that you studied various subjects in school, largely because their place in the scheme of education was traditional. Our present curriculum can be traced back, in an unbroken succession, to the schools of Rome and Greece. The schools of the ancient world had, for their chief aim, the training of the orator. At its best, this training was broad, rich, and inspiring. It was, however, distinctively a linguistic training; and the educated man, *par excellence,* was the man of words. Moreover, that training did not long remain at its best. Form and elegance came to seem more important than fruitful, cogent thought. And the teacher grew content to purvey chiefly the dry bones of formal grammar, artificial rhetoric, and stilted elocution. During the middle ages, when the great literatures of an earlier day were no longer available, the principal subjects of study were, at first, grammar, and later, dialectic (that is, logic). For a moment it seemed that the Renaissance, with its re-discovery of the ancient cultures, and its enthusiasm for literature, might bring a better day. But this hope swiftly faded; and the great revival of learning only fastened grammar study still more firmly upon education. In one of the most famous schools of the sixteenth century, ten consecutive years were given to the study of Latin, with the overwhelming emphasis upon the formal structural aspects of the language. When we call certain types of schools "grammar schools," we use a phrase which strikes deeply back into educational history. Language study has been the great stand-by of formal education for many centuries.

With the nineteenth century, many new subjects began to press more and more strongly for a place in the curriculum. Slowly we find the vernacular languages and literatures, modern history, and the sciences entering the picture. But in no case did they win their place without a long and bitter fight, whose scars they still bear.

Until recently, modern foreign languages were taught as closely as possible on the model of the old fashioned presentation of Latin and Greek. English teachers have been disposed to make much of language analysis, classical reference, and scholarly antiquarian interest, rather than the values of human communication and literary content. Effective laboratory work, and the applications of science to actual situations and social needs, have been far less prominent than textbook knowledge, which has tended to assimilate even science to the old linguistic tradition. New subjects indeed, were added; but the old central emphasis upon language as the core of education, remained.

So, many of the subjects which we studied in school, are taught, not because of any plan, not because anyone thought the matter through, and decided that they would yield the highest returns for our time, but just because they always have been there, or else because the conservatives could not keep them out. Here, indeed, is the most striking of all instances of that divorce of the school from life, that identification of education with an institutional tradition, which we discussed when explaining the place and purpose of the school.

From the fact that our present curriculum is largely the product of tradition, rather than constructive, rational insight, come its two great defects. It is a far less effective educational instrument than it might be, first because it is ill chosen, second because it is ill organized.

A. The present day curriculum is ill chosen in the particular sense of being quite inexcusably out of touch with the realities of modern life. All about us are issues of the most momentous importance. Prodigious economic forces are shaping the destinies of individuals and nations. Our best minds are wrestling, almost in desperation, with the reshaping of society. Science is creating agencies which will either elevate human life, or utterly destroy it. Surely a dispassionate observer, untrammelled by tradition, might suppose that the schools would find it their most urgent mission to convey to all children a sense of these things, and a wisdom concerning them. What else could it mean to be educated? But it is not being done. Those language studies which were the staple of the Greek sophist, still make by far the heaviest draft upon the pupil's time.

As to the elementary school, it is notorious that its studies fail in many ways to achieve the results which the public has a clear right to expect. To quote Merriam: "Non-schoolmen have their impressions of the schools and express them. Considerable credit must be given laymen for their educational thoughts, which have been developed by our democratic government. The supervisor of apprenticeship schools of the Santa Fe Railroad System complains that the public schools fail to develop in the pupils ability in spelling, writing, and arithmetic; that more attention is given to 'culture' than to insight into social and industrial conditions and to training in attitude towards work. . . . Samuel Gompers, President of the American Federation of Labor, is quoted as saying: 'The old cultural ideals of education, dealing with the abstract only, denied to the great majority of children an education adapted to their minds and natures, and hence failed to fit them for the duties and possibilities of the work of life.' The superintendent of schools at Solvay, New York, once asked twelve firms, representing employments into which pupils leaving the Solvay schools would probably go, what fractions were used in their industries. The answer included only the following:

$\frac{1}{2}, \frac{1}{3}, \frac{1}{4}, \frac{1}{5}, \frac{1}{6}, \frac{1}{8}, \frac{1}{10}, \frac{1}{15}, \frac{1}{16}, \frac{1}{24}, \frac{1}{25}, \frac{1}{36}, \frac{1}{64}$

This is, of course, only an implied criticism upon the school arithmetic."[1] While, of course, lay opinion is not necessarily well informed, or well considered, yet often it has a stimulating directness. In this case we should heed it.

As to the high school, George Counts, on the basis of a study he made of some of the finest schools in the country, reports: "For the most part, the boy or girl who attends high school today engages in a study of English Composition which is often formal and unrelated to his needs, of English literature which possesses literary interest rather than human interest, of a foreign language which will never be used, of mathematics which is designed to prepare for the further study of mathematics, of natural science which is organized from the standpoint of the scientist, and of history which presents but a partial account of human achievement. In most schools new

[1] Merriam: *Child Life and the Curriculum:* World Book Company, 1921, pp. 64-5.

materials have been introduced into the program, and the ordinary pupil usually enrolls in some courses which are not included in this list; but the foregoing picture gives a fair impression of the emphasis of the senior high school curriculum today." [2]

Harold Rugg, too, has forcefully insisted upon the lack of relationship to living, pressing problems manifested by the present day curriculum. He finds, for example, that current geography texts devote, on an average, five pages to the British Isles, and no space at all to the British Empire, one of the most significant structures of the modern world; and that, in social science and history, only a bare, schematic account, at the best, and perhaps none at all, is given of such supremely important matters as the westward movement of our people, the causes of the World War, or the causes of unemployment. And he continues: "The method of the encyclopaedia dominates also the treatment of our insistent domestic problems. A chapter to the westward movement. Thirty paragraphic pages to the problems of American industry and business. Not only is the treatment of critical matters inadequate and brief, but its emphasis is on form and structure—not on the driving forces of American life." [3]

So you would be justified in believing that many of the subjects, and much of the material you studied in school, was not of the highest educational worth, and was only remotely related to life.

B. The present day curriculum is ill organized for educative purposes. This is the second defect arising from its traditional rather than rational basis. In older times, when the schools offered little but the classics and some mathematics, the problem of organizing the curriculum was a simple one. But, little by little, new subjects have been introduced. And as we have seen, they were not introduced because they had a recognized place in a complete, well-considered scheme of education, but because it was no longer possible to keep them out. Subjects have come into our curriculum in the way that laws have come into our statute books—at haphazard, and without unifying design. In both cases the result has been the same: a steadily advancing chaos.

Looked at from the outside, it seems a fine thing to have an

[2] Counts: *The Senior High School Curriculum:* The University of Chicago, 1926.
[3] *National Society for the Study of Education:* 26th Yearbook, p. 150.

enormous number of different subjects taught in a great high school. And there cannot be much doubt that a curriculum ought to be as broad and rich as possible. But, as things are now managed, the result is often sheer bewilderment for pupils, teachers, and advisers. If an individual child is to be satisfactorily educated, the first necessity is to help, induce, and compel him to make a wise choice of a sequence of studies. But on what basis shall he choose? Certainly he does not know. Leave it to him, and his program card will be a joke, or a tragedy, according to your point of view. Moreover, the curriculum itself offers no adequate answer. There are certain series of prerequisites, but their controlling educational necessity is often far from clear; and the way the various courses actually dovetail into one another is something about which we had better not ask too many questions if we want to avoid trouble. Then there are certain sequences within the general curriculum, such, for instance, as the courses for college entrance credit. These are associated with a hazy, unrelated penumbra of electives. But, all in all, the system offers no clear guidance. It fails to indicate to the individual how to go about converting all this mass of available raw material into an integrated education, and to point the way towards coherent mental growth.

Our curriculum has developed towards enrichment—which is good. But it has done so in the wrong way—which is bad. We have mountains of food, but few well planned meals. We have a tangled forest, choked with matted thickets, through which lead a few vague trails and wood roads, rather than an orderly and intelligible plantation.

What then is needed? Clearly, we must seek to substitute a curriculum based on a reasoned insight into the aim and tasks of education, for one which arises largely out of tradition blindly modified under the pressure of new material which, somehow, seems vaguely valuable. As a matter of fact, we have, ready to hand and clearly formulated, the underlying conceptions which must guide the work of reform; even though there must still be a vast deal of experimentation before we know just how to apply them in all details. But these conceptions have not yet been used. Changes have been forced, rather than deliberate; haphazard, rather than determined in accord with some intelligible scheme. We know how to go about reorganizing the curriculum for the sake of making it a more effective educational instrument. But the actual job has never been undertaken in a really large way. Only here and there do we find curriculum revision attempted in a thorough-going manner.

It is remarkable how slightly educational theories have affected the curriculum. The old idea used to be that the function of education was to train the mind. But the subjects studied in school were by no means deliberately chosen and introduced on account of this theory. They were there long before it became popular. And while it had some considerable effect upon the way they were taught, yet in the main it was brought in merely to justify the existing program. Latterly, however, some of the brethren came to feel a little uneasy about formal discipline—some of them, not all. Their dreams having been disturbed by echoes from teachers' conventions, and other noisy places where an inconvenient wisdom utters her voice, they began brokenly to talk a modern social philosophy of education, and to murmur about adjusting pupils to life. But does their idea of a proper choice of studies change? Hardly at all. The very curriculum which, a few years ago, was so admirably adapted to strengthen the mental muscles, is now just the thing to secure better home membership, fuller civic participation, and a superior adaptation to industrial civilization. Counts, on the basis of his investigation (*Op. cit.*) points out that many teachers have changed their words, but not their ways or their minds. When it comes to a practical decision, education still means to them the old, traditional content, accepted because it exists. This is why they are capable of calling a modern educational philosophy just a new "jargon." To them, this is all it is!

Clearly, this will not do. It is necessary to translate our new educational conceptions into effective action and, above all, to apply them to this vital problem of the curriculum. How much of traditional curriculum will be retained, and how much will be eliminated, it is hardly possible to say. Probably the extent of alteration will be very different at different levels—different, that is, in the elementary school, the high school, and the college. The study of these somewhat detailed matters belongs properly to a book chiefly devoted to the subject. What I shall now try to do, is to show what the application of our conception of education to the curriculum actually means, in regard to determining its proper content, and indicating its most effective organization.

2. What principles should determine the content of the curriculum?

If we seriously wish so to manage the school that it shall yield a maximum opportunity, and render a maximum service to the pupil, there is one simple, inexorable, and arduous condition to be met. We must make available to him, from the wealth of intellectual capital, only such items as have an explicit, assignable relationship to his life problems and needs. The intellectual resources of civilization exist, not for their own sake, but solely to secure for the individual the best adjustment to its institutions. They are far too vast to be possessed in completeness by the wisest and ablest of us. Therefore we should choose those elements which will serve us best. This will be the content of the ideal curriculum. And to approximate it as nearly as may be for all children in the school, is probably the greatest single enterprise of modern education. Some account of the aims of education as institutional adjustment, we have already given. So you should have at least an intimation of what kind of concrete undertaking lies before us. Our goals are the institutions of society. Our means are the intellectual resources of society. Our task is to organize the one to achieve the other.

Take any proposed item of curricular material you like—the Latin conditional sentence, the study of Roman life, the solution of simple equations, the appreciation of Shelley's *Skylark,* the mastery of compound interest, the spelling of English words, the mastery of the Evans Gambit in chess—and there will always be two questions which we must ask.

Of these the first is: *What is its relationship to social adjustment?* If we cannot answer this explicitly, definitely, and in a spirit of realistic common sense, our failure is a danger signal. Perhaps we have no idea what bearing the item in question has on adjustment. Perhaps the only reason we can think of for learning it is that pupils need it to master a subject in a certain logical order. Then we must suspect—though we cannot yet be quite sure—that it has no place in our curriculum, that it stands for a waste of human energy, and ought to be scrapped. Perhaps we find that it will affect only a very few pupils in the great business of their living. Such would, for instance, be the case with a grammar rule in foreign language; for we know that even among doctors of philosophy, only a few actually use their foreign languages at all extensively. Then the item is not proper curricular material for all our pupils. Perhaps, again, we find that many of our pupils may have a use for this item in their institutional adjustments, but only very seldom; an instance being, perhaps, the calculation of the present value of a note. Then we will feel that it may have a legitimate place, but only after many more important things have been learned. There are by no means all the points of view from which we ought to assess each curricular item, in terms of the aim it is to achieve. But the discussion serves to show you how definite, how factual, one must be, to avoid that ever-present menace of the teacher—self-deception about the value of what is being taught.

The second question we must ask about every item in the curriculum is this: *Granted that it really helps some important life adjustment, would some other item do this better?* A great many teachers, as soon as they hear about institutional adjustment as the aim of education, at once begin to busy themselves in making out a case for their own pet subjects on this basis. Interestingly enough, they always succeed! The reason is simple. Everything the schools have ever taught—nay more, every last crumb of intellectual content—has some relationship, somewhere, somehow, to human life in the midst of civilized institutions. But some items have a much more direct relationship than others. And, by and large, directness pays. For instance, a teacher of Greek may say that to study the career of Cleon will facilitate a very valuable element of civic adjustment, namely a certain attitude towards demagogues. So it may. But why not develop this attitude by studying, in social science or American History, some of our latter day demagogues? Notice that I do not say that pupils should not know about Cleon. I only claim that, if what we want is to protect them from demagogues, they should know about other awful examples first. We have exactly the same argument from teachers of Latin, and modern foreign languages, when they say that their subjects tend to improve English. Possibly—or better, not impossibly—they may. But surely, when we ask why not do all this by studying English, we raise a baffling question. There is something both ridiculous and pathetic about these defences of educational deviousness, these claims that the shortest distance to a given point is round some barn somewhere. For we nearly always find that the teachers who advance the claims are the owners of the barns!

So much for our fundamental controlling principles. But how ought we to go about applying them? We must build up a specific picture of the actual, detailed adjustments which we consider desirable, and then set to work to bring them about. We must carry our principle that the institutions of society are the goals of education down to its ultimate, detailed consequences. This means that we cannot rest content with vague talk about adjustment to civic, economic, or family institutions, and the like. Such talk is good and helpful, but it does not take us very far. It does not tell us exactly what curricular items we should prefer, and what we should reject. Suppose you wish to promote, through the schools, the very finest type of family life; what must you know before you can sit down and, with any confidence, plan the items which should go into the curriculum? Clearly, you must know just what "the finest type of family life" actually is. You must carry your very proper and desirable aim down to concrete cases. You must draw up a bill of particulars.

A very great deal of work is now going on along this line. Many studies have been made, and are being made, which seek to explore and formulate the details of institutional adjustments. At first the investigators who applied these ideas naturally chose very simple problems of curriculum building. One of the earliest studies undertook to determine the best methods of training bricklayers. It was found that, while an expert might, himself, know very well what to do, he often failed to convey his skill to a novice, even with the best will in the world. So slow-motion moving pictures of highly skilled bricklayers were made; and from these was developed a sort of composite notion of the ideal expert. At once it became possible to show the novice exactly what he ought to do, and exactly where he was dissipating efficiency; and the whole training process was greatly aided. In other words, the essentials of the industrial technique could be sifted from the unessentials, and economically imparted. This simple case is most instructive, for it shows very clearly the germ idea of this whole method of attack on curriculum problems. We have, first, the type of adjustment called expert bricklaying. Then we have this adjustment analyzed into its component elements. And this gives us, in specific form, the goals of educational effort.

The idea underlying this procedure has been widely applied. Many other jobs besides bricklaying have been so analyzed, including various types of clerical and secretarial work, and, more recently, even the work of the school teacher. Moreover, it has been applied to situations other than total vocational adjustments. The question as to what spelling lists should be used in the grades has been answered by such a method as determining the words most frequently misspelled by children and adults. What items of English grammar should receive attention has been decided by studying grammatical errors as they occur in themes and letters. Current literature has been scanned for historical and scientific references, to provide some clue as to what portions of the content of history and science are of most worth in present day living. And, far transcending these modest efforts, we have the tremendous undertaking of assembling a complete list of the characteristic activities of an entire community, as the basis for the curriculum of its public schools.

Attempts at the scientific determination of the content of the curriculum have moved pretty largely along such lines as these. Such attempts are admirable and essential. But they contain an inescapable limitation. Briefly put, all these studies of the detailed facts of human adjustment offer us an account, not of the *ideal,* but the *actual* activities of human beings. And we must seek for a curriculum which will promote activities and adjustments, which, if not wholly ideal, are at least better than those now found. To build education upon the actual only is to abandon the hope of progress. It is a great and serious fallacy. And assuredly, some of the statements made by experts who have used the various fact finding techniques to which we have referred, do not seem adequately to guard against it. Thus, one of them has said: "Find the activities which men perform, or those which they should perform; and train for those."[4] Now it may not be too difficult to find out what activities are actually performed. But information of this sort, valuable though it may be, is not all that we need. Taken alone, it cannot furnish any proper foundation for an educational structure. It deals only with human adjustment to life problems, as it now is. But everyone admits that such adjustment is most seriously defective. We know that boys and girls read much fiction of the type of adventure stories, detective stories, and love stories, but only very little poetry; but does this mean that our schools should not actively encourage the reading of poetry? We know that few inhabitants of a typical American community ever read the notation of the musical score; but this fact, in itself, is no argument for not teaching the notation in the elementary schools. To take over an illustration given by Bode,[5] Governor Bradford knew that a great many people in his day were much given to reading; but he did not, therefore, conclude that everybody ought to read; on the contrary, he bitterly deplored and denounced it as a pernicious habit.

Education, then, must seek to bring about a better adjustment to life than that found at present. It seeks to change both the individual and society. And so, in planning our curriculum, and determining its proper content, we must not use our knowledge of the current nature of human social activity directly or immediately. On the contrary, we must build from it an account of the sort of improved activity which may be considered desirable and possible.

To understand how this may be done, let us go back to the very first essay at applying the technique of "job analysis"—the case of the bricklayers—where everything is seen in simplest outline. The education of the bricklayer aimed to produce, in the novice, a certain type of adjustment. But it was an adjustment which no one expert possessed completely. So mere watching, mere copying, mere modelling one's self on the *status quo,* was not enough. An ideal mode of education was not established, until a technique had been

---

[4] Bobbitt, F.: *How to Make a Curriculum:* Houghton Mifflin Company, 1924.
[5] *Modern Educational Theories:* Macmillan Company, 1927.

PLANNING THE CURRICULUM 387

found to set forth the ideal adjustment, which nobody actually possessed. And this is the true way to provide for all education a foundation of valid aims. Our fact finding techniques can, and do, tell us an enormous lot about how human beings actually behave—how they buy clothes and automobiles; how much of their incomes they spend for rent; under what circumstances they call a doctor, or visit a chiropractor; how apt they are to vote in a primary election, or to obey the letter and the spirit of the traffic laws; and so on, endlessly. But here we have only the raw material of educational wisdom. There still remains the greater, harder, and more thrilling task of determining, in view of how men do act, how they ought to act. Fact finding only gives us a picture of relative inefficiency. What we want is to educate for efficiency.

In some cases it is certainly more feasible to tell what the ideal adjustment is than in others. I have already called your attention to one notable enterprise along this line, Harap's *The Education of the Consumer,* which combines masterly scholarship and insight in the attempt to decide the nature of wise consumption of food, shelter, and clothing. Snedden's *Civic Education,* too, gives suggestions as to similar procedures in another field, for he proposes to decide upon the goals of civic training by ascertaining the civic deficiencies of various social groups. But, of course, our ignorance of the ideal course of life and adjustment vastly outweighs our knowledge. He would be rash indeed who undertook anything more than general statements of how human beings ought to behave in most of the problematic situations of daily life.

The only ultimate means of determining the proper content of the curriculum is a social philosophy of life. Indeed, such a social philosophy of life is exactly what we are trying to convey to the pupil. It is what education is for; since its great aim is to teach him how to live. The curriculum must be made up of those materials which most immediately serve and promote the best available ways of social action. To find out what those materials are, we must have some picture, some ideal, of what social action ought to be. Our ideal must surely be founded upon fact. Otherwise it can never be feasible or applicable. It must be an interpretation of society as it now is, of life as it is now lived. But mere facts are not enough.

Education is interpretation and prophecy. And interpretation and prophecy have their essential place in curriculum building.

3. *What principle should determine the organization of the curriculum?*

A curriculum is not a mass of material, any more than an automobile is a mass of metal. It is an active instrument for bringing about a flexible, creative, progressive adjustment to the institutions of society. Its purpose may be defeated just as surely by putting it together in the wrong way, as by making it out of unworkable stuff. Hence the importance of our present question.

The principle which must determine the organization of the curriculum can be stated very simply. *The curriculum must be so arranged and operated as to bring about mental growth.* If this is not done, it fails as an instrument for education. Mental growth means the fuller and fuller use, by the individual, of the intellectual resources of civilization, for the ends of living. The intellectual resources of civilization, in themselves, are nothing at all. They exist solely to promote more effective adjustments. When a child learns them merely to pass an examination, he does not become educated. He makes them ends in themselves, not means to an end. So treated, they become merely so much sterile subject matter. They must be acquired in a certain way, and in a certain setting, or the outcome is failure. So, no matter how wisely and well we choose the content of our curriculum, if that content fails to minister to mental growth, we have our pains for nothing.

For instance, we know that science has enormous potential value for raising the level, and increasing the enlightenment, of any person's life. We try to choose from the great body of scientific resources those items of information, those attitudes, and those skills, which we believe will have the most worth. So far, so good. But if we then merely organize this material into a series of formal lessons, pointing to nothing but tests and marks, everything becomes hopeless. It is no use saying that this is very valuable material, and that if the child learns it now, he will use it later on. Unless he sees the point, and feels the force of it now, he is very unlikely to use

PLANNING THE CURRICULUM

it later on. He will probably just forget it. The spectre of the cold storage fallacy rises to confute us. The child must be brought to use our well chosen scientific materials for progressively better and more intelligent living. We cannot too often remember that, while education is impossible without intellectual content, it by no means consists in mastering even the most potentially valuable content for its own sake, and stowing it away for use on a future occasion. Education consists of mental growth. And for this we must provide in the organization of our curriculum.

In our earlier discussion of mental growth, we saw that it always begins with the sense of a vital problem; and also that it is a movement from the fragmentary and incomplete, towards the unified and the complete. Let us see how these ideas may be applied to guide us in organizing the curriculum.

A. Mental growth always begins with the sense of a vital problem. It starts with contact with reality, with genuine experience. For this we must definitely provide in the organization of our curriculum. Just what does this mean? It means that we can never rest content with our plans, until we have found ways and means of tying in life experiences with the subject matter which the child is learning. One way in which this is done is by using projects. When a boy studies mathematics to find out about the trajectory of his rifle bullets—when a class learns biological and social science in connection with discovering the causes of typhoid in a farm home—when a group of children develop a play dealing with the landing of the Pilgrims—we can hardly be in doubt about a relationship existing between subject matter and life. We have gone far towards producing the essential condition for the beginning of mental growth, the sense of a genuine and compelling problem, though we may still defeat ourselves by mismanagement.

Some enthusiasts have suggested that the project method is the only way of achieving this result, and that the whole curriculum ought to be grouped about a series of such undertakings. So much, however, does not seem necessary. Unless such a procedure is handled with the utmost skill and insight, it will fail, because it may become all project and no subject matter. And there are other ways. For instance, we may systematically and carefully plan contacts between things learned in school, and the child's life out of school. Thus music, art, literature, and much science, may be definitely related to many home interests and activities. Certain topics in social science may be made fruitful if considered about the time the tax bills are due, or during a political campaign. Many other suggestions of a similar sort will readily occur to you. Or, there is a still more obvious means at our disposal. The sense of a connection between subject matter and reality can certainly be developed by the right kind of reading. The content of civics can be made meaningful by readings all the way from the level of *The Dutch Twins* to *Mr. Crewe's Career* or *An American Tragedy*. Why confine geography to a textbook, when the local public library has the files of *The National Geographic Magazine?* The daily press and the current periodicals, too, provide a mine of potential vicarious experience, ready to be used for our purpose.

What we need is a curriculum less formally and restrictively organized than of old—a curriculum organized with the thought that it deals with the concerns of life. We are not bound to go the full length of a pure project organization. Yet we are likely to depart more and more from the traditional organization of separate courses. The inevitable tendency of the course is to emphasize subject matter for its own sake, and to treat its relationship to life as a side issue. The modern curriculum, all the way from the elementary school to the university, is coming to be organized far more flexibly. There is a tendency to break away from the rigidly compartmental traditional scheme, and to lead the pupil to attack large and significant problems, without being particularly careful whether he strays over the boundary lines of the conventional subjects.

Before passing on, notice three things. (i) It is essential that the contact between subject matter and experience be organized and directed. We must not think it enough to give both, and trust to luck that the pupil will see the connection. In this connection lies the force and value of education. We must use life experience, of whatever kind may be available, to rouse the sense of vital problems which can be solved only by mastering intellectual content. (ii) All this implies that subject matter must be so planned that

PLANNING THE CURRICULUM

it can be assimilated to genuine experiences possible to the child at his present level. The whole conception fails, if we try to teach the child material so complicated and remote that it cannot possibly mean anything important to him, as he now is. (iii) Subject matter ill chosen, subject matter remote from our current life, immediately renders this whole plan nugatory. If our curriculum is made up of the wrong materials, nothing we can do will make it truly educative.

B. Again, mental growth is a movement from the fragmentary and incomplete towards the unified and the complete. And this, too, must be considered and provided for in planning our curriculum. Enlightened action and affective social adjustment depend upon an organized mental background. But it is impossible to convey that background ready-made. The effective use of the vernacular depends unquestionably on a grasp of the principles of grammar; but if we try to produce it by drilling little children on formal grammar, we shall fail. The ability to use arithmetic freely and certainly as a tool of thought, is impossible without working insight into the laws of numerical relationship; but the way to convey these laws is not to place them at the beginning of the child's arithmetical development. Mastery of natural science, of algebra, of geometry, or of history, undoubtedly means a logically organized, systematic mental grasp; but this is the end, rather than the starting point, in learning these subjects.

So, in the first two grades, we should have very informal, fragmentary number work closely associated with the natural interests and activities of the children, rather than the beginning of formal arithmetic, which may come in the third grade, and may even be postponed still longer. In the first grade, emphasis may well be upon reading, and oral language, with writing taken up in the second grade. Geography may be introduced, very freely and informally, in the third grade, and made more formal in the fourth and fifth. A free, fragmentary treatment of American history is appropriate for the fifth grade, and when the children enter the sixth grade, they are given a more highly organized, systematic presentation, associated with a wider background. In the junior high school, the tendency is to commence science with work in general science, leaving the study of the special sciences to a time when the pupils' minds are ready to assimilate and understand the more systematic aspects of the field. In the same way, we have modern geometry courses starting, not with the familiar axioms and postulates, but with much directed experience in dealing with concrete space relationships; and courses in foreign language, which make as little as possible of the grammar at first, and strongly emphasize reading, with grammar treated incidentally. Curriculum planning has more faithfully and completely recognized this principle of mental growth as a movement from the fragmentary towards the unified, in the elementary school and the junior high school, than in the senior high school and the college. But even at these higher levels, we find it. Many of the orientation courses now given to college freshmen have this thought behind them.

In this connection, there is one thing to which I particularly want to call your attention. You must not suppose that, because we begin with the fragmentary, the casual, the unsystematic, we believe for a moment that mental continuity and firmly organized grasp are not vitally important. Present day plans for curriculum reorganization and educational change are often criticized on this very point, but those criticisms are not wholly justified. That is to say, some such plans may fall into this error; but serious educational thinkers know very well that it is an error. By all means education requires a systematic, orderly grasp of the logic of science, mathematics, history, and so forth. Without this, we cannot have that mental background which is the only possible means of effective life adjustment. The whole point is, that we must work towards it rather than trying to begin with it. Of course, some schools and some teachers do, in fact, begin with the fragmentary, and never work away from it. But this nullifies the entire plan. But an equally serious criticism lies against schools and teachers where the effort is made to begin with the systematic, the logical, the complete. This mode of ignoring the claims of mental growth is by far the more common of the two. There is only one way in which the child can effectively inherit the racial intellectual wealth. He must come to own it through a long process of growth. And we must plan our curriculum for the patient fostering, and the wise guidance, of such growth.

4. *What must be the characteristics of the new curriculum?*

Let us now try to indicate somewhat more concretely what kind of curriculum we may expect to have when the principles we have been discussing are applied.

First of all, the new curriculum will be organized about a core of social studies, in which all children in school will participate. This is its most striking difference from the traditional curriculum, which was organized about language requirements. From the point of view we have been developing, it is obvious that the social studies have greater educational claims than the language studies. The supremely important thing for citizens of the modern world is to understand how the social mechanisms work, how current social conditions have arisen, how life has been lived in other ages, how it is now lived in other parts of the world, and what are the implications of social problems and failures. To regard a person as well and wisely educated, simply because he has an outstanding language mastery, although he is oblivious to the ebb and flow of the social forces in which he must bear a part, is inadmissible. The school must stand, above all else, for social interpretation and enlightenment. On this its curriculum must be built.

But this means something broader than social science as ordinarily conceived. It means teaching a wide range of content in terms of its social significance. The barrier between social and natural science will be broken down; for, as we have insisted, natural science becomes educative chiefly when its social significance is appreciated. The techniques of industry will be imparted, not for their own sake, or for directly vocational ends, but for the sake of developing understandings of characteristic social problems. Music, art, and literature, will be closely related to the core curriculum, because they are largely social in outcome, though not necessarily so in content. They will be taught chiefly for appreciation and for human values, rather than in the interest of technique. This will be the main stem of the curriculum, continuing on probably to the second year in college.

B. In the second place, the new curriculum will seek to serve the ends of general education; but not in the traditional sense of that time-honored word. General education has usually meant the study of certain subjects which have no specific vocational reference, such as language, pure science, and history. Often it has implied a scheme of education which is cultural in the sense of being impractical. Now the modern curriculum will be practical, because it persistently and essentially deals with the great issues of living. The learner himself will learn to see its practicality, because it will be so organized that he finds himself consciously dealing with the issues of life. But still it will be general, because its aim is total social adjustment. Its generality will lie in its outcomes rather than its content. As our educational principles work out towards their fulfillment, the sharp distinction between culture and vocation will steadily recede. Vocational choice will come as the result of increasing social enlightenment and self knowledge. And special vocational preparation will follow from a valid choice, and stem out of the central social core of the curriculum.

C. In the third place, the modern curriculum will be an integrated rather than a departmental curriculum. This means that the pupil will be led to perceive the relationship of each thing he studies to all the rest—the relation of mathematics to literature, of science to music, of history to language, and so on. The need for this is obvious, and cannot be disputed. Again and again it has been urged that if we study any subject in a water-tight compartment, we greatly reduce its value. And it has been insisted that education must find the means to recognize this essential one-ness of all knowledge. The great obstacle has been the organization of the curriculum into separate courses, as the mechanism of the credit system. And it has been thought that the way of salvation lies in what has been called "correlation." That is, efforts have been made to bring the separate courses the pupil studies into touch with one another. They are not wholly satisfactory, because the very organization of the curriculum into courses is the root of the trouble. What we need is a radically new plan, not a few mechanisms grafted onto the old system. We must seek to organize the student's work in broader, more inclusive units, which cut across the traditional subdivisions of the intellectual domain. But no mere paper reorganization will be enough. All we shall do will be to create a different set of subdivisions, just as harmful in the end as the old ones. We must create a curriculum which presents a selected picture of society. We must block out significant aspects of this social picture, and make these the units which the pupil studies. For instance, we set up classical civilization as a massive study-unit in the high school. Our students learn about its political and social institutions, its great personalities, its literature, its art, its architecture, its science. They gain a grasp of subject matter; but always in relationship to a social condition. And they see the relationship of one field of subject matter to the rest, because they see its relationship to society itself. In a word, we cannot adequately recognize the one-ness of knowledge in our educational processes by the correlation of water-tight, subject matter courses. We can only do so by building up a socially integrated curriculum.

D. In the fourth place, the new curriculum will be organized about a scheme of requirements. Some people have argued that, because modern educational thought recognizes, with unique force, the significance and uniqueness of the individual, there should be no trace of curricular requirements of any kind. If our curriculum must be organized so as to provide for the mental growth of the individual pupil, why should we require every pupil in school to study certain subjects? One college, at least, has been reported as going to the extreme limit in getting rid of requirements. For it has advertised that each student may have his own personal curriculum. This, however, indicates a very superficial understanding of progressive educational principles. There are, in fact, three cogent reasons for setting up a sequence of curricular requirements for all children in school.

First of all, certain studies are of supreme value for promoting an effective social adjustment and creating a common way of enlightened living. The more intensely we believe in the social purposes of education, the more in earnest shall we be in trying to have everybody learn these things. We cannot, for a moment, admit that education means simply learning anything that one happens to fancy. The core of social studies has a paramount claim. And we believe that any pupil who denies this claim on the basis of individual interest, and the supposititious right of absolutely free choice, is in error. Second, curricular requirements are necessary in order to organize and integrate the education of each individual. For the sake of mental growth, it is essential that a pupil's work in school shall be built around a solid core. It is not, indeed, necessary that everyone shall study exactly the same things as everyone else. But some organized, sequential plan there must be; or individual development will fail. Third, curricular requirements are necessary for the sake of discovering the interests and aptitudes of the individual. This principle is now being applied, with some success, in the exploratory courses set up in various junior high schools. Clearly, if we allow each pupil to follow any sequence he happens to follow, we may not only have a program intolerably scattered and unintelligible, but we are likely to have a program unduly and fatally narrow.

Curricular requirements are only bad when they are arbitrary. When students feel outraged at being forced to take certain studies, this is because the underlying reason is not apparent to them. Only too often that reason is not apparent, because it does not really exist. The requirement is supported on the basis of tradition only. But if we have a thoroughly rationalized curriculum—if we have a curriculum constructed of socially meaningful elements, organized to foster and favor mental growth—its essential reasonableness should be as evident to the pupils as to anyone else concerned. Curricular requirements, under such a system, can be made appealing, simply because the genuine need for them is obvious to any intelligent person; simply because they are not felt as the dead hand of an inherently indefensible tradition.

E. In the fifth place, the new curriculum will be planned with an eye to flexibility. Some educational thinkers have argued that the curriculum should not be planned at all; and that the decision as to what each child should study, ought to be left to him and to the teacher. The arguments against this kind of extreme individualism have already been presented. Our position is that the curriculum must, indeed, be planned in advance, and planned for all children, not as a mere matter of practical necessity, but because to do so is educationally sound. But if we do not think of education as the performance of set tasks in a given time, we certainly cannot lay out a course of study with the kind of rigidity often found. We must recognize that mental growth takes time, and that we cannot tell in advance just how much time will be needed in any individual case. Moreover, we must also recognize that, while the ultimate end of all mental growth is social adjustment, and while this indicates its general course, yet there may be wide differences in detail. For instance, if we set up classical civilization as a unit of study, there is no good reason why every pupil must cover exactly the same ground. One may want to write an essay on classical architecture; another may wish to spend time in studying some of the literary masterpieces of antiquity; another may delve into the legal system; and so on. What we want is not the uniform covering of ground but a general enlightenment. So, instead of prescribing exactly what books must be read; exactly what theorems learned; exactly how many compositions written; and exactly how much time must be spent on every detail; we block out our curriculum in terms of the mental processes to be affected, the outcomes in the way of attitude and enlightenment to be achieved. And while we lay out units of study, we permit variations of subject matter within them.

F. The sixth, and last, of the characteristics of the new curriculum on which I wish to comment is not entirely parallel with the others I have been discussing. Yet it is very important. For that curriculum must be *created* as well as, or perhaps even rather than, *selected*. Curriculum construction requires the expert, who surveys the available material and chooses from it those items most suitable for current needs. But also, it requires the man of creative vision, who sets forth new interpretations, and perceives new relationships between intellectual content and human life. Our curriculum, as we have already said, must ultimately embody a working philosophy of living. But this is something which cannot simply be found ready-made, no matter how expert the search, and how adequate the techniques. To obtain it, we must look for men of creative mind who see things in new and illuminating aspects, and who constructively add to our enlightenment. As Harold Rugg has pointed out, new curricular materials of the first order have been brought into being in America within comparatively recent years. New schools of art, and music, and historiography, and literature, have arisen. Their common message is their interpretation of the American scene. And such materials are, to a peculiar degree, meet for the uses of modern education.

So the ideal curriculum is not something static or finally attainable. On the contrary, it is something always changing and forever in the future. Curriculum reform is one of the modes of action and thinking by which a social order comes to understand its own purposes and meanings. The perfect curriculum would be the perfect expression of what human life might and should be. This we can never have. As soon as one insight has been achieved, others open up. Here we have, once more, the process of mental growth, which is, in essence, endless. So we must think of the task of ordering and planning the curriculum as endlessly creative, a never ending search for better ways and more perfect understandings, a continuous adventure of discovery, a task never to be terminated, never to be laid aside as complete.

5. *What should be the relationship of curricular to extra-curricular activities?*

One of the most inherently indefensible of all the distinctions which our present system of education has developed, is that between curricular and extra-curricular activities. It has become such a definite stereotype in our thinking that we have trouble seeing how absurd it is. So let us try to imagine the impression it would make on our convenient, fresh-minded observer from Mars. He would find that some of the things pupils do in school are treated with great and solemn respect and are importantly made matters of permanent record; while others seem to go on somewhat at haphazard, and to be outside the system. "What is the reason for this distinction?" he would ask. "Are these 'curricular' activities important, while the others are not?" To this we would have to answer no. To work on the school paper; to take part in a debate; to be a member of the school orchestra; to organize a fraternity chapter; to be a member of the football team;—such experiences are as significant as any well can be. Why, then, are they outside the charmed circle? There is really only one reason. They do not fit into our scheme of academic bookkeeping. They cannot be given a value in terms of credits. The distinction is one of accounting, not of educational values. It is highly artificial and arbitrary.

Just because there is no clear and sane distinction in principle between curricular and extra-curricular activities, we find great, and quite unintelligible divergencies in practice in different schools. Some schools give credit for instrumental music; others withhold it; some give credit for debate, others do not; some give credit for dramatics, others do not. And so on. There is no clear uniformity, because the distinction itself is not logical. Our schools have come to operate on a system which treats only a certain limited range of experience as educationally valid, when the clear fact is that all experience has an educative effect.

Our great structure of extra-curricular activities has grown up largely because of the narrow way in which our schools have conceived the educative process. That structure has been brought into being by the pupils rather than the teachers. Inter-collegiate football, which began some sixty years ago with a game between Harvard and Yale, was originated entirely outside the official auspices of the colleges themselves. The same has been true of the fraternity system, which was created as a necessary measure, when the colleges simply washed their hands of all responsibility for the social lives of their students. The reason why the fraternity system has gained no foothold in English universities is that those institutions have deliberately, and very successfully, planned for the social activities of their students, so that an outside organization is not needed and has no place. At first our schools were simply indifferent to what their students did when they were not studying. But as extra-curricular activities became more and more important and highly organized, a certain attitude of hostility developed on the part of the faculties. This was perfectly futile. The tide kept coming in, despite the injunctions of the educational Canutes. And while some grumbling may still be heard, a better and more constructive insight is in the making. It is coming to be seen that a school has not done its full educational duty, when it has merely undertaken to teach a certain mass of subject matter. That duty has not been done until the school has made itself over into a community where the pupil may live a full and fruitful life, and where he may find a focus of influence, which shall guide all his social relationships.

When we make a mere bookkeeping, non-educational distinction between curricular and extra-curricular activities, we do harm on both sides. On the one hand, our extra-curricular program continually tends to run wild and swamp us. We have athletic sports, tending towards the status of gladiatorial combats, whose only motive is the will to win. We have fraternity chapters which may throw a formal pinch of salt on the altar of academic standards, but which often exercise an anti-educational influence upon their members. We have a student journalism which constantly tends to run amuck, and a student social life whose main aim seems to be to spend more and more on formal parties. We invite, in short, exactly the kind of situation we might expect, if we turned over the curriculum itself to the tender mercies of unguided management by the pupils. We have an educational nightmare.

And also we weaken the curriculum. This false distinction is one of the chief reasons why study seems boresome and unmeaning. Consider how pleased students are when an instructor cuts a class, although they are being deprived of the very thing for which they, or their parents, have paid good money and made sacrifices. Is there not something topsy-turvy about a situation which can create such attitudes? Is not the reason simply that their studies are for a bookkeeping record, and so lack the appeal of activity which is a genuine part of life?

One of the best ways of making subject matter seem real is to take it out and give it an airing. We need far more informality in our handling of subject matter; far more and closer relationships to the ordinary doings of life. If we can teach it in situations which resemble our present extra-curricular activities, rather than our conventional class activities, we shall almost certainly teach it far more effectively, far more vitally, than we do. The supreme task of the school is the integration of intellectual content with activity. And hence, we must look for an educational statesmanship which plans all the activities of the school for the ends of social adjustment, mental growth, and enlightened living; and which abandons the distinction between the curriculum and the extra-curriculum. All the activities of the school ought to be regarded as educational: *all,* not some!

Notice that when I advocate the abandonment of the distinction between the curriculum and the extra-curriculum, I am advocating something very deep-going, very disturbing. For what is involved is nothing less than giving up our treasured credit system itself. On that system the distinction turns. So long as we enter in a permanent record, for the sake of determining honors and awards, only some of the things a student does, the dualism will continue to plague us. I do not think we can banish it with a wave of the hand. But I do think that this is the direction which American education is bound to take, and that a far better mechanism than our present credit system will be forthcoming. But I must postpone this for a later chapter.

Short of a treatment of all the activities of our school population as educationally significant, there is no solving the problem of the extra-curriculum. Most of our present efforts are merely grotesque. We pass rules that a pupil must have a certain average, and must carry a certain number of courses, to be eligible for the school team or for membership in some social organization. We have other rules which limit the number of extra-curricular activities in which a student may participate. At the best, such regulations are mere palliatives. They are essentially ridiculous, because they bring together completely incompatible elements. What possible inner connection is there between a mark in history and playing quarterback on the 'varsity team? Or between a knowledge of the Periodic Law and eligibility for a fraternity? Obviously none. It would be just as sensible to work things in reverse, and refuse to admit to courses in history and chemistry, those who did not make a certain number of touchdowns, or who were excluded from the blessed privileges of Greek letter societies.

All our rules do is to patch up a poor system. We cannot let extra-curricular activities alone. If we do, we shall land in most certain disaster. And so we set up artificial and negative controls. There is only one solution. We must coöperate with the pupils in planning a well considered program of activities, through which they can be helped to learn the secret of enlightened living; and we must forget the bookkeeping distinction between the curriculum and the extra-curriculum. In our chapter on recreational adjustment, I pointed out that the fact that play is activity carried on for its own sake, does not mean that it needs no regulation or guidance. So, in a still broader sense, we cannot simply make over to the pupils half our educational kingdom and expect good to come of it. Our school must be a unitary whole, if it is to have anything like its full potential effect and its proper influence.

Chapter 18

WHAT ARE THE IMPLICATIONS OF THE EDUCATIONAL LADDER?

1. *What is the general significance of the educational ladder?*

Many of the greatest educational thinkers of past ages dreamed of a system of schools, which, beginning with early childhood, should carry the pupil onward and upward, in a continuous sequence of mental development, to the highest levels; an "educational ladder reaching from the gutter to the university," to quote the classic, if slightly startling phrase. It has been the happy destiny of America to see this dream come true. And this educational ladder is the second great instrumentality which we must consider.

So accustomed are we to our scheme of education, with its threefold sequence of elementary, secondary, and higher schools, that we fail to understand as we should, how new a thing it is in the affairs of men, and how pregnant with meanings and possibilities. In spite of the urgings and strivings of the most forward-looking minds, it remained almost everywhere else in the world no more than a vision until after the World War. Even now it exists in but fragmentary form in most great European nations. With them, the distinction between elementary and secondary education does not lie chiefly in the advancement of the work done, or the age of the pupils, but in a division of social classes. The son of the professional man, the government servant, or the landed aristocrat, attends a different school from the child of the artisan or the farmer. He is, at once, in line for educational privileges denied to the child less fortunately born. Two or three years of study with a tutor, or in a preparatory institution, serves to induct him into one of the great secondary schools. And this, again, leads to the university. But such opportunities are not for the mass of the people. The child of parents humbly placed begins his formal education in the people's elementary school, not the preparatory school. He may, indeed, go on to do what we would consider work of secondary grade. Opportunities for this have greatly increased in the past ten years. But he will do it in a school of entirely different type and standing from that attended by a boy from the higher ranks of society—a school which, in France for instance, is called a "higher primary school," and which has neither the prestige nor the advantages of the secondary school. To be sure, if he has unusual brains, he may win a scholarship to one of the secondary schools. But he will be apt to find himself seriously out of place. Also he may be able to qualify for entrance to the university. But in Europe this again is pretty much the preserve of the privileged classes, who come to it with a very special educational background. None of the major nations of the old world have a full counterpart of our sequence from the public elementary school to the public secondary school, and thence to the university. Since the war, England has come to approach it; but even there, the enormous prestige of such schools as Eton, Harrow, and Rugby, and of Oxford and Cambridge, which are definitely class institutions, stands in the way. In the newer countries we find it—in the great self governing units of the British Commonwealth of Nations, and to some extent in Soviet Russia. But in the main, the educational ladder is still a social and cultural novelty.

As I say, Americans naturally take their system of schools for granted, without seeing anything particularly remarkable about it, or looking upon it as the outcome of a great victory, and the fulfillment of the hopes of centuries; or understanding very clearly its far-reaching implications. This means that, both as individuals and as a society, we do not get from it nearly all the benefits it can bestow. And we hardly value it as we should, or think about it as a most precious social achievement, to whose defence against foes within it and without, every good citizen should rally. So what

IMPLICATIONS OF THE EDUCATIONAL LADDER

want to do in this chapter is to explain, as well as I can, what the educational ladder implies, and what sort of education we may expect to have, if we carry through its logic to the end. In this section, I will state three basic ideas which it realizes in administrative form.

A. First of all, the educational ladder seeks to practice the great democratic precept that educational opportunity must not be determined by class distinctions. It is directly contrary to the conception of a society organized on caste lines, with its system of special privilege. It does not, to be sure, in and of itself solve the problem of educational opportunity. But it represents the first necessary and liberating step towards such a solution.

B. Then, the educational ladder implies that education should not only be generally available but substantially the same for all. This is the doctrine of a common education for a common purpose —namely, the elevation of the group mind and the direction and enlightenment of group action. It is the belief that all, whether rich or poor, whether bright or dull, whether male or female, should above everything reach a common understanding of one another, and fashion together a common way of life in which each may have his share.

C. Lastly, the educational ladder seeks to recognize and implement the truth that all genuine education is continuous. Here again, we have not yet reached perfection or worked out to the full the implications of our system. The break between the elementary school and the high school, and between the high school and the college, is far too sharp. But again, the pull of the system is towards providing conditions for a continuous mental growth. At least we are not proud of our defects. We know them for what they are. And we are setting out to correct them.

Such is the very general significance of our mode of school organization. Further to understand its meaning, I shall ask you to consider the peculiar functions of its three great constituent units, the elementary school, the high school, and the college.

2. *What should the elementary school seek to accomplish?*

The elementary school is not the school of the three R's. It i[s] the school of childhood. Its great task is the social adjustment o[f] all the children of the community. This is an aim far wider tha[n] that which tradition has assigned to it. According to the old con[-]vention, elementary education existed chiefly to cure the socia[l] disease of illiteracy. Children went to school to learn to read, an[d] write, and to acquire an elementary skill with numbers. The ide[a] that all boys and girls should have even this much was once con[-]sidered rather more than questionable. One reason why it ha[s] always been popular in America is the influence of Protestantism[,] which regarded ability to read the Bible as supremely important[.] Nowadays we not only accept without question the notion tha[t] everyone must be made literate; we also think that he should ge[t] a great deal more from the elementary school.

This shift towards a broader conception has been brought abou[t] by the impact of many complex forces. Life in our frontier com[-]munities was both simple and hard. The services of children wer[e] urgently needed at home and on the farm. Only a little of their tim[e] could be spared for schooling. Moreover, there seemed no partic[-]ular point in any wide culture or more than a minimum of "boo[k] learning." Everyone was too urgently occupied in conquering na[-]ture and making a living. But, as the frontier was driven farthe[r] and farther back, and at last wholly eliminated, children becam[e] more and more free from the immediate demands of hard pro[-]ductive work. They were given more and more time just to b[e] children. And it became increasingly obvious that the elementar[y] school could do much more for them than the bare minimum[,] which once seemed desirable.

Then, too, as life became easier, and freedom from the figh[t] against nature became greater, it also became more complex. Com[-]pared to the conditions of today, early America was a very simpl[e] society. Our far-reaching, bewildering tangle of social, industria[l,] and political relationships barely existed. In the course of only [a] few generations, a veritable jungle of problems has sprung up al[l] around us; and our only possible chance of finding the way is b[y] dint of disciplined and instructed insight. Take this in conjunction with the increasing freedom of childhood, and you have a point which only a blind man could miss. Obviously, the elementary school is under challenge to take fuller advantage of its new opportunities to meet the new and growing need.

Again, many of the institutions which touch the life of the child have become educationally impoverished. This is notably true of the home. A recreational center in connection with an elementary school would have been considered crazy in a frontier community. So would an extensive program of school music. So would work in manual arts. And a part of the reason was that such interests were cared for by the home and the church. Now, even if we abolished the home by constitutional amendment, and burned down all our churches, children would still have to be taken care of. And, as other institutions serve them less and less, the elementary school must serve them more and more.

Lastly, it has been growing more and more evident to thinking men, that we must have a universal, common, democratic education, if American society is to survive. The differences between the country and the city, between the rich and the poor, between men in varied occupations and varied races, have been greatly intensified by our industrial civilization. If we simply let such differences work out to their ultimate conclusion, it does not take a major prophet to see what will become of our social order. To elaborate a common way of life, and a mutuality of understanding, is imperative. And the job becomes bigger each day. So it is that the elementary school is recognizing a wider and wider duty, and filling a larger and larger place in our culture.

These massive forces have already had a great effect. If a man who had lived about the year 1800 could come back to earth today, he would probably consider a modern elementary school nothing less than fantastic. He would find that children no longer go to school for a few months in the winter, when they have nothing better to do. He would notice a great increase in the length of the school day. These things, quite apart from the size of the building, and the expensiveness of its equipment, would surely impress him. But, although very much has been done, the new conception of the elementary school as the school of childhood, rather than the school of the three R's, has not yet been completely applied. In our best grade schools, more than half the time of the children is still devoted to reading, writing, and arithmetic. Other subjects, to be sure, have been introduced in considerable abundance. But they are not usually treated as of the first importance. If anything must give way, if anything must have a poor place on the schedule, some of these newer studies are indicated. The business depression has revealed most strikingly how strongly intrenched are the three R's in the prejudices of the public. They are still considered the chief, though perhaps not the only, business of the elementary school. Contrast this with the following statement made by John Dewey: "What the best and wisest parent wants for his own child, that must the community want for all its children. Any other ideal for our schools is narrow and unlovely; acted upon, it destroys our democracy."

How may such an ideal be realized? By putting into operation two controlling principles. We must have a broad curriculum, including the whole range of the intellectual resources of civilization, taught for the sake of social adjustment. And we must create and maintain an educational situation such that the children learn what we want them to learn, chiefly through direct social participation, and to a secondary extent, by vicarious experience gained from the right kind of reading.

The traditional elementary curriculum was exceedingly limited. Moreover it was taught chiefly by direct drill, and for the sake of subject matter itself. This conception is hopelessly inadequate for present needs. If the elementary school is satisfied with doing no more than this, it is failing in its most essential task.

For instance, we believe that oral speech should have a place of the very first importance in the concerns of the school. This item from the means of communication has usually been left to the tender mercies of other agencies—the home, the general community, the neighborhood gang, and so forth. It should be regarded as a definite responsibility of the school, and a most important item in the creation of the social personality. There should, indeed, be little in the way of direct drill. But an improved mastery of the means of oral communication should come incidentally, though still according to plan, out of the general activities of the school. Again, reading, writing, and arithmetic should be far more closely connected with actual social activities and participations, than is usually the case. We must bear in mind that when we teach a child to read or to write, we must try not only to make him *able* to do so, but also *inclined* to do so. We must not be content with conveying mere subject matter. Rather we must seek to provide the tools for life activities and life adjustments which would be impossible otherwise. And this can be done today, to an extent that was not possible yesterday, because of the longer time that children spend in school. Music and art, too, must have an essential place in our program, simply because they are natural agencies for a better life for the child. Too often, however, they are formally taught, with a disciplinary emphasis, and for their own sake alone. Music is apt to mean concentration on the technique of note reading; art, the copying of conventional forms. What we need is rather a direct participation in musical activities as the heart and soul of the program; and art handled as a means of personal self expression. Natural science, and also social science, including geography and history, have their necessary place as well. These, too, should be handled very largely in terms of direct participation and activity. Studying the Constitution of the United States, learning various facts about American history, and memorizing the products of foreign lands, have very little significance of any kind for children. Not by such means as these do we make social science live in their lives. Rather we must seek to reveal to them, more and more completely, the significance of their own group endeavors; to bring them into touch with the life of their own community; and imaginatively to convey to them the lives of people in other times and other lands. Here, of course, vicarious experience through reading plays a part. But always the reading materials used must be interesting, human, vital, and of a character naturally to appeal to children. The old time textbook of geography, or civics, or American history, is dust and ashes. And no vicarious experience, however excellent, can be a substitute for direct participant activity. In the same way, natural science must mean a progressive acquaintance with nature and her laws, and not a mere acquaintanceship or knowledge, but an understanding of the social meanings of those laws. This must be obtained partly from well directed projects, partly through readings carefully chosen. Then too, the school must have a concern for the techniques of recreation. The playground should be considered an educational opportunity of high importance, rather than a place of release from serious and significant activities. Finally, we cannot neglect the prevailing ideals, the folkways, and the mores. Indeed, in a sense, these are the most important of all. If they are not rightly conveyed, we tend to raise a generation verbally literate, and morally illiterate. These elements of our common culture are to be acquired chiefly through the entire planned life of the school. But, in addition, literature offers a great opportunity here. On the old tradition, the elementary school was much concerned about good reading, and very little about good literature. Few things could be more worth doing than deliberately to stimulate and incite children towards the free reading of books which can broaden their horizons, deepen their sympathies, enlarge their understandings, and fashion their moral standards aright.

Keeping this general scheme in mind, there still remain certain qualifications which must be stated, and certain dangers to be avoided.

(i) When a definite and important skill is to be acquired, we should not rely altogether upon incidental learning. This is particularly the case with reading. Children must have a considerable amount of direct drill in the reading process itself, or they will acquire it both slowly and wrongly. We cannot simply set up various projects in the performance of which they must read, and leave them to pick up the art without special and expert guidance. At the same time, their growing ability to read should be made significant to them, and should be far more than a mere development of skill for its own sake. And this is brought about only by associating it, constantly and closely, with appealing activities which involve reading. Much the same comments apply to writing and number work.

(ii) Vicarious experience gained from books becomes a more and more suitable medium through which to learn the natural and social sciences, as we advance onwards through the grades toward the sixth. But it is of the highest importance that the materials be chosen for their natural interest, and their human appeal to children. I have already suggested elsewhere the great possibilities for the teaching of civics and geography of such books as *The Dutch Twins* and *The Swiss Twins*. Readings of this kind have far more educational value than the old fashioned conventional textbook, with its cut-and-dried lists of facts laid out for memorizing and recitation.

(iii) Another point is that so far as possible, any studying from books is best done on an individual plan, rather than as the mastery of assignments for ordinary class recitation. To read, to enjoy, and to learn from a book, is an experience of an essentially private kind; although one may benefit greatly from social opportunities to do something about what one has read and mastered. So individual work tends strongly towards converting reading into a natural, rather than an imposed and distorted actvity. This applies both to the kind of free reading designed to broaden the child's horizon and enrich his experience, and to much pencil and paper drill work which involves following out written instructions, as in arithmetic.

(iv) Sharp subdivisions and compartments of subject matter have little place in the work of the elementary school. Our controlling thought must be that children come to the school to learn basic social adjustments, not to master arithmetic, and reading, and geography, and history, and music, and rudimentary natural science. Concretely, what this means is that all learning must arise out of the matrix of school activities and projects, without any rigid subdivision of the time schedule.

(v) The elementary school must not be allowed to become a "finishing school"—a school, that is, the whole sense of whose work and spirit indicates that it brings a sequence of education to a definite end. In the past, this has been the case, simply because the school offered a limited program of studies, beyond which comparatively few were to go. The old time eight grade elementary school was essentially a finishing school. It restricted its curriculum so narrowly to the three R's that the seventh and eighth grades had to be loaded with a great deal of deadly review work, and with the most formal and theoretical aspects of grammar and arithmetic, to keep them going. Its pervasive suggestion was that education came to a natural terminal point at the end of the eighth grade. And it deliberately confirmed that impression by holding graduation exercises for those who had finished eight years of work. But, if we enrich its curriculum, then clearly the implication must be incompleteness rather than completeness, and the impulse for further education will be set up by the school policy in every possible way. And with the modern elementary school, which broadly initiates a social adjustment, rather than narrowly teaching a small range of subject matter, eighth grade graduation is seen for the absurdity which it is.

Such is our conception of the place and task of the elementary school in the educational ladder. It should be an environment which provides a rich mental growth, common to all children; a place where children take part in multiform, but integrated and co-ordinated, guided and enlightened activities; where they learn to live better by living widely and well; rather than a place where they sit quiescent, and stuff their minds with knowledge dug from the dull pages of textbooks.

3. *What should the secondary school seek to accomplish?*

The secondary school is the school for youth. It continues the work of the elementary school at a higher level, and for an older group. What it should seek to accomplish is the adjustment of youth to the institutions of society.

Here again, we have a conception much broader than the traditional one. In the past, the secondary school has been dominated largely by the purpose of serving the special interests of a select and privileged social class, many of whom are going on to college. It has not been organized for the education of all the youth of the community. Twice in the history of American education, there has been a definite break with this tradition that preparation for college is the task of the secondary school. During the early colonial period, the American secondary school was of the type known as the Latin Grammar School. Its great staple subject was just what its name indicated—Latin Grammar, though it paid attention also to Greek. No one who did not intend to enter college would derive much benefit from it. And so it served a very limited group of patrons. During the latter half of the eighteenth, and the early half of the nineteenth centuries, a new and different type of school arose, and at last, for a time, dominated the scene. This was the Academy. Its chief concern was not to fit its pupils to enter college, but to train them for "the great business of living," as the prospectus of one of the academies put it. And accordingly, it offered a very much broader curriculum, and appealed to a far larger proportion of young people. Then again, early in the nineteenth century, the public High School came into existence. In its original intention, it had nothing at all to do with preparation for college, and, in principle at least, sought to render a universal service.

But so strong has been the pull of the college preparatory tradition that first the academy, and then the high school, became to a large extent college preparatory schools. Among the older academies which still survive are some of the most exclusive of American private schools. The original, strongly democratic spirit of the academy movement has pretty well evaporated. And even with the high school, there has been some movement in this direction. After the Civil War, it became the chief type of American secondary school. In a great many communities the public high school was the only available secondary institution. It had to take care of pupils who intended to enter college, as well as of those who did not. And, almost inevitably, it began to concern itself in a very special way with the interests of the former group. For one thing, the college preparatory students in the high school came from the most influential local families. For another thing, they were the largest compact group in the school with a definite, unifying purpose; and even though they were in a minority, still they exercised the traditional power of organized minorities everywhere. Lastly, the ability to get students into college was a tangible index of the standing and success of a high school. It might fail in the larger purpose of adjusting its pupils to life, and no one would hear much about it. But let it fail with the College Entrance Board, or prove unable to meet the standards of the great accrediting agencies, and somebody was about due to lose his job. To be sure, the high school has never accepted the status of a college preparatory school pure and simple, although the smaller schools have often amounted to little more. But its policies have been quite unduly influenced by the needs of the college preparatory group, and too little concerned with anyone else.

You may have heard it said that the business of the high school is to train leaders. This is simply an alibi, a way of rationalizing, explaining, and excusing the domination of the school by the college preparatory group. Its clear implication is that the school must not be a school for all, but rather for the privileged. Up to about 1918, it might have seemed as though secondary education in America were destined to move in this direction. But since that time, there has been an enormous increase in numbers. Secondary school enrollments have more than doubled. Multitudes, who have no intentions or prospects of going to college, are pressing in. And the high school is being forced, by a kind of mass movement which it cannot control, to return to its original ideal of secondary education for all the youth. Not without bewilderment does it accept its destiny. The full implications of what is happening are not yet grasped, still less translated into adequate practical planning. The dead hand of the academic tradition is still heavy upon it. But there is now little doubt of the prevailing tendency, or the ultimate outcome. Three years of depression, which, strangely, have brought another vast influx of students, contribute still more to the rout of the conservatives who would cling to the ideal of secondary education for the few. Palpably, inevitably, the high school is becoming what it was always meant to be—the school for all the youth.

Clearly to understand what all this means, let us ask in what respects the high school, as the school for youth, will resemble and differ from, the elementary school, as the school for childhood.

A. Let us begin with the respects in which the secondary school should resemble the elementary school.

(i) First and foremost, the school should plan its work for the educational service of the entire body of youth, rather than of a select group. That this is rapidly coming to pass, may be clearly seen from the figures, which are extraordinarily impressive. For many years, new high schools were set up in the United States, at the almost incredible average rate of one each day. The secondary school enrollment has mounted very much faster than the population. Since 1918 particularly, this increase in numbers has been very rapid. And we may predict that, when we are able to take stock of the effects of the lean years through which we are passing, it will be found that the movement towards universal secondary education has been still further accelerated. Forty or fifty years ago, our secondary schools probably enrolled about ten per cent of those who were of an age to attend. But now more than fifty per cent are in these schools. It has been very truly said that the swift and vast development of American secondary education is one of the most notable social and cultural developments of the modern world.

Strange to say, however, the high school itself presents certain obstacles to its own universal appeal. Of course it does not deliberately plan to keep young people out. But its work is organized in such a way that many consider it hardly worth while to enter; or, having entered, leave early in disappointment. This is particularly due to the strong emphasis upon preparation for college. To be sure, the curriculum of a large modern high school is broad enough, in all conscience. But it is broad in the wrong way. It presents a great many more or less unrelated elective studies, when what we ought to have is an integrated educational sequence, appealing to as many as possible. The interests of those preparing for college are still served better than those of any other group. The traditional academic subjects, taught in the traditional way, still have the greatest prestige. The full implications of the democratic idea have not as yet been organized into the curriculum and methods of the high school.

In the junior high school, indeed, this is much less true. Here we have the prototype of the truly universal secondary school. It definitely undertakes to set up for its pupils a core of studies aiming at adjustment to social living. The school builds its work about education for health, for recreation, for home life, for civic life, for economic enlightenment, for culture in the sense in which we have come to understand the term. We cannot be satisfied till the senior high school follows this lead. It is the manifest logic of its destiny.

"But," you may ask, "if the high school is to organize its work so as to appeal to the entire body of youth, will not this mean a lowering of its standards?" It is true that, if everyone of the proper age attended high school, many would be intellectually and temperamentally unfit for the academic curriculum and the college preparatory course. Should we, then, sacrifice the interests of those who can benefit from the study of algebra, geometry, foreign languages, and Latin, for the sake of those who cannot? Clearly, this is something we must not do. And there is no need for it. We are, in fact, facing a false dilemma here. Standards must not be denatured, but reorganized. We need a significant core curriculum, together with a large freedom for each individual to proceed at his own pace and do his own work. And, as we reach the higher grade levels, we need more and more opportunity for specialization. If we cease to think of standards in terms of mass competition and average results, and deal with them in terms of significant individual achievement, we shall find it possible enough to create an educational environment in which both bright and dull may live for six years, to their very great advantage.

(ii) Again, the high school must stand for a continuation of a common, integrating education. It must simply go on with the work the elementary school has begun. It is not, in the main, a place for specialization, though, as I have said, opportunity for this should be provided as the pupil advances upward. But its chief contribution must be an educational experience common to all. The elementary school, dealing for six or eight years with young children, can indeed do something to create a common outlook, and a common way of enlightened living. But it cannot do enough to meet the needs of our complex, diversified modern world. If children are to be brought up so that, as adults, they will understand one another, and be able to live and work together as citizens of the Great Society, they need richer and deeper elements of culture in common than the elementary school can possibly supply. Institutional adjustment in matters pertaining to health, to recreation, to civic activity, to economic understanding, to family living, to the building of a common morality and a common culture sturdy enough to withstand the divisive influence of modern civilization, cannot be achieved by any school which deals with children only between the ages of six and twelve or fourteen.

(iii) In the third place, the high school resembles the elementary school in that it must teach subject matter for the sake of life, rather than for its own sake. Here is one of the great changes which cry aloud to be made in secondary education. The average high school teacher has been trained for his work in an academic environment, where the tendency is to exalt scholarship as an end in itself, and to regard knowledge as more important than action. And he imports this false point of view into the secondary environment. So we have history taught merely for the sake of knowing history, science studied merely for its formal laboratory techniques and its great accumulations of fact, and language learned with the main emphasis on grammar rather than on use. While this is allowed to continue, the high school cannot possibly universalize its appeal. It is not even offering the proper kind of college preparatory work. It is aiming at the education of pedants, rather than of human beings. And we cannot wonder that young people in such an environment gradually and vaguely come to feel that something is very far wrong, and either drop out, or else continue without much vital enthusiasm or a very firm belief that the whole thing is really worth while. The point, of course, is to make secondary education, not narrowly practical, but socially and humanly significant.

B. Now let us consider some respects in which the high school should be different from the elementary school. All the valid and justifiable differences come from just one thing—the fact that it is dealing with older pupils.

(i) One of the most striking differences that this seems to involve is that the high school can, and ought, to rely much more extensively than the elementary school upon vicarious experience gained through reading. But here again, the same points made regarding the elementary school are important. The reading done by pupils must be of a vital, interesting, and significant type. And it should be largely individual and free, rather than mechanically assigned for the sake of mass recitation and testing. I once discussed with a student his experiences in studying English history. He said that he learned about and recited upon the facts of the reign of Elizabeth in the ordinary way, using the ordinary compendious textbook. And it meant very little to him. Then, by some means, he was induced to read Lytton Strachey's brilliant book, *Elizabeth and Essex*. At once the entire Elizabethan period came to life in his mind. The whole history of the times took on a new and vital meaning. And whatever he read after that about Elizabeth, assumed a very special significance. In another case, a boy became interested in reading Macaulay's historical essays; and though he did not gain from them a logically coherent grasp of history, his reading did give him a life-long attitude towards the historical process and the study of history, which seems to me the essence of what is educationally desirable. How unnatural the ordinary assignment-recitation treatment of reading actually is, we may see from the fact that almost no student will undertake to begin by reading his textbook through from beginning to end, which is an obvious procedure when one thinks of it. Reading is apt to be made the taking of measured doses of knowledge, rather than a significant and illuminating experience.

(ii) But the high school should by no means give up the use of actual social participation, and direct opportunity, as a medium for education. It must be remembered, however, that the social activities of older pupils are more highly organized, more definite, and in a certain sense, more formal than those of elementary school children. The school should continue to be a place of multiform significant activity and experience. Managing the school paper, participating in the orchestra or the choir, organizing social events, and carrying on the program of athletics, should all of them be definitely tied to the educative process. Bear in mind always that the school educates by providing a full, significant, and enlightened way of living; and the true and abiding importance of all activities, whether "curricular" or "extra-curricular," will become evident at once.

(iii) We must expect to find in the high school considerably more in the way of departmental instruction, and the subdivision of subject matter, than prevails, or should prevail, in the elementary school. This is for the simple reason that, by the time the tenth grade is reached, much of the work is so advanced that it begins to demand special expertness and knowledge on the part of the teacher. But we cannot regard our present situation as desirable. What we actually tend to have is not a mere beginning of subject matter subdivisions, but just so many water-tight compartments. Again the junior high school, with its courses in general science, general mathematics, general literature, and general history, is showing us a better way. But what is wanted is not so much a mechanical reorganization, as a new spirit. A man may be teaching English, or history, or mathematics, or science, as a special subject. What is always necessary, if he is to serve his pupils as a secondary school teacher should, is that he perceives, and constantly seeks to convey to them, the broader significance and the meaning for life and society of what he presents.

(iv) A fourth distinguishing mark of the high school is that in it we must expect to find the beginnings of true specialization. Mental growth, if it is real, culminates in making interests definite, and in focussing them in specific ways. As the pupils enter into the various common experiences provided by the school, they begin to discover their own bent, and to know their limitations and possibilities. Some will be led to decide for college; and their minds may become set towards some field of academic specialization. Others, again, will see that, for them, the course of wisdom will be towards some vocational institution. Their general secondary education must be for them, a process of self discovery. It must be a revelation of what is in them. And it must serve to show their teachers and parents what is wise and best.

Such is the controlling conception of the secondary school in the democratic scheme of the educational ladder. It stands for a continuation of the processes of mental growth which were begun in the elementary school. It should serve all the youth, in the interests of the social whole and of a common way of enlightened living. It has been admirably called "the people's university."

4. *What should the college seek to accomplish?*

To promote intellectual achievement for the sake of broad and deep social outlook, and a completer understanding of oneself, is the mission of the college. Its aim must be the stimulation of intellectual concerns, interests, aspirations, and growth. Often we think of college graduation as the end of education. This is profoundly false. The man or woman who has lived four years in the environment of the college should be far better able to achieve a continuing development throughout life, than he or she to whom such a privilege has been denied. If the student's mental growth stops as soon as he receives his diploma, then, to commit an Irishism, it has never really taken place at all. The institution has failed, and the student has wasted his time.

The college differs from the lower schools in its special emphasis upon intellectual interests, and upon theory, and logical relationships. It resembles them in that its essential purpose remains social. And here lurks a danger. For intellectual interests are so compelling, that they easily tend to be followed purely for their own sake. Many members of the faculties of our universities are men who have devoted years to intensive research. They have become increasingly engrossed in a range of problems which must be rather narrowly limited, if they are to achieve anything at all. It may be that they themselves perceive the bearing of their specialties upon the broader whole, though only too often they do not. But they tend to teach their students simply what is of interest to them as research specialists. So, instead of an intellectual interpretation of life, we find a dead intellectualism which is the essence of pedantry, rather than living scholarship. Sometimes the question is asked whether the college should produce citizens or scholars. My answer is that it must seek to produce both, and in the same person. As Chapman and Counts have put it: "To be able to see two sides to a question, to realize ignorance, to appreciate expert service, to feel an abiding obligation to study and direct the course of social life, to be public spirited, to recognize the claims of national and international obligations, these are the hallmarks of the man whose education has made him free. Only as our colleges submit their students to broad, generous, and humane learning, calculated to foster these virtues, can they hope to send forth free citizens."[1] Only such can be the purpose of a college which is to deserve the noble name of liberal.

How, then, may such an end be accomplished? By providing for the student the conditions necessary for four years of the intellectual life. Now it should be pointed out particularly, that to live the intellectual life does not mean becoming a bookworm. It does not mean doing nothing at all but studying. It will involve much free and enjoyable social intercourse with one's fellows. The claims of the body will not be neglected. There will be much social responsibility, much sharing in corporate undertakings, both as leader and follower. But everything will be keyed to one great aim, which gives significance to the whole. The freedom, the fullness, the joy, of this most ideal way of human existence becomes less than nothing and vanity, unless it is all suffused with a mastering and living concern for the things of the mind. This is what makes a college different from a country club.

Here the American college has swung between two poles of error. In older days, the faculties felt no responsibility to furnish a wide and balanced program of social, cultural, and athletic activities as part of the institutional life. Their whole concern was with study, which seemed to them not merely the chief business, but indeed the sole business of the student. They treated him, not as a human being with wide and manifold interests, whose satisfaction was the only means of an adequate personal growth, but as a mind pure and simple. Such an emphasis meant the glorification of the grind as the ideal college type. It was educationally false, simply because the intellectual life carried on in a vacuum defeats its own ends and loses its social and moral values. Then came a strong reaction. What the college failed to provide was a necessary part of the scheme. Nature, expelled with a fork, came rushing back. And the students created for themselves a program of varied activities, which were set over against the intellectual purposes of the college, instead of being integrated with them. College athletics and the fraternity system are two instances of contributions to the corporate

[1] *Principles of Education:* Houghton, Mifflin Co., 1924, p. 487.

life of the institution, brought about by the initiative of the students themselves. Little by little, these interests, so improperly regarded as "outside" activities, came to dominate the situation. As Woodrow Wilson once put it, the "side shows" began to overshadow the "main tent." And this too was exceedingly unfortunate. Many students lost sight of the main purpose of their four years of college, and gave themselves up to an engrossing and dizzy round of essentially meaningless doings. In quite a number of cases, going to college proved to be a misfortune rather than a blessing, simply for this reason. It has been remarked with much truth, that our way of thinking of "college activities" as including everything but study, is a supreme irony and a proof that something is seriously amiss with the system.

What, then, is the cure? Certainly we cannot abolish "outside" activities. Even if it were possible, we should not wish to do so. What we must seek is a reorganization of attitude, so that activities cease to remain on the "outside," and become an intelligible, working part of the entire scheme. This cannot be brought about by any plan of arbitrary and mechanical regulation, such as imposing fixed limits upon the number of activities in which a student may engage. Such plans rarely work well, and in any case are not constructive. What we want is to shape up the conditions and influences of the place, so that students may not be dazzled and led to follow false gods, by the joys and doings it offers; and, on the other hand, so that they may find in their four years of college, an exhilarating experience of living on a high plane, made significant by a continuous mental growth and a steady gain in intellectual grasp and insight. Intellectual purposes must be paramount, but not monopolistic. The claims of the mind must be made so authentic, so appealing, that they are not smothered under competing interests, and accordingly can tolerate, nay welcome, a wide range of activities which are to be regarded as propitious rather than detrimental. How may this be achieved? I will mention four points which should be considered.

A. We must have a more significant college curriculum, a curriculum which is palpably an interpretation of life and of society, rather than a huddled collection of fragments of subject matter.

The great weakness of our present curriculum is excessive subdivision. At the level of higher education, this is particularly hard to avoid. A college instructor must be a specialist in his field. And this makes it difficult for him to see anything beyond it, or to reveal such wider things to his students. Much of his power lies in his being an intensive cultivator of a limited domain. But much of his weakness lies here too. He is not training prospective research workers, but educating human beings. And for this it is absolutely necessary that he make clear the broader relationships of his field within the whole range of knowledge, and its bearing as an interpretation of human life. To meet this need, many of our leading colleges and universities are developing a new type of course, which deals broadly with contemporary civilization, with world literature, or with general science. More than a formal change of organization is required, however. These new courses may be just as academic, just as divorced from life, as were the older ones. If all we do is to pour the old wine into new bottles, we are not much better off. We must have a determination to present material in a broader, more significant manner; and a recognition that its whole power to educate turns upon its immediate and recognizable relationship to experience. If this can be done—and it is being done—much will have been accomplished in the way of making the things of the mind authentically appealing to the students. It is not the least use scolding them for not being as much interested in their "lessons" (atrocious word!) as in their fraternity and athletic interests, when their "lessons" have been made arid and narrow. If we wish to organize and sustain the conditions of a rich, free intellectual life on the college campus, we must bring it about that every student can recognize and respond to the curriculum, as having a message about and a bearing upon those vital problems which he feels around him in the real world.

B. Along with this, our colleges must give up relying as extensively as they do, upon external incentives. Faculties are wont to exclaim about the pity of students working for credits and marks and degrees. But they continue to give marks, and to make the accumulation of credits the chief aim in life. President Lowell of Harvard once commented on the very small number of students who enter our colleges as undergraduates, merely with the purpose of learning and with no special concern for a degree. Does this not suggest that the college measurably tends to be a degree-granting institution, rather than an institution of learning? The only cure is steadily to exalt the things of the mind for their own value and significance; to do our utmost to make intellectual enterprises seem worth while to our students; and to do away with such external incentives as credits and degrees as fast as we can, for essentially they are childish things, which hinder rather than help the fullness of the intellectual life.

One important attempt that is being made in this direction is to set up comprehensive examinations for the degree. The value of this plan depends entirely on how it is operated. If we simply impose another and longer test on top of a system where there is too much testing already, we shall do harm rather than good. There is also the danger of encouraging our students to become examination passers, which is just about as bad as being credit grabbers. My own personal view is that the system of comprehensives has roused in the breasts of American college educators a premature and somewhat naive enthusiasm, due to a failure to recognize its manifold difficulties and dangers. If, however, the writing of an impressive examination can be made the significant culminating point and crown of two, three, or four years of continuous intellectual growth, then indeed its effect upon our academic manners and customs will be admirable. But we must always remember that the educational value or lack of value of the plan does not lie in the examination itself, but wholly in the mental processes which the examination engenders.

C. Along with excessive reliance upon extrinsic motives, we must get rid of a whole jumble of school-mastering traditions and processes. The assignment of daily "lessons," for instance, is an affront to any student who possesses intellectual initiative and purpose. So is the mechanical requirement of absolutely, or nearly absolutely, regular attendance at classes. An institution whose chief concern is with the intellectual life, should make one master requirement, and one only—that the student learn. What would you say of a college student who took the position that an instructor had no right to insist on his having read certain material by a certain date, and argued that he was both able and willing to do so in his own way and at his own convenience? Is there any adequate answer to such an attitude? Is it not just about what the college ought to want? It is no use saying all the time that our students are not ready for freedom; that we must guide and direct every step they take; that they must be kept under tutelage a while longer. This is just an excuse for refusing to change our ways. We must begin by beginning.

D. The fourth condition for the promotion of a strong and appealing intellectual life is that the student must be given freedom to discover and follow his own interests. This is very far from implying that he should be allowed to choose any courses he pleases, on a basis of free election. On the other hand, our present system of arbitrary traditional requirements is unsound. What we must have is a curricular core of subject matter organized definitely as a systematic social interpretation. In studying this the student comes to discover his own interests, not on the basis of mere whim, but because he is able to see the broad meanings of possible lines of specialization. The college must educate its students towards significant educational choices, and then must respect those choices, once they are made.

Such are the four chief conditions on which we may promote a genuine intellectual life in the college, and rouse a commanding enthusiasm for the things of the mind. But there is here a very fundamental pre-supposition without which this, and every other scheme for the improvement of the college, will surely fail. We must have a selected student body. Here occurs the one great break in the continuity of the educational ladder. The college, by virtue of its essential purpose, is not, and never can be, the place for everybody. Only a certain limited number have the capacity and disposition, the qualities of heart and head, which make four years of intellectual living a propitious adventure for them. The college is not the school for young adults, as the high school is the school for youth, and the elementary school is the school for childhood. The college is the school for those with intellectual aptitudes, capacities, and aspirations. To admit droves of the unfit is disastrous all round. It makes virtually impossible the achievement of the true conditions of the intellectual life, even for those who would benefit by them. The dull and the unwilling must be driven. They must be given little daily tasks, and threatened and scolded when they do not perform them dutifully. And this spoils that freedom which is the essential atmosphere of independent intellectual growth. Moreover, to admit the unfit to college is no kindness. For their best life interests, these people need something else. All that college can do for them is to unsettle and discontent them permanently, and transform them into unhappy hangers-on at the outskirts of privilege. Unless the college is a select environment, its work fails, and its whole character and contribution becomes lost.

Now the problem of selection for higher education is one that can be solved only by the total, focussed operation of the entire school system. As we have seen in our discussion of educational opportunity, it is impossible to tell in advance who should go on, and who should drop out. But this does not mean haphazard elimination. It means that in a vital educational system, progressive self revelation will become an integral part of the drama of mental growth. Chapman and Counts, speaking of rigid college entrance requirements, have said: "Against such a narrow conception of entrance conditions evidence is accumulating that fitness to pursue the college course is less a matter of meeting formal requirements, than one of possessing a high level of intelligence, superior facility in reading and in oral and written speech, good habits of study and thought, and earnestness of purpose. Given these qualities, which the rigid college conditions measure very indirectly and inaccurately, success in college is practically assured." [2]

[2] *Op. cit.*, p. 453.

Chapter 19

WHAT USE SHOULD BE MADE OF MEASUREMENT IN EDUCATION?

1. *What is the effect of our conventional use of measurement?*

With the use ordinarily made of measurement in school work, almost everything seems wrong. My house stands about a block from a large elementary school, a school rather unusually well conducted, and fortunate in a staff of excellent teachers. Once every month I see from my windows an interesting spectacle. Little children troop home, each one with a report card in his hand. On these cards appears, first, a list of subjects, and then a number of personality traits. And opposite each there will be a mark assigned by the grade teacher, an A, or a B, or a C, and so forth. There is something very sacred about these cards. They must be taken home; parents must sign them; and then they must be returned to the school. A serious ritual, indeed, to be devised by teachers who tell their pupils not to work for marks! Also the cards are very intriguing. Parents will boast about the number of A's obtained by their offspring. Children unlucky enough to draw a good many C's, D's, and F's from the educational grab-bag, are likely to be twitted by their schoolmates; and often one may enjoy the edifying sight of beholding them thus reduced to tears. The teachers, the principal, and the superintendent will all agree that what is valuable in education is significant experience, and that the only adequate motive for learning is a sense of the value of the thing learned. So the report card scheme, apparently, is one of the clever dodges they use to make intellectual achievement for its own sake dominate the mind and impulses of the child.

The college on whose faculty I have the honor to serve, deals with people who are supposed to be pretty well matured. But every nine weeks, the entire student body is reduced to the status of so many little children with report cards in their hands. How is this done? Very simply. The college requires, each nine weeks, an official report of the mark of every student in every course. The place boils with a feverish excitement. Students rush wildly from professor to registrar to dean to president. Cries of joy and anguish are heard on every hand. Members of the faculty hide from view, and pass futile rules which forbid instructors to announce grades to students. This seems a peculiar way of holding up the great ideal of authentic intellectual achievement before young men and women. I presume that if an American college student, or an American professor, were transported back into the Middle Ages by the time machine, and there beheld the seething excitement of the mob of students surrounding Abelard, he would imagine that the distinguished teacher had just marked a set of tests, and had in his hands a sheet of paper, with mystic but potent symbols after each individual's name. What else could possibly arouse such interest, unless it were a football game or an automobile accident?

Any unprejudiced person who will give his eyes a good rub, and try to see things as they are, cannot for a moment doubt that such spectacles indicate a great educational abuse. We tolerate them, partly because we are used to them, and partly because we cannot think of anything else to do. Any teacher in his senses can recognize that there is obviously something very wrong with that system of testing and marking which constitutes the conventional use of measurement in our schools. Something is exceedingly rotten in our educational State of Denmark, or such scenes would not take place. In this chapter, I shall try to show what it is, and how we may get rid of it. We shall, I think, come to see that, while measurement is a very important and essential tool in education, and while its proper use may do a great deal of good, its misuse is an evil great enough to be quite capable of nullifying all efforts for a thorough-going and realistic school reform. We can by no possible means have

MEASUREMENT IN EDUCATION 429

a sane and progressive educational scheme, so long as we stick to our present practices in the matter of testing and marking.

2. *What is the central error in our conventional use of measurement?*

Schemes and methods of testing and marking may be criticized from many points of view. But all of them exhibit one great and central error. They are based, essentially, on the classification of students on relative standing within the school or the class. A method of marking which does not do this cannot be properly worked at all. The very essence of any mark is that it indicates how well or how poorly a student has done, in comparison with his fellow students. If a teacher is going to mark at all, this is what he must accomplish. And if he tries to do anything else—if he uses the system with another purpose in mind—he makes a bad mess worse.

Let us assume the mantle of invisibility, and enter the sanctum of a teacher who is about to go through the series of statistical and administrative manoeuvers necessary to work out a set of grades for his class. We will say that this teacher knows what not everyone in the profession knows, i.e., his business; so that he will do the job in the very best and fairest style. Let us watch him through the process.

His first step will be to concoct a test. This test must present exactly the same challenge to every member of the class; for, if some pupils have a much better chance than others, the result will evidently be unjust, and the resultant marks will not represent the real differences in achievement. So he will write it out and have it mimeographed, rather than putting it on the board or dictating it. Moreover, he will make it cover an exactly specified body of readings and other work. If anyone has read on the subject beyond assignments, his virtue must be his own reward. The test must have a limited aim, the aim of showing how well the pupils have done what they were told to do. Should it contain questions not within the well-pounded area, there will be protests; and they will be justified. For everything turns on equal opportunities for all. Moreover, our teacher will feel strongly, and most properly, that his marks on the test ought not to reflect his personal whims and fancies, his likes and dislikes for individuals. The persistent whisperer and trouble maker must have the same break as the eager, smiling, coöperative, docile person; even though the teacher curses him in his heart, and longs to flunk him. So the questions are made very specific. The instructor labors to frame them in such a way that he can tell, beyond a reasonable doubt, exactly how well each pupil answers every one of them. It may be that he prepares an entirely "objective" examination, made up of true-false statements, completion items, and the like, which are so impersonal that they can be scored by a clerk or a janitor. It takes hard work to make such an examination; and the teacher feels that he has earned the appreciation of his students—as indeed he has—whether he gets it or not. Then comes the great day. The class arrives, stuffed with highly temporary knowledge, and jittering with anxiety. The papers are given out; faces lengthen; silence falls; pens scrape. The instructor carefully proctors the room. He has already seated his students alternately, to prevent copying. But someone might attempt the unheard of device of writing from notes! He will not encourage the kind of inquiry: "Please, professor, what does question six mean?" For if he gives extra hints to one or two, this puts them in a preferred position. Soon the exodus commences. At last only a few meditative individuals remain, sitting with the persistent hopefulness of broody hens on china eggs. Finally they depart; and the instructor retires, sighing, to wash the dirty linen. If he has made out a fully "objective" test, his task is easy, though dull; for all he has to do is to apply his scoring key, and count up the right answers. But he can also do very well with a competently made "essay" test. It contains, perhaps, ten questions. He assigns to each question a maximum of five score points; for, being expert on his job, he knows it has been well established that one cannot accurately discriminate much more than five shades of excellence in such answers. Instead of reading through each paper from beginning to end, he reads first all replies to question one, then all replies to question two, and so on. This greatly increases the accuracy of his work, and also its labor; and, as he revises all his scores after working through the whole mass, he feels justifiably certain that not many errors have been made. Next comes the great business of working out the marks; and here the principle of relative standing enters the drama. The best pupil has a score of forty-eight out of a possible fifty; the worst has a score of twelve; and the average score for the class is thirty-nine. Fair enough! Probably the best student should have an A, and the worst an F, and the average a C. But how many should receive an A? How many a B? How many a C? And so on. As our instructor thoroughly knows his job, he will not commit the obvious crudeness of simply giving the best five per cent an A, the next twenty per cent a B, the next fifty per cent a C, the next twenty per cent a D, and the rest an F. This is what is known as "grading by the curve." It may be a little better than just guessing. But it is far too rigid. He uses a statistical device, which I have described and explained elsewhere,[1] and which enables him to cut off from his list a certain proportion to which to assign each grade, although the actual proportion varies with the achievement of the class.

This is absolutely the best way of marking. Within its limits, which are the limits of the system, it is entirely just. The teacher can feel every confidence that all the marks he gives are as "fair" as marks can be. Indeed, the marks are not "given" at all. An objective situation, the same for all, is set up; and what each student does in that situation wholly determines his mark. The method is impregnable to internal criticism. If a disgruntled individual comes along, and complains of receiving a D, the reply is that seventy-five per cent of the class did better, which is pretty fairly crushing. If someone asks that a grade be changed, so that he can "make the team," the instructor shows the whole layout of scores and grades, and says, very truly, that he cannot do this without injustice to others. If you want really to mark, this is the way to do it. If, however, you want to be able to juggle marks for personal reasons, by all means avoid this method. There is only one real criticism of it—the claim that we ought not to mark at all.

Now I want to point out again, and insistently, that the whole procedure turns on determining the relative standing of the pupils.

[1] Mursell, J. L.: *The Psychology of Secondary School Teaching:* W. W. Norton Co., 1932, ch. 13.

The test is constructed with precisely this in mind. It is made on a basis of complete equality for all. Moreover, the skilled instructor will make it just hard enough so that there will be a big difference between the best and the worst paper. If he should make it so very easy that everyone got every question right—something I have known to happen—then he could not tell whether everyone should have an A, or an F, or a C. In other words, he could not grade at all; for he would have the limiting case, where all relative differences would vanish. Which would be quite awkward.

Moreover, our instructor works out his grades definitely on the assumption that they symbolize relative position within the group. He does not vainly imagine in advance the existence of a mythical A paper, a mythical C paper, and so on, which he can recognize by some mysterious insight and wisdom. Notice that. It is very important. Of course, a teacher will not always use quite such an elaborate and conscious procedure. But still, he will be controlled by relative standings, by the standards created by his class rather than formulated in advance in his own imagination. Let us suppose that, instead of marking a test, he has the job of grading a set of English themes, where there are no points to count up, and where everything depends on a judgment of quality. His first undertaking will then be to read through the whole mass, or at least a good many samples, to find out the average performance. This charts his course, and prevents him from expecting too much. The marks he assigns will be determined by the relationship of each individual paper to the group average. To be sure, some teachers, less well trained than our paragon, think they can mark papers on an absolute standard. But we have convincing reason to believe they cannot. Always they are influenced, and very greatly influenced, by the performance of the general mass of the class. We know this because it is a fact that a mediocre paper will receive a better mark if it is in a set of mediocre papers, than if it is in a set of very good ones. The teacher may not always be fully aware of what he is doing; but the pull of relative standings, and the influence of the average performance, is too strong to resist. So the procedure I have described displays, in all its nakedness, the essential logic of the marking process. And if you are going to mark at all, and want to do it "fairly," the more you control yourself by this logic, the better your work will be.

I have insisted that this system is impregnable to internal criticisms. But you may doubt it. You may think you see a certain objection. "What if the highest score on the test were only thirty, instead of forty-eight?" you may ask. "Would not this indicate that nobody should have an A? And would not your system automatically give this undeserving person an A? And is not the converse true? What if the lowest score were thirty? Would this deserve a failure? And would it not receive a failure, in spite of representing a tolerable achievement, if the system were applied?" About this there are two things to say. If all the scores are very low, this may indicate that the test is very difficult; if they are all very high, it may indicate that the test is very easy. For instance, in the finals in mathematics at Cambridge University, the highest honors can be obtained if one does only a very small proportion of the whole paper, simply because it is made exceedingly difficult. So this partly undercuts the objections that have been suggested. Then secondly, we must understand that the "normal curve" need not be used rigidly in marking, in order to mark on relative standings. Any instructor who used it in this way, and who simply cut off a certain percentage of the scores for each grade, would prove himself a statistical incompetent. It is technically quite possible to avoid all the absurdities which have been pointed out. No, the system is water-tight.

But educationally, it is very bad. It is bad, precisely because it substitutes the motive of beating Johnny, for the motive of doing things because they are worth doing, and learning things because they are worth learning. It glorifies the mass. It puts the mass, and the achievement of the mass, in the forefront, when what really matters is the achievement of the individual. If a boy has really done something worth while—if he has written a bit of English which may not in itself be so very good but in which he finds the thrill of improvement and creation—if he has achieved an insight into history or social science or language—if he has broadened his horizons and gained a new appreciation of social meanings—need we bother either ourselves or him so very much about whether his work is a little better, or a little worse, than that of somebody else? If we do so, shall we not take much of the joy out of his life, and the value out of his achievement, and the good out of his education? Are we not setting up for him false gods, and directing him towards something which is not really in his own best interest? Is it wise to set up an intricate examination system, which forces to the forefront of his consciousness the question of whether he can beat the other fellow? Does it matter supremely whether he manages to do so, or not? Is not something else much more important? And should all the records of his education be kept in terms of relative achievement, so that all his chances of privilege, eligibility, and promotion, and recommendation, are made to depend on just that? Surely, to such questions there can be only one reply.

Moreover, the system of marking on relative achievement perverts the whole social spirit of the class and of the school. The school and the class should be societies of happy and coöperative learners. It should be a joy and a privilege to contribute something to the doings of such a society; to have it admired, appreciated, used. Teachers think that this is just a bit of pretty but impossible idealism. So it is, as long as we persistently wreck the whole social spirit of our pupil groups, by emphasizing nothing but relative achievement. Under such a system pupils become so grade-conscious that they think they ought to have some sort of mark every time they sneeze. What possibility is there of free, creative, social teaching, in such an atmosphere?

In the schools of the Jesuits there was introduced a particularly remarkable system of competitive motivation. The class was divided into two sections. Each boy in the one section had a "rival" in the other; and the business of this rival was to catch his *vis à vis* in a mistake when he recited. Well, what the Jesuits achieved by a brilliantly cruel method of classroom organization, we achieve by the use of tests and statistics. We glorify competition, rather than individually worth while effort and the spirit of coöperativeness. And the logical outcome of our scheme is the damnable spectacle of a little child on his way home from school, crying because he didn't beat Johnny.

3. What is the chief fault in our use of examinations and tests?

Examinations and tests are extremely useful educational instruments. One of the great and valuable contributions of the new "science" of education is their improvement. But we use them quite wrongly and we dissipate most of their real worth, when we employ them chiefly to secure competitive marks based on relative standing. Moreover, as I shall try to show, the real meaning of the modern scientific testing movement is that we ought to give up this way of dealing with pupils, and substitute something very much better and educationally far more constructive. To begin with, let us understand why it is an abuse of examinations and tests to employ them chiefly to secure competitive marks.

A. For one thing, any examination on which marks are to be based, must be objective. This means that it must be constructed and handled in such a way that the rating of the pupil depends not at all on the teacher's private, personal, subjective whim. Without this, it becomes violently unfair. There are a great many cases reported in the research literature, where the same examination, graded by a number of competent teachers, has yielded quite different marks. This happens even in tests so important and carefully handled as those given by the College Entrance Board. It is a great injustice. A candidate's success, his eligibility, let us say, for entrance into a college he wishes to attend, may easily depend upon the highly fallible personal opinion of the examiner. For this there is no defence. If marks are to be given at all, and certainly if they are to be made very important, they ought to register the actual performance of the pupil, not the subjective opinion of the examiner.

But how are examinations made objective? Simply by making them very specific, very definite. What are sometimes called "objective tests" *par excellence* represent the limiting case, and the ultimate logic, of this effort. When we make up an examination in which all the pupil has to do is to indicate whether certain statements are true or false, or to fill in certain omitted words, or to reply to a question with a single word, or to pick out the best of several short answers, the personal judgment of the examiner is banished from the stage. Everyone who marks such a test will come out with the same results, barring sheer errors, which can be corrected. The fashion of calling tests of this kind "objective" is not a sound one, because it is quite possible to make out an essay-type test which is also highly objective. This is done by avoiding questions beginning with "discuss," or "tell what you know about," and using very definite questions, which can be answered correctly in only one way, or in a very few ways. Teachers who know their business quite understand the need of making their examinations objective if they are to avoid the gravest and most obvious injustice in their grading.

But here comes the catch. In order to make a test objective, we must make it definite. And in order to make it definite, we must greatly limit its scope. We cannot ask questions designed to stimulate original thought and creative expression. We cannot use a question as a sort of urge or hint to the pupil to write whatever happens to be in his head. It is not true to say that even the ordinary "objective" tests in the narrow sense are pure memory tests, and that they cannot in any way call for thinking. Many kinds of problematic thinking may be quite definite enough to be reducible to the objective form. But there is a severe limitation on the kind and amount of thinking which can be demanded by even the most expertly constructed objective test. And such tests, as they are ordinarily used, assuredly do greatly emphasize memory knowledge and facts, simply because these things obviously lend themselves to definite questions.

McCall, in the opening pages of his book,[2] says that everything which exists at all, must exist in some amount, and so be susceptible of measurement. There was a time in the history of mankind, when no way of measuring the distance between Boston and New York existed. We have been clever enough to find ways and means of measuring weights, distances, the amount of electricity consumed by a bulb in an hour, and a great multitude of other things as well. McCall's point is this: that if only we were clever enough, we could also measure the creative genius of Shakespeare, the moral force of Martin Luther, and the aesthetic feeling of Michael Angelo. These subtle, baffling entities have really existed. They have existed

[2] *How to Measure in Education*: Macmillan Company: 1923.

in some definite amount. Theoretically, therefore, there is no reason why we cannot measure them. The only trouble is that we aren't yet clever enough to do it.

I am willing to admit this argument, though a metaphysician might have one or two little comments to make about it. But the real point is the admission that we are not clever enough to measure a great many very important things. Some human abilities we certainly can measure. For instance, we can find out just how many items in a bit a prose a child will retain after reading it for five minutes; or how many arithmetic problems he can do in a given time. And these things may be well worth knowing. When we make a test objective, we simply limit it to dealing only with such measurable things—*practically* measurable things, I mean. And when we take another step, and make our whole grading system depend on objective examinations (whether in the narrow sense of true-false, completion, or short answer tests, and the like; or in that wider sense which includes some kinds of essay tests), we get a record of the pupil's education, based on some few of the mental abilities which he ought to acquire, and only on those. We are not marking him on his most interesting, and socially valuable abilities —insight, creativeness, social-mindedness, and so on. Indeed, we deliberately refrain from doing so in the name of fairness; because we have no way of measuring such abilities, and so working out comparative marks based upon them.

I want you to notice that I am not arguing against objective tests and examinations. A subjective test is not a test at all; it is a fake. It cheats pupils and teachers alike. It falsifies everything. If we are to use tests, they *must* be objective, or else simply crazy. My argument is that when we base marks upon objective tests—as we must, if we are to have valid comparative marks at all—we misuse an instrument otherwise very valuable.

Another reason why tests should not be used for getting comparative marks is that when we do this, we emphasize ground covering, and set in motion the most unfortunate intellectual and educational tendencies. In the next examination you give, try putting in two or three questions which do not relate to anything taken up in class, or in assigned readings. You know what will happen.

There will be a universal howl, and a justifiable one. To read widely and freely is most admirable and desirable; but this is quite irrelevant to the situation. The test exists, not to explore the pupil's intellectual resources, but simply to find out whether he knows what he is supposed to know, whether he has covered the assigned ground. If we are going to mark at all, it cannot reasonably be done on any other basis. The system of testing and marking, in fact, is the greatest single bulwark of the ground covering fallacy. We must give tests and comparative marks, otherwise pupils will not cover the assigned ground. We must give definite quantitative assignments as the very heart and soul of our educational procedure, otherwise how can we mark? The circle is complete. And teachers go on and on and on, repeating endlessly the same old unbreakable automatism, like madmen with a tic.

I have already said so much in these pages about ground covering, and the worship of subject matter mastery for its own sake, that I am not going to burst into any further polemics here. I will only point out this: when we associate ground covering with examinations and marking, we instantly and inescapably produce that monstrous educational perversion known as cramming. When teachers admit, on the one hand, that education depends wholly upon worth while experience; and then on the other hand, calmly accept a system which makes subject matter cramming—the worst possible kind of subject matter learning—just as certain as the dawn, we simply have another illustration of the capacity of the human mind for entertaining incompatible notions. We can go one way; or we can go the other; but not both. Either we commit ourselves to a mode of education which centers entirely on worth while experience; in which case we give up grading on relative standing and its supporting mechanism of examinations, with their consequences in cramming. Or we stick to our tests and examinations, and turn our backs on constructive educational reform.

C. The third reason why tests and examinations should not be used as instruments for working out comparative marks is that this degrades and poisons the whole social life of the school. Why is it wrong to bring notes into an examination room? Simply because the whole meaning of the examination situation is equal opportunity for everybody to beat everybody else. But if we don't care how the pupils rank—if all we care about is how well each one does in his own right and on his own motion—if our emphasis is an individual quality, and not on competition—then it doesn't matter if they write from notes. The whole bugbear of cheating is removed, because there is nothing to cheat for. A natural and legitimate aim is substituted for an unnatural and illegitimate one; and the whole social and moral atmosphere clears up.

Or consider the appalling effects produced by the practice of oral quizzing. If a class is habituated to expect that it will always be marked on its oral responses, so that each class meeting is regarded as a test, coöperative learning is made virtually impossible. Teachers say that if you don't quiz the pupils on their work and mark them on their responses, they will not study, and the class period will be a total loss. Could anything be more perverse? It amounts to an admission that the things taught in class have no intrinsic appeal, that they cannot be handled in such a way that the pupils will want to learn them. This, in turn, comes pretty close to saying that education itself is impossible, for only what we learn from direct interest is likely to be of much permanent value to us.

The whole effect on the social life of the school of using examinations, oral or written, as the means of getting the all-important comparative grades, is to convert every class meeting into either a cramming meet or a spell-down. It defeats the very possibility of constructive, coöperative social motivation. It weakens and impoverishes the relationship between teacher and learner. And it saps the very life of the school.

4. *What is the value of tests and examinations?*

It may seem to you that the practical advice which would come from our preceding analysis should be: Have nothing whatever to do with tests. But this is far from being the case. Tests and examinations cannot tell the whole story of a person's education. Indeed, I am sure that they cannot tell even the most important part of that story. This is due to the simple fact that they must be made objective and precise. Theoretically, perhaps, every mental capacity and attitude can be measured. But as a matter of practice, the range of abilities we can measure with precision is quite limited. So, no marks based upon examination results can possibly represent everything, or nearly everything, which one has achieved as a result of his education. But what tests can tell us about a person may be very well worth knowing. The modern testing movement has done the cause of education an enormous service by furnishing us with precise instruments, which give us indisputable and impersonal information. We are greatly in the debt of those patient workers who have developed and perfected our tests and the technique of their use. Only when these instruments are wrongly used, only when the very partial information they yield, is treated as if it were the whole story, do they become harmful. The best and most progressive schools will assuredly find many uses for tests and examinations.

A. For one thing, tests can be used for diagnosis. Suppose you are teaching a course in history, and you find that some of your pupils seem to have persistent difficulties. If you are a real teacher, you want to know why rather than simply blaming them as indolent or stupid. You give your class a reading test and also an intelligence test. And you find out that some of the pupils who are disappointing you are bright enough, but are defective in their ability to read an assignment and get the meaning out of it. This shows you something worth knowing. And it ought to show the pupils something worth knowing. You can set to work coöperatively to correct this weakness. Again, you have a pupil in second year French, who has great difficulties. He does not quite know why, and you are none too sure. You give him a test and find that his grasp of the fundamentals of the language is very poor. Again, you both have some valuable information, which shows you what needs to be done. Innumerable instances of this kind may occur, where the alert teacher finds a published or a "home made" test a means of saving the situation for some pupil. There are certain tests definitely called "diagnostic" because they are specially designed to reveal the nature of defects in a pupil's mental equipment. But many tests, which do not have this name, can be used for the purpose.

Notice that the more creative and free the teaching, the more use you may have for precise educational diagnosis. If your teaching is nothing more than subject matter coaching for the passing of a conventional examination, then this will tell the whole story so far as it interests you. Everything is definite and precise, and, for that very reason, bereft of some of its greatest values. But if you stimulate free discussion and creative contribution, and encourage all kinds of digressions, then, unless you are careful, your knowledge of the exact points of strength and weakness in the mental equipment of your pupils may be so hazy that you will not guide them aright. So here objective tests are worth much to the progressive teacher.

B. A second important use of tests is for prognosis and guidance. You will often be not quite sure just where to place a pupil in reading, or arithmetic, or algebra, or language work. For instance, a pupil may be ahead of others in many respects, but lag behind them in reading ability. You need to know this for certain, if you are going to treat him correctly and give him his fullest educational opportunity. A test may exactly reveal to you the state of the case and be the foundation of a constructive program. Or you may have a pupil who cannot seem to "get" algebra. Is it due to lack of native intelligence, or something else? You give him an intelligence test. This shows that he is quite bright enough to succeed with algebra. It tells you in advance how he may be expected to react, if given a good chance and good teaching. Many of the predictions, and the decisions arising from them, which you make with regard to pupils, must be based on the precise knowledge furnished by tests.

C. A third very valuable use of tests is to reveal to the pupil just how much or how little mastery or knowledge he actually possesses in a given direction. Not very long ago the Carnegie Foundation sent out to a number of colleges a test of general knowledge. It was in no legitimate sense competitive. No one could prepare for it specifically; for it contained thousands of questions, and covered a vast range of information. But taking it was a very valuable educational experience, for it revealed, both to the student himself, and to everyone else concerned, the range and limitations of his information. Tests may be used for this purpose on a much less ambitious scale. For instance, during a course in general science, taught largely by the project method, it may be worth while to give some sort of achievement tests, not for the sake of marking the pupils, but simply to reveal with precision the actual status of their scientific masteries.

D. Another use of tests is to help the teacher estimate, in part, the effectiveness of his work. It often happens that after one has delivered a public lecture, one would like very much to give the audience fifty true-false test items bearing on what one has said. The aim would not be to embarrass them but to help one to see more clearly the excellences and defects of one's own presentation. Tests can serve exactly this purpose in the school. In the conventional scheme, the teacher regards them as ordeals for the pupils. But really, they should be ordeals for the teacher. They are often put to just this use. For instance, the attempt has been made to ascertain whether the methods of teaching employed in a so called "activity school" give the pupils a better, or a worse, grasp of the "fundamentals" than those in a conventional school. And the only way to do this was to set up a carefully planned program of testing in the two schools.

E. Yet another use of tests is to furnish a very valuable and sound form of motivation—that is to say, competition *with oneself.* A pupil may be strongly stimulated and his efforts may be given a very precise direction, if he is furnished with materials for self-testing in some fields which he is studying so that he can actually watch his own progress towards mastery.

F. A final use to which tests may be put is specific self direction. It has been my experience that often, when an objective examination is returned corrected to the class, points for discussion turning on the assignments will be raised with much more precision and interest than has been the case during the ordinary class meetings. Part of the reason undoubtedly is that a long objective test picks out a great many points in a sequence of readings, and forces them strongly upon the student's attention. Why, then, should we not use such tests deliberately as study aids, rather than as agencies for marking?

Notice, as I close this section, that most of the above purposes will certainly be frustrated, if we use tests for securing comparative grades. As soon as we do this, the pull of the false motive is so potent that everything else is in shadow. Use tests for grading, and you will find it hard to use them for anything else.

5. *How does the marking system falsify the record of individual achievement?*

Up to this point, I have been arguing that our system of examining and marking is bad, because it leads both teachers and pupils to worship the false god of competitive excellence, instead of the true god of worth while individual achievement and personal growth. But there is still another way in which it perverts our educational thinking and makes sane, straightforward educational practice very difficult. It sets up a false ideal of individual achievement, *because it defines that achievement in terms of averages.*

Let us say that we are offering a course in history, and that it consists of ten topics or units. Bob secures a grade of C in each of these units, which are all followed by a content test. John, on the other hand, secures a grade of A on five of them, and a grade of F on the other five. When we compute the final grade on the course, we simply strike an average. Both Bob and John have an average rating of C, and it stands against their names on the registrar's books. This is an utter absurdity, because their actual intellectual achievements are quite different. Bob has known something about all the units of the course. But John's utter ignorance of Charlemagne has been compensated by his thorough knowledge about Napoleon. This may be sensible statistics, but it is a kind of educational lunacy.

Moreover, it will certainly warp the feelings, both of Bob and John, towards the realities of their education. For John the gaining of a real mastery and the finding of a real interest and thrill in studying the campaigns of Napoleon, is a splendid thing. It is real education. He has learned something. He has changed and grown. He will be a better person all his life long because of it. But there is absolutely nothing in the official record to show that it has happened. The school does not recognize it in any way, and does no kind of honor to his genuine achievement. It bundles it up, and smuggles it out of sight by averaging it in with the things he has not done. Bob, on the other hand, has, in effect, been taught that the important thing is to do just enough all the time to "get by." It may be that he felt some real stir of interest when he came to the unit on the Renaissance. But, after all, this was only a tenth of the course, counting just ten per cent towards the all-important ultimate record. There was no particular incentive to let himself go and to follow his inclination. To have done so would have meant authentic intellectual and moral growth. But the system did not encourage this. What it did encourage him to do was just to jog along for a "gentleman's mark." It has emphasized average rather than distinctive achievement; quantity, rather than quality.

Or consider how a student's "standing" in his studies is determined. If a man wants to be somebody in the world, he must become able to do something or other really well. He may be, and should be, a fairly all-round person. He may touch life on many sides; but somewhere, somehow, he must show distinction. Our Einsteins, our Paderewskis, our Henry Fords, are great figures, not because they are men of high average achievement, but because of really superior excellence in some respect. But in school, under the marking system, the whole emphasis is placed upon the average achievement. A smoothed curve is drawn between the peaks and the valleys, and this determines the student's standing; whereas the really important things about him are, precisely, the peaks and the valleys.

Consider how students are picked out for scholarship awards, or for membership in Phi Beta Kappa, or for graduation *summa cum laude*. The steady tendency of the system is to favor the industrious plodder, at the expense of the person who discovers and follows up valid interests of his own. An important academic award may be, and often is, determined by a single decimal point in the average grades of the candidates. A man may have done poor work in a single course—a course perhaps, which he should never have been forced to take. Throughout all the rest of his school career, he may have shown high and increasing distinction. He may obviously be the sort of person apt to amount to something later on. He may have proved his possession of an outstanding mind. It does not matter. The adding machine reveals the fatal flaw; and all his progress, all his distinction, count for nothing.

Look at the situation from still another angle. A student may enter a school, and at first do poorly. But, year by year, he may adjust himself better and better until, at last, his achievement is admirable. If we say that education is guided growth, this surely ought to please us very much. He has done just what we should hope for any growing being. He has cancelled past defects, and attained a present excellence. On any sane basis of valuation, one would think that this present excellence was all that ought to matter. But the registrar, like a dark recording angel, has a permanent record of his sins. His weaker past has ceased to live in him; but it lives on in the books. A little grudging credit for success he gains; for it does raise his average standing. But the actual picture of his education, on which, for many important purposes, he will be judged, is definitely and undeniably falsified.

6. *What can we substitute for marking?*

Whenever one assails the marking system, one is sure to meet with the question: What else can we do? Teachers admit its defects. But they recognize, and very properly, that there must be some organized mechanism for setting standards. And they can think of no substitute. They cling to the system, not because they like it, or, after mature reflection, have come thoroughly to believe in it, but just from helplessness. So we have here an essential question.

To reply in a word, we must substitute for marking a method of record keeping which places its central emphasis upon the actual educational and intellectual achievement of the individual, rather than on his relative achievement compared to the mass.

A concrete instance of how this may be done is furnished by the University of Chicago High School. In this school, all the courses are planned and subdivided into a number of "mastery units." Each student in each course must learn each unit, up to what is known as the "mastery level," before he goes on to the next. This naturally means that the class does not all move abreast. When a pupil "masters" a unit, a record of the fact is made. If he goes beyond the "mastery level" in some unit, shows great interest and initiative, and achieves specially high excellence, this also is made a matter of record. If an educational test is given, his standing on that test is also entered. And at the end of his course, the school has on its books a direct, realistic record of the achievement of the student. This principle can obviously be extended. If a student, of his own initiative, prepares an excellent essay, or writes a short story, or is active in the production of a play, or gives a distinguished musical performance, it also may be written into his record. The fact that some such things are "extra-curricular" means nothing. And this is as it should be; for they are authentic parts of his education. They are deeds which prove that his time in school has been well spent. The entire distinction between curricular and extra-curricular activities, essentially artificial, vanishes under such a system. The school simply recognizes what the student actually does. It applauds excellence, wherever and whenever it appears.

Notice that this is not just another kind of marking. It is something quite different. In the Chicago University High School, there are no failures; neither are there any A students. The reason is that there are no grades—no F's and A's at all. Instead of an interest in competition, there is an interest directed towards learning. Instead of a deceiving average, there is a direct account of achievement.

Exactly how far and fast any particular school or system of schools will be able to move in the direction of abolishing the old grading system and the substitution of a saner and more realistic plan of accounting, will vary in different cases. We must remember that transfers and so forth have to be made in terms of grades. And only a few favored institutions will be able to go the whole way at once. Still, a number of practical evolutionary steps are possible. (a) We must seek more and more to organize school work in terms of undertakings whose manifest importance motivates the pupils, irrespective of grades. (b) We must organize our work in broader units, which permit and encourage individual variations within the unit. Our whole group may, for instance, be studying Egyptian civilization. But they need not all read the same material, or deal with the same aspects of the matter, or make the same reports, or undertake the same projects. This change, in itself, destroys the basis of old fashioned grading, which depends precisely upon uniformity. (c) We shall probably prefer a five point grade scale (A, B, C, D, F), or even a three point scale, to the old "number grades" running from 0 to 100. In and of itself, a change in the scale does not mean a reform. One can grade as rigidly and uniformly on a five point scale as on a hundred point scale, and usually this is done. The point is that this is a step in the right direction. It makes possible an increasing flexibility of treatment, and gives us a chance to make grades less and less important in the scheme of things. (d) Side by side with the ordinary grades, we shall perhaps keep a much more realistic record of the pupils' actual achievements, similar to that described by Morrison at the University of Chicago High School. We may have to report to other schools, and to colleges, in terms of grades. But in assessing our own students, in advising and promoting them, we shall use the superior type of record. By every means in our power we shall try to make grades less and less important, and actual direct individual achievement more and more so. (e) We shall work towards a conception of graduation not determined by grades, averages, and credit hours, but by actual educational and personal achievement.

There is a widespread sentiment among American educators that the grading system has proved highly unsatisfactory. Changes along the lines I have indicated are being made. At least one important school system has entirely eliminated grading in some of its chief units. Most schools are probably not ready to go the whole length at once. But it is a change clearly indicated by our prevailing philosophy. And it should be courageously pushed.

Now, in the face of such a proposal, there will surely be some questions to ask. Let me try to anticipate them.

A. What would be the effect on the students if we gave up marking altogether and emphasized individual achievement as the vital thing? When you criticize the marking system to teachers, you may be sure of hearing one thing said. They will admit that the system is bad. But they will certainly say that, as a matter of practical common sense, the students will not work without it. Now in this there is some truth. I am quite sure that if one were to go into an elementary school, a high school, or a college, and, by fiat, abruptly eliminate the marking system, the teachers would be helpless and the place thrown into chaos. For this there is an excellent reason. From the first grade onwards, we have persistently and ingeniously educated children to work for marks. We have succeeded here much better than in some other pedagogical endeavors. Our students have been most effectively trained to a monstrous mark-consciousness. If marking were taken away, what would the poor things do?

But suppose, instead of undertaking to change everything over night, we try quite another tack. Suppose that, with equal persistence, ingenuity, faith, and skill, we emphasize individual achievement. Suppose that we plan our curriculum in such a way that studies seem worth while and important. Suppose that we provide constant opportunity and incentive to do appealing and valuable things. Suppose that we revise our classroom procedures so that our teaching is not police quizzing, but the stimulation of group activities. Suppose our school records are kept so that each start of genius, each achievement, is recognized at its own worth. Will the pupils fail to respond? It is impossible to believe it. The only reason why pupils work for marks, and why we think they will work for nothing else, is that we have never consistently tried to give them some better goal.

B. What would be the effect on the teachers, if we gave up marking altogether and emphasized individual achievement as the important thing? It would be exceedingly tonic. It would force them to teach, instead of permitting them to slave-drive. The teacher who could not organize and present material in an appealing and significant way; who could not handle individual work in such a manner as to give the pupil a feeling of progress and achievement; who could not direct a group learning situation constructively, would fail. And his failure would be starkly evident. He could not mask it by cracking a whip, for the whip would be taken from him. To abandon marking would be a tremendous and an inspiring challenge to every teacher to do that for which he is paid.

C. What would be the effect on parents, if we gave up marking and emphasized merely individual achievement? Teachers often defend the marking system by saying that parents expect it. But must the schools be eternally dominated by the educational fallacies of the lay public? Have they no function of leadership, no courage in their own convictions? And is it really true that parents would protest, if they found that the child was happy in school; that instead of having to be driven there, he wanted to go; that his life was filled with the delight of achievement; that instead of being crushed and narrowed, he was expanding mentally, emotionally, socially, and morally under a sane and beneficent regime? If we can guide the children of America in a more excellent way, the parents will tread it with us.

D. What would be the effect on the higher schools, if we gave up marking? Here we come upon one of the great strategic points of defence for the marking system. Colleges demand a record in the form of grades. But here again, the answer is clear. What we must have is a system of elementary schools and high schools, which are good enough to command the respect of the college. It has been proved many times that specific preparation in subject matter is not the best guarantee of college success. The qualities of the ideal college student are high mental ability, genuine intellectual interest, seriousness of purpose, and moral integrity. To benefit by the privilege of four years of college, one ought to be the sort of person who seeks and values intellectual attainment. If we can have a system of lower schools whose chief aim is to promote this very attitude, and if they are staffed by teachers fit to stimulate such attainment and to recognize it when they see it, then the formal demands of the college upon such schools may, and will be, relaxed. Those demands, after all, have been, in part at least, for the sake of sheer self defence. Let us have elementary schools and high schools where individual achievement is exalted, and where high excellence is known for what it is and wins acclaim, and the colleges will think themselves fortunate to enroll such as prove themselves worthy in this environment.

Chapter 20

WHAT IS THE SIGNIFICANCE OF METHOD?

1. *What is the basic question to ask about method?*

When we discuss method, the usual, and often the only question, is: How? How shall we set about teaching French by the direct method? What ought we to do in applying the project method in a course in chemistry? What procedures should be used in the phonic method of teaching reading in the second grade? What sequences should be observed in the inductive development lesson? How shall we use the blackboard? How shall we give assignments? How shall we ask questions in class? How shall we check on collateral reading? Such problems of procedure are endless. And often they are taken to be the most characteristic and basic problems relating to classroom method.

But there is an altogether different question which can be raised—the question: Why? What good should come out of the project method? What reason is there for choosing the direct method? What is the value of the inductive development lesson? Why use such and such a procedure or device? This is really a more practical question than the question: How? For *how* we use a given method depends on what we want it to do—depends, that is to say, on our answer to the question: Why? Books on the technique of teaching often say that a well managed project involves four steps—purposing, planning, executing, judging. The classic inductive development lesson, again, is supposed to begin with the step of preparation in which familiar material bearing on the new topic is called to mind; to pass on, through the presentation of new material, to the drawing of conclusions from it; and to end with verification and further applications. But where did these rules of procedure come from? They were not laid down arbitrarily by some committee of experts, and then humbly and universally accepted. They were developed as the best means of realizing the purpose of the project method, or the inductive lesson. They depend upon answering the question: Why? Why teach inductively, or according to the project method? We believe the project method, or the inductive lesson, capable of yielding certain values. Experience indicates that such values are most likely to accrue if we apply the method according to certain rules of procedure.

This question: Why? is certainly the basic question in regard to method. No one can hope to teach very well by following rules of thumb. The situations which occur in the classroom are so various, and so unpredictable, that one must always be ready to modify one's approach at a moment's notice, and to extemporize new procedures. Of course, general advice from experienced teachers on what to do and how to do it, is immensely useful. But one will not be able to use it effectively unless one understands the reason for what one is trying to do. A teacher may certainly gain some valuable professional dividends from studying the "how" of method. But he is likely to gain still greater ones by understanding its "why." And so the fundamental problem here is concerned with the underlying purpose of method. This is the problem with which we are to deal in the present chapter.

2. *What is the purpose of method in general?*

To avoid any possible misunderstanding, let us define our terms. By "method" we mean those procedures, devices, and techniques which are used in the classroom in the act of teaching. What we want to know is the end to which they should all be directed. What are we doing, when we try to teach?

Let me try to answer this concretely, by analyzing a teaching situation which everyone would admit to be first rate, and which the ordinary teacher would be only too happy to be able to duplicate. A football squad is being given blackboard work by the coach. Outwardly, the situation is not very different from what we might see in many a class. Moreover, the material the pupils are studying is not very different in kind from some academic subject matter. But the kind and quality of the learning which goes on is certainly far from typical of that ordinarily familiar in school. The boys are all keen to understand and to know. They put forward intense effort. And they are very likely to achieve results of analysis and comprehension which would startle their academic teachers.

Now for an illuminating contrast. Imagine for a moment that football was a game played only during the Middle Ages, and that our squad is a history class faced with a lesson on this interesting mediaeval sport. The teacher is very anxious to do his best. He gives far more care and thought to details of procedure than the coach. Just how can he give the assignment with the greatest effectiveness? What will be some stimulating questions? How shall he check up on the thoroughness of the pupils' preparation? And so forth. But, with all this trouble and effort, he is very likely to achieve far less. If twenty per cent of the class seem, for the moment, to have reached some understanding of the principles of the antique game, he can be happy. But probably eighty per cent of them will remain stolidly content with a job of learning which would earn them a tongue lashing from any coach, and jeopardize their positions on the squad.

Here we have two teaching situations, outwardly not dissimilar, but one an almost perfect success, and the other, relatively speaking, a failure. It needs no long discussion to demonstrate this. The difference in educative effect leaps to the eye. What we want to understand is the essence of the contrast. Why do we so instantly perceive that, in the case of the squad, the teaching procedure succeeds, while in the case of the class, it fails? Certainly it has nothing to do with the use of techniques and rules of thumb taken from books on method. Indeed, if we rated the coach and the class teacher on such a basis, the latter might often show a great superiority. He takes great pains to do what the authorities advise in handling his work, while the coach seemingly cares not a rap. So we must look elsewhere.

SIGNIFICANCE OF METHOD

The difference, which so dramatically forces itself upon us, even without our fully understanding it, comes to this. In the history class the chief concern is with subject matter for its own sake. That is to say, the pupils learn about the game and its rules, for the purpose of meeting some sort of examination on it and being graded. The football squad, on the other hand, studies subject matter as a means, not an end. The boys are learning something which they can use and apply. Their knowledge is for the sake of a compelling life adjustment. Here we stand on the great divide between success and failure. It is the contrast between conventional schooling and genuine education. So long as the techniques, devices, and procedures of the classroom are shaped up and directed towards the mastery of subject matter for its own sake, they fail of educative effect. No refinements of procedure will save them. But the moment the activities of the classroom are so adjusted that the learner perceives a relationship between subject matter and life, they succeed. Here we see the real purpose of all real teaching. To put it in a sentence: *The purpose of method is to make subject matter educative.*

3. *How can we tell whether a given method is good?*

If you continue in educational work, the time is sure to come when it will be important for you to form estimates of the values of classroom teaching. You may visit the class of some teacher, and afterwards he may ask for your opinion. You may get a job as supervisor, which puts you in the position of a professional judge of method. And in any case, you should constantly apply critical standards to your own procedures. On what basis should you try to estimate any method? What should you look for, and how should you look? What particular kinds of excellence should you be on the alert to discover? How can you tell whether a given method is good? What are the characteristic marks of a good method?

Your safest and most constant clue should be the principle we worked out in the preceding section. Always remember that the very purpose of method is to make subject matter educative. And so your first and most general question must be: Is this being done?

But, of course, this is a very general question indeed. And you will feel the need of more specific and definite guidance. Moreover, it is not an easy question to answer. To tell to what extent subject matter is really being made to live in the minds and lives of the learners is an extremely subtle matter. If you really want to get at such a fact, you cannot for a moment be content to concentrate on the obvious. You have no right to say that a method is bad, just because you do not happen to like what the teacher seems to be doing. Nor must you say that he is teaching well, merely because he is following the book procedures. You must manage to go down to the human aspects of the whole situation. You must find out what kind of living development is taking place in the experience of the pupils. This is far from easy. But it must be done if you hope for a valid estimate of any job of teaching. More than this, you can hardly hope to appreciate the actual educative effect being produced, if you visit a class only once or twice. This may be enough to give you an inkling. But it cannot do more. The value of any method depends upon the long-time influence which it exercises on the pupils. On the day of your visit everything may seem like very stupid routine, but the total effect may still be good. Or, conversely, you may come on a day when unusually good and interesting work is being done. Teaching itself is a most subtle undertaking. And it cannot be reduced to crude and obvious standards of evaluation.

I have particularly emphasized the complexities of forming a valid estimate of any method, for two reasons. In the first place, it is easy and tempting to rush to conclusions on the most superficial and inadequate grounds. This is something which happens continually in school work. A sound understanding of educational principles should help us to avoid it. In the second place, I want you to see the importance, not only of the general criterion already proposed, but also of carrying this down into particulars, which I am now about to try to do. If you want to tell whether a given method is good, you should, indeed, always remember that its purpose is to render subject matter educative. But beyond this, there are at least three definite questions which it will be helpful to raise. Does the method secure a linkage between subject matter and life? Does it recognize and properly consider marginal learnings? Does

SIGNIFICANCE OF METHOD 455

it direct primary learnings economically and expertly? These questions I shall now explain and discuss. If you can answer them affirmatively, then you have a good method, which is fulfilling its primary purpose.

A. Does the method secure a linkage between subject matter and life? Is subject matter treated always as a selection from the intellectual resources of civilization, whose whole value lies in its effect upon human adjustment to the social environment? Or is it being treated merely as subject matter; as an end in itself, to be learned merely to pass examinations and secure marks? If the first condition obtains, then no matter how crude and amateurish the teacher's work may be, we must pay homage to him as a real teacher. If the second condition obtains, then, no matter how smooth and slick the procedures, the spirit of education is not in them.

It does not much matter *how* the teacher gets this linkage with life, so long as he gets it. The actual procedure may, and indeed should, differ with the subject matter involved, with the abilities, temperaments, and interests of the pupils, and with the personality and aptitudes of the teacher. Sometimes it may be secured by the project method. Sometimes quite elaborate social procedures will be used, as for instance, where the class in American history is organized on the model of the Continental Congress. Sometimes the magic will enter in so seemingly simple an affair as wisely administered collateral reading. A boy at one of our great preparatory schools has told how the mere inflection of his teacher's voice in reading a stanza from Horace, threw the very light of life upon classical learning. We must not become infatuated with any one way, and try to insist upon it as the sole means of salvation. Above all, we must not be too much impressed with elaborate and far-fetched schemes, and disparage teaching where no great outward show is put on. The moment we do this, we turn away from the essentials to the externals, and forget the simple yet subtle essence of the teaching process, which is to make subject matter live.

Are these children, who are being taught to read, being given material which interests them? Are they being given opportunities to express themselves creatively, in word and deed, concerning the things they have read? Is there a consistent effort to do more than merely teach a skill? Is the classroom a place where they make the growing ability a part of the realities of their living? Is this writing lesson being handled as if the sole aim were a type of motor coordination? Or are the children being stimulated to say things they want to say in writing, and to find in the new skill a joy and a liberation? Is arithmetic presented as the formal observance of formal rules? Or is it being made a means for doing better the things which children want to do, and will do anyway? Is this course in history a series of lessons integrated about a series of tests? Or is it full of inspiring stories from the past, full of meaning for the present? Is it a chance to visit an Aladdin's treasure cave, or a process of forcible feeding? Is algebra being presented as a sequence of complex techniques, with absolutely no apparent relationship to the real concerns of a real existence? Or is it a progressive revelation of the meaning and value of rigorous thinking for the individual and society? These are the kind of questions to ask in evaluating any method.

Notice too, as we have seen before, that the linkage of subject matter with life means far more than an anxious search for alleged life situations with which to correlate every lesson taught. If we are teaching a unit on Japanese geography, there may be some point in having children bring to class Japanese curios which they have in their homes. But, to speak very conservatively, this is not the only way of making the content live in their minds. And it is often not the best way. The thing may often be accomplished simply by having them read collateral items of fact and fiction, bearing particularly on child life in Japan. Such books as *The Swiss Twins, The Dutch Twins,* and others of the admirable series, do more to make geography and social science live in the minds of young children, than much visiting of museums, clipping of newspapers, and organizing of group projects. The point is not to *find* life situations, but to *create* them. Life is not something which goes on exclusively outside the classroom. It takes place inside as well. Our real question is whether subject matter is being handled, *somehow,* in contact with the life interests and tendencies of the pupils, or whether it is being presented as something to be learned for its own sake.

B. Does the method recognize the importance of marginal learnings? This notion of marginal learnings has been brought to our attention particularly by Dr. Kilpatrick. Its meaning can best be explained by an illustration.

Let us suppose that we have three grades, all learning to read. One is taught by the old fashioned methods, which involve learning the alphabet as a first step; which make much of oral reading; and which use primers neither intrinsically interesting nor particularly well printed. Another is taught by one of the modern systematic methods, beginning perhaps with words rather than separate letters, and using interesting, attractively manufactured books. A third is taught much more informally. The same materials and psychological approach found with our second group are employed here. But also the children are stimulated to relate their reading to all kinds of enterprises. They are encouraged to read at home, and to tell the class what they have read. The faster workers are permitted, perhaps, to work out and put on a little play. Many other books besides the series of primers are available. Everything is done to make reading a natural and enjoyable activity.

Further, let us suppose that each group is brought up to exactly the same level of reading ability, so that when they are given a standardized reading test, they rate the same. (This will not happen, as a matter of fact; it is a purely theoretical assumption.) Have they all learned the same thing? By no means. Many of the first section will probably have begun to gain an actual dislike for reading and a negative attitude towards it, which is likely to handicap them later on in school, and may remain throughout life, unless powerfully counteracted. Most of the second group will like, or at least tolerate, their reading. And with the third group the ability to read will already have gone far towards an effective integration with social attitudes and adjustments of many kinds.

These extra effects, beyond the mere mastery of the subject matter, are what we call marginal learnings. They are supremely important. No method which ignores them can possibly be good. It may be important for a child in school to be able to read. But it is just as important for him to want to read and to prefer certain kinds of reading. Mastery of the skills of algebra is part of the story of learning—or being taught—algebra properly. But it is a part only. Unless the pupil also gains the inclination to use these skills, their mere possession will not help him much, and anyhow it will soon be forfeited. To have learned the causes of the Thirty Years' War may be a fine thing, but not unless one occasionally thinks about them in some connection. When we set up a method which ignores such considerations, we inevitably defeat the purpose of all teaching, which is to bring subject matter to life.

How can we take proper care of these marginal learnings? There is no routine way. It does not depend on any standardized procedure. We may do so by using the project method or the socialized recitation. But also we can do it without them. What we must have is a total situation in school which puts natural human values, relationships, and interests first. Marginal values in learning subject matter depend upon the total setting of the pupil's activities.

For instance, the teacher must conceive of himself as a human being dealing with human beings, not as a policeman clubbing pupils through textbooks. The kind of reading materials provided may well have a decisive influence. If nothing but textbook reading is assigned, we need hardly be surprised if pupils unconsciously assume that school studies are somehow against nature. Why not use wide and free collateral readings in almost all courses? Why not use them in science? Why not in mathematics? This leads to a far more natural and fruitful learning than the intensive study of compendia. Again, the whole physical setting enters into the situation. The entire furnishing, arrangement, lighting, and general aesthetic atmosphere of many a classroom is antagonistic to a free and rich mental development. And of course, we must have a spirit of freedom in the entire administration of the school. Could anything be more flagrantly contradictory to the purposes of marginal learning of the right kind than a system which requires a definite lesson to be covered on each day of the school year? Under such a regime, the teacher must discourage questions from the class; must refuse to pause even in the most delectable spots, or to follow any by-paths, however enthralling. He is the slave of an educational method perverted by the efficiency expert, whose one idea is that education means ramming a given amount of material into the children's heads in a given time. Method so conceived is actually anti-educational; for it tends directly towards making children hate subject matter. The marginal learnings are set in an actively negative direction. But in order to make subject matter educative we must provide for positive, propitious marginal learnings.

C. Does the method direct the primary learnings economically and expertly? This is the third question to ask in forming an estimate of the educative value of any teaching situation. A teacher who knows his business can take a pupil, and help him to learn to read, or to solve problems in algebra or geometry, or to translate Latin sentences, or to understand and use chemical formulas, or to appreciate poetry or music, far more readily and far more completely, than he will if left to himself. Golf professionals often say that an adult beginner who never takes any golf lessons, will seldom be able to bring his score much below ninety-five. Whether or no this is partly sales talk, it certainly illustrates one aspect of teaching, which ought, among other things, to aim to facilitate mastery.

This contrasts completely with the old disciplinary point of view in education, according to which hard work was considered beneficial in itself, and difficulties regarded as desirable. Some of the disciplinarians actually opposed reforms in method, on the ground that they tended to make learning easy, and so did away with valuable opportunities for mental exercise. For them, it was even of no great consequence if the pupil never really mastered what he was supposed to be learning, so long as he worked hard at it. For us, however, the actual mastery, the skill or knowledge itself, is essential. And the more readily and completely it is achieved, the better.

So obvious does all this seem, that it is astonishing to find a great many teachers who never see method in this light. Some few years back, there was launched what is known as the supervised study movement. Supervised study is a plan by which some or all of the pupil's preparation is done in school. Its leading idea is that the teacher can undertake few things more beneficial than showing the pupil how to learn. For, in a supervised study group, each pupil is actually learning rather than reciting; and the business of the teacher is to help him learn better than he could by himself. Such a system is clearly sound in principle. It ought to work. But very often it has turned out disappointingly. And the reason usually is that the teacher does not have the right point of view; and when he has no lesson to hear or recitation to conduct, but must actually and intimately show his pupils how to learn better, finds himself helpless. In the same way, one of the chief obstacles to the efficiency of individual work, where it is made possible for each child to study by himself and move at his own pace, is that the teacher does not know what to do. Method, for far too many teachers, means simply a scheme of procedure for running a recitation; and its excellence consists in keeping things going smoothly and avoiding obvious trouble.

Now method must direct the primary learnings economically and expertly, and show the pupil how to achieve definite masteries, if it is to fulfill its great purpose of making subject matter educative. Half learned, half understood material cannot favorably affect a life adjustment. I have no doubt that many of you who read these pages have a strong aversion towards mathematics, and a pretty complete unawareness of the human significance of rigorous thought, simply because you were taught so clumsily that you had little chance of mastering the subject. It is no use talking about the linkage of subject matter with life if there is nothing to link. Nor can effective marginal learnings ever take place in a situation where the primary, direct learnings are breaking down.

At the same time, we must be on our guard here in one important respect. Just because a teacher is directing primary learnings expertly, we must not conclude that his work leaves nothing to be desired. This is sometimes done in educational investigations, and perhaps rather less often, in supervisory work. Two teaching procedures, say in algebra, are compared; and it is found that by the end of the year, the first has produced in the pupils a larger measure of algebraic skill than the second. But this does not, of itself, prove that the first method is the more desirable. What if this superiority in the direct skills has been brought about by ignoring linkage with life, and shutting off marginal learnings; by refusal to follow side lines; by never assigning interesting and valuable collateral readings; by eschewing any kind of approach by projects or any emphasis on applications? In this case, we may have paid a most exorbitant price for our primary learnings. A much more free kind of teaching may produce far more in the way of real "mathematical-mindedness" than our driving, business-like method, which goes between two points by the shortest way possible.

The whole point can be put very definitely indeed. No method can be counted successful which fails to achieve primary masteries, and to bring them about with an economy of effort. But many kinds of teaching may produce such masteries, and still completely fail. The reason is not hard to understand. Such methods may make the mastery of subject matter an end in itself instead of a means. Teaching and learning of this kind reminds one of a man who sacrifices everything to the one goal of becoming rich, and then, when he has made his fortune, finds that he cannot enjoy it.

These, then, are the questions which you should ask, if you wish to form a worth while opinion as to the educative value of any method, whether used by yourself or someone else. Notice once more their subtlety. To know good teaching when one sees it, demands something more than superficial insight or a concentration upon the obvious. We have to do with a process which most intimately and inwardly affects human life. The first impression of that process is often most deceptive; for what looks good may be very bad, and what looks bad may be good. To recognize certainly the excellence or deficiency of any job of teaching calls for a clear insight into its informing purpose and a sensitive, trained, and humane perceptiveness.

4. *What are the values and limitations of some current methods?*

For the sake of adding point and concreteness to the general principles we have been discussing, I now wish to bring them into contact with a few teaching plans which have been worked out in recent years. Specifically, I shall consider the project, the socialized recitation, and individual instruction. Of course I cannot pretend to give, in the short compass of this section, a complete and rounded estimate of any of the three. My purpose is to show, in a very general way, how they exemplify the broad principles of method.

A. Let us begin by considering the project. What has come to be known as project teaching seems to elude precise formulation. One distinguished authority has defined a project as any wholehearted purposive activity. But the trouble is that this seems to include any and every kind of educative activity. Another well known way of defining it is to say that it is "a problematic activity carried to completion in its natural setting." This, at first sight, seems a good deal more specific. But we become doubtful when we consider, first, that almost every conceivable activity is in some sense problematic, and second, that in the broad sense, every setting is "natural"—for what can be outside nature? Yet another definition is that a project is a "practical problem." So we might go on.

After all, however, the game of definitions, though fascinating, is not particularly fruitful. We may have a very good time discussing the question: "When is a project not a project?" But it will not get us very far along the road towards improved teaching. We can recognize a project clearly enough for all practical purposes when we see one. When a class in general science disassembles the engine of a Ford car; when a fifth grade organizes a "Viking Day"; when a ninth grade in social science undertakes a community survey, or makes a set of posters; when a twelfth grade group coöperates in organizing a Good English Drive in the school; when a group of junior high school pupils work out plans for beautifying the school grounds; when children in a Russian rural school handle the local mail, or formulate better agricultural methods; there is no doubt in anyone's mind that we are dealing with projects, even though we may not be able neatly to distinguish them from non-projects.

What is the value of such undertakings in the scheme of education? Clearly, they have, in and of themselves, no magic; and they may even be a sad waste of time. What they are good for, if they are good for anything, is to furnish opportunities for making subject matter educative. Their intelligent use in connection with school work is, in fact, the most ambitious and revolutionary attempt that has ever been made in this direction. If we decide to use a project, we should be quite clear as to just what we are trying to do. We are trying to get away from the treatment of subject matter just as subject matter, and to make it take its proper place in the mental economy of the pupil as a means of more effective adjustment. This is what will determine the success or failure of our adventure in teaching. We are seeking to create an opportunity for linking subject matter with life, in a peculiarly direct and compelling manner, and for the propitious guidance of marginal learnings. The value of the project will lie in its relationship to subject matter.

Now a project may have two kinds of relationship to subject matter—*causal* or *expressive*. And these are quite different. When an elementary school group undertakes to study the causes of typhoid in a farm home, they learn a great deal of natural and social science in connection with their activities. The subject matter is made incidental to the project. Here we have the causal type of relationship, because the project is made the impelling cause of whatever subject matter mastery is obtained. This is a complete contrast to the situation where a fifth grade class in history decides to organize a "Viking Day." They are not learning history through these social activities—at least not in the former sense. The activities are the outgrowth, the *expression,* of the history they have learned. Now which of these instances is an example of the correct and desirable relationship between project and subject matter? Frankly, I do not see that we are forced to choose. I think that either may be excellent. For little children, I would decidedly prefer the causal relationship, because their approach to subject matter ought to be informal, unsystematic, piecemeal, if it is to be of value to them. To try to teach community civics in a systematic manner to a first grade class, would be a flagrant absurdity. But they may pick up a surprising amount of it by a well managed project of making a model village. With older children, the expressive relationship has an increasing value. To try to teach high school English entirely *through* dramatizations, and other project activities, or high school science entirely *through* visits to factories or the manipulation of machinery, will probably fail, because it will render continuity difficult, if not impossible to attain; and as we advance, continuity becomes increasingly essential. But opportunities to write and act historical plays, the making and careful documentation of collections, the assembling and disassembling of machinery, the study of current political issues, the well planned visit to a factory, may be just what is needed to add new light and vitality to the things they have been learning out of books. The real importance and value of the project—and it is a very great one—lies in its being an opportunity for the pupil to see subject matter in its actual, concrete, working relationship to everyday life.

There are some enthusiasts who insist that the only way to make subject matter live is to reorganize the entire work of the school into a series of projects. With this I am unable to agree. In the first place, it makes a systematic, firmly organized grasp of subject matter virtually impossible to attain. Learning naturally begins with the unorganized, the scattered, the diffuse, the vague. So the place, if anywhere, for a pure project curriculum would be the elementary school. But as we advance, the claims of system become paramount. Project work should still be retained. (Indeed, we find it at the highest level of formal education; for what is a doctor's thesis but a project?) But its whole relationship to subject matter changes.

In the second place, the plea for education by a pure project curriculum ignores the obvious fact that this is not the only way of making subject matter live. If you happen to be interested in educating young communists, you may think that the experience of working in a factory will be very valuable in determining how they learn social science. But surely it will also be valuable and vital to read such a book as *New Russia's Primer*. If we want to bring Roman history to life, our sole recourse is by no means to activities such as the writing and acting of a play in which Cæsar, and Cicero, and Clodius make their appearance. If the right kind of motion picture comes to town, see that the class attends it, and have them talk it over afterwards. Get them to read, and discuss together, some historical romances or some interestingly written essays dealing with Roman life. Stimulate them to read and think about parallels between ancient Rome and modern America. Read them Tennyson's poem *To Virgil*. If the history of Rome has meant something in your own life, you surely should not be at a loss in making it mean something in the lives of your pupils. Of course the play or other project may be enormously worth while. But do not cling to it like a drowning man to a spar. It is not your only hope. For these two reasons, I would emphatically conclude that, while projects should have an honored place in a scheme of education, a doctrinaire insistence that they are the sole means of salvation is absurd.

To bring this discussion to a head, let us see how the project method stands the test of the three questions suggested in the preceding section. Does it secure a linkage between subject matter and life? Certainly it may and should, though its actual relationship to subject matter may be of two quite different kinds. Indeed, we may say that if it fails here, it fails completely. Does it propitiously regulate marginal learnings? Again the answer is yes, whether it is set up as a causal or an expressive agency. In either case, it tends to make subject matter more real, more compelling, more worth learning. Does it secure the expert direction of primary learning? Here we hesitate. There is a further distinction to be drawn. If we are thinking of an individual project, such as a doctor's dissertation to mention the most extreme type, or indeed any piece of independent research, then indeed we could hardly wish for a finer opportunity for such expert direction. But with the group project, which is the kind ordinarily used in school, the case is different. The characteristic weakness of such undertakings is precisely that they tend to make the primary learning, the actual mastery of subject matter, fragmentary and haphazard, and to remove it from the direct control of the teacher.

B. Now for the socialized recitation. The thought behind this plan, as is true of all valid schemes, is really very simple. If we have a number of children together in a room, this is an opportunity for social experiences and activities. To make the most of it is no more than common sense. We may do so in a very elaborate and ambitious way; for instance, by organizing a social science class into a city government. Or we may do so very simply; for instance, by having the class listen to a poem or a piece of music and then talk it over together. And between these two extremes, endless degrees of elaboration are possible. But always the principle is the same. We take advantage of the physical "together-ness" of the pupils to have them act and feel as a social group.

As good a way as any to estimate the educative value of the socialized recitation is to ask what the alternative may be. The alternative is the policed recitation, the quiz recitation. Of course you may have a number of children together in a room, and decide not to emphasize social possibilities or to incite social behavior, at all. You may treat them simply as so many individuals. This is done crudely in the ordinary study hall, where each pupil is supposed to work at his own task, while the teacher merely tries to keep order. It is done effectively and constructively under the various plans of individual instruction, of which I have spoken elsewhere. But, if we want to bring out the social possibilities of the occasion, there are just two ways, in general, in which it can be done. We may take measures to set up a socially interacting group. Or we may have a squad drill.

I would not be prepared to say that the old fashioned recitation, which was really an oral quiz administered to a group, has no place in education. Occasionally it may be convenient and valuable. But its place is certainly not a very large one; and it should occur, at most, infrequently. For assuredly, it is not the only, nor at all consistently the best, use to which we can put the social opportunity offered by the class. When we have a class before us, we should see it as an opportunity, not to test, but to teach. Group experiences and enterprises have a natural and very valuable effect upon mental development; for mental development, as we have seen, is profoundly social in its implications. Such experiences should be promoted definitely for the purpose of making subject matter more truly educative than it could be if the pupils did nothing but lonely study.

The great value of social interests and activities seems to lie in their effect upon marginal learnings; and also in the linkage they provide between certain sorts of subject matter and life. For instance, one of the great difficulties in teaching English composition is to give the pupil the mastering sense of saying *something* to *somebody*. This may be at least partly achieved by having him say something to the class—which simply means organizing the class as an audience group, or a coöperative study group, where the pupil may bring his contribution. Again, if one has enjoyed a book, or a poem, or a picture, or a piece of music, what could be more natural than to want to talk the experience over with others, some of whom may have had it, and some of whom have not? Surely, such a social opportunity will tend to make appreciations of all kinds more genuine, more truly and deeply educative.

The limitation of the socialized recitation is much like that of the project. It does not greatly favor the expert direction of primary learnings. For this reason, one cannot say that it is the only adequate way of teaching, or that a whole course should be conducted by no other procedure.

C. When we come to individual instruction, we are dealing with a plan of teaching which is strong exactly where the project and the socialized recitation are weakest. Expert direction of primary learning obviously implies a very intimate relationship between teacher and pupil. Class instruction is always a clumsy means to this particular end, simply because the problems of one learner are not necessarily those of another. It is instructive here to consider certain developments in music education, where class instruction in violin and piano have been attempted. Such group instruction has an indubitable value. It should be continued. But it should be continued on proper lines, and for the aims which it is inherently capable of achieving. If what we want is expert direction of the primary learning, then it cannot compete with individual instruction. A first rate teacher can do a surprising amount in teaching the mastery of a musical instrument to quite a large group. But he cannot do anything like as much as if he took them one by one.

But while individual instruction is strong where the group project and the socialized recitation are weak, we should not jump to the conclusion that it must be weak where they are strong. In the first place, it can, and most certainly should, be a means of linking subject matter with life. A person may read and master a book in the deepest solitude; and yet have his whole understanding of and feeling about the world completely changed. If a high school pupil is studying passages from Wells's *Outline of History,* or Goldstein's *Art in Everyday Life,* he may be having an educative experience, complete in almost every essential respect. If a third grade child, learning arithmetic under a scheme of individual instruction, is supplied with materials which constantly suggest the life applications of what he is studying, the essential linkage may be set up in his mind, even without any project work at all. It all depends on the content which the pupil is learning under our system. To be sure, we may supply him with material consisting of the dryest reading and the most formal exercises. Then, about all that can be said for our plan is that it gives us a fine opportunity for coaching him in his primary learnings. But there is not the very slightest need to stop short here. The individual method is well able to secure very extensive and very fruitful linkages between subject matter and life.

In the second place, the individual method can and should be propitious to marginal learnings. As a matter of fact, this is one of the chief arguments of its defenders. They say that a child is apt to enjoy his work far more, and to show more satisfactory attitudes, if he is free to go at his own pace, and receives help from the teacher only when and if he needs it. We must admit that the class is a very unnatural situation in which to carry on many of the most valuable types of learning. A third grade child of unusual excellence in reading, for instance, may actually be better off at home, freely reading whatever he likes, than held to an annoying routine, based inevitably upon average performance. A scheme of individual instruction is a practical recognition of this. It gives the child what perhaps he needs more than anything else for the developing of favorable marginal learnings—and that is freedom.

This is far from meaning that we should use nothing but individual instruction. Just because it has rich and varied values, and is a highly flexible teaching instrument, it fits in admirably with projects and with socialized procedures. The Dalton Laboratory Plan, which is the most extreme individual method in use, has been sharply criticized on the ground that it eliminates all social experience and group activity from the learning process. It has been intimated that, for this reason, the Dalton Plan must be regarded as simply a device for cramming pupils with subject matter, while ignoring its educational values and its relationship to life.

SIGNIFICANCE OF METHOD

Such a criticism is probably unfair. To be sure, any individual procedure can be used for just this end, simply because it is the ideal situation for the guidance of the primary learnings. But, as I have pointed out, it can be made to subserve rich and living values as well. Nevertheless, the objection to the Dalton Plan on the ground of unduly minimizing group experience, does often seem to be valid, as that plan is actually applied.

Individual instruction in the public schools is entirely within the range of practical possibilities today. One must make use of specially prepared materials, to be sure. And one must take the trouble to learn just how, as well as why, to use the method. But an adequately trained teacher, working under proper conditions, can direct the work of as many as forty children in a room, each one of whom is studying on a basis wholly individual and moving at his own rate of speed. So do not suppose that, in advocating individual instruction, we are talking about some ideal but impossible tutorial scheme, with as many teachers as there are pupils. It is now very successfully used in some of the largest school systems, here and abroad.

There are a few points which arise in connection with this discussion of methods actually in use, which it may be well to comment upon, as we close this section. First of all, it is clear that no method can be regarded as ideal or suitable for all occasions. Probably the ideal situation in any school, or any course, would be a rather free and informal combination of rich individual instruction involving the use of vital and truly educative materials, and projects and social experiences. The relationship between the project work and the social undertakings on the one hand, and the orderly sequence of subject matter learning involved in the individual instruction on the other, need not be stereotyped in any way. Sometimes a project might stimulate subject matter learning. Sometimes subject matter learning might evoke a project or make a social recitation seem desirable. The aim would be, not to follow any set rule or pet theory, but to bring subject matter continually into relationship with life.

Second, it is clear that we cannot even begin to consider method apart from the content to be taught. Just because a socialized procedure may be excellent in a course in social science, it by no means follows that a closely similar procedure will be effective in chemistry. A health project may have a positively startling value in making the content of the course in physiology vivid and vital. But this in no way obligates us to use the project method in teaching algebra. Moreover, such terms as project method, socialized recitation, and individual instruction are really blanket words, covering a multitude of divergencies. Not all projects or socialized recitations are alike, nor is individual instruction invariably of one type only. Different types of content demand differences of treatment. One teacher has a genius for one approach, but another who tries it, makes a failure of it. The possible ways of bringing subject matter to life are endless. There is no such thing as one single method, or even a few standardized methods, which can be fruitfully applied everywhere and anywhere.

Chapter 21

HOW SHALL WE INTERPRET THE WORK OF THE TEACHER?

1. *What is the task of the teacher?*

A few years ago, the Music Teachers' National Association was actively considering a change in its title. The proposal was to call it the Music *Educators'* National Association. This proposal was defeated, largely because the word "educator" seemed strange and awkward. So much we may admit. To tell Johnny that he must wash his hands, and hurry off to the music educator's, does strike us as a little queer. And yet the essential idea is wholly sound. The teacher must think of himself as an educational leader. And he cannot be satisfied with his place in the scheme of things, or do the work that needs to be done, until everybody concerned—principals, superintendents, pupils, parents, school boards, and the general public—thinks of him in just this way. Educational leadership is usually considered the privilege and responsibility of administrative officials, superintendents of schools, university presidents, publicists, scholars well known for extensive research and publication—almost everybody, that is, whose chief work is not the day by day guidance of the pupils. The teacher is relegated to the position of a humble follower, who obeys orders, who carries out policies framed by wiser heads, who assigns and hears lessons from textbooks in the selection of which he has had little say, who rejoices in the mediocre status of a non-commissioned officer. So long as this condition prevails, education can never carry out its full mission. We cannot expect great and creative teaching from robots. The teacher must grow into the educator.

This assertion is not mere dogmatism. The moment we bring the entire thought of these pages to a focus on the work of the teacher, it becomes obviously and necessarily implied. The teacher's task is to secure for each child a progressive, creative, flexible adjustment to the institutions of our modern world; to convey the intellectual resources of civilization as agencies for more enlightened action. This simply cannot be done effectively by a person whose whole responsibility is to carry out orders without discussion, no matter how well such a responsibility may be discharged. Suppose you are teaching American history in the grades. You are given certain materials, including a textbook. Your job is to put the pupils through the work in a given time, and to get them to learn their lessons as well as possible. Almost certainly you will concentrate on subject matter for its own sake. Even if your school has introduced some plan of individual instruction, subject matter will still remain the chief concern; the only difference will be that not all the pupils will cover the same amount of ground. Ground covering, lesson learning, will remain still the center of the picture. But American history has not begun to be *educative* until it actually affects the social dispositions of the pupils. It must give them a critical insight into the vast drama of life going on around them, in which they are increasingly to participate. It must create in them certain attitudes towards political and social questions, towards industry and its place in the American scheme, towards our dealings with foreign nations. This, in part at least, is what we mean when we say that American history must contribute towards effective social adjustment. But to bring such things about, you yourself must have a real understanding of American social conditions. You yourself must have thought about, and be thinking about, those very life problems which your pupils will have to face. And you must see how your subject relates itself to them and contributes towards their solution. You must become an interpreter, at the mental level of your pupils, of American society. You must know what items of material to choose, and what to subordinate; what emphasis to employ; what lines of reading, and discussion, and activity to set up for the sake of bringing home to your pupils the social meaning of your subject. Of course you cannot do this all by yourself. You must have guidance from the administrative staff, conferences with fellow teachers, and a knowledge of what is being tried elsewhere. But neither can you be content with just going through a standardized, predetermined set of lessons, handed to you from on high. You wish to put your pupils in the way of acquiring certain insights and attitudes. Unless you yourself have these insights and attitudes, you cannot do it. And you must have freedom to help your pupils to see what you see. If you fail here, then, no matter how skilled you are as a hearer of lessons or a director of individual study, your teaching will be dead. Against you will be directed that most terrible of all criticisms, the criticism of pupils, who, twenty years after they leave school, say that they studied with a teacher for a year, and learned nothing worth remembering. You must have the point of view and the mental equipment of the educator, and also his status and freedom.

To convey subject matter, not for its own sake, but for the sake of mental growth and enlightenment, requires in the teacher an adjustment to his work that is flexible, creative, and progressive. Let us see why this is so.

A. The teacher's adjustment must be flexible. In a very great many cases, this is lacking. Whenever it is proposed to introduce some new plan of teaching in a school, one of the greatest practical difficulties is to get the teachers to change their ways. Such a sound idea as supervised study often fails, simply because, when they must give up the routine practices of the conventional recitation, they are at a loss. Individual instruction may be no better than ordinary class teaching, because of the helplessness of teachers when they cannot apply the usual devices for handling pupils all moving abreast of one another. These are sure signs of rigidity. It is exactly like the case of a certain nurse, who insisted on wakening a patient at seven o'clock to bathe him, although he had just fallen asleep after a disturbed night. Such rigidity always comes from two sources; a meager insight into and grasp of the subject to be taught; and a bag-of-tricks method. If one knows only just enough of American history, or science, or mathematics, to be able to check up on the rightness or wrongness of the pupil's responses to conventional test questions, one can have no freedom with it. One cannot flexibly and confidently vary one's presentation to suit the interests of the individuals with whom one is dealing. One cannot make it an interpretive power in their lives. And if one has been taught to teach, simply as a matter of always going through certain motions in a definite way, one cannot flexibly shape up an educational situation for desirable and significant ends. Always such rigidity means the routine teaching of routine content in a routine manner. It means failure in the task of making subject matter the agent of mental growth and enlightened living—the failure of that interpretive function which is the teacher's supreme obligation.

B. The teacher's adjustment must be creative. Always the great teacher-personalities have tended to create new procedures, new methods, new administrative patterns. Pestalozzi shattered the old forms of individual instruction to bits, and perfected, over many years of effort, a new pedagogy. Comenius was possessed by a new thought, and gave it expression in the first series of illustrated textbooks ever published. Froebel could not be satisfied with the education of his day; and his creative spirit, ever seeking new and better things, gave the world the kindergarten. Horace Mann crystallized a vision of educational service into the administrative scheme of our modern public schools. Now you may never produce anything as ambitious as this—although also it is possible that you may. You may never invent a Montessori System or a Dalton Laboratory Plan. But your work, if it is to be properly done, must partake of this creative character. You must build up an authentic vision of human needs and of the contribution which your subject can make to the great business of living. And you must find out what, for you, is the best way of making it effective in the minds and hearts of your pupils. Of course this is very far from meaning that you must flout authority and go your own way regardless of protests and advice. But it does mean that your following of authority must be coöperative, not servile. You can convey no vision you do not see, nor any insight you do not possess. The teacher must take the right way, not because he is told to do so, but because he perceives its rightness. Otherwise his work cannot be done. Even though a million teachers have done the same thing you are doing, yet it must be your own original discovery, your own original choice, made because you perceive it to be right, and not because someone tells you so.

C. The teacher's adjustment must be progressive. One of the dangers involved in issuing teachers' certificates, is that it so easily conveys the idea to the holder that he is now "trained." Many teachers work pretty much on this assumption. Of course they learn a good deal from general experience in their first few years of work in the schools. But they do not anxiously and urgently seek professional and personal growth as a great necessity. They read little professional literature. They attend teachers' conventions chiefly to have a good time and to find another job. And they do not grow, monthly and yearly, in their subject itself. This is the sure road to routine, and so to educational death. No one fresh from college or normal school can possibly have more than a glimmering of the human significance of any of the great subdivisions of our intellectual resources. Indeed, he is lucky if he has that much. This simply means that, as yet, he has little to teach. He can go through certain motions. He can seek to please by his "personality." But he has not yet the mature wisdom of the interpretive educator. To attain this is a life-long task. And if one never sets out upon it, what happens is that one's work becomes school keeping rather than education, and one's personality, be one male or female, dwindles down towards the crabbed nonentity of the neurotic old maid.

Here, then, is a picture of what teaching must mean in any progressive educational scheme. The teacher must not be treated as a cog in a vast machine. He must not be a routinized personality, carrying out orders in blind subservience. When this happens, everything tends towards the appalling picture which Chekov has given us of a teacher of his, without creative mind, bound down by routine, treating the children as his foes, filling the school day with unrelated learning of bits of subject matter, resulting in a junk shop mentality.

It may have seemed to you that certain of the ideas presented in the pages of this book are impractical. In some cases this may be so, due simply to my own lack of wisdom. But the general scheme advocated is impractical only on one assumption—that we are doomed to accept the services of routine-bound, ineffective teachers. If we want a genuine scheme of education, whose evident power and vitality no one can question, we must have teachers who are genuine educators. To make this possible is the great responsibility of all who deal with the teacher. His own instructors, his official superiors, and also the public, must strengthen his hands for the great task. And there is a responsibility upon him also, which he cannot shirk, to seek such things and to be content with nothing less.

2. *How may teacher training help the teacher to perform his task?*

Teacher training in America is profoundly unsatisfactory. It flagrantly fails to apply to itself the very principles which it advocates. It preaches one thing, and practices the very opposite. This is not due to sheer hypocrisy, for those responsible are often ardent believers in a humane, significant, and progressive type of education; but rather to a strange helplessness. In the past, jobs have been many, and suitable candidates few, and no one could see how to do much about it. Moreover, the training of high school teachers has largely been in the hands of the most conservative unit in our educational system, the liberal arts college, which indeed renders lip service to the social ideal, but whose action is often dominated by disciplinary and intellectualistic prejudices.

When we look at teacher training, what do we see? On the one hand, subject matter courses, organized in narrow and mutually exclusive subdivisions, and taught for the sake of something called scholarship, which usually means subject matter purely for itself; on the other hand, courses in the field of education, which almost perfectly exemplify the cold storage fallacy, and which have no particular relationship to subject matter mastery. The entire scheme is highly mechanical. Valid ideas about education, culture, and social living may be, nay, assuredly are, presented to the student. But the whole suggestive force of the system, its whole atmosphere, and all the incidental and marginal learnings it engenders, tend in the opposite direction. It is exactly the wrong kind of educational situation for the results we desire to achieve. How then can we possibly expect that teachers so trained will effectively comprehend, really believe in, and ardently wish to apply the ideas we advocate? Let us begin by giving them an actual taste of these ideas, instead of merely teaching their sound.

It is quite true that many superintendents and principals speak approvingly of our present system of teacher training. Various studies, in which the questionnaire method has been used, show this to be the case. But what, after all, does it mean? Does it not merely indicate a lack of urgent vision in these men? Does it not mean a tame willingness to accept what is, as pretty good, and perhaps the best for which we can hope; and an inability to imagine anything very much better? Discontent rather than content should be the indicated attitude. For where freedom ought to be, there we have routine. In the whole range of undertakings in which our schools engage, the education of the teacher should be the shining instance of education for creative living by creative living. Its controlling principle must be that effective professional adjustment to the work of teaching comes only by way of mental growth, and that the conditions of mental growth must be provided and sustained. The weakness of our present system all comes back to this. The conditions of mental growth are constantly falsified and ignored. When they are fulfilled, teacher training will become what it ought to be. Let us see more specifically what this means.

A. First of all, we must have academic courses which give a living mastery of subject matter. For flexible, creative teaching, the mastery of subject matter is an absolutely indispensable condition. To give an instance, it is impossible to teach French by direct conversation, unless one can talk the language freely. This is one of the most obvious illustrations of our point; but the assertion applies everywhere. One great reason why mathematics is so atrociously taught, and why it seems so dull and forbidding to numbers of our brightest students, is certainly that so many teachers have no real competence in and enthusiasm for this subject, and no vision of its life significance. Again, no one can present science as an interpretation of life and a method of thought, rather than as an assemblage of dull facts, unless he himself has a genuine competence in scientific thinking and is growing in scientific insights. Nor is the necessity for a mastery of the material to be taught confined to the higher levels. In teaching reading in the first and second grades, it is not enough just to set up a skill, and trust to providence that the children will find uses for it. We want to create in them a desire and a disposition to read and to grow by reading. And this presupposes a teacher who is himself an enthusiastic and an increasingly discriminating reader. In grade school music, our great aim should be to foster an understanding love of the art. But how can this be done by a teacher who knows and cares little about it? Whenever a teacher does not possess a living mastery of the subject matter to be presented, at once we have the teaching of a textbook, rather than the interpretation and application of an intellectual resource.

"But," you may say, "have we not heard of students with excellent academic records, who make very poor teachers? Are not holders of Phi Beta Kappa keys quite apt to fail with a high school class?" Yes, indeed; these things are so. Scholarship is not enough. Indeed, it may even be harmful. What more, then, do we need? A knowledge of routine method? Certainly not. This can never in the least compensate for ignorance. How can a knowledge of various devices and procedures, or even a recitation mastery of various educational doctrines, help a person to interpret to others a subject of which he knows little, and perhaps cares less? What we must have is scholarship of a certain type; grasp of subject matter in its broad human and cultural relationships, and in its bearing upon the enterprises and meanings of life. Having a strong major in science should not only mean a competence with the kind of techniques required by the research worker; it should also mean an appreciation of the fertilizing relationship of science to social progress. Being a scholar in English up to the level of the bachelor's degree should not mean a half way house towards a doctorate, and a recondite thesis. It should mean being a wide and discriminating reader, with literary enthusiasms which one is eager to convey to others. Biology teaches us that only life can produce life. This principle applies also to education. The only person fit to teach any subject is one in whose life it actually lives, and whose thoughts and actions it progressively shapes.

There is no difficulty in indicating where the great weakness in the average teacher's training in subject matter may be found. It lies in the fact that he has studied his subject matter in a sort of mental compartment. The ordinary major in science, or history, or mathematics, or English, is set up and organized as if science, or history, or mathematics, or English, were the only thing in the world, and as if mastering one of these fields meant no more than competence with its technical detail and familiarity with its facts. College instructors, who have specialized for many years in a single field of learning, often have this point of view and allow it to permeate their work. Often they take a positive pride in staying strictly inside their own intellectual fences; and seem to regard it as a sort of professional trespass to cross the boundary lines of learning for any reason whatsoever. Students thus trained in compartments inevitably tend to think in compartments. They are aware only of the internal, technical aspects of their field of specialization, and not of its broader meanings, and its bearings upon human affairs. No matter how "scholarly" a person may be in this sense; no matter how well he tills his narrow domain; no matter how many A's and honors he reaps; he does not know his subject as a real educator needs to know it. Indeed, it sometimes almost seems as if the better he is in this respect, the worse he becomes as a teacher. This at once explains why some of the highest ranking products of the college fail miserably, when put in responsible charge of an educational situation.

What the teacher needs, above everything else, is a broad and fundamental grasp of the materials he must convey; an awareness of it, not only as a field full of fascinating technical problems, but also as a part of the intellectual heritage, whose whole meaning and value is in its effect upon action. You will probably have noticed that this is exactly what I have been arguing for, as the basic meaning of culture. Culture does not signify knowledge, or technical expertness, or artistic insight, for its own sake. It means all these things, but for the sake of human social adjustment and enlightened behavior. And, above all, the teacher must have a vital culture, if he is to create and sustain a living cultural environment.

"But," you may ask, "when a person studies a subject for the purpose of teaching it, should he not know it in a different way from the person who studies it merely as part of his general culture?" The answer often given is in the affirmative. And so, in many of our best teachers' colleges, a serious attempt is being made to work out what is known as "professionalized" subject matter. This means subject matter specially organized and presented with a view to the needs and interests of those who learn it for the sake of teaching it. What shall we say to this proposal? Is it educationally valid?

Our answer must be that, if by "professionalized" subject matter, we mean subject matter broadly treated as a tool of the mind, then the ideal is legitimate and should have our enthusiastic endorsement. Take history as an instance. It is exceedingly enlightening to know the motives which have led to the writing of history—sometimes as mere compilation of facts dealing with the deeds of dynasties, sometimes to support a set of political opinions, sometimes as nothing less than a philosophy of human life itself. To be aware of such things brings history to life in the minds of those who study it. It ceases to be so much impersonal material, and becomes colored with human passions, and instinct with the hopes, and fears, and aspirations of mankind. To acquire such an attitude towards it is enormously enlightening, and brings to its study quite a new significance. It is, as a matter of fact, precisely the attitude of the creative and interpretive historian. And every student of history should share, in so far as in him lies, in the feeling the historian has for his subject. In the same way, the study of the development of science, or of mathematics, or even of the psychology of the scientist or the mathematician, can add something of very great value to the work of any student who specializes in these fields. So, if by "professionalized" subject matter, we mean subject matter taught with special attention to its significance in human life, its history, its psychology, its literature, and its value as an agency for culture, then we find it extremely desirable. We may, however, protest against subject matter so treated being called "professionalized" in any narrow sense. These are just the things which should receive attention in every student's major concentration, and in every sequence of work leading to the doctorate. They work powerfully against narrowness and pedantry, and towards a true and living cultural apprehension. So far, we have nothing which every student may not most fruitfully share with him who studies a subject in order to teach it.

But we may go farther than this. There is no reason at all why, in every major field, certain courses should not be set aside, which deal more specifically and in detail with the professional aspects of the subject—with the organized materials which exist for teaching it at an elementary or secondary level, with the tests which have been accumulated in connection with it, with the peculiar difficulties which it may present to the immature mind. Such courses may still be taught in a manner sufficiently broad to illuminate the wider issues of the field. One may become aware, in a new way, of the human significance of history or of mathematics, if one wrestles with the problem of how to make it live in the minds and lives of boys and girls. One must simplify without denaturing; one must sift out essentials from unessentials. In order to form a valid opinion of whether a given subject matter test is good, or whether a given high school or elementary school textbook is what it ought to be, one must have nothing less than a philosophy of the subject involved. Still, such concerns, and the courses which deal with them, are hardly germane to the interests of those who do not plan to teach in the field. At the same time, there is no clash of interests and points of view. Always, our purpose must be to help the student perceive the wider human significance, and the inner meaning, of the subject he is studying. The only real question is how far to go in the direction of specific detail. And here the vocational purpose of the person concerned must guide us. The thing to remember is, that, on the one hand, no person can be said to have an ideal grasp of any subject unless he is fit to teach it, while on the other, fitness to teach a subject depends precisely on this perception of its worth and place in the human drama.

B. In addition to the kind of academic education in the subject matter to be taught which has been described in outline, it is necessary for the prospective teacher to undertake a study of the theory and practice of education. And the central aim of the courses in education which implement this need, must be what I might call "educational-mindedness" rather than a stock of information about teaching and its problems. That is to say, the student must be brought to understand what it means to be a teacher, and to feel a personal need to master the various techniques, devices, administrative plans, and scientific doctrines which are to be his special professional tools.

When we consider the courses in the field of education in the light of our controlling principles, there are three great errors which it is evidently necessary to avoid.

(i) In the first place, we cannot be content with any kind of cold storage preparation, or any plan whose essential aim is to stock the student's mind with knowledge and ideas which he may put into practice two or three years later. And it is no use saying that such prospective preparation is allowable, because we are dealing with practical matters; for our pedagogy will cancel our practicality. This is what often happens. Consider, for instance, the course in educational psychology, commonly given during sophomore year. For some time there has been a growing tendency to bring the content of this course more and more closely into contact with the actual problems of the working teacher. This is entirely desirable. But it is entirely wrong to imagine that a student can learn all about such matters as a sophomore, and then have them pop into his mind when he needs them four years later. For one thing, he will not learn them as they must be learned if they are to be effective; for, with the best intentions, both on his own part and on that of the instructor, he cannot. The situation itself forbids it. Much that is presented to him is too far removed from his present experience and his immediate needs. For another thing, he will surely forget a great deal that he has verbally learned, no matter how thorough his work may be and how well he passes the tests in his course. The course in educational psychology is probably the most serious instance of the cold storage fallacy in teacher training. But the same criticism applies elsewhere.

(ii) In the second place, our courses in education must not be made so academic that they do not apply anywhere. Some professors of education, irked by the criticism of their colleagues, have undertaken to build up their work on the conventional academic pattern. The result has been courses which are neither one thing nor the other, which are academic in form, without even the small excuse of a long tradition, and an absence of specific vocational intention. A case in point is the work in the history of education, which used to be a staple of the teacher training curriculum, but which has now receded into the background. Certainly our courses in education must present general ideas, but never in the conventional academic spirit. They must be general ideas which apply to a very specific situation, and which gain meaning and vitality from their applicability. Otherwise the learning of the student will be verbal rather than real; and the only outcome, a temporary capacity to write an examination, rather than a permanent modification of disposition and attitude. There is no doubt that the study of the mediaeval curriculum, or the educational ideas of Plato or Milton, can be extremely illuminating. But there is also no doubt that, if such matters are presented and learned just as so many facts without any bearing upon our present problems and preoccupations, they will be in no vital sense educative.

(iii) In the third place, our courses in education must not be "practical" in advance of a felt need, or in the sense of being wholly and brutally specific. Here we have another tangent on which professors of education have gone off. They clearly see that their aim is vocational. And they conclude that their chief business must be training teachers in rule-of-thumb methods. This involves two fallacies. First of all, a rule of procedure learned in advance of the situation where it is to be used, is badly learned. It becomes a mere routine. The student cannot even discuss it intelligently, as anyone knows very well who has tried to talk over some high school teaching problem with a class of college sophomores and juniors. The essential exceptions, the shades of meaning and intention, fail to register. And the best result we can hope for is the memorizing of rules of procedure which will later be applied as routines. The second fallacy is that practicality in this narrow sense means pure empiricism, which is always wrong. What we need is *enlightened practicality*. Procedures must be understood in terms of purpose. And mastering them must be part of a wider undertaking—the comprehension of the educational enterprise itself.

The root reason why our work in teacher training is so unsatisfactory is that it is either out of contact with real experience, or has the wrong sort of contact with it. Where then may such contacts be sought? And how should they be capitalized? Where shall we look for the kind of experience which may make our education courses seem real and cogent to our students? Opportunities of this kind may be found in two directions: first, in the student's own educational experience up to the present; second, in actual contact with teaching situations.

First consider the capitalization of the student's own educational experience. By the time he has come to be ready to take his first course in education, every student has had many years of direct, concrete educational experience. Why not take advantage of it? Here is a neglected gold mine. Teachers of education tell their students that the educative process is the reconstruction of experience. Every student before them has had a wealth of experience in the very field being considered. He has been what we might call a professional pupil for something like fourteen years. And yet the instructors do nothing about it, except in the most casual and incidental manner. I would suggest that the early courses in education should turn very largely on a critical interpretation of the student's own wide educational experience.

Notice that such courses will have a far wider appeal than one confined to prospective teachers only. They will deliberately set out to make the student self conscious about the very activities which are, for the time being, his chief business in life. And in this way they will have meaning and value for everyone in the institution. May we not very properly maintain that everyone, before he graduates from college, should have been led systematically to reflect about the whole business of education, and to achieve an enlightened attitude with regard to it, in the only possible way—by an interpretation of his own experience through the great body of knowledge, doctrine, and insight regarding schooling which has accumulated through the ages? Is it not rather shocking to allow people to leave college without any well considered ideas about the meaning, the values, and the defects of their principal life activity during the past sixteen years? May not such well considered ideas be properly regarded as a part of their living culture? Will not the probable outcome be more intelligent attitudes in regard to the education of their children, and their duties as citizens towards the schools?

I believe that work so organized can be exceedingly vital and illuminating. Consider how eagerly student audiences will listen to brief discussions of educational topics in the form of semi-popular lectures. Consider how actively they discuss among themselves the merits and defects of their teachers, of the procedures on which their work is planned, and of the educational policies of the institution. That the study of education has a wider mission than one confined to prospective teachers is more than suggested by the fact that many of our greatest minds, from Plato onwards, have been concerned with it, though they often had little reference to the actual work of the instructor. The wide popularity of the educational writings of such men as Everett Dean Martin, Bertrand Russell, and H. G. Wells is still further indication of a felt and genuine need. Why should not our courses in the field of education deliberately take advantage of it, and capitalize the experience of the student in the interest of their own vitality?

Then, too, the student who intends to teach must have contact with actual educational situations in the relationship of the teacher rather than the pupil. This is secured by various plans of supervised observation, practice teaching, and field teaching. The idea is sound enough. But too often it is misapplied, and fails of its full possibilities.

For one thing, such contacts often come altogether too late. This is more particularly true in the training of high school teachers in our colleges and universities. Here the usual plan is to give the students various sequences of book courses, culminating in observation and practice teaching in the senior year. This may be a logical sequence. But psychologically it is unsound. Concrete experience is the beginning, not the end of mental growth. The whole meaning of what the student learns in educational psychology, secondary education, principles of education, tests and measurements, and school administration, lies in the concrete teaching situation itself. When we postpone experience with that situation until the final chapter, we relapse into the cold storage fallacy. Something may be done—in many of our best teacher training institutions it *is* done—by requiring a general review in connection with practice teaching. But even this is artificial and enormously weakens and devitalizes the preceding learning.

And there is an error in fundamental aim. The fallacy is suggested in the very term "practice" teaching. What the term seems to indicate is a rehearsing of various activities and routines, which, later on, the student will undertake for pay. And this is precisely wrong. What actual contact with teaching situations should secure for the student is an opportunity to grasp the meaning of educational principles, doctrines, and theories, which nothing else can supply. The aim should not be practice at all, but enlightenment. The ordinary teacher has an abundance of practice; but he fails to grow because he has a paucity of enlightenment along with it. Here, as everywhere, concrete experience must be interwoven with theoretical interpretations. The intellectual content illuminates the experience; the experience renders vital the intellectual content.

If we could place students who intend to teach in an institution where, from the first, they had intimate contacts with actual teaching, beginning as observers, and assuming more and more responsibility as they showed the capacity for it, we could convey the intellectual elements of their training far less formally and far more effectively, than we manage to do in our ordinary sequence of courses. In a certain teachers' college this has been tried, with very interesting results. Selected students were simply turned loose to observe and participate in the work of the experimental school, without a word of guidance. Just at first, they were bewildered. But in a very short time they began to ask questions and to seek sources of information. They came to the director of teacher training, asking, "Why do this? How meet that problem? How deal with such and such a child?" Their whole training in educational psychology, methods, tests, and so forth, was built about their aroused interests.

Whether such an informal scheme would, in all cases, be successful, I am not prepared to say. But the principle is admirable and sound. It means bringing about a development towards "educational-mindedness" in and through the interpretation and revaluation of significant experience.

As I close this rather long discussion of teacher training, there are three points on which a word should be said.

First, teacher training as I have tried to envisage it here, cannot be carried on adequately in our existing institutions, and more particularly in our colleges and universities as at present organized. Much of the weakness of our courses in education is due to their being placed in a hostile environment and taught cheek by jowl with academic subjects. The conditions for their full effectiveness cannot, under these circumstances, be supplied. This means, specifically, that much of the professional training of teachers should be carried on in graduate institutions, where vitalizing educational contacts become possible. Some of the work, however, should remain on the undergraduate level. And this should be concerned, particularly, with the critical interpretation of the student's own educational experience, which, as I have insisted, has a value and appeal by no means confined to prospective teachers.

Second, notice how our whole discussion seems to render almost meaningless the great problem of the proper number of courses in education. The American Association of University Professors has recently recommended twelve semester hours as desirable for a high school certificate. But some of our states require almost twice as much. Now so long as the department or school of education is competing with the academic departments for control of the student's time, we shall have no adequate solution at all. But our principles point towards a very different set-up. Some serious work in the field is eminently proper for the undergraduate. Indeed, its possible values, and the plausibility of its claims, are so great that it may even be an appropriate collegiate requirement. But such a broad study of education would fit in and coöperate naturally with a sane scheme of liberal higher education, rather than constituting a dissonant, competing element. And the more specific and definitely professional activities do not belong in the undergraduate college at all. Hence the competitive issue of the number of hours of education to be required is avoided.

Third, notice how our principles tend to resolve the conflict between the courses in education and the academic work. To reflect in general about one's own educational experience and career is surely a step in the direction of making one's culture vital and meaningful. When one assesses gains and losses, and ask what it has really meant to study various subjects in various ways, the broader meanings of those subjects become more and more apparent. As one moves on from this level, and considers education more definitely from the standpoint of the teacher, one does far more than merely learn a number of techniques. One sees, in sharper and sharper relief, the significance of intellectual content, and its applicability to human needs. As one grows in understanding of what it is to be a teacher, subject matter ceases to be so much inert material, and becomes an intellectual resource for the enlightenment of action. Growth towards educational-mindedness means growth towards a living, focalized, functioning culture. And intellectual content, properly understood, is understood in terms of its true place in the drama of human education broadly conceived.

In such ways as these may the conditions of mental growth be maintained in connection with the education of teachers. Only so may the teacher be trained for his task. As has been most truly said: "If teachers' colleges can train students to understand the best educational principles, to appreciate their full significance, apply them both consciously and unconsciously, and make such principles a part of their teaching and being, more will be done for good teaching than has been done in the history of the profession."

3. *What should be some of the chief results of teacher training?*

A valid scheme of education for the teacher should bring about certain general results, of which I will here mention three.

A. First and foremost, teacher training must lead to a continuous professional growth. In the preparation of teachers, there has been far too much emphasis upon an immediate outcome and the securing of maximum efficiency during the first year of teaching. This has been due, in part at least, to the conditions in the profession itself. Beginning teachers are often given little special supervision. They are thrown very much on their own resources. They are paid salaries unduly high in proportion to the later salary levels. The whole point of view of the schools concerning them seems to be that they are fully trained and ready to work under full normal conditions. This, of course, puts heavy pressure on the teacher training institutions to prepare, not for a life of teaching in which there will be a long course of professional growth, but for a first year to be gotten through not too discreditably.

This leads at once to a false practicality and a narrow vocational emphasis, which is most unfortunate. The tendency is to regard nothing as properly belonging to the training of the teacher, if it cannot be definitely put into use within six weeks of the time he accepts and begins work in his first position. Of course, teacher training institutions do not go the whole distance in this direction. But such is the prevailing trend. Now, if we are concentrating merely on helping the teacher through his first year or two, perhaps very specific advice, and many rules of thumb, are indicated as the most desirable things under the circumstances. Certainly there will be little opportunity for the recognition of the full bearing of controlling generalizations and basic principles; this is a matter of years of growth, and thought, and experience. All that we can work or hope for is the establishment of some kind of routine, which will carry the teacher along and not disgrace the institution which trained him.

As a matter of fact, the first year, or probably the first two years of teaching, should be definitely probationary in character and very intimately related to the formal activities of training. And the great aim of all training should be continued growth in breadth of view and expertness of technique. If a teacher can cash in completely on his preparation in his first year or two of experience, that preparation has not been worth very much. Its full values should just be beginning to appear after, perhaps, twenty years.

This question of continuous professional growth, or, as it is called, "improvement in service," has received wide discussion. Usually it is dealt with in a somewhat mechanical way, and taken to mean reading an occasional professional book or article, and attending summer school sessions. Such things are all very well in their way; but they are the merest externals. There is one central, essential way in which a teacher training agency may seek to promote the continuous professional growth of its graduates. It can set about arousing in them a genuine enthusiasm for the life and work of the teacher. This comes as students are brought to see more fully what teaching means and what its opportunities and responsibilities are. Beginning with ordered reflection upon his own educational experience, the student is led step by step into closer contact with the actualities of teaching, which give point and meaning to his growing knowledge of educational theory. By the time he is ready to take an appointment, he should have some understanding of what teaching, as an interpretation of social life and the application of intellectual resources in the interests of enlightened action, really means. He should perceive both the possibility and the desirability of planning his work on sound progressive principles. And he should feel an enthusiasm for so doing. If his adjustment to his job is of this character, no one will have to force him to take advantage of the agencies of professional growth. Professional reading, further study of his subject matter specialty, the examination of new methods and procedures and plans, and experimentation in his own work, will follow naturally.

B. Another thing to be accomplished by a scheme of teacher training organized in accordance with proper educational principles is to render serious and valid the vocational choice of the prospective teacher. A great many students now plan to enter the teaching profession for very superficial and insufficient reasons. It seems to offer a quick and easy opportunity to earn a little money. Or else they can think of nothing else to do. Often the student gives no serious consideration to his fitness for the work and has no sort of understanding of what the calling of the teacher really involves.

From every standpoint, this is most unfortunate. First it impairs the professional standing of all teachers. No profession, many of whose members are in it for essentially unworthy and ulterior motives, can maintain high standards before the public. Imagine what would happen to the medical profession if physicians were recruited in such ways. Then, it means a constant tendency to sacrifice the interests of the pupil to those of the teacher. No person who enters teaching reluctantly, or with the idea of staying in the work for a few years for the sake of accumulating a little money, is likely to have the attitude of serving, first of all, the personal interests of the pupils. Third, it has an unfortunate effect upon the academic teachers who deal with the student in college. They know very well that they are not dealing with a person who has made a serious life decision. This makes them disinclined to modify their work for the sake of his interests and needs. Much of the resistance to "professionalized" subject matter, even in the broad sense, comes from a feeling that, after all, the peculiar needs of the prospective teacher are not to be taken too seriously. Unfortunately, there is considerable justification for this. The student must not complain if others do not give great weight to his choice of a calling, when he himself is perfectly willing to enter it for trivial reasons, and with mental reservations in regard to the permanence of his adjustment. Fourth, it casts a blight over all courses in education. No human being, though he were a combination of Socrates and Abelard, could overcome the ill effects of sheer indifference and veiled hostility on the part of his students. Effective teaching is a coöperative undertaking, in which the attitude of the students is as important and determining as the work of the teacher. When students enter courses in education under protest, without any vital curiosity, and lacking a serious purpose, they need not altogether blame either the instructor or the subject, if they find the work dull and sterile. Fifth, a shallow and trivial vocational decision has a most evil effect upon the individual. To enter such a profession as teaching for ulterior motives is an essentially immoral act. It strikes at the very roots of personal integrity. Teaching should be a calling in which one finds an increasing personal satisfaction and stability, and an ever widening opportunity to do one's best work. But if chosen on trivial grounds, it fosters cynicism, rationalization, and the division rather than the integration of purpose.

How then shall we remedy this defect? By remembering always that a valid vocational choice comes from mental and personal growth. When a high school senior writes down on a college enrollment blank that he wishes to become a teacher, this decision should by no means be treated with contempt. On the other hand, it should by no means be regarded as final. Probably the student does not yet know either himself or life in general well enough to be sure of his choice, or to give it any very great and ultimate validity. Still, it is one of the natural organizing points of his mental development. He ought to begin learning, as soon as possible, something of what education means, something of the significance and the reality of the teacher's life. This is one reason why I believe it would be a serious error to postpone all work in the field of education until after college graduation. The education of the teacher must be conceived as a means of finding himself. And this may well begin as early as sophomore year in college. If, after such preliminary work, in which he is led to a better understanding of the educative process in the individual and society, chiefly by a reflection upon his own educational experiences, he still desires to enter teaching, then indeed, his choice has gained something in stability and enlightenment. By his own act, he has selected himself for further training. His mental growth has gained specificity and direction. But even yet, it should not be regarded as a final choice. What we want is to postpone finality as long as possible, and to bring about a steady growth in certainty. The plan I have suggested of a vital institutional training, projected at least one year beyond the bachelor's degree, would seem to satisfy this condition about as well as can be done, particularly if a year's probationary teaching be imposed to crown the system. Notice that there is more here than the mere heaping up of obstacles, though this will not be without its valuable effect. The pathway into teaching should never be made too easy. Our aim, however, is positive, not negative. It is not merely to exclude the unfit, but to encourage, enlighten, and inspire the fit. What we want is a plan of teacher training which will lead, progressively, to self discovery on the part of the student.

C. The third thing which a valid scheme of teacher training will accomplish is the healing of the breach between method and content. I have mentioned this already in the present chapter, and it is implied elsewhere in the book. But the point is so important, and so often discussed, that I wish to refer to it again. To think of teacher training as concerned with method apart from content is sheer travesty. Teacher training is concerned with education. And education means the use of intellectual content for social ends. Whenever subject matter and method part company, both become sterile. To grasp subject matter aright for educational ends is to grasp it aright intellectually. To understand method properly is to see how subject matter may be made educative.

4. *What should be the status of the teacher in the school?*

The most important learner in the school is the teacher. Any educational system which denies this, which treats him as an unrespected employe hired to perform a routine duty, which does not regard his personal growth as a paramount concern, and which fails to safeguard and encourage that growth in every way possible, is false to its ideals and condemns itself to unescapable mediocrity.

Does this statement seem to you startling? Does it even seem wrong and shocking? "Have we not," you may ask, "often been told that the school exists for the pupil, not for the teacher?" In a sense, this is true. Many teachers enter the profession as a not unbearable preliminary to marriage, or to pave their way towards some other occupation. Others are anxious chiefly to earn a living with the least possible trouble to themselves, and resent special calls on their time, or suggestions as to professional reading and study. Still others are chiefly interested in promotion and a career. In each case, a wrong is being done. Such teachers are deliberately sacrificing the pupils to private and personal ends. Always we are bound to protest. Always we must insist that no one has even the glimmer of a notion of what it means to be a real teacher, unless he feels it his greatest responsibility to serve the pupils.

What sort of service must he render to them? Clearly never a menial service. It was once my pleasure to know a college freshman who proclaimed to all and sundry that she regarded the faculty just as so much hired help, about on the same level as her father's butler and chauffeur. Such an attitude, we instantly say, was wrong and pitiable. No teacher can do his proper work, either as a slave or a jailer. On the one hand, his way must not be shaped merely by the wishes of his pupils or of their parents. He must have a wisdom of his own, and see more clearly, and know better than either the pupils or their parents, what is best and most desirable for them. On the other hand, coercion will never serve his ends. His work is one of coöperative persuasion, of salesmanship, in the highest sense of the word. He must know his pupils better than they know themselves and lead them on to fuller self knowledge. He must understand life, and the supreme meaning of the mind as the controlling power in human living; and aid them to grow up towards the same vision and insight. He serves them as a guide and elder brother.

How can he render such service? Never by neglecting his own inner, personal growth. As the years pass over his head, he must become, not only older, but also wiser. He must come to know more of the material he teaches, not merely, or perhaps chiefly, in the way of technical grasp, but in its broader aspects, and its wider place in the scheme of life. He must see more and more in his subject matter as an educational medium and opportunity. And he must become more and more sure in his judgments of human nature and his estimates of human possibilities and needs. And this means that he must continue to learn. On the continuance of his learning depends his whole effectiveness and value. This is why he is the most important learner in the school.

If all this is so, then it becomes a matter of supreme moment for the schools to help the teacher learn aright. All too often he learns wrongly. He finds out that he must conform, that he must keep silence and refrain from criticism, that he must, above everything, be tame and inoffensive, that he must accept and execute orders which affront his educational conscience. Often he is the passive observer of policies carried out by his principal or superintendent, which he does not understand, and which seem to him wrong and timeserving. And so he comes inwardly to believe that the real business of education is just following out dictated routines, whatever his outward professions. He moves in the direction of cynicism, and grows from less to less, instead of from more to more.

This is a very real tragedy of which the leaders in our schools are far too little conscious. It works powerfully against all that is best in the educational enterprise. It means the deliberate depletion of what is finest and most hopeful in the human and moral resources of the school. Of course, any contact with realities is apt to come as a shock to the young spirit. This we must expect. What the teacher learns in the idealized atmosphere of a fine teacher training institution, and what he finds in the daily round of the ordinary school, are two very different things. And so long as we have an imperfect world, this must be so. But contact with rough reality can work upon a person in two quite opposite ways. It may shatter his beautiful but as yet unsolidified idealism. Or it may lead him to a growth in wisdom, and tolerance, and insight, and show him more and more clearly how and where to apply his effort. Which of these effects experience will have upon the young teacher depends very largely on the status and treatment which the school accords him.

A. The most important single condition is the attitude of the administrative officers. One of the greatest defects of our public schools is their use of an industrial pattern of efficiency. The executive regards himself as the proper source of all light and leading. He assumes all responsibility and hands down orders to be obeyed. If our business is the manufacture of shoes or automobiles, this may be the best way of doing things. But the school is concerned with processes, not results, first of all. Its aim is to develop a way of life, rather than turn out a product. And to achieve this, the personal development and contribution of each member of the staff must be considered essential. So, if he is to perform his task adequately, the teacher must be treated as a responsible partner in a joint enterprise. It may be necessary to make decisions in which he does not concur. But his opinion should be taken and his voice heard. And this is for the sake of his own growth towards the full stature of an educator.

It is sometimes said that principals and superintendents object to any independent thought or activity on the part of their teachers. A good deal of attention has been attracted to a certain investigation, in which administrators indicated the characteristics they considered desirable in teachers. It seemed that they preferred the passive virtues, such as considerateness, amiability, promptness, neatness, and cooperativeness, to the active virtues of open-mindedness, scholarship, and initiative. Yet I doubt whether they do, in the main, really object to those active virtues, which surely should be the mark of the excellent teacher. It may be that they have all too little chance to get to like them. There is no doubt that if our training institutions were to send into the profession people with a real zeal for education and an ardent desire to seek the best things, many of our present administrative patterns would have to be changed. Perhaps administration would be more difficult. But also it would be more worth while. The demands upon leadership would be greater, simply because more active and intelligent followers demand more constructive leading. But I would be sorry to believe that our superintendents and principals would be hostile to the change.

The staff of any school should be regarded as a self educating, democratic body. This is peculiarly important for the sake of the younger teachers. They need to have a sense of personal responsibility, not only for their class work, but also for larger policies. Only so can they really understand what is being undertaken, and grow in educational vision and practical idealism. When the teacher is treated as a colleague rather than an employe, it strengthens his relationship with his pupils, who are exceedingly sensitive to his status. And it strongly promotes his own professional growth. We cannot expect very much in the way of personal development from one who is the mere subject of an autocratic regime. If our schools are to serve the cause of democracy in the world, they cannot hope to do so without adopting democracy as the watchword of their own internal government.

B. Then the teacher's tenure of his position is a vital element in his personal and professional growth. It is essential that his right to differ be safeguarded. Not only may the school, like every other human institution, benefit from responsible and informed criticism. But also, if the teacher is forced to avoid "dangerous" words, and tempted even to suppress "dangerous" thoughts, his professional growth is stifled. It may be that administrators will say that teachers are at present unworthy of the privilege of free comment on school policies. The reply is that they ought to be worthy of it, and that they never will be if it is forever withheld.

Specifically, what this means is that the teacher must not be liable to arbitrary discharge for frivolous or concealed reasons. In particular, the common system of annual contracts is professionally detrimental to a high degree. It is a constant threat hanging over the teacher's head; a constant force making for conformity and the suppression of personal views. In some systems, the teachers have been able to organize and insist upon a scheme of life tenure. But neither is this satisfactory. It takes an angel in human form to avoid the subtle temptation to loaf on the job, if he knows that the job is almost absolutely certain, and that he cannot be removed for anything less than gross misconduct. What is usually recommended is a system of indefinite tenure, coming at the end of a few years' probation. This means that the superintendent must always take special action to remove a teacher, rather than merely not appointing him again at the end of the year. Reasons for such action must usually be given. And in any case, the dismissal of the teacher always must come up as a serious and definite issue for official action. Of course this plan, like any other, can be abused by unscrupulous persons. But it offers a far better practical safeguard than the scheme of annual tenure, without the extreme and undue fixity of life tenure. This is exactly what we want for the promotion of professional growth. The teacher needs to be protected against random and personal attack. He needs to be safeguarded sufficiently, so that he will feel able to think about and discuss school policies without constant fear of losing his head. Otherwise, how can his development fail to be compromised? If we ran our classes and treated our pupils on an analogous basis, what outcomes would we obtain? On the other hand, his position is not so impregnable that he cannot be removed short of legal action.

C. The third condition of professional growth is adequate salary. The winning of salary advances is often spoken of as the major professional victory won by the teaching profession in America. This may seem to some a rather materialistic triumph. Yet, as far as it goes, it is real and important.

We must always remember that the relation of reward to effort is different in a profession from what it is in business. In business, it is roughly and theoretically possible to estimate the money value of an employe. But in a profession, this is not even theoretically possible. What, for instance, is the appropriate reward for a doctor who saves your life, or a lawyer who establishes your innocence in a murder trial? Figuring it on a business basis, you owe him all you now have, and all you will ever earn. What, again, is the cash value of the services of a teacher? It is impossible even to guess. How then shall we calculate the cash value of the debt which society owes the teacher? Our answer must be that the teacher's salary must be sufficient to enable him to live as he must, in order to discharge his true functions, and to rise to higher levels. If, with the exercise of reasonable prudence and frugality, he is not fairly free from financial worries; if he must pinch to buy a few necessary professional books, or to attend meetings where his horizons will be broadened; if he cannot look forward towards the support of a family and provision for his old age; then, most certainly, his professional development is compromised. Another item to be considered is the cost of his training, which is a legitimate part of his expenditure for professional living. If we take progressive educational principles seriously at all, if we believe in the supreme importance of the classroom teacher in the educational scheme, then his work must be so managed and so rewarded as to offer the material basis of a satisfying lifetime career.

5. *What should be the status of the teacher in the community?*

I have insisted again and again that the aim of all education is the enlightenment of social action. And so the teacher must be regarded as the interpreter of the communal life to the children of the community. His task is to bring to bear the intellectual resources of civilization upon the problems of current living. This is to be accepted quite literally. And often it is a somewhat dangerous undertaking. It may involve the critical discussion of tolerated abuses, and the consideration of many things which vested interests would prefer to shroud in silence. It may become the duty of the teacher to deal with such matters as evolution, the League of Nations, the recognition of Soviet Russia, the tariff. Some would say that the teacher should avoid dealing with such issues, and that he should steer clear of controversial and "political" matters. The answer is that if we remember and believe in the social function of education, he cannot do this. If he does avoid such questions, he fails in his essential task. He is not bringing intellectual resources into contact with the real issues of the pupils' lives. And he is back to teaching subject matter for its own sake, insulated from social applications. Moreover, the tame neutrality which so many others advocate and observe is really not neutrality at all. It is taking sides with the *status quo*. Such being the case, the schools must take courage and deal with current realities. It is the obligation of the schools to fight for the right of the teacher to guide the pupils' thinking on controversial and immediate issues. This is not only for the sake of free speech; but because, if our education fails to come into contact with just such matters, it is false to its own essential purpose.

These must be the matters of concern to the teacher. It is his difficult yet inspiring task to deal with them in terms, not of partisanship, but of intelligence. In the ancient Vedic civilization, the teacher was a mature man who had performed the duties of soldier, citizen, and head of family, and who had lived widely and wisely enough to be an effective guide for youth. In Plato's Republic, those who taught had, for fifteen years before, carried the highest responsibilities of the state. Surely, in such notions, the ideal is clear. What we wish is neither callow radicalism nor cowardly conformity; but a mature and temperate wisdom, which can guide the young in dealing with the real issues of life.

INDEX

ability, individual, 235 ff.
abilities, special, 251 ff.
academy, 413
academic courses, 477-81, 488
adjustment, 5-7, 328-9; human, 10 ff.; racial, 21; static, 7-8
advance through school, 250, 257, 266, 396-7
Africa, 44
age of arrest, 58-9
American culture, 304-5
apperception, 62-3, 66-7
apprenticeship, 99-100
Athens, 116
athletics, 198, 358
average, 443-5

background, 62 ff., 154-5, 391-3
Bagley, 41, 111-2
bank crisis, 352-3
banks, 41
Battling Siki, 41-2
Belloc, 200
Bennett, 146
biology, 4-5
Bode, 386
bookishness, 103-4
books, 266-7
bread-and-butter aim, 33
bright pupil, 357-8, 348-9

capital and labor, 160-1
career motive, 294
Chapman and Counts, 426
Charters, 371
cheating, 284

children, attitude to, 176-7
choice, 250; v. specialization
Ciceronianism, 105
civic adjustment, 122 ff.; education, 138 ff., ch. VI
classes, 135 ff., 259 ff., 467
cold storage, 107-8, 179-80, 222-3, 482
college, 182-3, 240, 420 ff.; preparation, 413-4
Collings, 52
common education, 245-6, 407, 416-7; needs, 243; way of life, 98-100, 287-8
community, 130-1, 132-3
competition, 433-4, 442
comprehensive examinations, 424
compulsion, 335-6, 346, 355-7
conformity, 33-4
consumer, 151 ff.
continuity, mental, 288; v. background
core curriculum, 249-50; v. social science
correlation, 394-5
cosmopolitanism, 128 ff.
Counts, G. S., 378, 381
course, 291-2, 394-5
Courtis, 267-8
craft system, 152
creative adjustment, 197 ff.
creativeness, 19-21, 36 ff., 160-1, 180, 474
credit system, 281-5, 394-5, 401-2; v. marking
cultural education, 246-7; studies, 310 ff.
culture, 246, 317-8, 479-80; individual, 306 ff.; social significance of, 301 ff.
culture epoch theory, 71-2
curriculum, 28, 104-5, 127-8, 133, 138-9, 154-5, 181-3, 200-1, 216-7, 220-1,

244-5, 249-50, 253, 281, 285-6, 290-1, 356 ff., ch. XVII, 422-3, 464-5; content of, 164-5; creation of, 397-8; defects of, 375 ff.; determination of, 76-7; elementary, 408-10; enriched, 257-8; evolution of, 376-7; flexibility in, 396-7; new, 393 ff.; organization of, 379-80; reform of, 380-1, 388 ff.; selection, 97-8, 382 ff.; use of, 431, 433

Dalton Plan, 264-5
Danish Folk High School, 38, 240, 294, 307
Darwin, 237
Deeping, 208-9
defectives, 347-8
definitions, 84-5
democracy, 103, 405; industrial, 159 ff.
Denmark, 136, 307
departmental instruction, 419
dependents, 172-3
Detroit, Mich., 264-5
development, stages of, 70-1
Dewey, John, 329
diagnosis, 440-1
difficulty, 78-9
Dimnet, E., 344
discipline, formal, ch. IV, 227, 365, 381
disciplinary aims, 33; studies, 343
disease, 205-6
drill, 91-2
dull pupil, 257
dynamic organization, 289 ff.

economic enlightenment, 163-5; insecurity, 170-1; institutions, ch. VII; intelligence, 158-9; order, problem of, 141 ff.; problems, 175-6
Edison, 186, 190
educated man, 10-11, 42
education, 3-4, 42 ff., 238; aims, 7, 29 ff.; hours in, 487-8; teaching of, 482-8
educational organization, 323-5; propaganda, 233-4; responsibility for health, 204 ff.; selection, 234-5; values, 200
effort, 296-8
elementary school, 181-2, 406 ff., 414 ff.
England, 120-1
enlightenment, 214 ff.

environment, 9-10
Erskine, John, 200
ethics, code of, 369-70
eugenics, 207-8
European education, 277, 407-8
experience, 370, 484-5; control of, 366-7; immediate, 365-6; life, 89-91
exploratory courses, 291
extra-curriculum, 201-2, 363, 398 ff., 421-2

faculties, 79-82, 252-5
family life, ch. VIII, 174 ff.; reconstruction of, 170 ff.
family, size, 172
Finney, Ross, 39-40, 155, 212
Fisher, W. A., 305
Fitch, 160
flexibility, 17-8, 34-5, 36 ff., 180, 473-4
Flexner, 311
followership, 247-8
food, 152-3
fragmentary approach, 391-3
France, 122
Franklin, B., 311
fraternity, 399
free elective system, 286-7

general education, 18, 62, 100, 150, 220-1, 394, 405
generalization, 86, 371
genius, 251-2
Germany, 122
goals of education, 25 ff.; v. education, aims
Goddard, 347
gold standard, 164
ground covering, 106-7, 437-8
group activity, 109-10; projects, 272
Gruenberg, 170, 177
guiding thought processes, 333-7

Harap, H., 152 ff., 387
hard work, 361
harmonious development, 32
health, ch. X; activities, 217-9; education, 216-7; habits, 211-2, 223-4; improvement, 212-3; information, 215-6, 224
healthy living, 221 ff.

INDEX

heredity, 236-7
high school, 413; v. secondary education
higher institutions, 449
home, 114, 183-4; decline of, 166 ff.
home economics, 181, 314
home work, 227-8
homogeneous grouping, 268 ff.
Hoover, H., 147 ff.
housing, 153-4
hygiene, 177

ideals, 368, 370, 371-2
identical elements, 86-9
individual, 21-2, 28-9, 43-4, ch. XII; contribution, 111; differences, 243-4; instruction, 263 ff., 271-2, 411, 467-8; method, 259
individuality, 309-10
industry, 115
inferiority feeling, 344-6
informational studies, 343
Inglis, A., 31
inherited structure, 12
instinct, 13-6
institutional adjustment, 194 ff., 208 ff.
institutions, 25-9
integration, 394-5
intellectual interests, 420-1; life, 421 ff.; resources, 39-42, 55-7, 67, 81-2, 127-8, 150, 320-2, 354
intelligence, 236-7
intelligence tests, 241
interest, 106, 110-1, ch. XIII, 396, 425; extrinsic, 281 ff., 295, 362, 423-4; intrinsic, 286 ff.
iron law of wages, 156
Italy, 122

Jesuits, 434
job analysis, 384-5

Kilpatrick, 457
kind of education, 242 ff.
Kipling, R., 80, 341
knowledge, 32-3, 108, 133

ladder, educational, ch. XVIII
laissez faire, 145
Latin, 312-3
Latin Grammar School, 412-3

Lawrence, T. E., 274
leadership, 247-9, 414
learning, 17, 18-9, 59, 71, 282-3; incidental, 410; marginal, 457-9; primary, 459-61
leisure time, 191-2, 308-9
lessons, 423-4
life, 5-7; conduct of, 367; divorce from, 101 ff.; linkage with, 455-6; situations, 292-3, 294, 456
linguistic studies, 250
Louis XVI, 200
Lull, 304

McCall, 436
management, 149
manual training, 314
markets, 157
marking, 278-9, 430-3; scale, 447; substitutes for, 445 ff.; system, 443 ff.
mastery technique, 445-6
marks, 362-3
measurement, ch. XIX
medical science, 210-1
memorizing, 85
memory knowledge, 128
mental growth, ch. III, 81-2, 108, 220-1, 288, 388 ff., 396, 405
Merriam, 378
method, ch. XX, 492-3
mental power, 80-1
mental tests, 236-7
mind, 205
modern life, 351-2
Monitorial plan, 35, 260
moral instruction, direct, 368 ff.
morality, ch. VI; meaning of, 350-3, 369
motivation, 442
movies, 304
music, 76, 78, 198-9

narrowness, 138-9
Neo-Platonists, 311
New Russia's Primer, 54

objectivity, 435-7
opportunity, ch. XI; problem of, 231 ff.
oral quiz, 439
oral speech, 408-9

ornamental culture, 307-8
outcomes, 298, 337-9
out-door schools, 227

paramecium, 5-6
parents, 449
passing courses, 282-3
patriotism, 128 ff.
Pericles, 38-9
personality, 24-5
personality relations, 170, 171, 173-4, 178-9
Peters, C. C., 44-5, 134, 174-5
physical setting of school, 226-7
physician, 206-7, 211
Plato, 311
play, 185 ff.
policies and personalities, 133 ff.
practicality, 293-4, 311-2, 483-4
practice teaching, 485-6
practice theory, 188-9
preparation, 221-4, 275-7; v. cold storage
prestige, 195
primitive life, 122-3, 128-9, 207
problem, sense of, 330-3, 389-90
procedure, classroom, 78-9, 292-3
producer, 146 ff.
prognosis, 441
progressiveness, 17, 18-9, 61, 180-1, 221
progressive schools, 8, 21-3, 57-8, 112-3
project method, 52-3, 90, 389-90, 462-5
propaganda, 139-40
psychology, study of, 178
public affairs, knowledge of, 125 ff.
public health, 209-10
pupil participation, 219-20
pure project curriculum, 291-2
purpose, 8-9

questions, use of, 343-4

reality in education, 138
reason, 352
recapitulation, 69-73, 187-8
recreation, ch. IX
recreational abuses, 197; adjustment, 194 ff.; facilities, 195-6; interests, 177-8, 192-3; pursuits, 202
reflexes, 12-3

refraction, 84
regionalism, 128 ff.
relative standing, 429 ff.
report cards, 427-8
requirements, curricular, 395-6
residual function, 96 ff.
research, 345-6
results, 337-8, 346-7
rigidity, 34, 140, 180-1, 223-4
routine, 334-5, 340-2
routine job, 161-2
Rugg, 379
Russia, 113-4, 122, 132, 294, 307

sabbatical leave, 191
scholarship, 478-9
school, 10, ch. V, 126-7, 217 ff., 241-2, 245, 256-7; and recreation, 199 ff.; and society, 116; danger of, 101 ff.; derived meaning, 109; health, 224-6; moral training in, 353 ff.; relation to other institutions, 112 ff.; size of task of, 94 ff.
schooling, 3, 95-6, 231-2, 238-9, 406-8
science, 313-4
seat work, 227
secondary education, 137, 163, 182-3, 412 ff.
selection of pupils, 163, 425-6
self direction, 442
seven cardinal principles, 29-31
sex, 14-5
Sisson, 125
situation organization, 53-4, 291
skill studies, 342-3
Snedden, 387
social adjustment, 100-1
social life of school, 355 ff., 438-9
social opportunity, 261 ff.
social participation, 418
social philosophy of education, 387-8
social science, 165, 249-50, 393-4
socialized recitation, 465-7
society, 23 ff.
specialization, 18, 163-4, 419
spectatorship, 198-9
Spencer, H., 10, 30
standard of living, 155 ff.
standards, 242, 273 ff., 359 ff., 367-8,

416; imposed, 361-2; low, 360-1; personal, 364
state, 114-5, 131; and education, 102-3
stay in school, 232 ff.
Steffansson, 42, 223
student self government, 357-8
subject matter, 42-3, 58, 68, 101, 108-9, 179, 242, 275, 332-3, 365, 400-1, 411, 463; aims, 324-5; professionalized, 480-1; values of, 75
sugar coating, 294-5
superintendent, 477, 494-6
supervised study, 459-60
supply and demand, 156
surplus energy theory, 187

task setting, 106
teacher, 35-6, 92-3, 183, 225, 269-70, 284-5, 334-6, 359, 363, 442, 448-9, 460-1, ch. XXI; adjustment of, 473-5; professional growth of, 488-90, 493-4; salary, 497-8; status, 493 ff., 498-9; task of, 471 ff.; tenure, 496-7; training, 476 ff.; vocational choice of, 490-2
teaching, 77-8, 329 ff.
techniques of amusement, 202-3
techniques of industry, 247, 321-2
tests, construction of, 429-30; value of, 439 ff.
therapeuton, 212
thinking, ch. XV
Thorndike, 59, 234-5
three R's, 407-8
transfer, 82 ff., 89 ff., 371-2
triviality, 343-4
tutoring, 259

units, 446-7

values, criteria for, 10
versatility, 253
vicarious experience, 410-1, 417-8
vocation, 159, 315 ff.
vocational choice, 318-20; education, 34, 91, 99-100, 246-7, 322-5; fitness, 175

wage levels, 156
wants, 159
Washington, Booker T., 159
worker, 162-3
workmanship, 148-9